T0248370

CARNIE KING

The Story of Patty Conklin and Conklin Shows

JOHN THURSTON

DUNDURN
PRESS

Publisher: Meghan Macdonald | Acquiring editor: Kathryn Lane | Editor: Susan Fitzgerald
Cover designer: Karen Alexiou

All interior images courtesy of the Conklin family.

Library and Archives Canada Cataloguing in Publication

Title: Carnie king : the story of Patty Conklin and Conklin Shows / John Thurston.
Names: Thurston, John Harry, 1955- author.
Description: Includes bibliographical references and index.
Identifiers: Canadiana (print) 20240335384 | Canadiana (ebook) 20240335732 | ISBN 9781459749924 (hardcover) | ISBN 9781459749931 (PDF) | ISBN 9781459749948 (EPUB)
Subjects: LCSH: Conklin, Patty. | LCSH: Conklin Shows—History. | LCSH: Carnivals—Canada—History.
Classification: LCC GV1835.3.C66 T48 2024 | DDC 791/.10971—dc23

We acknowledge the support of the Canada Council for the Arts and the Ontario Arts Council for our publishing program. We also acknowledge the financial support of the Government of Ontario, through the Ontario Book Publishing Tax Credit and Ontario Creates, and the Government of Canada.

Printed and bound in Canada.

Dundurn Press
1382 Queen Street East
Toronto, Ontario, Canada M4L 1C9
dundurn.com, @dundurnpress

Contents

Preface:
A Carnival Kingdom

The carnival has a place in the memories of most North Americans. Whether on the midway of a county fair or at an event like the Canadian National Exhibition (CNE), many of us have been touched, however briefly, by the carnival spirit. The fantasy of running away with the carnival persists, and some still live it out. Chances are we encountered our carnie spirit on a midway attached to the Conklin Group, which was for many years the largest carnival company in the world. Conklin Shows, spanning a shifty, shifting side of the outdoor entertainment industry in the twentieth century, is the legacy of James Wesley "Patty" Conklin. This is the story of a carnie king and his kingdom, and their place in the history of the carnival and of the last century.

The history of the North American carnival has been explored unevenly, with little attention to the carnival in Canada.[1] Tracking the evolution of Conklin Shows offers the opportunity to recount a substantial slice of this story, and to give it focus and scope. The activities of this carnie king and his company encompass scores of other carnival outfits — partners, rivals, competitors, victims, collaborators, employment pools — that have struggled to survive in an industry that was dominated in North America for much of the last century and a few years into this one by the Conklin enterprise.

The story of Conklin Shows parallels major trends in the evolution of North American culture. Country fairs and city festivals offered the show its first Canadian homes, and it accompanied Canada's transformation from a rural to an urban society. The show contributed to the viability of many agricultural fairs.[2] Patty Conklin took over the CNE when Toronto was a backwater provincial capital with a really big agricultural and industrial exhibition, and his descendants stayed with the city as it grew into a global metropolis and the Ex became the world's largest fair.[3]

Patty Conklin grew into the myth of the self-made man while his fellow citizens with newly gained disposable income and leisure time coalesced into a market for mass amusements. Carnival companies like Conklin & Garrett fed on the developing relationship between people of middle income seeking diversion and those forced to the margins who found a way to make a living by satisfying desires they could not share. The lives once lived on carnival lots fascinate for their disreputable, outsider mystique, their attachment to another time, and their uneasy transition into this one. While many of us have retained the fantasy of running away with the carnival, this book explores the reality.

The carnie way of life and its changes reflect broader trends. Throughout its evolution, the carnival industry, Conklin Shows at its centre, has played a significant part in the social history of North America, absorbing, initiating, and disseminating an array of clichés and devices, symbols and trends, gimmicks and tricks that are now part of our cultural environment. Patty thrived within the showbiz world of vaudeville, dime museums, and nickelodeons — eccentric, garish, and local. His grandson, Frank, belonged in the mass entertainment world of the television, film, and music industries — standardized, bland, and global. This book attempts to portray the history of Conklin Shows by following how the show and the carnival industry as a whole responded to trends in popular culture.

My personal history with the carnival began when I worked on the midway of the CNE as a young teenager, when the Ex was at its peak. I continued to work with Conklin Shows for over 10 years at the Ex and on both the eastern and western road shows. This work partly funded my university education, during which I learned the research techniques I have employed in producing this book. Much of what I know about the show I learned orally, including through a series of over 30 interviews conducted with Conklin staff and associates. That knowledge has been substantiated by research in newspapers and in books and periodicals about the carnival, especially *Billboard* magazine, reaching back to the 1910s and forward to when it became *Amusement Business* in 1961 and then ended publication in 2006. I had access to the Conklin family archives, which contain letters, telegrams, account books, contracts, newspaper clippings, and other documents. For the Renker family, I researched vital records in the New Jersey State Archives in Trenton. I have resisted reproducing stories I knew orally but for which I did not have documentary sources. The main exception is the series of vignettes included at the beginning of each major section. These passages are either imagined reconstructions of events known to have happened or, in the later chapters, come from other sources, especially interviews.

The story of the Conklin carnival brings into focus part of the amorphous entertainment environment. Unlike other entertainment industries, the carnival industry in North America is circumscribed and a representative story is available through a single company, the beginning and end of which aligns with an epoch in the industry's history. Conklin Shows provides the opportunity to follow a range of characters, from Patty, his brother Frank, and their lot bosses to some of the less-reputable souls who called the carnival their home, and on to later generations of Conklins. The story of this carnie king and his kingdom appeals to our curiosity about how others live, differently from us while in our midst; people with whom we have had contact, usually unsatisfactory, but enough to make us wonder who they were behind their carnie personas. This book presents one version of that story.

The Apprenticeship of Joe Renker

(1892–1923)

Before he became himself, Patty Conklin grew up as somebody else. He was born Joseph Renker in 1892 to parents who had been four years in the United States, having escaped poverty and poor prospects in their native Germany. His early years were like those of many a son of immigrants, not all of whom found the better life they sought in their adopted land. He had a collection of colourful stories about his boyhood and teenage years, most of which cannot be confirmed through other sources and some of which seem attempts to redeem what were probably squalid beginnings. As the rechristened Patty began to exploit the opportunities he found on the midway, he discovered the talents that would help him conquer the carnival world.

BEFORE THE CARNIVAL

As the SS *Gallia* lists and creaks, and the engines thud, the huddled mass of misery in steerage settles in unevenly for the night. A young couple, Karl and Maria Renker, share a tiny berth with their eight-month-old son, Charles Jr., and their single suitcase. Overwhelmed by the murmur and stench of hundreds of humans confined in the hold, they try to clean and calm their baby and get some sleep.

In their berth is another German, a Jew on his own with two daughters, three and one, his fortunes otherwise unknown. The Renkers have each other and keep their health for most of the voyage. They do not have a clear idea of where they will end up or what they will do, but the ship is full of their compatriots, and they exchange plans and hopes and fears. Some have relatives or friends who will meet them in America, but not Karl and Maria.

Whenever they can, they try to get above deck for air, but when the weather is heavy, which is often, they are confined below. The roiling seas and mountainous waves, the filth and terrible food, the crowds and constant discomfort, the ever-present illness and death — all are only bearable because their duration can be counted off in weeks, rather than months.

★　★　★

Joseph's parents were among the hordes fleeing the militarized Prussia into which they had been born, Karl August Renker in 1861 and Maria Ana Kaiser in 1865.[1] Karl grew up in Ronsdorf, just beyond the Rhine Valley where Maria lived. The year Karl was born, Wilhelm I became King of Prussia. Prince Otto von Bismarck, the king's Iron Chancellor, soon forged a unified Germany, dominated by the industrial and military might of Prussia after its expansive growth and three aggressive wars. Karl and Maria married in 1886. Partly motivated by the threat of being conscripted to serve in the Prussian army, Karl convinced his young bride to leave their homeland. The Renkers arrived in America in April 1888, a month after Wilhelm I, by then emperor of Germany, died and was succeeded by Kaiser Wilhelm II.

The large-scale development of coal mining and heavy industry in the Ruhr district had begun just before Karl's birth. The political, social, and economic upheaval attendant on German unification and industrialization contributed to the Renkers' decision to emigrate. Textiles had long been an important industry in the region in which Karl was born, and before he emigrated, he had learned some of the dyeing trade he would follow in his new country.

By the 1860s, 800,000 German speakers made up Kleindeutschland — Little Germany — in New York, after Berlin and Vienna the third largest German community in the world. When the Renkers left Europe in 1888, they were part of the second wave of immigration to the United States, largely from England, Ireland, and, especially, the west of Germany. Over five million Europeans arrived in the United States during the 1880s, one and a half million from Germany alone. The Renkers arrived in the midst of America's greatest period of industrial expansion and population growth, and faced some of the same problems they were trying to escape. Many of their compatriots pushed on to the Midwest to homestead their own land, while those like the Renkers who stayed in the East became part of a pool of surplus labour from which a few individuals and corporations wrung enormous wealth, while also building the monuments to itself that wealth demanded.

The SS *Gallia*, a steamship that sailed under its three masts whenever the wind was favourable, could carry 300 in first class, but only had 17 when the Renkers boarded. It left Liverpool on March 27, with a stop at Cork to top up its steerage deck to almost its full complement of 1,200. Liverpool had become the main embarkation point for European immigrants to North America and somehow the Renkers made it there from Hamburg with an infant son. After a voyage of 10 days, they arrived at the Port of New York on April 7, 1888, and came through the Castle Garden immigrant processing station at the tip of Manhattan Island.[2]

Instead of joining New York's Little Germany, the Renkers continued on to Paterson, New Jersey, site of a smaller German community. Just 12 miles west of New York City, Paterson had been planned as an industrial city to take advantage of the Great Falls on the Passaic River. It became an important manufacturing centre for textiles, locomotives, and machinery. By the time the Renkers arrived, Paterson was home to over 20,000 residents, mostly immigrants at work in the silk mills that were by then producing more than half of the silk made in the United States. Germans had been flocking there for decades and the Renkers would have learned through the network of German immigrants that there was work in Paterson.

Renker gave shoemaker as his trade on the passenger list for the SS *Gallia*, but by the end of 1890 he was calling himself a dyer. He had given his name as

Carl on entry into the country and changed it to Charles by the year he turned 30. He was not one of the skilled silk workers the mill owners advertised for in European silk centres, since even 10 years later he remained a dyer's helper.

The insatiable demand of the silk mills for labour met Renker's need to feed a growing family. Maria had given birth to Charles Jr. in Germany. Alvina was born in the summer of 1889 and Adelia in Paterson early in 1891, although Adelia died soon after. Joseph was born on April 27, 1892, in Brooklyn. He was the only Renker born in Brooklyn and there is no record of the family ever living there. The street on which Joseph was born was occupied by German immigrants and had a branch office of the *Brooklyner Freie Presse*. Charles might not yet have had steady work in Paterson and the Renkers were likely visiting friends in Brooklyn when Joseph was born. Charles still gave silk dyer as his occupation on Joseph's birth certificate, as he did for another son, Rudolph, born the next year.

The stock market panic of 1893 and ensuing depression account for why Charles was out of work and in Jersey City when Rudolph was born. With few possessions to burden them, immigrant families easily moved from dwelling to dwelling, town to town, looking for work or better housing or communities where they could feel at home.

There is a continuous record of residence for the Renkers in Paterson from the late 1890s on, although they changed addresses often, perhaps moving up to something that had electricity, available throughout the city after 1914, better plumbing, or other modern conveniences. His four surviving children forced Charles to settle into 12-hour days at the silk mills, earning little more than a dollar a day. He resisted any urge he might have felt to wander further afield in search of other opportunities.

After Rudolph, Maria Renker, now called Jenny, as was both her own and her husband's mother, gave birth to five more children: William in 1896, Catherine in 1898, a stillborn child in 1902, Frank in 1903, and Henri in 1905, when Jenny was 40. With no pensions available, a poor man's old age security could only be bought with children.

In 1904 Charles might have been temporarily laid off from the mills because that year he identifies himself, like he had on the SS *Gallia*, as a shoemaker. His foray into independent business lasted no more than a year before he went back to silk dyeing. The silk mills employed children as young as eight. Charles Jr. had been contributing to the household economy since he was 12. By 1905 he was a silk weaver, a skilled trade, and Alvina and Joseph had entered the workforce, she as a silk winder and he as a labourer. He was 13.

By 1910 the Renkers were in the house on Water Street, where the parents would spend their remaining years. Charles, Alvina, and Joseph had moved out, and the family had room to take in four boarders, three of them from Germany and one a friend of Rudolph's.

Joseph later spoke with respect of his older brother. Charlie was a well-read, chess-playing, studious sort. With an abundance of motivations, in his early 20s he had tried to escape Paterson, heading west to Detroit, with brief returns to Paterson to work as a weaver. He settled back in Paterson in his late 20s and stayed for the next 20 years. After the death of his parents, he moved to New York City to become an apartment building custodian. From Charles, his senior by five years, Joseph learned the spirit of restlessness that characterized his entire life.

Life in New York City

Joseph ran away at 14 in 1906 to fend for himself in New York City or, in some versions of the legend he created, Jersey City.[3] According to stories he later told, he lived for a time with a Taft family, who were Jews. He would not have been alone among immigrant sons who ran away at an early age for life on the streets of New York. As social worker Jane Addams wrote about this period, "Never before have such numbers of young boys earned money independently of the family life, and felt themselves free to spend it as they choose in the midst of vice deliberately disguised as pleasure."[4] The streets of the city teemed with youth living brutal and dangerous lives, exposed to the darker side of humanity from which the survivors picked up the wiles they would use to eke out their existence. It was here that Joe Renker gained the street smarts he would later exercise with such skill and exuberance.

Joe first worked outside the original Madison Square Garden, built in 1890 and dedicated chiefly to boxing. He later talked about selling bags of peanuts at the gates. The bags were half filled with empty shells. Before a customer could discover the ruse, Joe had disappeared into the crowded streets. He boasted that he could make $26 an hour in sales. In other stories he said his peanut-selling days were spent at baseball games and Grand Central Station. He claimed that when his voice competed with the train announcer, he was offered the job but turned it down because it did not pay enough.

Joe developed a lucrative sideline to the peanut business with three other street kids. "The Four Gentlemen" worked the main entrance to the Garden: "We called ourselves that," he later explained, "because on rainy days we'd carry umbrellas to escort people to the entrance. We did all right, between $6 and $8 each for an hour's work a day, while other kids were getting maybe $3 a week in regular jobs."[5] With the money he made, he left the Taft family to rent a room, likely in a flophouse colony of his peers.

In the early 1900s, the New York theatre district was centred on Madison Square Garden. When the *New York Times* built its offices at the intersection of Broadway, Seventh Avenue, and 42nd Street in 1903, and New York opened its first subway line in 1904, running beneath this intersection, Times Square was born. In less than 10 years, the square became the new centre of entertainment in New York, a transition Joe Renker witnessed. With his competitors and colleagues, he made his living off the crowds that thronged the entertainment districts. He would also have spent some of his money on the abundant recreational opportunities in the area.

Vaudeville and nickel theatres, among the earliest forms of mass entertainment, flourished during these years.[6] Young Joe can be imagined among the "gallery gods" in the scores of vaudeville theatres in lower Manhattan before the war. These youngsters peddled newspapers and hustled and scavenged on the streets, then used their earnings to buy seats in vaudeville galleries, where they hooted, stamped their feet, and hurled all manner of objects at the stage to signal their approval, or otherwise, of the acts. Despite attempts by theatre owners to suppress them, their spirit was never fully expunged from vaudeville. On amateur night, many of them would show up on stage with their own acts. Joe tried his hand at singing on some of these occasions. This was his first taste of being the centre of attention, his first experience of holding a crowd in thrall. He liked the feeling and would seek to replicate it throughout his life.

The first nickel theatre, or nickelodeon, in New York City opened in 1906 in the heart of Joe's stomping grounds. Youth from the streets came in gangs, especially during the afternoons and early evenings, turning the nickelodeons into their social centres and clubhouses. When the lights went down, Joe and his peers shouted, screamed, howled, laughed uproariously, and bounced about in their seats.

The newspaper boy or "newsie" was the quintessential street urchin of the period. Hawking extras at all hours, fighting rivals for street corners, and doing odd errands for shady characters, the newsie has become a folk hero of the early twentieth century. In later stories, Joe Renker took on a share of this iconic status, recounting how he sold papers to passengers on the elevated rail platforms in New York in 1907 and 1908. In one version of his legend, he next got in the business of selling kewpie dolls, just as they were becoming the national rage around 1910. Patty had a story he later told about working under the Manhattan Bridge. He watched in admiration as a thief lowered a fishing line from the bridge and hooked one of his dolls. The image is filtered through his years of witnessing similar feats of prowess at his carnival games.

Patty claimed a connection with another cultural icon of the period, this one of a different order. The amusement parks of Coney Island — Steeplechase Park, Dreamland, and Luna Park — flourished from the late 1890s to the start of the Great War, peaking in popularity around 1910.[7] Coney Island drew more visitors later, but never again for the classic parks. These parks, inspired by the Midway Plaisance at the 1893 World's Columbian Exhibition, appealed to an urban middle class, eager for exciting yet wholesome entertainment that could evoke and satisfy their desire for sensory stimulation and emotional release, sharing that entertainment in a new type of public space with thousands of fellow citizens. On Coney Island, American males found their need for amusement justified and catered to by commercial enterprise on a scale to match the rapidly growing population. Grown men were for the first time encouraged to play — if they could afford to pay.[8] This emerging trend would be essential to Patty's future career.

Patty later talked about working at roller coaster maintenance on Coney Island and being there after a big fire, describing how the coaster went faster when in flames. The most notable fire of the period was the night that

Dreamland burned to the ground in May 1911 and caused $4.5 million in damages. There were many roller coasters throughout Coney Island and he could have worked on any number of these. He also occasionally claimed to have been a sideshow talker, although this allegation is especially redolent of personal mythologizing. He nevertheless would have spent some time as a young man at the parks of Coney Island.

While in Manhattan, Joe was little more than a long walk from his family in Paterson. Indeed, for the pageant in support of the silk strike of 1913, 800 strikers walked the 23 miles from Paterson to Madison Square Garden where the pageant was held.[9] That strike would have involved the Renker family.

Paterson was rife with labour troubles, often instigated by skilled silk workers who resisted the mechanization of their trades. The Industrial Workers of the World (IWW or Wobblies) helped to organize the strikers in 1913 around the issue of an eight-hour workday and was successful in uniting skilled and unskilled workers representing many nationalities, mainly German, Italian, Irish, Polish, and French Canadian.

The strike engaged New York intellectuals for the first time in working-class unrest. They travelled to Paterson to witness rallies of up to 25,000 strikers at strike headquarters, which was less than a mile from the Renkers' home. New York writers and artists wrote and produced the pageant, held in June at the Garden, in which 1,000 strikers sang their own songs in one language. Over 15,000 attended the event and it led to greater financial support for the strikers. To further assist the strikers and their hungry families, the IWW arranged for as many as 700 children to be cared for by families in New York City and Elizabeth, New Jersey.

After keeping the Paterson mills closed for five months, in July the workers capitulated to the owners who had been using mills in Pennsylvania to replace lost output. The dyers were the first to give in and went back in total disarray without receiving any concessions. Nevertheless, the strike remained a symbol for class solidarity across ethnic boundaries.

Charles Sr., Charles Jr., and Alvina were all in the silk industry at the time, although Charles Jr. would leave Paterson for the West in 1913, possibly because the strike left him without work. Rudolph was a machinist living at home, but the collapse of Paterson's economy would have affected him too. Frank and Henri could have been among those children sent out of the city, possibly to German friends in Brooklyn. Joseph's exact whereabouts during the strike of 1913 are not known with certainty, but it is unlikely he was with his family.

By 1915 the family had been reduced from 11 to six. Rudolph married early in the year and had a son by its end. William and Catherine were still at home, and they too had begun to work in the silk industry. Frank and Henri were at school. The family had one boarder. Around this time, Jenny was diagnosed with a brain tumour. There was little that medicine of the time could do to treat her condition and the family would not have had the money to pay for what treatment was available. The family economy would have been stretched to buy something to relieve her pain.

Jenny did not live to enjoy the security and comfort children might have brought to her old age. After suffering from the disease for over two years, convulsions brought on by the tumour killed her in July 1918, two weeks after her 53rd birthday. Two months after that, Catherine married George Brocco, the son of Italian immigrants, and left the family home. Charles, William, Frank, and Henri stayed with their father. With the United States in the Great War since 1917, his status as a German immigrant provided another obstacle to his ability to earn a living or integrate with the society around him.

First Job on the Midway

Joe was not there for his mother's funeral or his sister's wedding. By this time, he had joined the carnival and was wandering further afield. *Billboard* magazine, the omnibus weekly for entertainment news during the first half of the twentieth century, had carried advice for circus and carnival folk without plans for the winter to open nickelodeons, which had become the new entertainment sensation. Joe might have heard about the travelling carnivals through hanging around nickelodeons or at Coney Island.

By 1912 Joe had begun working with a carnival playing the oil boomtowns of Texas and Oklahoma. He was a partner with W.H. "Bill" Rice and Roy Marr, running gambling games on midways. The partners catered to oilmen flush with cash they were eager to spend. The games were uniformly dishonest, giving the players ample opportunity to part with their money and then retaliate by attacking the carnies. Men went to the midway expecting fights, which would have given them as much excitement as they could hope for on a night out in a Texas oil town.

The western route through the oil towns was rough, even by the standards of the early carnival. The partners, along with Rice's wife, their bookkeeper, travelled in railway baggage cars between spots. They slept with a gun, as there was nowhere else to store the take and they could not leave it unguarded. This was but one of the survival tactics the group learned, each day facing crowds of rowdy men, taking their money without the restraints or protections of any established legal authority. During these years, the state, distracted by the troubles in Europe, ignored the need for law and order in the territories.

Joe might have made his first trip to Canada during these years. He said he booked games on his first Canadian route when he was 19, which would have been in 1911.[10] He often reported that he had had a game at the first Calgary Stampede in 1912. Carnival companies travelling into Canada were required to deposit $2,000 with Canadian immigration authorities as a guarantee that all of their employees would return to the United States when the fairs were over. In the fall of 1914, a company called the Rice and Dore Carnival complained to *Billboard* that Canadian immigration authorities were unfairly holding their bond. The authorities said that the company had left some of its American staff behind. If this was the company with which Joe visited Canada, he was not among those who stayed behind.

The partners made a good deal of money before the outbreak of the Great War. Joe and Bill Rice saved much of theirs, while Roy Marr drank his away. After three or four years on the road, Joe returned to New York City, intent on finding a wife. The Rices stayed in Texas for another year, then returned to their home state of Arizona. Joe was unsuccessful at finding a wife upon his return to New York. But he did have a substantial kitty and a wealth of experience in the field where he would build his own empire.

THE FIRST CONKLIN SHOWS

James Conklin, an old man in a window booth, nurses a bourbon. He is not relaxed in the plush leather seat, but leans over the table, shoulders hunched, looking out at New Orleans's rue Royale, gazing absently at the thin trickle of people flowing through the Quarter in the dim, late afternoon light. He slips a hip flask from the folds of his waistcoat and tops up his drink, the ice almost gone.

His wife joins him, and he looks up as she sits down, rubbing her brow. Their eyes do not meet.

"I don't know why we had to come down here to winter. We can hardly afford to stay in this place — you think it gives you something to brag about to the help." She sighs and wipes her forehead with a handkerchief, takes off her glasses, and rubs her eyes. "This heat and damp is terrible for my nerves."

A waiter comes and she asks for water and ice. The man across from her strokes his moustache and looks at her with passive, hooded eyes, then turns back to the view out the window. The setting sun casts a yellow glow over the city.

"Go back to New York anytime you want," he says.

The March 16, 1915, issue of *Billboard*, the carnie bible, had the following announcement:

> An aggregation new to carnivaldom, known as Clark & Conklin's All Feature Shows, will tour the Eastern territory the coming season. This aggregation is under the personal supervision and direction of James W. Conklin, a veteran circus showman. While Mr. Conklin is not very well known to carnival folks, he has a wide acquaintance in the circus world.

James Wesley Conklin, born in 1861, the same year as Joe Renker's father, had at one time owned the Family Theater in Woonsocket, Rhode Island.[11] He had worked in a management capacity with both the Ringling Brothers and the Barnum & Bailey circuses. He had been the assistant manager to J. Harry Six on his carnival in 1914. A portly, avuncular man with a bushy grey moustache, he sometimes took the show owner's honorific of "colonel." Between 1915 and 1920, Joe Renker joined Clark & Conklin Shows, adopted his surrogate father and began his transformation into J.W. "Patty" Conklin. The character who would transform the North American carnival industry would appear just as the industry was ready for him.

The Foundations of the Carnival

The precursors of the carnival are ancient and legion. Records of annual gatherings that combined commerce with entertainment reach back to the Roman Empire. These events attracted shows, rides, and games, the main components of the modern carnival. By the second millennium, Christian seasonal festivals had become huge events throughout Europe. A few hundred years later in the United Kingdom, festivals had taken on the contours of what we know as the fair, an annual event organized by an agricultural society to celebrate productivity and perseverance. Because it generates needed revenue by feeding the desire for diversion, entertainment — spectacles, thrills, and gaming — has often dominated fairs.

Agricultural societies, part of the commercialization of European agriculture in the eighteenth and nineteenth centuries, used fairs to promote "progressive" farming practices. These societies and the fairs they supported sprang up along the eastern seaboard of the United States in the early nineteenth century. The government of Upper Canada sponsored its first agricultural exhibition in 1846 and fairs spread throughout British North America, along with settlement. By the end of the century, fairs were important annual events for many new communities.

Then came the world's fairs, the first of which was London's 1851 Crystal Palace Exhibition. Exhibitions in Paris (1889), Chicago (1893), and St. Louis

(1904) confirmed the economic value of world's fairs and produced a market for a type of entertainment only they could satisfy. While Montreal's Expo 67 was Canada's first world's fair, in 1878 Toronto politicians founded the event that would become Canada's de facto world's fair. The Toronto Industrial Exhibition, unofficially the Canadian National Exhibition from 1907, formally became such in 1912. A force all its own, the CNE set international records for attendance and midway grosses throughout the middle of the last century, reigning for decades as the largest annual outdoor exhibition in the world and attracting over a million visitors for each of its three weeks — a weekly attendance that no world's fair has ever matched.

The agricultural and world's fairs had entertainment, but the type of organization that North Americans know as the carnival came together in the last years of the nineteenth century. The North American carnival, centred on a midway run by showmen-entrepreneurs like Colonel Conklin, incorporated practices from the circus, the dime museum, the nickelodeon, the amusement park, and Wild West and medicine shows, but the world's fairs of the late nineteenth century were the catalyst in the formation of the first carnival companies. The carnival evolved throughout the last century, largely in connection with fairs and exhibitions, without breaking from the tradition begun by the first carnivals in the midwestern United States in the late 1890s.

One of the outdoor entertainment industries, the carnival has had a cultural and commercial presence in North America comparable to that of annual festivals, spectator sports, and outdoor concerts. The social and economic impact of these industries has provoked extensive reportage and commentary. The carnival has not received the same scrutiny. "Because of the splendor and prominence" of other outdoor entertainment industries, a sociologist of freak shows writes, "and the carnival's own reputation of being cheap and sleazy ... the carnival has taken a back seat in the chronicle of popular amusements."[12]

Early branded the poor man's entertainment, the carnival's "cheap and sleazy" reputation partly accounts for its neglect. But despite its marginal status, the carnival spectacle has previewed trends that reappear throughout all strata of the industries of diversion. The carnival became a mass entertainment industry before the technologies that enable the production of mass audiences were available, expending tremendous effort to reach its multitudes town by town, appealing to their appetite for novelty, excitement, sex, spectacle, risk, titillation, wonder, and thrills, bringing the world — or an illusion of the world — to the farming communities and oil towns of the West, and the newly industrialized towns and cities of the East. Carnivals reached audiences by travelling to them. By the end of the twentieth century, with the explosion of the industries of amusement, what type of mass entertainment was not for the poor man?

The word "midway" was first applied to a collection of outdoor amusements at the World's Columbian Exposition, held in Chicago in 1893, a year late to celebrate the quadricentennial of Columbus's voyage to America.[13] The Paris world's fair four years before had introduced the Eiffel Tower and proven the economic benefits entertainment features at a world's fair could reap, but the organizers of the Chicago fair were loath to play to the mob. As a sop to popular taste and the showmen ready to exploit it, they grudgingly allowed the "Midway Plaisance" to be set up outside the grounds, attached to the exposition proper at the midway's eastern terminus. The Chicago world's fair drew 27 million people, but the mile-long midway was the most popular area, saving the fair from financial failure.

The Midway Plaisance contributed more than a word and a concept to carnivals. George Ferris, an engineer for a Pittsburgh firm who aimed to rival the Eiffel Tower, constructed on the Chicago midway the first wheel that would be known by his name. Over 250 feet high, it weighed a thousand tons and had 36 cars, each the size of a streetcar and able to hold 60 passengers. It was not a portable machine and was scrapped after the fair, but it was the prototype Ferris wheel, providing the model for the device that would soon be identified with the midway. Under its concocted international theme, the Midway Plaisance featured the exotic sideshows, animal acts, and foreign villages that would also survive into the travelling carnival.

Middle America first saw belly dancing at the Chicago world's fair. Fahreda Mahzar, dancing as "Little Egypt," became the most celebrated and sought-after entertainer on the midway. Outraged journalists and commentators supplied Little Egypt with a notoriety that saved the fortunes of many show operators. After her debut, every show on the Midway Plaisance had a "hoochie coochie" dancer and girl shows would remain a midway feature for decades.[14]

The North American carnival was born in the back alleys of the Midway Plaisance, where outdoor showmen first talked about co-operating in peripatetic organizations to exploit the demonstrated public taste for their attractions. The first travelling carnivals aimed to bring the wonders of the Midway Plaisance to Americans who had not made it to Chicago. Several conglomerations formed soon after 1893, but they failed to solve the logistical dilemmas of the travelling midway. Frank Gaskill, a Canton, Ohio, hotel keeper, is credited with founding the first successful carnival company when in 1898 he booked a collection of attractions for a street fair in Canton sponsored by the Benevolent and Protective Order of the Elks. The Elks and other benevolent societies were soon supporting and profiting from a slew of carnival companies, including Canada's Conklin Shows when it came along. Lodges across the United States and Canada sponsored carnivals, as they were good fundraisers, and some even produced their own midways.

Gaskill's Canton Carnival Company went on the road in May 1899. George Chartier's Exposition Circuit Company followed Gaskill out. Both companies carried exotic and animal shows, a few games, unadvertised dancing girls, and little else. That summer, Frank Bostock, a British animal trainer who had transplanted himself to Coney Island, and Victor Levitt, who had worked with Bostock at Coney Island, formed the Bostock Mighty Midway Company, the third carnival in the field. These shows began to solve the problem of portability, organizing their operations like circuses and travelling by railway.

Rides were coming. The Eli Bridge Company in Jackson, Illinois, manufactured the first travelling Ferris wheel in 1900 — thriving on that innovation unto the fourth generation more than a century later. Although it would be a few years before many carnival owners could afford one, the Ferris wheel, along with the merry-go-round, unmotorized versions of which had been around for centuries, soon became icons of the North American carnival and no show could afford to travel without at least one of each. The appeal of mechanical wonders, often with a fractured sheen of futurity, became another appetite the carnival identified and exploited.

Convinced they were witnessing the birth of an industry, showmen and promoters with experience gained through the first three carnival companies fathered their own companies. The Supreme Council of the Elks banned street fairs in 1902, mainly to appease the moralists who from its beginning found the carnival an irresistible target. The ban was more honoured in the breach until the spread of the automobile effectively drove street fairs off the streets.

Carnival owners quickly discovered in agricultural fairs and industrial exhibitions a more enduring venue than the street fair, a recognizable midway appearing, for instance, at the Toronto Industrial Exhibition in 1903. That year, the Winnipeg fair was the first in North America to book a travelling carnival. The Minnesota State Fair followed the next year and within a decade every major fair was expected to have a midway.

The annual carnival season evolved into a mix of muddy urban lots, street fairs, and sponsored celebrations in the spring, and exhibitions and agricultural fairs in the summer and fall. Shows go "in the barn" or winter quarters when the cold descends. As street fairs disappeared, the concept they represented evolved into the "still date" or "still" — a spot booked for early in the route, before the fairs begin. Still dates give the owner a chance to work the kinks out of his show and put his staff far enough in debt to ensure they stay with him for the rest of the season. Still dates are usually held under the auspices of a local organization in return for a percentage of the take. A still might have no other attraction than a midway, unless the sponsoring committee can fabricate a parade or contrive some excuse for a festival. Good sponsorship could turn a still date into a profitable engagement or "red one." Early on, however, fairs and exhibitions became the heart of the carnival season and carnies relied on them to pay the bills through the off-season.

There were 22 travelling carnivals in the United States by 1903 and some of them visited Canada. All of them travelled by railway, many as "gilly shows," which were shows that had no transportation equipment, so they were loaded on rented railway boxcars then carted to and from the lot by local draymen. Better-equipped carnivals had their own wagons, loading and unloading them directly on the lot, pulling them between the lot and the rail yard, and carrying them on carnival-owned flatbed rail cars and boxcars.

By this time, a merry-go-round builder from Kansas, C.W. Parker, had expanded his carnival company to require 26 railway cars. He used a steam engine tractor to haul equipment between the lot and the yard. When not busy hauling, the steam engine generated electricity to light the midway. Parker's show was one of the first to carry a ride, a merry-go-round he had built. By 1904 his was the biggest outfit in the industry. Three years later Parker had four shows out on 83 railway cars and employed over 800 people.

In 1905 there were some 45 midway companies travelling North America. An economic downturn cut the number in half by the end of the decade, but by the time Clark & Conklin formed in 1915, over 200 carnivals wandered the continent. Even after the economic and social turmoil of the 1920s and '30s, there were still "300 Carnivals To Tour!" in 1937, as a headline in *Billboard* magazine shouted on April 10. Exact numbers are impossible to calculate as companies formed, dissolved, and reformed under various names, some conglomerations so ephemeral they left no record at all.

Clark & Conklin's All Feature Shows

When James Conklin took his company out to compete with the 200 other carnivals that set out in the spring of 1915, he brought along some of the people and acts he had associated with during his circus days. They included Commodore Benjamin H. Schlomberg's Water Carnival and Circus, and Charley Alpert's show with "some genuine freaks, and a banner flash that will do credit to any midway."[15] Clark & Conklin also had a Girl in the Moon illusion show and an athletic show. For rides, the show carried a new merry-go-round, a Trip to Mars, and a "circling wave," all owned by other operators. Despite the grand announcement of its launch, the company began as a "suitcase show," with little equipment of its own.

The Clark in the show's name came from Conklin's wife, born Ella May Clark. In one listing of the roster, E.M. Clark is the assistant manager. Ella was active in running the show, and is often presented as treasurer and concessions manager, sometimes appearing as Mrs. E.M. Conklin. She might not have been legally married to Conklin but was his steadfast partner.

Clark & Conklin's All Features Shows opened its first season on Thursday, May 1, 1915, at Ossining, New York, a small town on the east bank of the Hudson River, 35 miles north of Manhattan. It went on to play "some of the best towns in the East," which, the March 16 announcement in *Billboard* claimed, had already been booked by the time the show opened. When it closed for the season, the show took up winter quarters in New York City, just north of the entertainment district. Joe Renker might have first encountered the show there, on the streets of New York, after his return from the oil towns of Texas.

The 1916 season took Clark & Conklin Shows west. They announced that they would begin the season on April 29 "in Western Pennsylvania."[16] This would have been an early start and there is no evidence it happened. They played Youngstown, Ohio, less than 10 miles west of Pennsylvania, for the week ending Saturday, June 3. Its population approaching 100,000, Youngstown was part of an important steel-industrial complex. Four main railway lines and four branch lines intersected the city, an essential consideration for a carnival. The show then went 50 miles west to Barberton, a suburb of Akron. It stayed two weeks, the second perhaps unplanned. After Barberton, the show returned to Youngstown for another week.

Such a route is evidence that the show did not have spots booked for the season and was relying on an "advance man" to work ahead of the show, booking spots week by week. This practice was common at the time, especially for small shows and during the spring, before the pre-scheduled fair season began. The Clark & Conklin advance man does not seem to have had much luck at the start of the 1916 season.

During the winter of 1916–17, James Conklin moved south, a practice typical of carnival and circus owners. He took up residence at the Hotel Monteleone in the French Quarter of New Orleans, where he and Ella would watch the passing crowd from a booth in the hotel's restaurant. The Clark & Conklin equipment was stored in Covington, Kentucky, across the Ohio River from Cincinnati.

Conklin came back to the Cincinnati area to oversee the refurbishing of the show's equipment for the coming season. As of March 1917, he gave "c/o of Billboard, Cincinnati," as his address.[17] *Billboard* provided a communications function for travelling show people. Letters could be sent to one of the weekly's offices and in each issue a list of people who had missives awaiting them was printed. *Billboard*'s outdoor entertainment office was in Cincinnati.

Conklin sent *Billboard* a note that "everything is hustle and bustle" at the show's winter quarters and it would open at Covington in late April with "twelve paid attractions and thirty concessions."[18] Playing an opening week in the same town as a show wintered was common, allowing the show to dust off its equipment without the expense of a rail trip away from its shop, where any maintenance problems could be addressed. The notice suggests that the company had not yet booked any of the independent ride contractors that had travelled with it during the two previous seasons. Such instability was endemic to the industry. Rides were less essential to a midway than shows and games. The "paid attractions" included a new Jungle Show, being built by another "oldtime circus friend of Mr. Conklin."[19]

Clark & Conklin opened in Covington and stayed for two weeks. They went on to Dayton, Ohio, and then Columbus. They had planned to move on to Lancaster, a small city 30 miles southeast of Columbus. The Lancaster date fell through, and they remained in Columbus for another two weeks. The show then played towns in northern Ohio, circling around later in the summer to a cluster of small towns and cities in the east of the state. The spots were booked week by week. The show did not leave Ohio.

A *Billboard* article on June 30 helps to explain the 1917 itinerary of Clark & Conklin Shows: "The railroad situation ... is becoming ... a bugbear to circuses and carnivals, practically all of the shows encountering ... trouble in getting moved." Mobilization for the European conflict had come quickly once President Woodrow Wilson signed the declaration of war on April 6. The railways were commandeered to carry America's industrial might to ports to be shipped overseas. Shows using equipment owned by the railways were particularly hard hit. Such "system moves" could be almost impossible to arrange. Clark & Conklin Shows had to wait until equipment became available before they could move on.

The Conklins wintered in Jackson, Mississippi, returning to Cincinnati in early March 1918. Conklin briefly considered a partnership with J. Francis Flynn, who had "taken a half interest in the attractions with Colonel Conklin" and would furnish the rides.[20] Three weeks later the partnership was cancelled because Flynn "desired to stay in the South until after the date set for the opening of the shows."[21] Conklin booked other rides to replace Flynn's.

Conklin ran an advertisement in *Billboard* on March 30 looking for more personnel. The ad noted that the show had a few more managers of circus fame, including Jack Ogden, who now had the freak show. They also had a new athletic show, managed by a Greek wrestler. Conklin was looking for a fat girl and a "good Geek to handle and lecture on Snakes." The ad also reached out for musicians and other performers, and agents for games.

The show opened in a suburb of Cincinnati late in April. In announcing the opening, the Clark & Conklin press agent repeated a statement made when the show began: "Colonel Conklin hasn't one of the largest and best caravans in the country, but what he has makes a very neat, medium-sized midway. Furthermore, he owns all of the canvas and fronts with the show, save the carry-us-all, which belongs to Bobby Burns."[22] The carousel might have been the only ride the show carried at this time.

Clark & Conklin next played Reading, another Cincinnati suburb, where the show was "notified by the Pennsylvania Railroad Company that it would be impossible to move them to Eaton."[23] After the previous season, Conklin was prepared for this contingency. The show moved from Reading to Eaton, a distance of about 50 miles, using 20 trucks. They had added a Ferris wheel to their lineup. The show also travelled by truck to Miamisburg, 25 miles from Eaton, but picked up railway cars there. Miamisburg was a street fair. That Clark & Conklin had gotten a street fair suggests that the advance man's luck was improving.

On July 13, Clark & Conklin placed another want ad in *Billboard* requesting shows, rides, and games, this time "for a long season South, at Fairs and independent doings." The following week the company took out a full-page promotional advertisement, boasting of eight shows, two rides, two bands, and an unspecified number of games on eight railway cars. Apart from the Conklins, management included a general agent, a superintendent of concessions, and a press agent, the presence of the latter accounting for the publicity.

The show continued to play Ohio, with a few spots in West Virginia, before moving into Kentucky. It entered Tennessee in October, but, as the war in Europe was coming to an end, another global catastrophe began to have an impact on the American entertainment industry. The Spanish flu epidemic had begun in Europe in the summer, and by the fall, with the dispersal of soldiers from the war, was raging worldwide. Before it was over, the Spanish flu would kill some 675,000 Americans, more than were killed in the Great War itself. Among other preventive measures, places of public amusement were closed.

Clark & Conklin opened in early October, in Humboldt, Tennessee, but had to close the next day because of the epidemic. They travelled to Memphis, planning to open the following week. The opening never occurred. Enduring "a little layoff until the epidemic conditions improve," the show's representative noted that "the city will more than likely be closed to amusements for the next ten days and possibly much longer ... as soon as the quarantine is lifted the show will again open, having some of the best towns in the Mississippi Delta contracted for the latter part of October and November."[24] The press agent had been laid off.

The next want ad that Clark & Conklin placed in *Billboard*, on November 30, confirms that the show was in difficulty. Seeking shows and concessions for the Mississippi Delta, it stated that "we have our own cars and stay out all winter." American carnival historian Joe McKennon remarks:

> This "winter trouping" was unpleasant and very little financial gain was ever realized from it. The brutal fact of the matter was that the show owners were afraid to close their shows. If they did close, they would never be able to hold them together and open again. Possibly some of them hadn't had a payday all season. If they closed, some of the help might want nonexistent cash and attach the show property for the same.... Meanwhile they were all cold and hungry ... eating from a common stew pot, if and when a few hardy townspeople visited the bleak midway and spent enough to provide the necessary components for the stew.[25]

To add to their misery, the Conklins were in a car accident early in December in Mississippi.[26] James Conklin's thumb was severed by the other car's windshield and Ella Conklin, while not injured, suffered shock. She fell ill in January 1919 and remained sick until spring, exhibiting a nervous frailty that would recur over the years.

The show's general agent left in January. The carousel owner had also left, taking his ride with him. Another carousel was brought on. The show saw at least one day of snow.

To keep his show afloat and no doubt willing to meet whatever conditions were laid down, James Conklin entered into the partnership with J. Francis Flynn he had contemplated the previous spring. The Conklin–Flynn United Shows placed a want ad in *Billboard* on March 15. While the ad declares that the show has its own "riding devices," it identifies needs in every other department. An announcement on April 19 notes that Mrs. Conklin and the concession manager had 10 games, down from a high of 30. The Conklin–Flynn partnership dissolved in July, although Flynn continued to furnish three rides to the show.

After opening in Tennessee in late March, Clark & Conklin did not inform readers of *Billboard* of its whereabouts during the rest of the season. There was news on August 9 that Mrs. Conklin had bought a minstrel show. She planned to "launch the new outfit early in October, playing one-night stands thru Mississippi, Arkansas and Louisiana." Although minstrel shows were often part of the carnival business, one-night stands were not. She was developing a sideline. In September, her husband bought three monkeys in Cincinnati, while playing Aurora, Indiana, 20 miles away. This information is the last that *Billboard* contains about Clark & Conklin Shows.

Campbell's United Shows, owned by H.W. Campbell and travelling on a 30-car train, wintered in Georgia. Campbell announced in *Billboard* on February 7, 1920, that people already with the show included "Mr. and Mrs. J.W. Conklin and son." Sometime in the fall of 1919, the childless Conklins had lost a show and gained a child.

PASSING THE BATON

Low voices fill the room as the mourners console each other. A young man, clutching his dangling hat in two hands, sticks close to the frail woman in black, her eyes wet behind thick, round glasses. A man with a notepad approaches them, taking off his hat.

"You're James Wesley Conklin Jr., right?" he asks.

"Yeah, right, they call me Patty, Patty Conklin."

"And this is your mother?"

"Yes, Ella Conklin, my father's partner. They used to own a big show together, a real big show. He was well-known in the business."

"I'm sorry for your loss, Mrs. Conklin."

The reporter asks more questions, but the woman is distracted. The funeral director comes out and speaks to Patty, who takes Mrs. Conklin's elbow, directing her toward a door at the back of the room. She passes by the coffin, pauses briefly and looks in, and then is led away.

After the loss of their show in 1919, Mr. and Mrs. J.W. Conklin and son were clearly eager to get back to making money when they showed up at the Campbell's United Shows winter quarters early the following February. The son referred to in the announcement of their arrival was Joe Renker, who might already have taken the name James Wesley Conklin Jr., at least part time. Having made his first appearance in *Billboard*, he was now part of the carnival community; he was "with it and for it." According to his account, the Conklins adopted him for business reasons in 1920. The adoption was never officially registered. A week after the Campbell press agent submitted the *Billboard* article, Joseph Renker was enumerated for the 1920 census under his birth name at his genetic father's home in Paterson.[27] He gave his occupation as "showman" on the census.

The February 1920 article is the first to document Joseph Renker's connection with the Conklins. For him to be referred to as their son, he must have been with them for a good length of time. He later said he was with the show for five years, so he probably joined them when they started it in 1915. He spent his mid-20s with the Conklins, helping out in the games as they struggled to make their show a success. Joe probably learned as much from their failures as from any successes they had. As he would later demonstrate, he learned from his adopted father the art of "fixing" a show with the authorities.

When the United States entered the war against Germany in April 1917, Joe would have been eligible for the draft. Possibly in an attempt to get an exemption, he joined the Elks a year later.[28] Sponsored by Conklin senior, he signed up as Joseph Renker with a lodge in Grafton, West Virginia, a little more than 300 miles from Cincinnati, in the latter of which the show opened at the end of the month. It is hard to see how "showman" could constitute a category of deferment and he later claimed to have avoided conscription with the excuse that he had "bad teeth." As an itinerant, he might not have registered for the draft at all.

For the 1920 season, James Conklin was a "legal adjuster," first for Campbell's United Shows and then for Famous Broadway Shows. Shows needed a legal adjuster, "fixer," or "patch" who made the necessary arrangements, including bribery, with the local police and other authorities to ensure that a show did not come into conflict with them. If a patron had a complaint, the fixer mediated between the patron, the show, and the law. Even shows that operated honestly needed to pay off the police, who had come to expect this kind of compensation from carnies. Having been a show owner for five years, with no one but himself as legal adjuster, Conklin had rare experience in the profession and could provide this service for other shows.

The Carnival Office

The many components of the carnival must work well together, and the show owner must coordinate and direct them. "The office" is responsible for securing contracts with committees and fair boards, booking rides, shows, and games, ensuring that everyone makes it from one spot to the next, and promoting the show to the public. The number of details can be formidable. A carnival's success can depend on the talent, experience, effort and, often, brazen bravado of the office staff.

At one extreme, probably close to where Clark & Conklin sat, the office might own nothing and book independents to bring in their attractions. The owner of a "suitcase show" owns no more than his suitcase full of bookings and contracts. At the other extreme, the office might own everything and hire staff to run it. The larger shows tended to develop toward this extreme, especially as it became necessary to professionalize as businesses to deal with increasing layers of scrutiny and bureaucracy from all levels of government. Having witnessed the desertion of independents from Conklin senior's show, Patty's ideal from early on was to be sole proprietor of everything on his midway, although he never attained it. As rides became more expensive, management was often the only surety for capital sufficient to finance them. The attractions on a midway can vary markedly over the course of a season, as independents come and go in response to the size and success of events being played, but a show owner needs to be able to guarantee a bare minimum.

The various office roles might be performed by the owner alone or by dozens of staff. The proprietor is responsible for overall coordination. The general superintendent or "lot boss" looks after day-to-day operations. The duties of the lot boss included assigning space to all the attractions, called "laying out the lot." Because the location a show, game, or ride gets can determine whether it makes money, the lot boss can be subject to considerable pressure from operators. A good lot boss ignores this pressure, unless it's accompanied by significant monetary enhancements.

The treasurer or secretary keeps track of the money. The general or contracting agent sets up contracts with committees and fair boards, and organizes the route. The fixer or patch, like James Conklin in 1920, attends to the local authorities, bribing them as required. The special agent or advance man travels a week ahead of the show, ensuring that arrangements have been made for its arrival in each community, a duty that might include scrounging up new contracts to fill gaps in the route, as the Clark & Conklin advance man tried to do. The press agent works the local media, distributing material to them, arranging for billboard posting, and providing updates to *Billboard*.

The office might employ a range of superintendents, especially for concessions and rides, the latter called the "ride boss." Large shows would have a "trainmaster" to make arrangements with the railways, maintain railway stock, and supervise the loading and unloading of equipment. Shows that carried marching bands for free entertainment down the midway had a musical director. Some early carnivals had a general announcer to talk at the main gate and move from show to show. Larger carnivals had at least one dedicated electrician and maybe a lights supervisor. There might also be security staff, including a night watchman to guard against the return after hours of disgruntled patrons.

The characteristic common to all office staff is that while working for the office they do not generate revenue. They are paid from general office overhead, a percentage of the take for senior staff or a fixed salary for more peripheral personnel. They might be given a show to run or have games concessions from which to draw profits, often free from the usual office tariffs.

Beyond profits from office-owned shows, rides, and games, management gets a slice of the independents' take. Owners of shows and rides pay a percentage of their ticket sales, something that can be easily quantified. Owners of concessions, including games, novelty joints, and food stands, on the other hand, pay a flat rate per foot of midway real estate, called a "privilege." Staff not connected with the office cover their own travelling expenses, in some cases paying the office directly for rail transportation between spots. The overhead for each attraction is the "nut" and once it is covered the operation is said to be "off the nut."

The relationship among the office, the "agents" who operate the games, and the public was generally tense. Games agents paid a privilege and not a percentage of what they made because that was often in inverse ratio to their moral rectitude, something that carnival management had difficulty regulating, and there was no way to reliably measure their take. The most consistent target for public complaints about carnies was gambling and dishonesty as practised by games agents. As the complaints were usually addressed to the office, customer relations fell to the patch, whose fallback position was that the agents were independent concessionaires over whom the office exercised no control. Management might make this excuse even when the agents were working office equipment. Games concessions were so problematic and such a risk to the office investment that there were frequent predictions they would disappear. Some owners experimented unsuccessfully with games-free midways.

A carnival is a largely self-contained itinerant community with a social structure that reflects its organization. The hierarchy runs from the office staff, down through independent ride, show, and concession owners, to sideshow performers, ride jocks, and games agents. The last group in particular, in which

Patty began, was once composed almost exclusively of outcasts and derelicts who were heavily exploited by their bosses — the office, for instance, being the sponsor for in-house gambling operations that kept them poor but hopeful. Regardless of their condition, these people felt a strong commitment to the one place, always moving, they could call home.

The main demarcation has been between those on the outside and those who are "with it and for it." Through much of the twentieth century, carnies fiercely identified with their own kind against townies and marks. The belief that they have found a community in which they can enjoy freedom and adventure unknown to the mundane world is at the root of carnies' attachment to their lot. The belief persists despite the fact that during the season carnies work long days, get little or no sleep when travelling between locations, have only a day or two off each week, and work every holiday. In the off-season, they are left to their own devices, with plenty of freedom but little money, living off their summer savings or welfare, pooling in enclaves of idle colleagues, waiting for the first spring still date so they can get back to making money.

The Death of J.W. Conklin Sr. and the Birth of Patty Conklin

Joe Renker, or J.W. Conklin Jr., was with his adopted father when the elder died of a heart attack on September 28, 1920. James Wesley Conklin Sr. expired on the job, working as the legal adjuster for the Famous Broadway Shows, which was playing the Great Lancaster Fair in Pennsylvania. He was 59 years old and had been in show business since he was 16. *Billboard* printed an obituary and an article on October 9. The article describes him as "a widely known member of the outdoor show world ... familiarly referred to and addressed by many friends as 'Uncle Jim.'"

The obituary notes that Conklin "is survived by his wife, Ella, and one son, Patrick, both of whom were with him at the time of his death." Joseph Renker had taken a third name, the one by which he would be known, but for the solemnity of the obituary "Patty" was transcribed as "Patrick." Having adopted a father and then buried him, Patty adopted an ethnicity with his nickname. Even though fair and blue-eyed, he slipped on a Celtic identity to avoid the nasty associations clinging to his Teutonic genes and name.

After a funeral service conducted by the Elks in Lancaster, James Conklin's remains were sent to Newburgh, New York, for interment. Newburgh was Ella Conklin's home, and she accompanied the remains.

Both Ella Conklin and Patty were accomplished games agents who could easily earn their keep, partly because they were not unduly scrupulous. Early in October 1920, Ella returned to Famous Broadway Shows, which was playing towns in Virginia, dropping into *Billboard*'s New York office on her way.[29]

Billie Clark and a partner had put together Famous Broadway Shows in 1916. When Clark bought out his partner in 1920, "the entire outfit, including all Pullman, box, flat and stock cars, wagons, horses, animals and riding devices ... was valued at $55,000."[30] Clark would build the show up into two units before closing it in 1926.

Famous Broadway Shows went into winter quarters at Greensboro, North Carolina, late in 1920, after 40 weeks on the road. Clark planned to add five flat cars to his train, bringing the number up to 25 cars for a show that employed 300 people. In preparation for the coming season, he announced that he would "not tolerate any form of gambling upon the midway, and only such shows as are fit for the entertainment of ladies and children will be presented."[31]

The issue of gambling and girl shows versus family entertainment had been with the carnival from its beginning. There were always a few "Sunday school shows" — a term borrowed from vaudeville — but there were more shows rife with shady and salacious entertainments. A carnival that allowed gambling, grift, and explicit girl shows was said to play "strong." The strongest hoochie coochie shows allowed audience participation, called "serving lunch."

A significant theme in the history of mass entertainment was the growing realization by amusement impresarios that they could reach mass audiences only if they eliminated the rough attractions that had won them their early popularity among sporting males. This theme runs through the early history of vaudeville and film. The movie industry has been especially adept at playing to a broad, middle-class, consensual morality, while still satisfying the lust for sex and violence. Similarly, the carnival industry would later reform itself to broaden its market. At one time midways attracted only the working class, immigrants, and other marginalized segments of society. They have long since completed their transformation into sites of "fun for the whole family," where the middle class can find leisure and lose money.

Promoters of a clean, honest midway were vocal in presenting their arguments. In the early 1920s, *Billboard*'s editorial board mounted a campaign to clean up the carnival business. They worked with the Showmen's League of America, founded in Chicago in 1913 in support of carnival and circus show people. Together, they established the Showmen's Legislative Committee of America and appointed a commissioner who visited midways and reported on whether they qualified as Sunday school shows. Shows would declare themselves to be running under the banner of the Showmen's Legislative Committee. At its convention in Toronto in 1922, the International Association of Fairs and Expositions passed a resolution "favoring clean fairs ... and that nothing be tolerated on our grounds of a degrading or dishonest nature."[32] Grift and sex continued to be widespread on midways until well after the Second World War.

Patty Conklin had no intention of operating under the principles of the Showmen's Legislative Committee. His talents ran more toward games than girl shows, grift rather than sex. One of his early claims to fame was inventing a new "flat store" — a game no one can win unless the operator wants them to. He developed the bushel basket game for the season of 1920 and a version of it still travels with most shows. The tension of the bottom of the basket could be adjusted to make it almost impossible to get a ball to stay in. The beauty of the game, as with all good flat stores, is that it looks easy, although it bounced balls out as if it were a baseball pitching machine.

In the fall of that year, Patty announced that he had "decided to manufacture and sell a limited number of the sensational one-ball bucket games concession which he introduced this season and with which he has been 'cleaning up' on H.W. Campbell Shows all season; also on the Famous Broadway Shows."[33] In January and February of 1921, he took out advertisements for the "Original Conklin One Ball Bucket Game."[34] He offered a bucket, baseballs, canvas top, and frame for $100.

Patty was testing the waters to see whether he could make a living supplying carnival equipment, an easier life than travelling with a show. His advertisements insist that he is "the inventor and sole manufacturer of this game."[35] He could not get patent protection for a flat joint and for the 1921 season two well-established carnival supply companies advertised a bushel basket game, the illustrations for which look like Patty's game. His ads did not appear again. He would have to stay on the road.

The initial announcement for his bucket game said Patty had a plant at 142 Water Street, Paterson, New Jersey, set up to manufacture the equipment, and the ads for the equipment provide the same address. This was his father's address. A want ad for Famous Broadway Shows gives this address for J.W. Conklin Jr., the company's eastern representative. As eastern representative for Broadway Shows, Patty had attained a position of some responsibility. That he appears in a subsequent announcement for the show reinforces this impression. News from the show's winter quarters in Greensboro mentions that "J.W. Conklin, Jr.," who "will have several concessions with the show," is "expected daily."[36] In the years to come, his arrival would often be anticipated in the show business press.

Broadway Shows, with two free acts, six rides, 20 paid attractions, and 90 concessions, played a few spots in North Carolina and Virginia before moving on to Washington in mid-April. They set up on a lot a mile and a half east of the grounds of the Capitol Building for three weeks. During the first two weeks they were in competition with Lou Dufour Shows, the first company ever to book the Capitol grounds.

Lou Dufour was a 26-year-old with a company he had formed the previous June and expanded to a 10-car show for the 1921 season.[37] Dufour had grown up in the theatre world in New York, worked Coney Island as a teenager, and joined the Foley and Burk Show at 18. He worked a number of shows and exhibitions before forming his own. He got the Washington spot by seeing an opportunity and having the foresight and moxie to seize it. He kept the spot through bravado and deceit, inviting the committee responsible for the engagement to a winter quarters in Richmond, Virginia, that Dufour shared with a much larger show and encouraging the committee members to assume that all of the equipment they saw was his. Dufour closed his show in 1924, filed for bankruptcy in 1925, and went on to fame as a sideshow producer.

Dufour's coup in 1921 raised the ire of many larger companies. After he advertised for games and shows to fill out his lineup, "Washington became flooded with general agents," Dufour recounts. They "represented thirty-car and forty-car railroad shows, the cream of the carnival industry. They were seasoned veterans, some old enough to be my granddad, at the top of their profession, big-salaried men. Who was this upstart to grab off the big plum of the upcoming spring season?"[38] The agent for Johnny J. Jones Exposition, one of the two largest carnival companies at the time, was one of the "big-salaried men." Another was the agent for Clark's Broadway Shows. Dufour was predating Johnny J. Jones Exposition, and these agents were attempting to undermine him. Broadway Shows settled with competing against him.

Patty Conklin took advantage of this convergence to jump ship, leaving Billie Clark for Lou Dufour. Dufour tells the story of being approached by "this young fella" — three years older than Dufour — who "looked as though he could use some eating money."[39] Dufour realized that he had known "his father" and so "felt kindly toward him." Dufour "asked for a nominal privilege," the fee for the privilege of playing with the show: "You know, this fella reaches into his pants pocket and hauls out a roll of bills that would choke a horse. And they weren't aces and deuces. It was all big stuff. I learned then, and never forgot, that no one ever had to feel sorry for Patty Conklin. He could always take care of himself." Patty had two big weeks with Dufour, visited in the course of them by Mrs. Conklin, who was still with Broadway Shows.

Despite his status on Broadway Shows, Patty's basket games had run afoul of Clark's determination to run a clean operation and Dufour had no such scruples. Patty and Dufour remained friends and business associates for 50 years. The Washington date ended the association of both Conklins with Clark. They had made sufficient cash to consider other options. They began their trek north as independent concessionaires.

On Decoration Day, May 30, the Conklins were in Newburgh, at her husband's grave. Writing from Toronto in the middle of June, they informed *Billboard* that they had "left the Broadway Shows with their six concessions to make a circuit of western Canada fairs. They also advise that their entire 'bucket' business is now being handled by Geo. Brocco, the chief mechanic at their new and enlarged factory, 473 Marshall street, Paterson, N.J."[40] At her husband's graveside, Mrs. Conklin had noted that "the floral pieces included a blanket of cut flowers which covered the grave, from his dear ones, Mrs. Conklin, J.W. Conklin Jr., and Frank Renker."[41] They had crossed into Canada with the youngster they would transform into the third Conklin in their entourage.

THE EARLY YEARS IN CANADA

The baggage handler throws the boxes out on the platform of the Canadian Northern Railway St. Boniface Station, just outside Winnipeg, ignoring the "Handle with Care" emblazoned in red on their sides. Patty and Frank, in white shirts and suspenders, fuss around, try to catch the boxes, stack them, impose some kind of order.

After the train leaves, Molly Lavoie pulls up on a horse and wagon, and greets them in his heavy French accent. They bicker back and forth, then load the boxes on the wagon, tying them down with whatever rope they can find.

"*Allez! On y va*," the Frenchman shouts and Frank finds his hat and climbs on the wagon.

Patty rejoins Mrs. Conklin, who has been waiting off to the side, and they walk through the station to find a taxi. As the wagon bounces down the dirt road, a celluloid doll spills out of one of the boxes and rolls into the ditch, its wide blue eyes blind in the dust and late afternoon summer sun.

★   ★   ★

On their trip from Washington to Newburgh in May 1921, Patty and Mrs. Conklin stopped off in Paterson to look in on his bucket business, which he had moved to his brother-in-law's trucking depot. Patty's brother Frank, who had left their father's home in 1920 when he was 17, might already have been travelling with Patty, who had been at home for the federal census the year before, or might have joined him at this time.

Patty was still answering to both his names. The *Billboard* letter list for July 2, 1921, notifies "Renker, Jos." that there is a letter waiting for him. As late as June 1923 he renewed his membership with the Grafton Elks as Joseph Renker. The next year he had fully become "Jas. Wesley Conklin," even to his brother Elks. Frank crossed the Canadian border under his birth name but would soon adopt his new family. He would grow up as Frank Conklin among the freaks and girl shows and mechanical wonders of the midway, becoming a carnie alongside his older brother.

Midway Attractions

During the first half of its history, shows were the midway's main attraction and the reason why companies that include the word "show" in their title use it in the plural. Exotic shows like the Streets of Cairo, the Turkish Theater, and Paris at Night, modelled on those of the Midway Plaisance and harbouring dancing girls, were replaced during the first 30 years of the modern carnival by more explicitly sexual shows. A carnival historian writes that "throughout the years, no matter what attractions, games, or rides came and went on the showgrounds, one constant carnival attraction was the girl shows. When you walked onto the carnival grounds, you knew you were going to find a merry-go-round and a girl show."[42]

The freak show evolved out of the late nineteenth-century dime museum — P.T. Barnum's start — which had presented fire breathers, contortionists, sword swallowers and walkers, midgets, giants, tattooed men, people with assorted physical deformities, and other such once-familiar fare. Single act shows were known as "pit shows." The "ten-in-one" — 10 acts for one admission — was forced into being at the 1904 Toronto Industrial Exhibition by shortage of space on the midway. Along with the freaks and performers, it usually featured a "geek." An ordinary geek simply handled animals, probably badly, but a "glomming geek" bit the heads off chickens, snakes, rats, and other small creatures. The ten-in-one, also called the "circus sideshow" or "museum show," became the freak show. By the 1920s they were the attraction on the midway, produced by the office and advertised by an elaborate banner line.

Athletic shows and motordromes were other early midway favourites, as were, a little later, water shows. The athletic show or "at show," where patrons paid to watch local contenders challenge carnival brutes, was a proven crowd pleaser dating back to European fairs but would die out with the growing popularity of professional boxing in the 1930s. Betting was encouraged and the results rigged to ensure that no matter who hit the mat management won. The motordrome, invented just before the Great War, featured motorcyclists racing their machines around the vertical walls of a wooden cylinder. Motordromes are one of the few early shows to have survived to the present. Water shows, presenting high divers, clowns, and plenty of women in bathing suits, drew big crowds from the late 1920s into the '70s.

Promoters exercised a macabre ingenuity in devising attractions. Every type of human oddity, real or imagined, has found a place on the midway. Crime, war, and drug abuse shows operated under the guise of educating the public, as did Dufour's baby shows with deformed fetuses in formaldehyde, and life shows with exhibits illustrating the "facts of life," somehow always focused on those related to reproduction. Various illusion shows have come and gone, as have wax shows, always hard to maintain in the summer heat.

Most shows, especially those featuring freaks and exotic spectacles, have disappeared, the former partly because of the turn in public morality against making a display of misfortune, the latter because of the availability through electronic media of all manner of the odd and exotic. The appetite for carnival freaks has been displaced into the grotesquery of horror movies, the directors of which have uncovered tastes unimagined even by carnies.

During their heyday, midway shows attracted the public with a "bally," a raised platform in front of the show upon which the "talker" presented his spiel. The talker — never barker — is one of the most recognized human icons of the midway and skilled talkers became legends among show people. The talker was assisted on the bally by performers, especially women, who previewed what the public could enjoy for the price of admission. The crowd gathered to hear the talker was the "tip" and, once gathered, the talker sought to "turn the tip" — to get everyone streaming to the ticket box. The shows paid their way by drawing patrons to the midway, but few made significant money and salary overhead could be high.

Shows used various means to augment their take. The "candy butcher" worked direct sales inside the tent, the "candy pitch" being that random boxes of candy had free gifts inserted in them. The gifts, of course, did not exist. A "blow off," the most profitable extra for a show if run with skill, was an added attraction positioned in a vestibule at the exit from the main show and requiring an additional fee. For girl shows, the blow off offered a more risqué feature than the main stage. The blow off was used to clear patrons from the tent while it filled with a new crowd and to ensure that as much money as possible was squeezed from the exiting crowd. The war show extra would be a shell game — a con game in which a pea is rapidly shifted under three walnut shells — operating in the back of the tent. When an old soldier came in, a fellow veteran would escort him to the shell game with a promise to help him pick out the right shell.

While seldom a draw on their own, the games became essential to the financial health of carnival companies, the take from them keeping many a show alive and adding substantially to the bottom line of many another. The first carnivals did not have games except those run surreptitiously inside the show tents. As the industry developed, the shows became little more than bait to draw crowds to be cleaned out by various types of thievery associated with the games. Rides later performed the same function as shows.

The layout of midway lots evolved to ensure that the games agents have first and last chance at the marks. The ideal midway is oval with the entrance gate at one end and, on either side inside the gate, the games making up the "front end." The rides and shows are the "back end," with the rides down the middle of the oval and the shows around the circumference. Lot bosses early learned that North Americans tend to walk down the right-hand side when they enter a midway, so shows catering to children, families, and other early arrivals are located on that side. The more powerful shows are at the far end, opposite the gate, to pull the crowd down the length of the midway. Noisy attractions like the motordrome are spotted along the left-hand side, to draw people into that lane.

The games agents get their first shot at the marks as they enter the gate. As people are funnelled around the midway, crowds move around the oval to congeal at the front end and the games get another stab at the thickening horde, a good portion of which is trying to find the gate. Designed as a dynamic human lobster trap, the classic midway is easy to enter, harder to leave.

The first games were "grind stores," relying on a steady flow of customers, none of whom would spend a great deal. Prizes were given out freely in the early days to keep people playing. Gradually, money replaced merchandise and many of the games became nothing more than rigged gambling operations.

Carnie agents, the more dishonest of whom were called "lucky boys," developed many types of fixed "stores" or "joints," other names for games. A "gaffed joint" was a crooked game. The "gaff" in a "G wheel" was the control on the wheel that enabled the operator to stop it wherever he wanted. A "count store" was any game where players selected numbers that the agent added up for a total score; the score could always be fixed by an agent who added faster than a player or who reversed sixes and nines. An "alibi joint" was a game of skill that was nearly impossible to win; the alibi agent provided alibis as to why a player had not yet won, advice for the next attempt or, if the player managed the impossible, an alibi to explain why the player really had not won and would not get a prize. A "flat store," like Patty's bushel basket game, was a game that could not be won unless the agent chose to let you.

Carnies early on developed techniques other than giving out prizes to draw players to their joints. A "shill" or "stick" was a carnival agent who posed as a member of the public. He pretended to play a game and walked away with a big prize to entice others to join in. "Hanky-pank" games attracted players with a prize every time, the prizes generally being junk or "slum." The most attractive prizes used to decorate a joint were called the "flash" and required dusting off between spots.

Pickpockets and short-change artists were common on early midways, the latter working ticket booths for shows and rides, sometimes receiving no pay other than what they could swindle from the public. "Jam auctioneers" or "pitchmen" developed elaborate shows of illusion and deception to persuade the public to buy unwanted and generally worthless merchandise. Pitchmen became an industry to themselves, working city street corners in the off-season.

In the early days of the modern midway, the Ferris wheel and the merry-go-round were almost the only mechanical devices on it. In 1915 William

Mangels, a Coney Island manufacturer, developed the Whip, the first portable thrill ride, in a New York machine shop. While other rides produced a uniform motion, the Whip delivered an oscillating motion. The cars, attached by spokes to a horizontal oval hub, whipped at greater speed at each end of the oval. Beyond the thrill, the increased speed threw passengers together. Any carnival man who has had anything to do with rides believes as a matter of faith that this forced physical contact between male and female passengers is one of the main draws of his devices. In the 1920s, public opportunities for physical contact were few. The Mangels Whip marked a change in midway attractions leading to the monster rides that began to show up after the Second World War. The Tilt-A-Whirl, developed a few years later, doubled the G-forces of the Whip, throwing friends together more firmly, and remains popular on midways.

Early ride inventors also realized they could offer couples a rare chance to cuddle in the dark. The Caterpillar, introduced by Spillman Engineering in 1922, had cars running on a circular, undulating track and got its name from the canvas hood on hoops that arose to enclose riders. A proliferation of dark rides and tunnels of love catered to this part of the carnival audience, soon dubbed "the tunnel trade." With these rides, sex became a participatory activity on the midway, not just the spectator sport provided by the girl shows. Here again, the carnival would eventually be made superfluous by the public morality it helped to loosen.

The Conklin Concession Company

Wortham's World's Greatest Exposition Shows was a big show with the latest rides and a good number of shows. The Conklins and Frank left Toronto in June 1921 for Winnipeg, travelling light and planning to join Wortham's as it began the A circuit of western Canadian fairs, which went from Winnipeg to Brandon, Regina, Saskatoon, Calgary, and Edmonton. In 1918 the Western Canada Fairs Association had coordinated its fairs in Alberta and Saskatchewan into circuits rated from A to E. A show could contract for the whole A circuit, making it the finest gem a carnival company in North

America could gain. That Prohibition was in effect in the United States from January 1920 added a special shine to the Canadian circuit. Johnny J. Jones Exposition had the A circuit in 1920 and would get it again in 1922. Clarence A. Wortham, Jones's only rival for ownership of North America's largest carnival, had several units, sending his number one unit to Canada. In business since 1910, Wortham also had the CNE — even then the world's largest annual outdoor exhibition — and the Western Ontario Fair in London.

While Patty's claim to have been at the first Calgary Stampede in 1912 is improbable, he had certainly "heard about all the easy money in Western Canada," so he decided to try it out for the 1921 season.[43] He and Mrs. Conklin financed the trip to Winnipeg with a $3,300 stake, partly derived from the sale of her husband's equipment, and arrived with a boxcar full of kewpie dolls. The Wortham concession manager did not, however, want the services of the Conklins. Dejected, the troop prepared to return to the United States, leaving the kewpie dolls behind. From the back seat of a taxi on the way to the train station, Patty spied a small, ragbag show in a dirt lot in St. Boniface, a francophone community just outside Winnipeg. He stopped the taxi and got out in the summer heat to inspect the show.

The International Amusement Company was playing the Winnipeg area up against three much larger shows. Besides Wortham's World's Greatest, the Al G. Barnes Circus and Sheesley Greater Shows were there. Patty talked to the owner of International Amusement, A.R. "Molly" Lavoie, reviewed his route list to ensure that the show had enough engagements to cover the season, then decided to book his games with the show. The Conklins opened on Lavoie's midway on Friday, June 24, St. Jean Baptiste Day. Lavoie, a francophone, would have been at home in St. Boniface on the holiday of Quebec's patron saint. The Conklins — Irish, German, American — not so much, but they were obviously adaptable.

Molly Lavoie had formed the International Amusement Company the previous year. It was a gilly show and seems to have changed its winter quarters almost every year. The show might have wintered in New Jersey in 1920–21 because its opening date was in Passaic, seven miles from Paterson. Patty likely first met Lavoie there and even talked about plans for later in the season. From St. Boniface, the show went to a string of C circuit fairs in the Prairies and fall fairs in British Columbia, finishing up in Kelowna the first week of October. This route would have been Patty's first in Canada, and he would cover much the same route many times.

The announcement from International's winter quarters at the Vancouver Fair Grounds published in *Billboard* on March 18, 1922, features the Conklins prominently, Frank now sharing the name: "James W. Conklin, Jr., together with Mrs. J.W. Conklin, Frank Conklin and a half-dozen agents, has been at quarters for a month and has completed a string of concessions which are almost the last word in attractiveness and beauty as well as utility of construction." Theo Forestall signed himself as the press representative, mentioning that, as well as being "auditor for Mr. Conklin," he "will handle the publicity for the show management." Theo would be Patty's secretary and treasurer, third in command of the Conklin enterprise, for two years.

Forestall, a year younger than Patty, a New Jersey native, and a graduate of Lehigh University, joined the carnival in 1917, and became secretary of Campbell's United Shows in 1919. His wife operated a concession on the show that year as well. The Forestalls returned to Campbell's early in 1920, around the same time as James Conklin Sr. and his family. Forestall accompanied the Conklins when they went to Canada in mid-1921. He ran a concession, as well as acted as treasurer, and could jump into a joint when needed.

Patty developed a habit of reaching out to people he knew and could trust. He persuaded at least one other American friend to come to Canada. He had met Joe "Jockey" Custock on one of the carnivals they worked together in the United States. Once he got established with Lavoie, Patty wired Custock in Georgia, asking him to join his lineup of agents. Custock agreed and eventually became a lot boss, staying with him for 20 years, and returning at the end of Patty's life in response to one final appeal.

International Amusement expanded for the 1922 season and had a respectable lineup of rides. They had bought a new Ferris wheel to go with their merry-go-round, Chair-O-Plane and Mangels Whip. Lavoie took his company from the late-March 1922 opening date in Vancouver to New Westminster. In Chilliwack, he treated the locals to their only exposure that year to the Whip. Likewise with the fairs the show played in the Prairie provinces. Residents of towns like Taber and Vermilion in Alberta, Humboldt and Rouleau in

Saskatchewan, and Neepawa and Carberry in Manitoba rarely had the opportunity to experience the shows and rides that larger carnivals were bringing
to the bigger towns and cities. That the rides and shows carried a surcharge
paid at the flat stores and gaff joints rounded out of the locals' experience of
big-city amusements.

Patty and his fellow games agents fleeced the local marks with gusto. He
later boasted that in his first two years in Canada he cleared $20,000, an enor-
mous sum for the time, especially when made with so little investment — stick
joints and canvas, a bit of apparatus, boxes of cheap prizes. Starting the 1922
season, Patty had seven games, Frank four, and a string of other agents one or
two each. Mrs. Conklin, getting on in years, ceased to work regularly in the
joints, although she too filled in when required.

The Conklins stayed with International through most of its western tour,
but left Lavoie when he took the show into Ontario later in the summer. By
early September, they had joined Snapp Brothers' Shows at New Westminster.
The Snapp Brothers had the western Canada B circuit, finishing up their
Canadian route at the Vancouver Exhibition and the New Westminster
Royal Industrial Exhibition. The last date for the Conklin concessions was
with Levitt-Brown-Huggins Shows at the Puyallup Fair, outside of Tacoma,
Washington, the second week of October. They would rejoin this company
the following season.

Molly Lavoie, his company wintering in Moose Jaw, Saskatchewan, announced at the end of the year "that he will put out two carnival shows the
coming season and that the No. 1 show will not carry concessions of any
kind."[44] If this "experiment" worked out, he would cease to carry concessions
on either show. He went out with only one show the season of 1923, and
that show had "several concessions," but not the Conklin games.[45] Lavoie
abandoned his experiment, carrying more concessions in later years, but declaring that he had "enrolled under the banner of the Showmen's Legislative
Committee" and would run his show "under its creed."[46] His ambition to
run an honest show might have led the Conklins to part with him, like Billie
Clark before.

Mrs. Conklin remained the Conklin best known to the show world, and
the closeness with which her movements are followed by *Billboard* attests to

both the esteem she retained with that world and her eagerness to cultivate it. After the Puyallup date in October 1922, the group stopped off for "several recuperation weeks" at Hot Springs, Arkansas, as Mrs. Conklin "had been ailing somewhat."[47] Besides its hydrotherapeutic facilities, the other attraction of Hot Springs for Mrs. Conklin was that it drew a substantial community of wintering carnival folk. The Conklins then turned north, passing through Cincinnati early in February 1923, visiting the *Billboard* offices and Mr. and Mrs. J.E. "Doc" Ogden. John Ogden had been a circus friend of Mrs. Conklin's husband and had a sideshow with Clark & Conklin Shows. They then stopped in Pittsburgh for a few weeks. Finally, Mrs. Conklin returned to her home in Newburgh, and Patty and Frank to their father's home in Paterson.

The Conklins did not stay long in the east, returning to the Levitt-Brown-Huggins Shows in the spring of 1923. Victor Levitt had been with the carnival industry since its beginnings, as general manager of the Bostock Mighty Midway Company in 1899. The Mighty Midway had no dates of its own, so it followed the first two carnivals, Frank Gaskill's Canton Carnival Company and George Chartier's Exposition Circuit Company, and found vacant lots next to them. Levitt subsequently went through a number of partnerships before heading a combination with W.C. "Spike" Huggins and Sam Brown in 1921.

The press representative for Levitt-Brown-Huggins Shows wrote *Billboard* early in May 1923 to pass on news. Among the 40 concessions on the show, "Mrs. Conklin and her sons, Paddie and Frank, have five."[48] The Conklins stayed with this unit through May and June, while it played still dates throughout Washington, including two pairs of weeks in Seattle. They must have operated through the office secretary, because their accountant, Theo Forestall, was with the K.G. Barkoot Shows that spring. Barkoot, a Syrian, had worked the Columbia Exposition in 1893 and started his own travelling show in 1903. Barkoot Shows played Ohio and Michigan in May and June. By the middle of June, Forestall was in Chicago planning to join the Conklins on the fairs in western Canada.

For the 1923 season, the Conklin entourage had become the Conklin Concession Company with "fifteen well-framed and elaborately flashed concessions" and "twenty-five people." They left Levitt-Brown-Huggins and in July and August played "independent dates," Patty reporting in early September that they had completed "two solid months of fair dates" before "starting the British Columbia fairs."[49] The Conklins finished August in Blairmore, Alberta, 12 miles from the Crow's Nest pass into British Columbia, and were in B.C. throughout September. Patty writes that they "made as many as five spots in one week without losing a day," which suggests they were playing very small fairs and were constantly on the move.

With only games to provide, the Conklin Concession Company could not have booked fairs on its own. For their western Canadian fairs, the Conklins had found another show to hook up with, one that did not send press notices to the trade weekly. Always convivial, Patty would have ensured that Molly Lavoie introduced him to Speed Garrett in the spring of 1922 when "Messrs. Galloway and Garrett, of the shows bearing their names," visited the International Amusement midway.[50] Garrett's small show was based in Seattle. Patty's business connection with him likely dates from the middle of the 1923 season, when Patty booked concessions with Garrett's show for small fairs in Alberta and British Columbia. Through Speed Garrett, Patty found his footing in the carnival industry, while Speed found his downfall. Within a year, Patty would become a partner with Garrett and, at the age of 32, a show owner for the first time.

Conklin & Garrett's All-Canadian Shows

(1923–1932)

His apprenticeship served, James Wesley "Patty" Conklin began to stake his well-publicized claim in the carnival industry. He briefly dragged Speed Garrett along as a partner but kept some events in their relations from becoming public. He rose during the period when early icons were carving out their places in the Wild West of the American media. Charlie Chaplin, Samuel Goldwyn, Walt Disney, William Paley — and Patty Conklin — were conjuring empires of entertainment out of the empty air. Like Gatsby and Goldwyn, Patty had changed his name and was ready to use anyone available to further his ambitions. A true American, he was inventing himself as he went along.

PATTY AND SPEED ON THE ROAD

After closing the show, tearing down in the dark, and stowing the equipment on the train to Drumheller, Patty and Speed head out the next morning in the company car with the show secretary driving. The arid rangeland, heated by the early June sun, is broken only by willows and cottonwoods along the Red Deer River. The road is unmapped, narrow, dusty, and rough, barely passable by the Model T, which can't go over 45 miles per hour anyway.

Speed suggests they try a little fishing. He's got a couple of rods in the trunk for just such an opportunity. They laugh to recall the huge sturgeon one of their carnies caught the year before on Vancouver Island. Patty, nimble despite the overalls he's pulled on, hops from rock to rock down the riverbank. Behind him, tall, gangly Speed picks his way stiffly in his rumpled three-piece suit.

They catch a half-dozen good-sized trout. Back at the car, they crack open a couple of warm beers and unpack their sandwiches.

"Will, get the camera and take a picture. It's in the trunk," Speed tells the driver. He sidles up to Patty and, the brim of his hat turned up, grins sheepishly into the camera. Patty, beer in hand, leans back and glowers. Pleased at this moment of bonding with his partner, Speed later sends the picture to *Billboard*.

★　★　★

Throughout the 1920s, the Conklins — Ella, Patty, and Frank, none of them born to the name — played western Canadian towns that had not existed a decade or two before. Even after massive immigration to the Canadian Prairies early in the century, the population of some of these towns numbered in the hundreds, although they served a larger rural citizenry. But they were on railway lines, which all but guaranteed their ensuing development and put them squarely in the crosshairs of the travelling carnivals. The Conklins rolled over these towns, waging the battle of carnie and townie year after year, conquering western Canada just as it was being settled.

A carnival was often part of an agricultural fair. The early western fairs became torn between their educational and entertainment functions, despite the acceptance that had grown elsewhere on the continent that a certain amount of amusement in the yearly routine was a right. The rationale for the agricultural societies running the fairs was to educate farmers by imparting better farming techniques. But the fairs also drew the new carnival organizations, ostensibly intent on entertaining the farmers — and that would give them a different kind of education.

As social occasions, the fairs helped to assimilate the huge influx of immigrants, many of whom were from eastern Europe. Carnies saw these immigrants as especially ripe for the plucking. Patty learned that one reason a carnival could make money in the Canadian West was because of "its many districts where the population is largely foreign and of peasant origin and to whom a show is an event."[1] Fairs were events of ambivalent significance. Patty and his kind were happy to help stage them.

As early as 1915, the *Farm and Ranch Review*, published in Calgary, called for the elimination of midways from western fairs: "One of the most repugnant experiences which can befall the average man or woman is afforded by a tour of the midway at any of our Western agricultural exhibitions.... The matter of abolishing the unquestionably immoral effect of the midway should commend itself to our social reform leagues."[2] Critics accurately equated the companies that ran midways with the shadier element from the United States, but midways drew the crowds needed for a fair's success and had to be accepted as necessary evils. The carnival brought the outside world to isolated farmers and settlers, and ensured they paid for the experience.

The towns the Conklins played in Alberta, Saskatchewan, and Manitoba with Molly Lavoie's International Amusement in 1922 had C circuit fairs. Galloway and Garrett had been playing small fall fairs in British Columbia for several years, the Conklin Concession Company with them in 1923. An individual concessionaire could make a lot of money at small fairs, but these fairs could not support a show of any size. International had larger fairs in the West and Ontario, and Patty asked Lavoie for an exclusive on concessions in the West for the 1924 season. Such an arrangement was "out of the question," Lavoie responded in a letter. "What do you expect me to do before I get West I wooden be able to contract no one and leave them flat after I start the fairs and I go in Ontario where wheels dont work and need more concessions there as they are use to have a lot and that is where my best fairs are."[3] Ontario restricted gambling, which would also be a problem if Patty were to stay with him on the eastern part of the route. Patty looked around that winter and found another opportunity for an exclusive on games in the West.

Season of 1924

Before the opening of the 1924 season, Patty became Speed Garrett's partner in a new company, buying out Galloway, Speed's former partner, for $1,500. At the Levitt-Brown-Huggins Shows' opening in Tacoma, Washington, in the spring of 1924, show people visiting the midway included "Mrs. Conklin and her two sons, [and] 'Speed' Garrett."[4] The Conklin–Garrett arrangement was not announced at this time, but was in the bag. Patty was the mover in the new partnership. Speed remained an active partner for three years before being sidelined by ill health. Patty, attuned to the importance of public perception, supplied the "All-Canadian" qualifier to this company founded and run by Americans, and Conklin and Garrett's All-Canadian Shows was born.

Speed Edward Garrett was born in Kentucky in 1875 and grew up in a small town near Boise, Idaho, where he later married and had three children.[5] He began in the entertainment business by buying film reels in Los Angeles and projecting them from the back of his truck for citizens of small towns throughout the West. He became the first movie theatre operator in Boise and also worked at carnivals that passed through the city. Before becoming a show owner, he had games in San Diego and was an independent concessionaire at the National Orange Show in San Bernardino. He likely formed Galloway and Garrett Shows around 1920.

Letterhead of Conklin & Garrett All-Canadian Shows with photos of the co-owners.

Beyond his own capital, and the 15 games and 25 staff of the Conklin Concession Company, Patty offered Garrett railway equipment and two rides. Lavoie had been trying to sell two railway cars, a Ferris wheel, a merry-go-round, and other equipment to Patty since the spring of 1923, pressuring Patty by claiming he was holding off other buyers. On an earlier trip to his father's home in Paterson, Patty had seen the equipment at Lavoie's Detroit winter quarters and found much of it worthless. Lavoie wondered how his staff "could break stuff like that in such a short time."[6] Patty was unable to return to Detroit, as Lavoie requested, so the negotiations were completed by telegram. In 1924 they closed the deal, Patty paying $1,700, less than half what Lavoie had originally asked. In mid-April, Canadian Pacific Railway delivered the equipment to Patty in Seattle, where Garrett had kept his winter quarters.

In 1924 the All-Canadian Shows was "a small two-car show" with a freak show, a miniature-horse show, a war show, an athletic show, a cow show, and Lavoie's merry-go-round and Ferris wheel.[7] The cow show was not always presented, but the Conklins' 12 games were. Patty arranged for the show to open in Vancouver early in May.

Vancouver had grown rapidly since the turn of the century. Although the depression of 1913 and the loss of trade during the Great War had hurt the city, it began to boom again in the early 1920s and by 1924 had a population of more than 120,000. Conklin & Garrett Shows would benefit from its association with the thriving city throughout the decade, as it replaced Winnipeg as the leading city in western Canada. According to Patty, however, the first year in Vancouver the show "lost considerable money."[8]

While the show was playing Vancouver, the company's advance man completed arrangements with the Empire Day Committee in Nanaimo on Vancouver Island to play five days there the following week. The main day of that celebration, Saturday, May 24, was marred by heavy rain in the evening. The resourceful Patty resorted to a daring, if risky, way of attracting customers. He set a fire — not his last — to a novelty stand. A crowd rushed to see what the excitement was, staying on the midway afterward to gamble at the concessions.

The fire brought out the fire inspector. Patty, "fast-thinking, quick on his feet, a hard, unyielding fighter when the chips are down," dealt with him easily:

There wasn't a fire extinguisher in sight. "What do I want with extinguishers?" demanded Patty indignantly. "Some jerk would just steal 'em." Then, looking around hastily, he saw a pile of sandbags, used to keep the tent covers in place. "Besides," he continued with the barest pause, "I got something better. Look at that." And he pointed virtuously to the sandbags. "You can't beat sand for a fire, can you?" The inspector retreated, apologizing.[9]

The show returned to the mainland for a number of small celebrations and fairs. They spent June and July in Alberta and Saskatchewan, and August and September in British Columbia. After a three-day fair in Nelson, a small town in B.C.'s Selkirk Mountains, they took the railway to Rossland, an even smaller town, for a still date from Saturday to Saturday, with Sunday off. They had another three-day fair in Kelowna, which had just been reached by the railway, before returning to Vancouver, where they put their equipment in winter quarters for the first time. Patty did not share Speed's ties to Seattle, and Vancouver had cheaper rents.

The end-of-season schedule illustrates Patty's resourcefulness in arranging a route that combined fairs and still dates to keep his crew together. The show was restricted to the dates established by fair committees when playing fairs but had latitude when setting still dates. The small western fairs were two- and three-day events. The Nelson fair ended on a Thursday. If Patty cut all his frontline staff free for three or four days over a weekend, the season's end in sight, many of them would disappear. So, he scheduled a still date with a Saturday opening, although they could not stay open on the Sunday. The gross receipts for the three-day fair in Nelson were slightly over $6,000; for the seven-day still in Rossland they did not reach $4,200, at least on paper.[10] No doubt they grumbled, but Patty kept intact the crew he needed to get the show into winter quarters.

After stowing the equipment in Vancouver, the Conklins spent a few weeks in Seattle and then moved on to Los Angeles for two months before travelling east in January.[11] In Los Angeles, Patty got elected to the board of governors of the Pacific Coast Showmen's Association, founded in 1922. He would further his ambitions through this organization over the next decade.

When in Seattle, Patty and Speed stayed at the Georgian Hotel. Among the other guests were show owners Spike Huggins and Sam Brown and their secretary-treasurer, Will Wright. As he did over the next decade in various cities, Wright opened a storefront sideshow that winter in Seattle, filling it with attractions he took out for his midway shows. Storefront shows descended from the dime museums popular at the end of the nineteenth century and were part of the genealogy of the sideshow. Patty convinced Wright to join Conklin & Garrett for the 1925 season. An Englishman who had come to the United States in his mid-30s, Wright was 48 when he went to work for Patty. He helped Patty direct the show over the next decade, handling various duties, including secretary, press agent, advance man, and general agent.

In 1925 the Manitoba fairs joined the Western Canada Fairs Association, and the B circuit was reorganized to enable one show to play 14 fairs at two per week. Garrett and his right-hand man, John J. Moran, attended the association meeting in Edmonton at the end of January. On the basis of the "All-Canadian" label and the promise of a larger show than they could field, they were awarded the B circuit fairs for the first time, taking them from the Levitt-Brown-Huggins Shows. The Conklin & Garrett press representative gave "a great deal of credit" to "the management" for "landing a plum the size of the 'B Circuit', especially in consideration of the fact that this is only the second year" for the show.[12]

Season of 1925

Although to a lesser extent than promised, the company did expand for 1925, doubling their railway stock to four baggage cars, adding two Pullman cars, buying a Chair-O-Plane swing and booking a Whip. They still had Lavoie's Ferris wheel and dilapidated merry-go-round. The show's press material announced eight shows. A former employee of Johnny J. Jones Exposition brought a motordrome show he had built. Wright put on his one-ring circus, Jungleland, a snake show, and, apparently an attraction all on her own, "his little horse, Queenie."[13] The show also added light stands to brighten up the midway and extend the nighttime action.

One Pullman had berths for the owners and office staff; the other was used as the "pie car." The carnie pie car, the staff lounge on trips between spots, went back to the circus trains of the late nineteenth century. A pie car held a cookhouse to feed and water the carnies, and management sponsored gambling. Slot machines and other gambling equipment were available, but in the Conklin & Garrett pie car, high-stakes stud poker, Frank's game, was the favourite. Patty and Frank took a cut of the action.

The show opened with a week in downtown Vancouver in late April. "Clean–Moral–Refined," read the ad on April 27, 1925, in the *Vancouver Sun* for the "Big Spring Fun Festival." Louis D. "L.D." Taylor, recently returned after 10 years out of office to his fourth term as mayor, officially opened the show with a florid speech under uncommonly sunny skies.[14] After the auspicious start, bad weather later in the week hurt attendance.

They then travelled by ferry to Ladysmith on Vancouver Island, where they spent the next week. Patty, now a seasoned pyromaniac, set another fire, this one to the old merry-go-round. Wright reported to *Billboard*: "There was a fairly good attendance on Saturday night, but a big fire which started about 9 o'clock put a damper on the business."[15] Patty's motive this time was to ward off the complaints of the B circuit fair committees to whom Speed had promised a larger show than they actually had. The show sent the committees newspaper headlines about the fire, implying that they should be relieved to see the company arrive with anything at all after such a conflagration.

The show played Victoria next, the British Columbia capital, which had not seen a circus or carnival in years. A local newspaper lavished "great praise as to the cleanliness of the many high class attractions."[16] Business was good, possibly because the press release's description of the show as "an aggregation of returned soldiers," however inaccurate, impressed anglophile Victorians.[17]

Conklin & Garrett invited the newspaper boys from the *Colonist* and the *Times* to be their guests on Friday night. Over 300 came out. Treating a city's "newsies" — even then a fabled brotherhood — to a free night on the midway had become a carnival tradition. A show gained free publicity, local goodwill, a break on advertising rates, and a guaranteed crowd. On the pages with the articles announcing the invitation, the Victoria papers printed the show's advertisements free of charge.

The *Times* quoted Patty's theatrical invitation to the newsies, while the *Colonist* quoted Moran, the show's lot manager and fixer. Moran, a small man who had come with Garrett, was thrusting himself into the spotlight a little more than Patty liked. After the show finished in Nanaimo, the chief of police wrote in a testimonial letter, probably requested by Moran, that "Mr. J.J. Moran, Managing Director, has always endeavoured to assist the Police, and if any individual within his province occasioned to get into trouble, Mr. Moran extended the excessive courtesy of seeing them out of their trouble."[18]

Hosting the newsboys of Nanaimo, the show received good publicity in the *Free Press*, including several photographs. Like most local newspapers, the paper published the show's press releases as provided, but one article was wholly original. In a two-column front-page story on May 23, 1925, the *Free Press* quoted at length the reactions of four newsboys to their night on the midway. Patty was their guide through the rides, shows, and food stands. They fended for themselves at the games. All of the boys were impressed by the motordrome. One mentioned "the big fish," wondering "how they could get such monsters out of the sea," and another was also impressed by the "huge sturgeon which was recently caught."

Someone on the show had caught the fish between Victoria and Nanaimo, and it was added to the other animals, living and dead, in the show's menagerie. Patty later recalled that the one on the Conklin & Garrett midway "was plenty big. And it created great publicity ... But after two weeks we had to get rid of it. Even we couldn't stand it any longer."[19] This sturgeon might have initiated Patty's infatuation with fishing.

After dumping the stinking fish in the Nanaimo harbour, the show returned to the mainland for a few still dates in the mountains before arriving in Drumheller, a coal-mining town on the rim of the Alberta Badlands. The town had not seen a carnival for 10 years. The show arrived just as the miners began a strike against wage cuts, but before their confrontations with the police became violent. Here was another Wild West location for the All-Canadian crew to conquer.

Drumheller was the first spot in 1925 that Conklin & Garrett played under the auspices — sponsorship — of the Elks. Conklin Sr. had been an Elk and played dates under their auspices. Patty had joined the Grafton, West Virginia, chapter in 1918. In Canada, he joined the Vancouver lodge, Canadian Elks Lodge No. 1, and began to cash in on this connection in 1926, when the show started to thrive on the fraternal society's support and patronage. Conklin & Garrett would play ever more towns under Elks' auspices and develop their Vancouver opening date as a big annual Elks event. Patty formed a close business relationship with Ernie Hand, the Grand Exalted Ruler of the Vancouver Elks from 1930 to 1933 and a friend of Mayor Taylor. Patty and Will Wright used the Vancouver lodge as their club when they were in the city, and Patty was active in the Elks off and on.

Conklin & Garrett played a few more still dates before starting the B circuit fairs at the beginning of July 1925, running through 14 fairs by the end of August. The Canadian Pacific Railway had just opened a spur line into Lloydminster, and the son of the vice-president of the company recounted what happened there during the fair:

> My father decreed that the railroad construction crews should be paid in cash and they were given a one-day holiday to attend the opening of the branch line. They came to Lloydminster — hundreds upon hundreds of them — in a special train.... It was some years later that I discovered why the Conklins always held my father in such vast esteem. Thanks to my father's instructions ... the Conklin & Garrett Shows mined $25,000 from their one-day stand in Lloydminster, a fact which, in those days, was akin to striking the Mother Lode.[20]

Flush with the hard-earned cash it took from the construction crews, the show returned to British Columbia for still dates and fall fairs, ending the season in Trail in early October.

Wright reported that "conditions on the prairies were a lot better than they were in 1924, with the result that the attendances and receipts of the B Circuit of Canadian fairs were in advance of recent years."[21] The receipts for the 1925 season reveal where the real money was made.[22] All of the rides and shows together made $69,500. After the fair committees took their percentage, a little more than $40,000 was left. The games grossed $120,000, from which the committees got nothing. Percentages from these receipts went to the 25 or so "lucky boys" who ran the games. From the receipts of over $160,000, $18,000 profit went to Conklin & Garrett.

Over the 1925 route the show collected a few dozen testimonial letters praising its cleanliness and good management, many written at the request of Wright or Patty.[23] Conklin & Garrett did not carry girl shows, which were expensive to produce and only paid their way in larger centres. But as to grift, the office was skilled at keeping it well concealed, the marks well deceived, and the officials well greased. The testimonials never mention the games. This silence speaks volumes. The raft of testimonials points to Patty's evolution as the show's promoter. Recommendations from upstanding citizens were money in the bank. The citizens, for their part, were happy to finally be able to speak up for an "All-Canadian" show.

The show went into winter quarters in Vancouver and Speed, the Conklins, and most of their staff returned to the United States. In California that winter, Wright joined Patty on the board of governors of the Pacific Coast Showmen's Association.

Patty attended the two main fair meetings in the Midwest. The International Association of Fairs and Expositions traditionally combined its meeting in December with the Showmen's League of America in Chicago. Most of the big American fair contracts were awarded at this meeting, as were contracts for the larger Canadian exhibitions in British Columbia, Ontario, and Quebec. Mrs. Conklin and Patty attended the Showmen's meeting not just to do business, but also to socialize, although this distinction would have been lost on Patty.

The Western Canada Exhibitions Association had been rotating its early February meeting among several cities. In 1926 the location was Regina. When no other show bid on the B circuit fairs for the coming season, Conklin & Garrett took it. Contract in hand, Patty returned to New York City to meet Frank, who was returning from a trip he had taken to South America for his health. The brothers and Mrs. Conklin went to Los Angeles for a month before returning to Vancouver.

Season of 1926

Conklin & Garrett played the 1926 season with four rides, 12 shows, and 30 games, travelling on 10 cars. To their three other rides, they had added two Missouri Mules, car-like devices that bucked up and down, developed in 1925 by Traver Engineering of Pennsylvania, then the world's largest manufacturer of midway rides. The new shows included an illusion show, a wax show, a collection of war relics and exhibits, and Underground China Town. Mrs. Conklin ran the war show, which had become popular on midways after the Great War. Underground China Town displayed a mock-up of an opium den, appealing to the public's appetite for racist scenes of debauchery presented under an educational guise. Opium dens were a problem in Vancouver — real, but also inflamed by the press. Vancouver also had a thriving Asiatic Exclusion League, of which L.D. Taylor, ex-mayor at the time, was an enthusiastic member, and which would have approved of the lessons Underground China Town dispensed.

Al Salvail took over the ten-in-one. He was a well-known sideshow entertainer and manager in the outdoor entertainment industry, coming from the circus and most recently from the Miller Brothers 101 Ranch Wild West, once a competitor with Buffalo Bill's show. Successful early in the season, Salvail added a second show for the fairs. Another old hand, Pete Kortes, in the sideshow business since 1918, brought a museum show and a reptile show.[24]

Like Wright, Salvail and Kortes kept busy in the off-season with storefront shows. Salvail stayed with Conklin & Garrett until 1933. Kortes left for Beckmann & Gerety Shows in the fall of 1931. He played other big shows and in 1945 bought Greater Sheesley Shows, the unit that had been playing Winnipeg when the Conklins first came to Canada. The industry was still small and anyone with the chutzpah and imagination to produce attractions that could draw in the public — never mind give them their money's worth — could fashion a career.

Conklin & Garrett's opening date for 1926 was the first annual Vancouver Elks Circus. Patty had promoted the event, not entirely selflessly, devoting "many weeks of tireless work … before any encouragement was given the proposition."[25] A week before the opening, the show began to see returns from Patty's new association with Canadian Elks Lodge No. 1 in the form of local newspaper publicity: "But this year, instead of coming from a foreign country and thence returning with Vancouver money," an April 20 article in the *Vancouver Sun* read, the midway will be provided by "an all-Canadian show and receipts will go to aid the B.P.O. Elks of Greater Vancouver in their work." Coverage continued the next day: "Conklin & Garrett … is well known throughout Western Canada and in the past 10 years it has acquired one of the best menageries, and admittedly the best sideshows, playing anywhere in Canada." The full front-page spread of the Saturday entertainment section was devoted to articles on and photographs of the event, with more on the Elks in subsequent pages. With this kind of coverage, printed by the paper as supplied by Patty, the show's half-page advertisement, probably provided free, was almost superfluous.

The *Sun* claimed the show had never before played Vancouver, even though during the same week the previous year it had been parked just blocks away from its current location. Beyond a larger show, Conklin & Garrett with the Elks added a car raffle, possibly the first show to do so in Canada. Each night, the winner of a $1,465 Pontiac was drawn from the admission tickets. The raffle paid off in publicity, as the *Sun* announced the winners. The show garnered further publicity in that paper on April 30 when "Mr. Conklin … entertained the inmates" of the Children's Aid Society Home and the Deaf, Dumb and Blind School, both recipients of Elks funds. Patty had discovered the promotional value of entertaining at his expense people who are marginalized.

The *Sun* had close connections with the Elks, often giving the club extensive coverage, and it carried articles on the Elks Circus every day during its run. Patty correctly predicted that this opening stand would become an annual event. The Elks' take for this year and the next two was "slightly in excess of $28,000."[26] Conklin & Garrett's share was much more.

The show went on to Victoria, playing under the auspices of the Native Sons of Canada, an Anglo-Saxon nativist organization. Although the *Colonist* claimed in an article on May 7, 1926, that the show was "increasing in popularity, and big crowds are thronging the grounds at both afternoon and evening performances," attendance was poor. The show continued to come to Vancouver Island after 1926 but played Victoria only once more in 1930.

The Victoria event in 1926 was such a "bloomer" that Patty resorted to his usual emergency tactics. A witness later told the story of the inferno:

> I remember standing by their almost deserted lot in Victoria one night. A parade was coming down Douglas Street, about three blocks away. At that juncture, an inspired genius threw a flaming box of matches into the mitt joint. The tent burst into flames; the Victoria Fire Department roared to the scene; the paraders on Douglas Street followed the fire engines; and starvation was temporarily averted on the carnival lot.[27]

A mitt joint, in carnie lingo, is a palm reader's concession. The owner of the Mystic Temple had not foreseen the end of her travels with the show and took the torch for the larger good.

Victoria proper had been such a wash that Conklin & Garrett cancelled plans for a date in its suburbs. To flesh out the season, they played the Elks card. They worked five stills besides Vancouver under Elks' auspices. They had been in some of these towns in previous years, sometimes during their fairs, but never with the Elks. When the Exalted Rulers of the lodges wrote their testimonials, they addressed Patty as "Sir and Brother."

Their first Elks still after Vancouver was in Courtenay, halfway up Vancouver Island's east coast. The road to Courtenay had been completed in 1910 and the railway's terminus reached there in 1914. Conklin & Garrett was the first carnival the town had seen. After they left, Patty would have understood the lodge brother who wrote to him that "it seems a bit lonesome in Courtenay now since you are gone."[28]

At Nanaimo, the Local Council of Women inspected the show, declaring that it contained "nothing of an objectionable moral nature." The show was there under the auspices of the Great War Veterans' Association for the Empire Day celebrations. On May 19, the Nanaimo *Free Press* confirmed that "the name All-Canadian shows, despite rumors to the contrary, is no misnomer." Advertising dollars and sponsorship went far in bending the truth.

Back on the mainland, travelling between Medicine Hat and Drumheller, Alberta, Patty and Speed did a little fishing and sent a photograph to *Billboard*. In it, they are standing in front of a Model T, holding a string of fish.

In Drumheller "a miniature cyclone hit the show ... playing havoc with various tops."[29] Carnies call such a storm a "blowdown" and Patty had "to give orders for complete abandonment in order to avoid loss of life."[30] The carnival is continually at the mercy of the weather. In early September, Conklin & Garrett ended a still date in Fernie, British Columbia, in a blizzard that dumped a foot of snow. Two days later they opened a fair 50 miles further west in the same conditions and lost money on the week. The local Gyro Club thanked them for the "business-like way in which they lived up to their contract."[31] Even if a show made no money, if it played a spot it had to fulfill its financial obligation to the committee.

The show's press representative, possibly Wright, reported satisfaction with business that season, "except the last five weeks in Okanagan Valley, which were played in snow."[32] After subtracting over $24,000 in depreciation from equipment valued at $100,000, they netted almost $16,000 on receipts of over $147,000.[33]

When arranging to play Trail under Elks' auspices that summer, Conklin & Garrett had not been able to find vacant land for a lot. Trail was expanding rapidly under the direction of the Canadian Pacific Railway's Consolidated Mining and Smelting Company and the land on which the show had set up the previous year had been developed. So, Patty bought 28 building lots just outside of town for $5,000. They used this land in 1928, 1929, and 1930. When Conklin & Garrett left the West, Crescent Shows not only took over many of their spots in British Columbia, but used the Trail property for free, until Patty found out and went after Crescent for rent.

The equipment was put in winter quarters for 1926–27 in Vancouver and the owners returned to the United States: Speed to Oregon, Patty to New York City and Paterson. Frank and Mrs. Conklin stayed in Vancouver, as did Moran. But before Speed and Patty could get away, they had another fire, this one at the winter quarters warehouse and with Patty not on site.

Moran looked after collecting the insurance. When the claim was paid, Speed found a property in New Westminster, a suburb of Vancouver. The site included a building that could be used as a shop and three acres for railway tracks on which to store the cars. On Speed's recommendation, the show bought the property for $7,500 and wintered there for the rest of the 1920s. Patty later claimed that he did not agree to the venture. The New Westminster and Trail properties would cause him endless bother through much of the next decade.[34]

Speed visited Frank and Mrs. Conklin in Vancouver later that winter. He was planning to go to the Western Canada Fairs Association meeting, but by the third week in January he was complaining that he could not shake a cold he had caught at the warehouse fire. Speed did not go to the meeting, nor did he spend much time on the road the next season. The cold he caught turned into tuberculosis.

PATTY RUNS THE SHOW

Conklin & Garrett has been open in Drumheller for three days and survived a terrible storm by the time the Barnes Circus rolls into town. After the last circus show that Saturday, the circus crew visit their midway friends. Al Barnes joins Patty in the Pullman stateroom for a drink. With the circus girls on the lot, the lucky boys lose interest in working the marks, who are not spending much anyway and are allowed to drift away.

After closing, the night heats up as the circus performers and carnies turn to entertaining each other with the talents of their trades. Two of the Barnes boys put on a wrestling bout in the athletic show top. The Elks sponsor a concert for the crew, and Spike Green, a midway concessionaire, charms the crowd with his fine tenor voice, which has more character after cajoling marks all day. The girls from both aggregations take the stage together to show some leg. The tent is jammed with show people.

Signs remain of the vicious storm that struck two days before. A few tent posts are held together by splints and there is a tear in the canvas top. The wind had threatened the Ferris wheel, but it managed to ride it out and none of the other rides had been damaged.

The carnies regale their circus brethren with stories of the cyclone they missed. The circus crew is from the South and they praise the benefits of California sunshine over prairie winds. The rain starts again and the night breaks up, with some pairing up for private nightcaps.

★　　★　　★

Patty attended the Western Canada Fairs Association meeting in 1927 with Moran, Speed's representative. Speed wired Patty to warn him that he had "private information" that the show must offer "five or more rides ten or more shows several others will bid with the number."[35] Patty worked his magic and lies, and Speed wired him after the meeting to congratulate him. Conklin & Garrett had the B circuit fairs again for 1927.

Season of 1927

The show's press material claimed they had "15 Double-Length Railway Cars, 7 Major Riding Devices, 12 Big Circus Sideshows," a stretch in every case. Four of the rail cars were Pullmans. They had added a Merry Mix-Up, which was an inexpensive swing ride, and a pony ride, for a total of seven rides, counting each of the two Missouri Mules. All the rides were show owned, except for the ponies. The Missouri Mules had a bad first week and did not leave Vancouver. Patty had been trying to sell them since the end of last season. He had also tried to book a Hey-Dey, a centrifugal force ride that was an update of the Whip, or Caterpillar. The accounts book for 1927 has preprinted headings for a Caterpillar and a Tilt-A-Whirl, but they never played.[36]

The company could come close to 12 shows, but not all of them opened at every spot. They still had the athletic show, ten-in-one, animal show, motordrome, war show, snake show, and oriental show. Although they promoted a wax show, they dropped it because it was impractical and replaced it with an outlaw show, another proven attraction, in which photographs, news clippings, and the paraphernalia of crime were displayed. This was a "pay as you leave" exhibit and the war show became one in a few years, relying on customer satisfaction or pity for its receipts. They added a monkeydrome in which monkeys drove little cars around a slotted track. An independent producer booked a mitt joint with them at some spots. In an ad at the end of the 1926 season, Conklin & Garrett had unsuccessfully looked for a jungle land and an illusion show.[37] Will Wright's World of Illusions and Jungleland were getting run down, and he was getting tired. Jungleland grossed low the opening week of the 1927 season and was dropped. The snake show did not open until six weeks into the season. The motordrome was gone from the roster by the end of June and the outlaw show by early September. If All-Canadian Shows could not keep shows, it was in trouble.

The accounts book contains numerous pay entries for Patty, Frank, Moran, Wright, and Kortes, among others.[38] Speed came out briefly, since there are

Studio portrait of Patty Conklin, 1927.

two notations in July for his salary. The rest of the office staff included an electrician, a trainmaster, a watchman, two or three general staff, and managers for several shows. Total staff for the season peaked at 175.

Mrs. Conklin was paid a salary for Vancouver at the beginning of May, but not after that. She had been suffering from ill health for years and although she claimed at the end of the previous season that she intended "to remain in the show business for many years," her days on the road were numbered.[39] She had been keeping the company's books. On October 23, 1926, Patty had appealed in *Billboard* for Theo Forestall, his erstwhile accountant, to contact him, but Forestall apparently did not respond.

On April 23, 1927, before the show's opening in Vancouver, the *Sun* carried a two-page feature on the Elks' second annual circus. The first page had a new studio photograph of Patty, handsome, dignified, and business-like, which he would use in promotional material for years, an article on "Conklin and Garrett's Diamond Jubilee Shows," one on the Elks' charitable work, and a half-page advertisement for the event. The second page carried articles on the Exalted Ruler of the Vancouver Elks, Ernie Hand, and two houses to be given away during the event.

The article on the show stressed the value that "a well organized, smooth-running, capably managed carnival" can bring to a community. It named Patty as the sole manager and briefly sketched the show's history. That "the show covers the same route every year … speaks well" for it. After meeting resistance because of "the manner in which shows of a similar nature conducted their business," Conklin & Garrett is now welcomed wherever it plays. "This feeling would certainly not exist if the show did not conduct itself in a right and proper manner," the article concluded.

The *Sun* printed an article daily for the first few days of the event. On Tuesday, April 26, it covered the opening, the excitement of which had been enhanced "when one of the clever monkeys succeeded in making its escape." Letting exotic animals escape was a publicity ploy, and the monkey was only at large for an hour or so. After this piece, the show was not specifically mentioned.

The show was scheduled to finish in Vancouver on Saturday, April 30, and move on to Nanaimo for the following Monday. By the end of the week, however, Conklin & Garrett had to inform the people of Nanaimo that they would be disappointing them. The *Free Press* uncovered the show's excuse: "At the last minute on Saturday night the plans ... were changed owing to the request of His Worship L.D. Taylor of Vancouver that the shows extend their engagement three days longer.... The crowds were so enormous that many thousands were unable to get on the grounds."[40] This explanation, repeated in an advertisement on the same page, could possibly have been contrived to cover a breach of contract owing to poor management, but Vancouver was at the crest of the greatest boom it had yet seen and L.D. was a friend of Patty, so the announcement was likely true.

Taylor was among the first of many luminaries Patty counted as friends, although their friendship might have helped tarnish Taylor's reputation.[41] Arriving in Vancouver from the United States in 1896, Taylor rapidly climbed to prominence. He helped bring the *Province* newspaper to Vancouver from Victoria in 1899 and bought the *Daily World* in 1905. He served 11 years as Vancouver's mayor over eight terms, running on platforms that emphasized both development and support for labour. Taylor had a reputation for speculation and intrigue and was often accused of unscrupulous dealings and association with unsavoury characters, which led to his defeat in the 1928 election.

After this defeat, Taylor's well-wishers among Vancouver's businessmen raised $5,000 to send him around the world on what they must have thought, given his 72 years, would be his retirement tour. To begin the tour, Patty welcomed Taylor on his private rail car for the trip to Edmonton.[42] In 1929 and 1930, Patty took him as a guest of Conklin & Garrett to the Showmen's League banquet in Chicago. Taylor returned to Vancouver for his seventh and eighth mayoral terms, and during the latter Patty named L.D. godfather to his son.

The show finally closed in Vancouver on Wednesday, May 4. They had promised Nanaimo a kids' matinee the following Saturday and managed to open the rides and a few shows on Friday night for an insignificant take. They listed their sponsor as the May Day Committee, although the May Day celebration was two weeks away.

From Nanaimo, Conklin & Garrett went to three small island towns they had played before. They returned to the mainland for a few more stills in

A Conklin & Garrett fair in Nelson, British Columbia.

British Columbia, Saskatchewan, and Manitoba, including Regina, Saskatoon, and Winnipeg, all under Elks' auspices. They began the B circuit fairs at the end of June in Carman, Manitoba, playing a straight run of 14 three-day fairs across the Prairies up to the end of August. They had more Elk still dates in the Prairies before finishing up with a couple of small fall fairs in British Columbia. Their last day open was September 24 in Nelson and they were in the New Westminster winter quarters four days later.

The show made good money for much of its stay in Vancouver. The stills on Vancouver Island were not money makers. They came into consistently good money with the B circuit fairs. Their best day was a sunny summer Friday in North Battleford, Saskatchewan, when they grossed $8,635. They played 19 fairs in 24 weeks. Patty bragged that their longest jump was 1,000 miles, and they travelled a total of 7,000 miles during the season.

The accounts book for 1927 confirms the extent to which the games carried the company, consistently contributing more than two-thirds of the total take — often much more — all rides, shows, and sales included.[43] Those amounts are only what were recorded, and the lucky boys pocketed much more off the record. On that Friday in North Battleford, the concessions brought in $6,535. On a slow day in Rosetown, Saskatchewan, total receipts were only $1,104, of which the games took in $958. Rides and shows brought crowds to the midway to have their pockets purged at the games.

Conklin & Garrett owned most of the games and the agents were paid a percentage of their receipts. The show provided them the opportunity to take the marks for as much as they could. Some were independent agents who paid a privilege, cost of transportation, and a percentage to the office, keeping the rest for themselves. Show managers had a mix of arrangements with the office, some being paid as office staff, while others received a percentage. Operators of office-owned rides were paid a straight salary, as were show performers.

In want ads in the fall of 1927, Patty sought to book specific concessions and rides, and these included a list of all the shows the company at one time had: "Law and Outlaw, Mystery Show, Jungle Land, Monkey Speedway, Wild West Show, Prison Show and One-Ring Circus."[44] He continued to try to sell the motordrome and Missouri Mules, dropping the price of the latter from $2,500 to $1,500. The ads also note that Pete Kortes can place "Fat Girl, Giant, Midgets, Tattoo Artist and Freaks of all kinds." Patty, Frank, Wright, and Moran visited Kortes's World's Museum in Seattle in November, where it stayed until after the Christmas holidays.

Patty travelled to San Francisco and Los Angeles. He was spotted in the lobby of the Sherman Hotel in Chicago, host to the big fairs convention, along with virtually every major show owner of the day. He settled at New York's Herald Square Hotel for December before returning to Los Angeles for the rest of the winter. He was "accompanied on his trip by his mother, who is his best pal at all times."[45] *Billboard* saw in him a rising star and encouraged him with publicity, mentioning his name in every weekly issue throughout December and January.

In New York, Patty booked some concessions, a few shows — including a freak animal and bird show and a Palace of Wonders — and at least one ride, a Whip owned by Ben Botsford. Botsford was a promoter working for the Wirth and Hamid agency, one of the largest agencies handling free acts for fairs and exhibitions. Botsford also handled promotions for Conklin & Garrett, working for both companies until he graduated to the William Morris agency in 1929.

Free acts included everything from a single high diver to a fully fledged grandstand show. Fair and exhibition boards put them on as entertainment covered by the price of admission. Patty announced that he would use the "Barnes-Carruthers class B free attractions in connection with the Winnipeg celebration."[46] He concluded that the Winnipeg date, again under Elks' auspices, "was a knockout for us on account of the free acts" and decided "to carry acts at all our still dates."[47] This was a new idea, although probably not his, for carnivals at still dates.

On the way back to Los Angeles, Patty and his mother stopped off at the Western Canada Fairs Association meeting, now held consistently in Winnipeg. Ella was sick, however, and Patty let Moran handle the negotiations for the B circuit while he cared for her. The show won the circuit over four competitors.

Patty did not go to Paterson that winter. The previous summer, his father had shot himself in the head.[48] Charles Jr. had found him. Karl Renker had lived alone since the early 1920s, eking out an existence as a used furniture dealer. Joseph and Frank had stopped by to see him in the off-season. His other children might have visited, but they were not the support in his old age that he had hoped for. Sometime before his suicide, he had been forced from the house where he had lived for 17 years, unable to pay the rent without help from sons or boarders.

It is not possible to know why, at 66, Karl would kill himself, but he was alone in a land that had refused to grant him the minimal success he had thought it promised. His wife dead, his sons and daughters gone, his English faulty, without income, he must have felt he had no reason or capacity to live. Patty, haunted by fear of his father's fate, made sure throughout his life that he had people around him, even if on salary. There is no record that he or Frank returned for their father's funeral. Playing the B circuit fairs in the farming towns of the Canadian West, they might not have found out about it until after it was over.

Season of 1928

When the show opened in Vancouver at the beginning of May 1928, Speed was on the lot.[49] By the beginning of June, he was in a Seattle hospital being

treated for tuberculosis. He came out to the show at the end of July, but soon
retreated to Seattle. His condition worsened and his doctor ordered him back
into the hospital. He had planned to return to the show or at least join it at
winter quarters but was unable to do either. In the fall, he wrote Frank a long
set of instructions on how to load and store the equipment at winter quarters.
Throughout the season, he and Patty kept in touch through telegrams and
letters, Patty providing updates on their company's fortunes.

The show advertised only five rides for 1928, despite the addition of
Botsford's Whip. The sideshows were much the same, although the animals had
been reorganized as "Dorothy's One-Ring Circus." They had a new funhouse.
The outlaw show had become "The Awakening," displaying "the awakening
from a life of crime and the terrible penalty one has to pay for such a life."[50]
They added a girl show for the first time, under the guise of an educational
exhibit on anatomy. Following a practice that had been started by P.T. Barnum
in the mid-nineteenth century, the *Sun* and the Nanaimo *Free Press* continued
to reprint verbatim, spelling mistakes and all, stories drawn from the show's
press material. The stories ignore the games, focusing solely on rides and shows.

The *Sun* provided its usual extensive coverage of the third annual circus,
but for the first time a note of controversy intruded. Minutes after opening on
Saturday, the police closed all wheels of fortune and other gambling games,
despite protests that they had been approved by city hall.[51] Quickly on the
scene, the counsel for the Elks secured an injunction restraining the city or
the police from interfering with the games, which the Elks' lawyer managed
to get extended until the show was over.

The Elks wanted the issue resolved, since they had a 15-year contract with
the city to stage their annual celebration. During the legal proceedings, it was
revealed that the complaint had originated with the operators of Happyland,
an amusement park at the Vancouver exhibition grounds, protesting that
the carnival was being allowed to compete unfairly with them. The British
Columbia Amusement Company had built Happyland in 1926 as an answer to
public complaints about the carnivals that had been brought in for the Pacific
National Exhibition in previous years. Levitt-Brown-Huggins Shows had been
the last carnival to play the exhibition, preceded by the Snapp Brothers. The
Conklins had worked with both companies. The exhibition board eliminated

Mrs. Conklin and Patty with the floral arrangement to celebrate their showing at the Elks still date in Vancouver, 1928.

games of chance from the exhibition and Happyland in 1928, again in response to complaints. The B.C. Supreme Court ruled that the Elks could continue to operate gambling devices, allowed by the Criminal Code for charity purposes, while Happyland could not. But in a few months Conklin & Garrett Shows would face more serious opposition on the Prairies for the same reason.

The show had dropped all Vancouver Island dates except Nanaimo. To make up the slack, they opened in Vancouver a week later than usual and then played South Vancouver, a bedroom community soon to be absorbed by the city. They were under Elks' auspices in South Vancouver, as they had been their first time in Nanaimo. The show was back in Nanaimo for the May Day celebration and received its best coverage ever from the local paper, including half-page ads and a front-page, bottom-banner announcement for the last day, May 13, 1928. The article that day noted that "yesterday Mr. Conklin received an invitation to exhibit his circus in Victoria, but owing to previous arrangements he was unable to accept the invitation." Patty remembered Victoria too well to want to return.

The show played the same Elks still dates as in 1927, with the addition of Edmonton, before hitting the prairie fairs in July. Despite rain and troubles with the city, they made money in Edmonton. In a letter to Speed, Patty explained: "We had a great deal of trouble at Edmonton but managed to get in four days with the wheels which was quite a victory. It cost approximately $1500.00 in legal fees to accomplish this. However we were well paid for our efforts as the show grossed ... $30,000.00 on the week."[52] Legal fees was one of the terms carnies used for bribery. Patty had to use the skills as a fixer that he had learned from Jim Conklin Sr.

Patty anticipated difficulty in keeping the wheels open in Saskatoon. He managed to operate them there, but not in Regina. As he feared, the Saskatchewan Department of Agriculture, which regulated provincial fairs, was strictly enforcing its gambling laws and the show could not always run all its games. Public complaints about carnivals were starting to be reflected in stricter legislation and enforcement.

Moran helped with the legal adjustments but added to Patty's troubles. Patty wired Speed from Saskatoon: "Moran on terrible drunk the last six days. If things keep going like they are I will be ready to go in the hospital when you get out."[53] This was just when Patty needed Moran most, so Frank stepped in to assist with the officials. In early September, Patty told Moran "to take a rest" and he disappeared for the rest of the season.[54] Patty warned Speed that Moran was in Vancouver in mid-September, telling him not to let Moran "do any work for our concern."[55] Moran wired Patty that winter, but Patty decided not to employ him again.[56] Late in 1929, Moran was put on trial for the death of a woman who killed herself after he had spent all her money, then refused to marry her. Speed paid for Moran's lawyers, and he was acquitted. Moran moved on to Royal American Shows to be their fixer. Patty had known Moran was trouble and had never gotten along with him. Moran was Speed's man and with Speed out of the action, Patty started making over company staff to suit himself.

Economic conditions on the Prairies were affecting the show's fortunes. Drought had plagued farmers throughout the 1920s and reached crisis proportions by the end of the decade. Southeast Alberta was especially hard hit. From a peak of 108 fairs in 1921, the province hosted only 63 in 1928, and at the end of that year 40 Alberta agricultural societies were dormant. In response, Patty switched some still dates in smaller towns to stills in the larger centres of Lethbridge and Medicine Hat, and Swift Current in Saskatchewan. It is doubtful that this produced the desired results, since the towns to which the show switched were dead centre in the Alberta dry belt and, despite their size, still dependent on farmers.

Patty managed to counter some of the bad news by changing the ride lineup. In June he sold the Chair-O-Plane for $4,000 and bought a Tilt-A-Whirl for $5,900. When he set the new ride up in Winnipeg, it immediately became the top grosser. The traditional midway rides — the merry-go-round and Ferris wheel — had been the top earners. In nine days in Winnipeg in 1927, the merry-go-round made $508, the Ferris wheel, $566. In five days in Winnipeg in 1928, the Tilt-A-Whirl made $1,750. "Is very pretty ride and should get off the nut this season," Patty wired Speed, the "nut" being the overhead or operating expense, including the cost of the ride.[57] It was uncommon for a ride to pay for itself in one season.

The Tilt-A-Whirl was the shape of things to come. It was new, it was fast, it caused great physical contact among riders, and it had good flow-through or capacity. The merry-go-round was a slow ride for kids and their parents. The Ferris wheel took a long time to load and unload. The Tilt drew thrill-seekers, and they were on and off quickly.

More rides like the Tilt-A-Whirl would soon be introduced to the midway. Equipment and technology had always been important to the North American carnival, from show fronts and stages to generators for the electricity to light the midway. But the technology of riding devices was becoming dominant. By the end of the 1920s, many carnivals were for the first time carrying as many rides as they did shows.

Throughout the 1928 season, with Speed in the hospital, Patty habitually asked for Speed's opinion on any change he had in mind. Speed never contradicted Patty. Patty tried to eliminate the show's financial obligations to Speed.[58] At the beginning of July, he sent Speed a cheque for $6,536 to cover the show's debt to him. He also paid off the show's debt of $10,000 to himself. Mrs. Conklin had lent the company money to keep it on the road, but Patty decided to let that debt ride. Because of her age and health, she was taking less of a role, leaving at the beginning of September, while the show still had five more weeks out.

The show went into winter quarters in early October. Patty bought a merry-go-round and a new Swooper from Sellner Manufacturing and tried again to sell off unprofitable equipment. He once more dropped the price of the Missouri Mules, this time to $1,000. He wanted to get rid of the Fun on the Farm funhouse the show had bought the previous season. The funhouse was developed by Spillman Engineering in 1926, but the gilly show version had only come out in 1928. Described in advertising material as "an imposing yellow structure with seven animated ballys to attract the crowds and draw them into its mysterious passageways," it did not live up to its billing.[59] Patty was also trying to sell some of the old baggage cars as part of his plan to go out on an all-steel train the next season. He later wrote Speed that "we never even got a nibble regarding the stuff we advertised for sale. It appears to me that it is very difficult to try and sell any show property."[60]

PATTY MOVES UP

Frank counts out 10 brass coins stamped with the company name and Patty's face and places them in two stacks on the counter beside the man slouching there. "Here you go, Rip. That should do you the rest of the week." It's the middle of the morning and the midway is deserted, except for a few roughies — manual labourers — on the way to the cookhouse.

"Shit, Frank, I need some real money to get by," Rip grouses.

Frank scowls at the man. "Quit yammering. You're lucky to get this after the heat you raised last week. I patch the law for your grift, then you gotta burn the lot by bashing that mooch for an easy beef."

"That don't mean nothing, I still need cash to get me through." Rip stands up and crosses his arms.

Frank throws his hat on the counter and his bald head shines in the sun. He coughs and spits in the dirt beside the joint. "I give you white money and soon as I'm back in the office, you're off to score hooch. Take the dukey. Get a drink at the pie car, you gotta have it so bad."

"What, the office coming up empty? On the square, I turned in half a yard yesterday, so when am I going to see some of that back?"

"Never mind about the office. We're doing just fine without you butting in. You'll get paid at the end of the season, like everybody else," Frank says. "You don't like it, you can screw."

Rip turns away and pulls out his grouch bag. Grumbling, he drops the bogus coins in it.

★　★　★

In the fall of 1928, Patty informed the carnival industry "that the show had a good season, although the gross intake was not as large as last year."[61] He visited Speed in a Seattle hospital in October to tie up business that required Speed's signature. He also arranged to become less tied to Speed's signature, in March 1929 instructing Ernie Hand to incorporate two companies, Conklin & Garrett Ltd. and Bazaars Ltd.[62] Patty and Speed transferred their assets to the companies in exchange for shares. They were the company directors, but at various times so were Wright and Frank. The incorporation was part of Patty's professionalization of the show, but it also gave him a freer hand to steer it.

In the winter of 1928–29, Patty represented Conklin & Garrett at the Showmen's League convention in Chicago, the Pacific Coast Showmen's convention in Los Angeles, and the North Pacific Fairs meeting in Vancouver. At the Showmen's League banquet, Patty sat with the league's executive at the speakers' table, as representative of the Pacific Coast Showmen's Association. On the board of governors of the association since 1925 and several committees since then, Patty was popular with showmen at the club. He liked to spend money and was particularly noted for his generosity in supporting causes promoted by the association. The new president inaugurated a series of special nights, for each of which a member covered all expenses. Patty paid for the first of them, which was named after him and at which "it was only natural that the plan of decoration should be green."[63] The German immigrants' son was now passing as a son of the Emerald Isle. He also helped pay for the party to launch the association's trip to the National Orange Show in San Bernardino.

Patty informed the association they might have a visit from Speed, and the different styles of the two men were remarked upon in a report on the association's activities: "Garrett is almost a stranger in Los Angeles ... while Paddy thinks nothing of jumping from Vancouver to Los Angeles three or four times each winter, where he is always assured of a royal welcome, and even at this early date the rumor is already out that he will be one of the contestants for the honor of being next president of our organization."[64] The prediction proved to be accurate.

Patty had connections to maintain in New York, New Jersey, and California, meetings to attend in Chicago, Los Angeles, Vancouver, and Winnipeg. He had become a compulsive traveller, enabled by the railways and the developing continental network for automobile and, soon, air travel. When the show was settled into winter quarters, his momentum kept him on the move so that even during the off-season, when most showmen were happy to remain stationary, no city was graced with his presence for much more than a couple of weeks. His addresses were hotels. His peripatetic habits would later make domestic life difficult.

On his way to the Western Canada Fairs Association meeting in Winnipeg, Patty stopped in Edmonton, Lloydminster, Red Deer, Lethbridge, and Yorkton to do "a little hand-shaking."[65] He was anxious about the tough competition he faced for the B circuit fairs. He had "information that there are going to be several other shows from the East who are going to try and get our Fairs." He had "a couple of very good angles" and thought the show stood "as good a chance as any of them." Frank and Wright were travelling with him to assist with negotiations. Speed stayed at his ranch in Waldport, Oregon.

Season of 1929

The B circuit was divided for 1929, nine fairs in the west and seven in the east. In the midst of the B circuit in 1928, Patty had written to Speed that he thought they would give these fairs a rest. He nonetheless bid on and won the western half of the B circuit for 1929. He added five C circuit fairs to fill out the route. Speed wired his congratulations to the team in Winnipeg.

The eastern half of the B circuit went to Royal American Shows, breaking into Canada for the first time. In 1922 Carl Sedlmayr had bought out a show that had gone flat and formed Royal American.[66] By 1929 they carried seven rides, 13 shows, and 25 concessions, about the same size as Conklin & Garrett. Sedlmayr had bid unsuccessfully against Patty for the full circuit the previous year. Getting half of the B circuit was a good break for Sedlmayr, who kept the circuit for the next three years, dropping it when Royal took the A circuit of western exhibitions in 1934. On that foundation, Sedlmayr built the largest carnival company in North America. For the next 40 years, the Conklins and the Sedlmayrs sporadically vied for the Canadian western fairs, the rivalry only settled when Royal lost the A circuit in 1975 and rapidly declined afterward. With that, Conklin Shows finally took the royal crown.

The *Vancouver Sun* began printing articles on the Fourth Annual Elks Circus three days before it was to be opened by the mayor, not Taylor this time. Besides the Swooper, Conklin & Garrett had added a Caterpillar to their Ferris wheel, merry-go-round, Whip, Tilt-A-Whirl, and Fun on the Farm. The newspaper singled out for special notice the Tilt and the Caterpillar, rides that brought couples together.

Vancouver booming, Patty and the Elks had come up with new features for the 1929 event. According to an article in the *Province* on May 4, five "purses of gold" of an unspecified amount were to be given away each day on draws of ticket holders. A fireworks display would be put on each night. The feature that got the most print, however, was the free act:

> One of the great Soderberg's sensational dives ... is considered one of the most daring and death-defying feats that has ever been attempted. Mounting the long slender ladder, over one hundred feet high, until he reaches the small platform at the top, Soderberg then dons an asbestos suit which is saturated with gasoline. At the same time gasoline is poured on the water in the small tank.
>
> ... all lights are extinguished and a match applied to the gasoline in the tank, at the same time Soderberg lights the gas on his suit and dives like a living ball of fire into the

flaming tank. The splashing water extinguishes the flames and the intrepid diver emerges smiling and unharmed.[67]

A photograph of a crowd watching the dive accompanied the article and the paper printed more pictures a few days later. In the off-season Charles Soderberg was assistant custodian for the clubrooms of the Pacific Coast Showmen's Association and he later worked in the movie industry as a stunt man. High divers were popular free acts in the 1920s and Soderberg was one of the best, travelling with Conklin & Garrett for the 1929 and 1930 seasons. Patty would do great things with other free acts in the future.

Patty was mentioned in several articles in the *Sun* in 1929, often with praise for his management. He appeared in a photograph with city aldermen at the official opening. A photograph of him before the office tent among floral tributes marked the event's close. An article ostensibly about the editor of a magazine published by the Elks had as much to say about Patty, quoting the editor from a different article in the magazine. The Elks editor had written that the Vancouver lodge had "come to feel that this show rightfully belongs to them, and Brother Patty Conklin says that is the way that he wants all brothers to feel about the show."[68]

The show's new publicity agent wrote to *Billboard* that Speed "is in poor health this spring and most of the detail work falls upon Mr. Conklin. 'Tis true," he added, "he has surrounded himself with some well-trained and fast-stepping lieutenants, including his brother Frank, 'the Beau Brummell of the City', who is Paddy's assistant; Will Wright, general agent and all-round handy man; Roy Draper, secretary; ... [and] Mrs. J.W. Conklin, treasurer and Paddy's very estimable mother."[69] Draper had joined the office inner circle after he negotiated the purchase of a truck-mounted calliope for $500 from Clarence Wortham's brother in California.

Conklin & Garrett did its usual run of still dates and fairs, but the show hit hard times. Most of the stills were down from the previous year, Edmonton by $8,000, and the fairs also turned out poorly. "Conditions on the prairies are in a terrible state," Patty wrote to Speed. "There are absolutely no crops and the farmers are all very down-hearted."[70] The winds were so strong during the fairs in Saskatchewan and Alberta that they had been unable to open on some days. Patty was building a business dependent on agricultural prosperity in the midst of an environmental crisis. He feared he would not be able to keep the show together. He cancelled two weeks of C circuit fairs for still dates in Regina and Calgary. He would have liked to close the show early but had to stay out to earn enough to pay off its debts to himself, Mrs. Conklin, and Speed. They had put up their own money to keep it running. Despite the conditions, by the end of July Patty could pay off Speed's loan to the show of $13,000 and his own of $14,000. There is no evidence that Mrs. Conklin received anything.

The expansion of the show's route meant criss-crossing the three Prairie provinces. Patty bemoaned the distances between fairs: "The schedules usually call for just about the maximum of shuttle movement."[71] After a fair early in the week in western Alberta, the show had to travel "halfway across Manitoba" for one later in the week. The farming population was also "very widely scattered," so that show agents had "to put up a lot of paper and do a lot of long-distance chasing around the country with it" to ensure that the show was "thoroly advertised."

Along with newspaper ads, billposting was the main vehicle for advertising. Patty bought "paper" from Enterprise Show Print, the only printer of posters for circuses and carnivals in Canada. Andrew King, a newspaper publisher who owned the company located in a tiny Saskatchewan town, had met Patty when International Amusement played there in 1923. King later recounted Patty's drollery at paying "the substantial balance owing on his season's printing account entirely in silver coinage." King stowed the 35 pounds of rolled coins in his pockets. He doubted Patty's "casual excuse that his partner had just taken all the folding money down to the railway station to pay for his train move to the next location."[72] Given the show's tight money situation, this could have been the real reason, as much as Patty's love of a practical joke. King retained Conklin Shows' business even after the show left the West.

The show saved on staff salaries by issuing meal tickets, redeemable at the cookhouse and in the pie car, and by paying staff with "brass." Brass, invented early in the history of the carnival, was show "money." When cash was short, brass coins stamped with the denomination and show's name were given to

Studio portrait of Frank Conklin, c. 1929.

employees in lieu of legal tender or "white money." Brass could only be spent on the show, but it kept staff fed until white money became available.

Patty was giving Frank more responsibility and was happy with his work. Frank had "complete charge of looking out after the stores and ... has done remarkably well."[73] The "stores" were the game concessions. Frank was tough, but friendly and slow to lose his temper, good traits for dealing with games agents. He was also doing some of the fixing. Wright was acting as general agent and Frank Bickford as advance man. Bickford, a Vancouver native, running the ten-in-one since 1927, was taking on general management work. At its peak in 1929, the show employed 200 people.

Patty managed to keep the show together until he got it back to Vancouver at the beginning of October. That fall he succeeded in selling the Missouri

Mules for $1,000 each and the Fun on the Farm for $1,500, reductions by almost two-thirds from his original asking prices. The Depression had arrived early on the Canadian Prairies in the form of drought and crop failure, and the show would be cut to 13 railway cars in 1930.

Health Issues

Along with economic difficulties, Patty faced poor health, his own and that of those close to him. Mrs. Conklin fell ill late in June of 1929 and returned to Vancouver for medical care. She remained sick until the end of the winter, which she spent in Los Angeles. Speed's health kept him off the road. The show's press agent died in the middle of the season and the office shipped his body back to Los Angeles for burial. In August, Patty came down with pneumonia. Early in the winter Frank became ill with tuberculosis and went into the Pottenger Sanatorium for Diseases of the Lungs and Throat in Monrovia, Los Angeles County, and was treated by Dr. Frances Pottenger, at the height of his fame as a lung specialist. Patty spent much of the winter in Los Angeles with Mrs. Conklin and Frank. All of this sickness was a strain on Patty's resources and spirit.

The Pacific Coast Showmen's Association posted notes in the October 5, 1929, issue of *Billboard* about the health of "our good friend 'Paddy' Conklin," wishing him well because the members were looking forward to his arrival for the November meeting. The association prepared for him as though he were a conquering hero, as reported by *Billboard* on November 9: "A large gold and silver sign, hanging in a prominent position, with the inscription, 'Welcome Home, Paddy', caused a buzz and a constant hum of mixed voices to circulate thru the clubrooms, and all minds, with but a single thought, 'Will Paddy be here tonight?'" He finally walked in "amid rousing cheers, smiles and handshakes." The report described at length his experience and innovations, and how his "humanly attitude toward his men has gained for him the confidence and co-operation of all members of the Conklin Shows." The meeting took place only five days after the stock market crash of October 29. The report concluded by noting the "considerable excitement" the crash caused in Los

Angeles: "Paddy Conklin sympathizes and advises the boys that now's the time to buy, whereupon the stock subject was dropped."

Conklin staff members were active with the Pacific Coast Association that winter. Patty continued to be "very much in evidence at the meetings … and solves many problems that arise."[74] He had been nominated for president and, with no opposition, was acclaimed in December. He wrote to Speed that he felt this would "do our show a great deal of good."[75] Frank and Sam Boswitz, who had been with Conklin & Garrett since 1927 and also wintered in Los Angeles, joined Wright on the board of governors. Patty was elected to the board of governors of the Showmen's League as well, a position that every major show owner had to occupy at some time.

In a letter from December 1929 that still refers to "our show," Patty asked Speed to meet him before the Western Canada Fairs Association meeting "to discuss very important business matters."[76] Speed was in Waldport and could not meet with Patty in Los Angeles in January, as Patty had suggested. They arranged to talk by telephone. After the conversation, Speed agreed to have a letter sent to Patty in Winnipeg confirming that Patty had full legal authority to make agreements for the show. Speed was getting out of the business. The doctors had told him that he could no longer travel with the carnival and should move to a dryer, warmer climate.

PATTY TAKES OVER

Sleet rattles the Seattle hospital's windows as Patty tries to explain how bad the season has been. Speed can't keep his thoughts together. "What about Moran, did he give you any trouble?"

"Speed, we got rid of Moran two years ago. You gotta realize what I been dealing with out there. The farmers are broke and a lot of the gazoonies are going without this winter," Patty complains.

"But the Tilt made good money, right?"

"Nothin' made any money — didn't even pay the gas. Just sign this and I'll look after it all. You're too sick, I don't want you to worry."

"I need money for groceries when I get outta here."

"We'll look after you when you get out. I'll make payments a couple of times a year, until I pay it all down."

"How much are you giving me for it?"

"Look, the junk needs a lotta work and I have to cover winter quarters, taxes, all that crap. I'm giving you what it's worth. Just sign these papers, will you, I gotta get back to the hotel."

"I hope I can get outta here soon; I can't even pay for this bed." Speed props himself up to sign where Patty points, then collapses in the bed.

"You need to get someplace where it's hot and dry, like California. And you need somebody to look after you." Patty stuffs the papers inside his coat and stands up. "Look after yourself, Speed." He turns and leaves.

★   ★   ★

For several seasons during the early 1930s, the health of Mrs. Conklin and Frank was precarious, so Patty was the only Conklin consistently on the road. For a short time, he was sole owner of Conklin & Garrett Shows. Speed had given him full power to bring in whomever he wanted as an active partner, if that person had capital to buy out Speed. Failing to find a partner, Patty announced his ownership of the show in January 1930. *Billboard* called the announcement "the most outstanding business deal in carnival circles."[77]

Patty and Speed Make a Deal

Speed made it from Seattle to Vancouver in mid-January of 1930. His condition continued to deteriorate. At his hotel in Vancouver, he had a nurse handle communications with Patty, and he soon returned to Seattle. On the way from Winnipeg back to Los Angeles at the end of January, Patty stopped at the Seattle hospital to see Speed, who was not in full possession of his faculties. The two signed the final papers of the agreement whereby Patty bought Speed's half of the show for $19,000.

Speed later complained, justly, that this amount was too little. The six rides alone were worth close to $30,000. They had bought the Tilt-A-Whirl in 1928 for $5,900 and the Caterpillar for $6,000; they had tried to sell the Ferris wheel, without its motor, for $3,000 and the merry-go-round for $4,200; the Swooper was new that season and the Whip would have been worth something. Besides the rides, there were 11 baggage cars, four Pullmans, and all the shows and concession equipment. Patty took advantage of Speed's condition to buy him out at a bargain basement price. Maintenance and storage had to be covered, but Patty ensured Speed shared those costs, while revenue accrued solely to himself.

Patty returned to Vancouver from Los Angeles by March 12. Speed travelled from Waldport to Los Angeles, arriving on March 19 and moving on to San Diego by the beginning of April. Despite their expressions of a desire to meet, they failed to do so. Speed stayed in San Diego for much of the next two years, returning sporadically to Seattle for treatment and Waldport to look after his ranch. He was living with his son, Fred, who transcribed his correspondence. To one such letter to Patty, Speed added a garbled postscript in a shaky hand:

> What was date of sale my part of show to you and what form and amount was it as there seams to be a mixup perhaps you can help me get it O.K. as my mind goes entirely away at times allso did I sign any papers conserning oil when you was there
>
> allso what did you and I agree on about our Company account write these things on a personal letter I can figure them out at times. [78]

In complying with Speed's request, Patty mounted a pre-emptive defence of the deal:

> I purchased your interest in the Show on January 29th. The amount that I paid you for your half-interest was $19,000.00; $4,500.00 on the signing of the contract; $5,000.00 on the 1st of April, 1930; $5,000.00 on the 1st of April, 1931; and $5,000.00 on the 1st of April, 1932. In doing so I bought

title, all moneys we had in the Bank, stock and Show in
its entirety, with the exception of our real estate at New
Westminster and Trail, and I don't mind telling you that I
think I paid an exceedingly big price for same, as I was again
compelled to spend ... $25,000.00 on fixing the Show up
again this year.

You also enquire in your letter if you signed any papers
in regards to oil. Oil was never mentioned during the entire
transaction, so evidently you must have that mixed up with
something else.[79]

Speed replied that he thought Patty had done well: "Had I not been sick and
down and out at the time I sold I would still own half interest in the Conklin
& Garrett Shows, as I did not then or until tonight, hear or understand a small
part in our sale."[80]

Despite Speed's vague sense that he had been taken, he remained on cor-
dial terms with Patty, at least as far as the correspondence reveals. Until his
death, he continued to ask Patty for money when he was flat and Patty com-
plied when he felt he could, which was not often. Befittingly afraid that Speed's
family would undertake legal action against him, Patty kept all of the documents on the deal close by him.

Although Frank remained in the sanatorium in California, Patty made
him his partner. "Since I purchased your interest in the Show I have sold same
to Frank," he wrote to Speed, "but this is not for publication or anyone's information other than your own. So please keep this to yourself."[81] Why he wanted
to keep the transaction private is not clear. Perhaps he wanted to be perceived
as the sole owner.

Throughout the winter, Patty added to the show. In Los Angeles, he contracted with Harry Meyers for a Freak Animal Show: "This attraction has a
frontage of 217 feet, with triple-decked banners depicting the interior pres-
entations. It is doubtless one of the most elaborate and greatest revenue-
drawing offerings in the outdoor field of entertainments."[82] Meyers, who had
had the cookhouse on Levitt-Brown-Huggins Shows, also got the cookhouse
concession with Conklin & Garrett. Patty bought another Ferris wheel and

planned to run twin wheels, a combination that had been successfully pioneered by Royal American in 1928. Of the $25,000 he said he invested, $20,000 was borrowed from the bank.

He expanded the show before the fair contracts for the coming season had been awarded. The western Canada B circuit, split just the previous year, was put back together for 1930. Royal American had expanded at a greater rate than Conklin & Garrett and at the Western Canada Fairs Association meeting won the whole B circuit for 1930. On February 1, *Billboard* reported, "This was a surprise, as Conklin & Garrett have had the contract for years, giving every satisfaction. In fact, at the banquet Wednesday evening regret was expressed by representatives of the circuit that it had been necessary to make a change." At a meeting in Moose Jaw in March for the C circuit and smaller fairs, Conklin & Garrett won the consolation prize: contracts for nine fairs, including four that had been demoted from the B circuit. Patty also booked still dates in two towns with strong Elks lodges that he had played as B fairs in previous years.

Through small touches that would impress the right people, Patty started to put his mark on the show. For the Vancouver event, he ordered complimentary admission cards with gold lettering and a fancy border. He had route cards printed showing every week booked until the beginning of October. He also sent Speed the advertising material and two books of tickets for the Vancouver date. And he had the show calliope out on the street two weeks before opening.

Season of 1930 and Some Weddings

At the Vancouver opening early in May, the show had much the same lineup as the previous year. There were seven shows and seven rides, although only a single Ferris wheel. Apart from the freak animal show and a bear show, the only other new show was Death on the Guillotine, run by Wright. Originally produced in Australia, it featured the illusion of a young woman having her head chopped off and carried into the crowd. Wright had a temporary North American exclusive on this show with six units out on other midways.

The show's office staff remained largely the same, although Frank, listed as assistant manager and superintendent of concessions, did not go out. He remained in the sanatorium until the middle of July, but after what *Billboard* described as "an extended vacation in the mountains and seashore," he visited the show in mid-August.[83] He then returned to the sanatorium. Mrs. Conklin's health had improved enough that she was able to spend time on the grounds with Patty in Vancouver and she went on the road. Patty described her health as "alright," but lamented to Frank that she "is very lonesome and seems to be worried all the time."[84] She left for Newburgh before the end of the season.

The show's spring dates were consistent with previous years. They played still dates from Nanaimo to Winnipeg through May and June. They began the C circuit fairs at the end of June. They added two more sideshows and had contracted with the circuit to provide the free acts, a one-ring circus and Soderberg's Dive of Death.

With the C circuit in 1930, the show had a much tighter route than usual. During July they worked five Saskatchewan fairs west of Saskatoon, none of which required a jump of more than 100 miles. They then moved on to four closely grouped fairs and a still date in Alberta. None of these towns was more than 25 years old and their populations numbered in the hundreds. They all had arisen through the Canadian government's campaign to settle the West, providing land grants to wheat farmers and the railways to get the wheat out, which had resulted in a huge inflow of settlers.

Although the route was compact, business was not favourable. The show was plagued by "constant rain and wind."[85] At one three-day fair, they had a dust storm the first night and thunderstorms the next two. Patty described the transformation of a lot "so dusty ... that we had to sprinkle it continually" into "a lake with things floating on it."[86] Their next fair was rained out on what should have been its best day. The show also had to cope with the depressed economy. "The country is not in any too good shape, and everyone seems to be crying that they have no money," he wrote to Speed.[87]

Both the office and the midway staff were hurting. Patty was having difficulty with "the help" because they were not making any money. He tried to salvage the office's fortunes by trimming. At the end of June, he cut the show from 15 to 13 railway cars, reducing overhead by $350 a day. In July he dropped a ride, three shows, and 10 games: "If things continue such as they are in the next week or so I am going to take off the caterpillar and at least two more shows and about 5 concessions."[88]

Patty was consoled to have the company of his competitors in this misery. Royal American was "in the same fix as we are," he reported to Speed.[89] Morris & Castle Shows had taken the A circuit of western exhibitions from Johnny J. Jones Exposition, the biggest show at the time. Despite this, Morris & Castle would be "very lucky" to "get back to the United States." The one bright spot was that the "Weed Inspectors" were not enforcing gambling regulations as strictly as they had the previous year, a relief that Patty attributed to the economic conditions.

Fights between carnies and marks, called "hey rubes," were another problem of running a carnival. Patty had to deal with one particularly nasty incident that season. Rip Weinkle had been a concessions manager with the show for a few years and in 1929 was listed as the show's musical director. Weinkle laid a beating on a local in Kindersley, Saskatchewan:

> ... someone got the fellow that we had the trouble with to make a complaint against Rip and got out a warrant for carrying concealed weapons also a warrant for common assault. As a consequence Mr. Rip was locked up and spent three hours in jail and I drove from Rosetown to Kindersley and arranged to have his trial and we beat the concealed weapon case without any difficulty and the complainant withdrew the warrant for common assault and had a new warrant issued for assault with violence and attempt to kill. After talking the matter over with the complainant and 12 of his witnesses, several stool pigeons, the Judge, the policeman, I managed to get matters adjusted and it cost $211.00 but it looked very serious as all of these fellows that appeared as witnesses were swearing Rip's life away.... Rip was as meek as a lamb when they had him in the cell and until the entire case was over.[90]

Patty's account of the legal proceedings suggests how savage a hey rube could be. Weinkle was not with the show the following year but continued to book concessions on other shows and circuses into his 70s, becoming a legend and occupying "Rip's Corner" at the Virginia State Fair as late as 1968.[91]

Soon after Conklin & Garrett finished its still dates in British Columbia and went into winter quarters at the beginning of October, *Billboard* printed a rumour about some "very interesting and pleasing events" to come in Patty's near future.[92] In the next issue, the Pacific Coast Showmen's Association revealed that he had gotten married, and the November 1 *Billboard* printed a full report of the wedding.

The bride, Edythe Marie Bell, 32-year-old daughter of Mr. and Mrs. William Bell of Nanaimo, was described as "a popular member of the younger social circles of Los Angeles, Seattle and Vancouver."[93] Like so many of her peers with good looks and potential talent, she had gone to Los Angeles with the dream of becoming a movie star. There she had met Edgar "Painless" Parker, a dentist-showman who had become notorious through his extravagant self-promotion.

Born in 1872, Parker had gone to dental school in New York and Pennsylvania.[94] Failing at conventional dentistry, he innovated with showmanship and chicanery. He hired P.T. Barnum's former publicity agent to create the Parker Dental Circus, a travelling medicine show he took from the east coast to the west, once being busted for practising without a licence in Victoria. He had moved to Los Angeles, where he expanded to a chain of 30 dental clinics along the west coast. Diverted from her screen ambitions by the need to make a living, Edythe was hired by Parker to help him open some of the clinics with demonstrations of painless tooth extraction using nitrous oxide, or laughing gas. Her son later said she assisted Parker "while he demonstrated the gas by a pulling a person's teeth on stage."[95] She acquired a licence to practise dentistry herself, but found she was aging beyond the conventional marriageable age and came home in the summer to see what she could do about that.

Patty and Edythe met in 1929 at the Nanaimo street fair, where she ran an ice cream booth for her father, who owned the Nanaimo Home Dairy. Patty never ate so much ice cream as he did that week. He donated a trophy for

Edythe Marie Bell at 18.

the winning parade float to impress her. He looked her up in Los Angeles the following winter and bought her a grand piano. Frank wrote to her in April 1930 and Patty often called her. Edythe sent flowers for the show's opening in Vancouver. Perhaps they were planning even then to marry once the season was over. She would have been comfortable with the show world through working for Painless Parker, who had bought a circus to ballyhoo his clinics on the west coast and had legally changed his first name to "Painless" when California passed a law requiring dentists to work under their legal title. From working for "Painless" Parker to marrying "Patty" Conklin would not have been a big leap. Patty said "they married to save long distance telephone bills," while Edythe joked that "it was a case of marrying him or paying a fifty-dollar concession fee that he was trying to extract for her ice cream booth at the Vancouver Fair."[96]

The couple were married on Tuesday, October 14, in the Congregationalist church in Seattle. Frank was best man; Edythe's sister was lady of honour. About 60 guests attended and more sent their congratulations, including Speed; Patty's brother, Charles Renker; and his sister, Catherine Brocco. The bride and groom flew to San Francisco, where they sailed for a honeymoon in Honolulu. Wright had wintered in Honolulu and Frank had vacationed there in the winter of 1928–29, so Patty had contacts there. He was treated like a celebrity, giving interviews about the outdoor amusement business in North America. He met E.K. Fernandez, Hawaii's sole carnival owner, for the first time during the honeymoon tour and praised Fernandez, among others, for his hospitality.

With Patty's wedding over, Frank felt free to go public with his own. He had married Lotta "Billie" Vylda Webb on August 1 at Santa Ana, California. She was a nurse at the Pottenger Sanatorium where Frank continued to receive treatment. The wedding was a private affair. Frank and Billie's honeymoon had been a visit to the show in Drumheller. Both the brothers' marriages lasted until their deaths.

Back on the continent, Patty, bride in tow, began his peregrinations to Chicago, New York, Los Angeles, Seattle, Vancouver, and Winnipeg, planning to rest in Los Angeles or Miami. The Showmen's League convention in Chicago was well attended, even though the past season was "generally conceded to have been one of the worst in the history of show business."[97] Patty sat at the head table again, this time with Edythe and Ella Conklin.

At the Western Canada Fairs Association meeting in Winnipeg, Conklin & Garrett won back the B circuit fairs from Royal American. The show also managed to get the Pacific National Exhibition in Vancouver, on which Patty had unsuccessfully bid the previous year. L.D. Taylor, back in office for his seventh term as mayor, influenced the decision.

Instead of heading west from the fairs association meeting, Patty and Edythe returned to the East. Ella was sick in Newburgh, and her condition was serious. The February 14, 1931, issue of *Billboard* noted her illness and also announced her death. Her loss, mourned by the show world, had been anticipated by her surrogate sons. With no one to execute her estate, the show's debt to Mrs. Conklin of several thousand dollars died with her. Frank and his wife were not able to make it to the funeral, but Patty and Edythe did. Ella Conklin buried, the newlyweds returned to Vancouver.

Patty had a strict rule about allowing wives and children on the road only if they were working. Andy Cullerton had been the show's electrician since 1926 and superintendent of lights since 1928. In 1930 he was able to get his wife a job on the show as the candy-floss operator. Wright's wife worked with him on the road and even his daughter was on a bally platform at the tender age of four. In general, however, wives and girlfriends were not welcome.

In the show's roster for 1931, the new Mrs. J.W. Conklin appeared as treasurer, replacing Ella Conklin and taking the job so that she could meet Patty's requirement. In another major change, Frank was listed as a proprietor for the first time. He went on the road without Billie, but his illness relapsed mid-season and he returned to the sanatorium. Frank Hopwood, dramatic critic for the *Vancouver Sun*, was press agent. Other than these changes, the office staff remained the same.

Season of 1931

For the May opening in Vancouver, Frank and Billie flew in from Los Angeles on Transcontinental and Western Air, only two years after commercial passenger flights began and a month after the first passenger plane crash in the United States. At the opening, the two new Mrs. Conklins played host with their husbands. Hopwood and his wife and daughter were also "very much in evidence" and the *Sun*, with his assistance, provided extensive coverage.[98]

Conklin & Garrett advertised eight rides and 12 shows for the Vancouver date. They included each of the twin Ferris wheels in the count. They had managed to find a Lindy Loop, a circular track ride brought out by Spillman Engineering a year after Charles Lindbergh's 1927 trans-Atlantic flight. Patty had been trying to book one since then and got this one only for Vancouver. The merry-go-round, Swooper, Tilt-A-Whirl, Caterpillar, and Merry Mix-Up completed the ride lineup. With the Elks, the show also provided a dance hall with a 10-piece orchestra that played until one in the morning.

Many of the shows were the same as the previous season, although at least three new ones were added. They had Madlyn–Arthur, a half-man, half-woman act. This type of act was usually faked — a "gaffed freak" — using clothing and makeup to produce the illusion of a different sex on each side. They also had Harry Attree's Flashes of 1931, billed as a musical comedy revue with dancing girls that had played New York City and the vaudeville circuit. This attraction warranted a photograph in the *Sun*.

The most notable new show was one of Lou Dufour's Unborn exhibits, which he had first produced for the Johnny J. Jones Exposition in 1928. These were exhibits of deformed fetuses in formaldehyde that became known within the carnival industry as "pickled punks." Sometimes they were made of rubber, in which case they were known as "bouncers." After pitching his pickled punks to the "approval and enthusiasm" of Henry Ford, Thomas Edison, and Harvey Firestone, Dufour knew he had a gold mine.[99] By 1931 he had franchised 16 units, booked with most of the major carnivals and several amusement parks. This sideshow genre remained popular into the 1960s. Since working for Dufour in Washington, Patty had kept up the friendship and welcomed one of Dufour's exhibits. On May 9, after the Vancouver event, the *Sun* remarked that "the 'Unborn,' an educational and deeply interesting lesson in the formation of life, has held people spell-bound at the work of nature."

At the end of the seven-day opener, the show moved a few miles down the road. The *Sun* explained that "there were thousands who were disappointed at not being able to visit" the show in Vancouver, so Patty "decided to move, bag and baggage" to Burnaby.[100] They next played Courtenay and Nanaimo on Vancouver Island, and then returned to the Vancouver area for a week in New Westminster. They headed out in June for the Alberta still dates, followed by the B circuit fairs, most of which they had last played two years before.

Patty had a serious automobile accident while in Courtenay. He had recently bought a $5,000 1930 Pierce-Arrow, the favourite car of statesmen, captains of industry, and movie stars. His later story was that he had hit a tree, while the rumour was that he had run a man down. The damages of

$315 he paid to a Courtenay man suggest something in between. The accident marked him for life. He never drove a vehicle again, preferring to rely on a company chauffeur.

The show's press release reported that receipts "were not so good as in former years, yet a few of the fairs gave the show average business."[101] The show had bought its own Lindy Loop for the fairs. After them, they spent a week in The Pas, Manitoba, at the time, according to the press agent, "the farthest north for a railroad show to go." The Pas was in a sparsely settled region on the extreme edge of the agricultural lands of the south. It was an accomplishment to get there and back. The show covered 1,300 miles in a few days to return to Vancouver for the exhibition.

Both of Vancouver's major papers covered the Canada Pacific Exhibition extensively. Conklin & Garrett had long been trumpeting its counterfeit "All-Canadian" status. That the Canada Pacific Exhibition would for the first time have a show with this label was played up. The *Province* remarked that the "Made in Canada" label was on prominent display in exhibit departments. On January 3, 1931, *Billboard* had reported that a Vancouver daily published "a lengthy article on … a sort of 'Canada First' proposition regarding amusements at next year's British Columbia exhibitions…. There has been a bit of 'all-for-Canada' propaganda afloat lately — which may have been 'adopted' by some amusement interests in this instance." This observation applied to Conklin & Garrett, happy to exploit the Canadian protectionist spirit, but the reporter had been disingenuous, since the Depression led to the same protectionism in the United States.

In an article bearing the unmistakable imprint of Frank Hopwood, the *Sun* helped Patty further in establishing his local credentials. Headlined "They're Vancouver Girls in Conklin Show at Fair," the article justified itself as "a news story, and not a theatrical critique" through its main point about the girl show:

> All the girls in Paddy's show are home-grown. They were born and raised here. They were trained here. And there's a reason for it all. Paddy has seen his hard times. He has eaten the husks. He hardly knew prosperity until he hit Vancouver. And then he discovered it.

> So today in all Paddy's shows, the talent is Vancouver
> talent. Perhaps Paddy is a sentimentalist.[102]

Patty was surely a sentimentalist, a trait that dovetailed neatly with his promotional abilities, and both characteristics could lead to unconcern for the strictly literal truth. But other values had already trumped any sentimental ties to the city he might have entertained.

As a final touch, Patty announced during the exhibition that he had hired as his general agent W.C. "Bill" Fleming, born in Peterborough, Ontario. Without mentioning that Fleming had moved to the United States when he was 13, the *Sun* described his appointment as part of "Mr. Conklin's determination to keep his organization 100 per cent Canadian, in departments where it is at all possible."[103] Fleming also added to a latent east-west tension internal to the show.

British Columbia's premier opened the event by boasting that "Vancouver's Canada Pacific Exhibition is now easily the greatest west of the Great Lakes and destined to become steadily greater."[104] Reduced to seven days from 10 in 1930, the exhibition's 1931 attendance of 244,385 came within 40,000 of the mark set the previous year. The exhibition association expected to make its largest profit ever, the association's president pointing out that, "with the exception of the Canada National Exhibition at Toronto, now in progress, every other Canadian fair has operated at a loss this year."[105]

For Patty, it was "the largest fair in his career" and, after the "hard times on the prairies," he was "a justly proud man."[106] But he never had the good fortune to play it again and would not be there for L.D. Taylor's election to his last term as mayor. In the December 5 issue of *Billboard*, he published an article titled "Carnival Problems in Western Canada." While his show would work the Prairies a few more years, for the 1932 season he was shifting his route eastward. The show left Vancouver the following spring, never to return in Patty's lifetime. He had made his mark on the growing city, and it had supported him, but the West was suffering from drought and depression, and he sniffed a whiff of prosperity rising in the East.

Turning to the East

·······························

(1932–1937)

·······························

By the early 1930s, the North American carnival was expanding in its classic period and the industry press was confident about its future. Patty Conklin's vibrant, brash personality and knack for self-promotion ensured he was thoroughly covered in carnival publications and often the mainstream press. He claimed his nickname came from how he could be trusted to stand pat on handshake agreements. But he had dealings he did not want publicized, and was obsessive about these transactions, keeping almost every scrap of paper related to them. Acutely conscious of the scams he was perpetrating, he wanted his documents handy in case his pedigree was ever questioned. He would become one of the bright lights shining in the carnival's tawdry universe.

CUTTING TIES ON THE COAST

Ernie cowers before the crowd staring up at him. A strange man holds his hand, speaking to the crowd and pointing at him. The little boy's mother had hugged him and told him not to worry, but he doesn't know where she is now; he hasn't seen her for a long time. He is too tired and scared to cry.

It is nighttime, and even under the glaring bare lights it is cold in the tent; goosebumps rise on his arms, and he shivers. The man yanks the blanket off Ernie's shoulders. With a shiny stick, he pokes at the tiny body and limp legs dangling from Ernie's stomach, talking to it, calling it Len, and pretending to tickle its feet. Ernie shrinks back, almost feeling the stick somewhere, on some part of him that isn't him.

"Mother Nature thought to give him a brother, then decided against it! A miracle of twindom and freak of Mother Nature, Ernie and Len are inseparable!" the man shouts. He keeps talking, saying things Ernie doesn't understand. Something about how special he is.

The crowd, mostly men and boys much older than Ernie, have curious, awed looks. They nudge each other and point and giggle, but they don't laugh out loud and only mutter among themselves. He would like to be with them but knows he can't. He wants this to end so he can go back to his mat in the trailer and maybe be given some food and a drink, and be able to get warm and sleep.

★　★　★

Conklin's All-Canadian Shows, with Speed off the books and the company's new name, began poaching on the territory of other shows, including the International Amusement Company and Wallace Brothers. At the 1931 meeting of the Showmen's League, Bill Fleming, the new general agent, floated the rumour that the Conklins were moving east. He had been general agent for Johnny J. Jones Exposition in the early 1920s, negotiating contracts with the Canadian National Exhibition and the Western Ontario Exhibition in London. He had gone to Rubin & Cherry in 1928, the year that show had taken the CNE and the London fair from Jones. Fleming had retired from the industry, but Patty persuaded him to come back during the 1931 Vancouver exhibition.

The Developing Carnival Industry

The carnival had scratched out a place for itself in North American society. With over 200 shows on the road — even if many struggled and were doomed to disappear — the industry was one of the first big dogs of outdoor entertainment to create a market among the masses. The Johnny J. Jones Exposition led the pack with major fairs across the American Midwest and western Canadian provinces. The Beckmann & Gerety, Morris & Castle, and Rubin & Cherry shows nipped at Jones's heals. Other shows expanded despite the Depression and by the mid-1930s, Royal American was the alpha dog.[1] No one foresaw the bite that Patty Conklin, starting with a 15-car gilly show, would take out of the industry.

Many predicted the end of the carnival, seeing the shows that were on shaky ground as representative. The overlap of the carnival and the circus shaped the perception that the former shared in the decline of the latter. The carnival had always had to fend off local politicians, businessmen, reformers, and other troublemakers. The conviction of would-be public figures — and the public and the press that encouraged them — that this industry would soon succumb to their attacks propped up prophecies of its imminent demise.

Such threats to their livelihood fed the self-image of those perpetual outsiders who, once they had found their carnival haven, felt they were finally in a place where they truly belonged. Townie animosity confirmed the carnie as its own world, one that a crafty and charismatic character like Patty could dominate and use to exploit the larger world that helped create it.

The industry recognized its weaknesses. Strong shows — gaffs, gambling, girls, and grift — were symptomatic of its most pernicious flaws. Throughout a 15-year bout of wishful thinking, *Billboard* magazine had been forecasting the disappearance of strong shows. Its spasmodically revitalized campaign to achieve this goal was futile until economics made cleaning up a good business decision, one that would transform the carnival into a family place, ready for the middle-class masses. Conklin Shows played strong until it made financial sense not to. Meanwhile, Patty's success with his strong show garnered the respect of his peers.

Patty also gained respect for some of his freaks. Showmen during this period were continually on the lookout for local oddities. In Winnipeg in 1931, Patty had heard of the birth of a double-bodied baby. Ernest Leonard Defort was born with a headless parasitic twin growing from his stomach. Patty found him on a Manitoba farm and when he was five months old his impoverished parents signed a contract with Patty. When he turned two, Ernie and "Len,"

Ernie and Len sideshow attraction, with banner, attendants, and the sideshow talker, c. 1936.

the name given to his twin, began their career as a star attraction on Conklin's All-Canadian. The labour laws against exhibiting children had not yet been written. By the time he was 12, Ernie's parents had made enough money from exhibiting him that they could afford the surgery to have Len removed, an operation that received widespread attention in the press.[2] Ernie later rejoined the carnival without Len to work as a games agent, earning much less than he had as a freak.

In these hardscrabble times, backyard shows struggled to establish their credibility, as movies, radio, and other mass entertainments became industries. Outdoor showmen turned to the examples of other organizations trying to disinfect themselves: Major League Baseball under Judge Landis, its first commissioner appointed in 1920, and the Motion Picture Producers and Distributors of America, begun in 1922 with Will Hays at its head. A few months after the Hays office opened, carnival owners began organizing to emulate "the motion picture and baseball interests of the country."[3] The

Showmen's Legislative Committee began operating in 1923, one of its primary goals to abolish "the 'rogue elephants' in the game." The committee petered out from a lack of commitment by some show owners and from attempts by others to use it against their competitors. By the early 1930s, the Hays office was recognized as little more than a public relations ruse, yet showmen continued to cite Landis and Hays as examples to follow.

Some showmen displaced the need to clean up the carnival's reputation onto a different problem, that of the increasingly exorbitant financial demands of the sponsoring committees as they became wise to the kind of money carnies made. These demands had to be passed down the line to concessionaires and ride owners. Committees played shows off against each other, giving their event to the company that would swallow the highest percentage or flat payment. Local officials expected favours just to allow a show to play, Sunday school or not. Some carnival owners justified "their grift on the ground that the high license fee and other extortions compelled them to run the rackets."[4] The carnies and the committees knew they had to find some kind of balance or both sides would lose.

To counter these ills, carnival men looked to another trend in the entertainment industries: amalgamation and vertical integration. The Theatrical Syndicate had dominated early twentieth-century American theatre. The United Booking Office, a centralized entertainment empire, controlled vaudeville until vaudeville's decline. By the early 1920s, the major Hollywood studios had integrated the production and distribution of movies.

Carnival owners sought the same goals for their industry as the United Booking Office promised vaudeville: sound business principles, regulated salaries, compact touring routes, and the end of competition. On July 2, 1923, *Billboard* announced that "the next logical step is amalgamation. Big businesses have found it to their interest to combine and there is no reason why the same governing principles cannot be employed in the show world." The article argued that the owners of major shows should "pool their mutual interests into a federation with a board of directors and managing head ... and give the country standardized amusement by the equitable routing of their units." *Billboard*'s editorial staff and the showmen who wrote for it frequently raised the idea.

While its exact details were seldom described, amalgamation of the carnival industry was to be a panacea. A central office would discipline strong
shows. It would stop competition among shows and present a united front to
fair boards, ensuring that the fees required were reasonable. It would negotiate
rates with the railways, rationalize routes, create compact circuits, and avoid
overbooking. It would promote the industry to the public.

Under pressure from a declining economy, some shows attempted concrete action. Late in 1930, the Rubin & Cherry, Beckmann & Gerety, Morris
& Castle, and Johnny J. Jones shows announced that they would merge into
the International Midway Corporation, which would handle their routing and
booking. The idea failed to materialize. Three years later, a New York lawyer drew up a proposal for a trade association, and in early December, the
American Carnival Association was announced, support for it pledged by 11
shows, including the four that had tried to merge in 1930, as well as Royal
American and Conklin Shows. The association appointed an executive, drew
up bylaws, and undertook activities, but failed to mount effective interven-
tions and, while it survived for many years, never became an effective force
for the industry.

The organizer of the American Carnival Association acknowledged "the
psychological objections which are usually raised in the minds of showmen
when organization is mentioned."[5] Among these are showmen's individuality,
independence, entrepreneurship, distrust, ambition, and competitiveness. No
show securely dominated the industry. Each owner had his own territory, but
each knew that, given the right circumstances, he could jump the fence into
a competitor's backyard. The constraints imposed by any co-operative enterprise would threaten his company's potential for expansion.

Season of 1932

The winter of 1931–32, Patty and Edythe travelled extensively, visiting Los
Angeles, Vancouver, Seattle, Toronto, Montreal, and New York, and taking a
Caribbean cruise. Patty and Fleming attended the Canadian fairs meeting in
Winnipeg in late January, the show bidding for the first time on the A circuit

and not the B. Competition included Rubin & Cherry and Royal American, but Castle-Ehrlich-Hirsch Shows, successor to Morris & Castle, won the circuit. The B fairs went to Boyd & Wirth, under whose name the free acts for the circuit were also contracted. At a point when Patty usually had his season fully booked, he had given up the western B circuit and had no more than a couple of untried Ontario fairs.

Boyd & Wirth was unknown as a carnival. Larry Boyd had worked for a number of shows, including as a partner of Jimmy Sullivan in a show sometimes called Wallace Brothers that had dates in Ontario and Quebec in the late 1920s and throughout the '30s. Boyd was known in Toronto for promoting Shrine circuses and, with Sullivan, for putting a midway on vacant lots around the city for as many as 10 weeks at a time. In 1931 he joined with two Wirth brothers from the circus to book free acts. Industry insiders speculated that Boyd & Wirth took the B circuit for a resurrected Boyd & Sullivan or Wallace Brothers' show. Sullivan, nervous about the competition, was doing everything he could to prevent a successful move by Patty into Ontario.

Fleming called on old contacts. By the end of February 1932, he could report that the fair route in the East was just about complete. He booked fairs in Fort Williams, Sault Ste. Marie, Cornwall, Peterborough, Stratford, Woodstock, Owen Sound, and Midland in Ontario, and Brome and Granby in Quebec, some of which he had once contracted for Johnny J. Jones. This route, equivalent to the western B circuit, covered the latter half of August and all of September, with a few gaps. Fleming asserted that he had "'bought' no fairs in this territory, all being booked on percentage, including Granby and Brome, which had heretofore been sold at flat-rate."[6]

In a letter dated March 8, 1932, Patty warned Speed that he would not be able to make the final $5,000 payment for Speed's half of the show, due at the beginning of April. To excuse his dereliction, Patty described his troubles putting together a route: "I am just beginning to line up things for the coming year. So far I have not contracted any dates in the West, our plans are centred in the East and we will be showing at least ten fairs in Eastern Canada and about five fairs in the Prairies." They still had the Vancouver opener. On March 26, Patty complained that "a good many of the dates I had contracted have been cancelled owing to conditions."

The contradictions encourage speculation. The C circuit of western fairs had not been represented at the Winnipeg meeting because its members could not afford to attend. They planned to establish carnival contracts later, although it was "doubtful just how many of these" would come in.[7] Patty might have hoped to get them, as he had in previous years, and they had fallen through. Sometime in April he made other arrangements.

When spring arrived, Patty announced in the April 30 issue of *Billboard* that he would play "his old stomping grounds" in the West before "extending his scope ... farther eastward than before." He had fairs in Saskatchewan and Manitoba, and some still dates to tie up loose ends. Fleming and the show's advance man would have to fill some stills week by week. Describing the last-minute scrambling to complete the route, *Billboard* noted on June 25 that Fleming and Patty "have certainly been stepping about." Even in July, there were still "stray ends" in their contracting.[8]

Seven of the fairs Conklin's All-Canadian Shows played that summer were on the western B circuit, contracted by Boyd & Wirth. On May 23, *Billboard* commented that "'Paddy' Conklin and 'Bill' Fleming may have featured fore-thought when they didn't bid on a certain fair circuit for this year." Whatever arrangement Patty and Boyd had for Patty to look after Boyd's fairs might have been brought up at the Western Canada Fairs Association meeting, but they likely did not finalize their arrangement until spring. This collaboration was the first of a long string that Jimmy Sullivan, Boyd's partner, would have with Patty. Frank handled the negotiations with Sullivan, and they eventually became friends.

Conklin's All-Canadian opened in Vancouver with the seventh and final Elks Annual Bazaar–Circus. Mayor Taylor and the city council had only been able to come up with the licence three weeks before. His health poor, Taylor had opened the recent council session from a reclining chair, flat on his back speaking to the ceiling. He was brought from the hospital to the show opening in a wheelchair.

Apart from the Swooper, which they had sold, the show carried the same rides as 1931 and some of the same shows. The motordrome; the half-man, half-woman act; the girl show revue; and Dufour's Unborn had been replaced by a war relic exhibit, a flea circus, "Dolly the Doll Lady," and an "Educational

Waxworks,"[9] replacements that required few staff and so met Patty's desire to "cut the nut down."[10]

The free attraction for Vancouver was "The Bombardment and Battle of Shanghai," a fireworks display. Fireworks were often designed and billed as representations of battles of record. "Preparations are under way with a Hollywood production company to film this presentation, sometime during this spring," Patty claimed in the *Vancouver Sun* on May 2. The fireworks display did not go on the road and its filming did not happen.

Conklin's All-Canadian avoided sailing to Vancouver Island in 1932 and after New Westminster headed for the mountains. The show had five still dates in towns it used to play as fall fairs on the way back to Vancouver. Patty would never visit these towns again. Perhaps he booked them for a sentimental farewell, sentimentality once again making good business sense. The show then played a series of stills in Alberta. Billie joined Frank, who had left the sanatorium at the beginning of May to go on the road, in Edmonton. Although cured for the time being, Frank was still weak.

On June 14, Patty wrote Speed that "business with us is so bad that it is beyond even anyone's own imaginary ideas. We have been grossing anywhere from $110.00 to $400.00 per day ever since we left Vancouver." He added that "conditions in the country are such that it is practically impossible for us to gross operating expenses at our Still dates. Plenty of people but no money. There are a number of people on the Show that are really missing meals." Writing to *Billboard* in the middle of July, after the beginning of the fairs, Patty reported that business was spotty, but the weather showed promise of "giving us a break soon, after which we hope to improve."[11]

The eastern leg of the route, including switching the closing date from Montreal to Hamilton, was finally settled by mid-July, when Patty sent route cards to Speed and the press. *Billboard* remarked on August 13 that route cards were "more circus than carnival." Another "circusy" feature was Patty's ability to move the show "from one town to another in the middle of the week, and arrive for each engagement on schedule." There was no need to point out that larger shows avoided this practice by playing events of a week's duration or more.

Despite telling Speed in a letter on July 25, 1932, that "things with us continue very bad," Patty publicly claimed that through the prairie fairs everyone on the show remained in "good spirits" and looked "forward to the new spots in Ontario and Quebec."[12] Turned out they had little to look forward to. They found "conditions in the east ... worse than we anticipated."[13] Patty did not know whether they would finish the season in Toronto or Hamilton, or in which city he would strike winter quarters.

At the start of the closing 10-day still in Hamilton, the show trumpeted its survival in the face of adverse circumstances. As reported in *Billboard* on October 15, Conklin's All-Canadian

> ... has successfully exhibited this year from the Pacific to the Atlantic Coast ... and travelled nearly 7,500 miles during a season of 24 weeks. No person with the show has missed a pay day. In this year of world-wide business depression the management is pleased that, although the show made but very little if any money, it has lost none. Manager J.W. Conklin gives as his opinion: "The only reason for our being able to accomplish what we have this year is that we own and operate everything on our show thru the office."

That was before the Hamilton results were in. On October 19, after a week of bad weather, Patty wrote Speed that "business with us has been so extremely bad that we haven't made any plans for the coming year. Our Showing here at Hamilton cost us over $3,000 and our trip in the East was not a success owing to our Show being far too large for the time that we were playing." Demoralized, Patty was thinking of packing it in. He put the show in winter quarters at the National Steel railway car shops in Hamilton. The office staff disbanded, Frank and Will Wright heading to Los Angeles, others to Vancouver.

Patty had been trying unsuccessfully to sell his car and his real estate in British Columbia, but he could still afford a seven-week trip to Europe with Edythe. Travel would clear his mind so he could plan the show's future. "Something new or the show will never do," he told *Billboard* on November 12. Married and entering middle age, he knew he needed to expand his horizons beyond North America and experience something of the world. After touring England, France, the Netherlands, and Germany, he returned with

Patty and Edythe Conklin on the streets of London, 1932.

"some ideas new to this continent."[14] What they were he did not say, but he had renewed his commitment to the carnival.

Frank and Wright continued to be active with the Pacific Coast Showmen's Association and Patty remained popular with members, but he was turning away from the coast. He fined himself for missing the association's banquets in 1933 and 1934, mailing in cheques to cover his misdemeanour. The money in the latter year paid for food and drink on "Paddy Conklin Night." While he visited the association whenever he was in Los Angeles, by 1933 he had turned to the Showmen's League of America, based in Chicago, as the theatre for his ambitions. But first he had to deal with Speed.

THE END OF SPEED

The agent hands the rings for the game to the mark. They look tiny and out of place in the man's big, calloused hands. He tosses a ring, and it hooks one of the clothespins lined up on the board across the back of the joint. The agent pulls the pin off the board and flashes it in the player's face.

"Twenty-one!" he shouts. "That'll give you 50 yards, this round. You're almost there, champ. Double down and take another shot! Come on!"

The mark digs into his pocket and takes out a handful of crumpled bills. He pulls a couple of tens and gives them to the agent. He throws another ring. The agent pulls out the pin.

"Ohhhh," he groans, "148, you missed it that time! No yards. You're gonna get there, boss, just give it another go!"

"Lemme see that board there," the mark demands.

The agent hands over a sheet of cardboard covered with numbers and formulas. The man peers at it closely and looks at the agent.

"I'll give you ten-to-one this time — it's your lucky day!"

A small group of spectators gathers. Sometimes the agent gives the man money back, but more often it goes the other way. The agent's patter is unceasing and confuses the man. As it grows dark, his wad of bills gets smaller. After two hours, he has had enough. He turns away, shaking his head and muttering as he wanders off the midway.

The agent calls over a mate to replace him and hurries behind the joint to the office, his money apron bulging.

If the finances of Conklin's All-Canadian Shows were bad in 1932–33, Speed Garrett's were worse. He was sick, in debt, and without income. He tried to get money from Patty and by liquidating his few assets. He begged assistance from the Elks. He died a pauper.

The Death of a Partner

The partners still jointly owned the winter quarters in New Westminster and the property in Trail. Patty had refused to become sole owner of the property when he bought Speed's interest in the show. He did not want to own real estate and had been trying to sell the land since 1929. Ernie Hand was looking after it, including insurance, taxes, attempts to rent or sell, and payment of a night watchman who lived on the New Westminster lot. Hand, Vancouver notary public as well as Grand Exalted Ruler of the Elks, had taken on the show's financial and insurance business in 1927 and his friendship with Patty had grown. Hand helped incorporate the two companies that absorbed the partnership and advised and assisted Patty in the transfer of Speed's shares.

In a series of letters from September to November 1931, Patty and Speed discussed the property. Telling Speed that he was "very short of money," Patty presented a bill for expenses incurred by their property. Speed replied that he was "willing to take most any kind of an offer on our Canadian holdings." Patty asked Speed to specify "the very least" he would take, warning him that "it must be very cheap," but when Speed set his price Patty balked: "Thirty-five hundred dollars in US funds is lots more than the property is worth." They had bought it for $12,000. No matter how low he drove Speed, Patty refused to accept. He left it up to Speed to do what he could with his half-interest. Speed could do nothing, and the Trail property remained unsold at his death.

Speed had remarried in San Diego early in 1931 and his new wife had a baby in October. The following March he left them there, rent in arrears, to return to his ranch in Oregon, where he could live rent-free, even though the climate was bad for his health. Writing to Patty, he insisted that he had to see partial payment on the $5,000 due in April. His continued credit for groceries was contingent on clearing his debts. Patty told him he had no money for him, so Speed would "just have to make some other arrangements." Speed backed off: "If there is any securitie behind the last note I will not forclose on you." Patty assured him that "the first money I can lay my hands on I will positively send you some part of it."[15] Well into the fall he was still promising payment.

Speed got something from the sale of an oil property, but, sick and desperate, he was taken in that transaction, too. He asked Patty to get the address of the men to whom he had sold the property because their last transaction with him "was not on the square."[16] Patty told him he had no way to locate these men.

Mrs. Garrett wrote Patty in September 1932 from San Diego with the news that Speed had died. Destitute and with a baby, she asked about the $5,000 debt. Patty assumed it would be taken care of when the estate was settled: "For your information," he replied on September 20, "Speed owes me quite a bit of money for advances that I have made him in the past two years."

Speed had not died, and his wife claimed she had misunderstood a telegram. Almost immediately after she announced his death, Speed wrote to Patty from Oregon to ask for "three or 4 hundred dollars" so he could get credit for the winter on his grocery account.[17] Patty sent the resurrected Speed a cheque for $300, the first payment on the last installment. A few weeks later, the show's secretary sent Speed a statement of account that showed he owed Patty $860 for expenses on the land. Meanwhile, Patty went to Europe for two months with Edythe.

Bill Fleming represented Conklin's All-Canadian at the Showmen's League banquet but had a falling out with Patty soon after Patty returned from Europe. Patty did the contracting for the rest of the winter. At the western Canada fairs meeting, the show won contracts for the B circuit, this time official, and a renewal for the Winnipeg Elks' annual event. Patty then went to the Ontario Association of Fairs and Exhibitions gathering in Toronto, where he signed 10 fairs, including many the show had played the previous year and new ones in Belleville, Lindsay, Collingwood, Kingston, and Leamington. He completed the lineup of fairs with a renewal of the Peterborough contract in March. The chance for another Elks event in Vancouver was held out until March. It did not materialize nor did any Quebec fairs. But Patty had been arranging still dates and by the end of April 1933 he had the season booked solid.

To augment its depleted coffers, for the first time the show put equipment to work in the winter. The penny arcade was set up in a storefront in Hamilton. Frank and Wright arranged to provide rides and games for an indoor bazaar in February 1933 in Sherbrooke, Quebec, "Queen of the Eastern Townships" and a textile centre dominated by English businessmen. The local contact for this engagement was Bill Foote, the Grand Treasurer of the Canadian Elks. On his national tour as Grand Exalted Ruler in 1930, Ernie Hand had spoken to Foote about Patty and Foote visited the show in Granby in 1932. Many kind words about each of them were exchanged among the trio, resulting in the invitation of Conklin's All-Canadian to play the winter bazaar and, eventually, the Sherbrooke exhibition.

Speed had been bedridden since September 1932. In February and March 1933, Patty and Agnes Tulloch, the woman who had been looking after Speed in Oregon for almost a year, exchanged a series of letters. Mrs. Tulloch renewed the attempt to get help from Patty, asking for "at least $400 soon." Patty could not send any money, claiming that "I really haven't got it." Citing a doctor who demanded payment while simultaneously advising that Speed be relieved of all business worries, Mrs. Tulloch begged Patty for assistance: "Mr. Conklin, I think you are a friend of his, also a brother lodge member and he is in dire need." Patty insisted he did not have any money and did not know where he "could raise some."

The show was nearly bankrupt. In the spring of 1933, Patty was turned down when he tried to borrow from the Imperial Bank of Commerce for operating expenses. Frank's wife, Billie, covered the payroll for opening week with a loan of $500. At the same time, Patty hired her brother, Malcolm McNeil Webb, as secretary-treasurer. Neil, as he was known, could defer his salary. An ordained minister in the Salvation Army with an encyclopaedic knowledge of the Bible, maybe he would bring the show some divine grace. Neil quickly found himself at home by stabilizing the show's finances, and he remained with the Conklins for 40 years.

The show scraped by. After a handful of still dates from southern to northern Ontario, Kitchener to Kirkland Lake, they opened in June in Timmins, a gold mining town in the north. Everyone on the show was broke. On the third day, a young miner came on the lot and began to play one of the count stores, where the agent adds up numbers. The agent scored over $3,000.[18] This kind of money does not come honestly. It went straight to the office, enough to cover the show's payroll and expenses for several weeks and save it from bankruptcy. For the next eight years, whatever the spring route, Patty made sure to line up a date in Timmins. The show would post a lookout for the anonymous saviour and although he came back to play, he never coughed up again like that first year.

With their resource base, the northern Ontario mining towns were not suffering from the Depression and late in June Patty had enough to spare $200 for Speed. As if sickness and poverty were not enough, Speed's uninsured house had burned down at the end of May. He moved in with the Tullochs and Mrs. Tulloch appealed to Patty for money for medicine: "If it is humanly possible could you send him what you can now. He will never need it worse. His health is not improving at present."[19] When Patty sent the cheque, he asked Speed to advise him of the balance due, but to "bear in mind that I have again paid the taxes and many other items in connection with the real estate." Patty was looking for "some kind of a reasonable proposition" so they could "settle this matter as soon as possible."[20]

Speed had forgotten that Patty still owed him the last payment for his half of the show. After the fire, he found a note from the bank that reminded him of Patty's debt:

> ... just now I am badly in need of at least $2,000 (Two thousand) as I must move to California before winter sets in up here as my health is steadily growing worse in this climate.
>
> Will you please make an effort to send same to me as it may be the means of prolonging my life.

Agnes Tulloch wrote the letter and signed it for Speed, perhaps more for her benefit than his. It did not reach Patty in time to help Speed. He died, this time for real, on August 29, 1933, three days after the letter was dated. He had just turned 58.

When Speed's son, Speed Eldene Garrett, telegrammed Patty the news, he asked for $500 for expenses. The man in charge of a Masonic service for Speed in Boise, Idaho, asked for $300. Patty sent the lesser amount. He summarized his account with Speed in a letter to Speed Jr. on September 8. The two payments to Speed and the funeral expenses, plus exchange and charges, and the accumulated expenses on the properties reduced Patty's debt to $2,687. Patty could not understand what had happened to Speed's money and he thought Speed "had at least $50,000 in cash and $10,000 worth of Hearst Publication bonds."

Because of the ongoing expense of maintaining the real estate in British Columbia, Patty was in no hurry to settle his debt to the Garrett estate. Ernie Hand died unexpectedly four weeks before Speed, so Patty had no agent to help him with the properties. Patty assumed that Speed Eldene Garrett would be the executor of the estate. Instead, his older brother, Fred, an unreliable alcoholic, was appointed. A long, messy correspondence among Patty, Fred, and an assortment of attorneys for the estate ensued, petering out without resolution over four years later. Fred went for months ignoring Patty's queries, which often involved getting the estate's approval for the disposition of the properties. When Fred did write, it was usually to ask for money to cover his activities on behalf of the estate. Patty paid for Fred to travel to Vancouver to meet him and look over the New Westminster land. The other heirs also had trouble with Fred and in early 1937 an attorney working for them contacted Patty.

The expenses on the real estate amounted to over $700 a year. In the mid-1930s, Patty let the taxes slip into arrears and almost lost both properties in tax sales. On January 29, 1937, he informed Fred that "my bill against your estate with the accrued interest, amounts to over $5,000." In one of his last letters to Fred, on December 30, he repeated his opinion that "it is a shame our affairs have been either neglected or forgotten entirely." He tried to reach Fred again in early 1938 but nothing came of his efforts. Eventually, Fred showed up in Toronto and Patty paid him off with $2,700 cash. In exchange, Fred gave him a document saying that his claim was settled. Patty carried the document with him for the rest of his life. Fred returned to Boise with about $500 left from what Patty had paid him.

Patty found agents in Vancouver and Trail to handle the properties. He was able to lease the New Westminster land in 1936 and sell it a few years later. The 28 Trail lots began to sell in 1937 and by 1939 only eight were left. He may have been justified in keeping the proceeds.

The Birth of an Heir and Season of 1933

The death of Patty's partner was preceded by the birth of his son, James Franklin Conklin, on May 2, 1933, in Hamilton. His nurse brought him out to see his father's midway in Kirkland Lake a month later. His inheritance would not have looked princely.

Business for Conklin's All-Canadian began to pick up halfway through the western fairs, beginning in Yorkton, Saskatchewan. A group of Cree who had an Indian Village at the fair initiated Patty into their tribe, making him an honorary chief. Fifty chiefs in traditional dress escorted him from the village to the grandstand where the ceremony was performed. This was their one outlet for cultural expression as Indigenous people were forbidden by the Indian Act to hold public ceremonies except at agricultural exhibitions.

Chief Patty filled in the last hole in his route with a two-day still at Indian Head, a small farming community east of Regina. They then began the Ontario fairs at Fort William–Port Arthur. Fairs that they had booked in Picton and Napanee were cancelled due to the economy, and they replaced them with a still date in Sudbury. Sudbury had been closed to carnivals for years and the show had to pay a heavy licence fee. The fairs in southern Ontario followed. They played a few more days in Hamilton before putting the show in winter quarters.

By the end of the season, the show had recovered financially. According to Patty, "business was better than last year and on the whole the season was profitable."[21] They had also been relieved of a significant expense. A negotiator for Castle-Ehrlich-Hirsch Shows, which was playing the western A circuit, had convinced the Canadian Pacific and Canadian National railways, the country's main rail carriers, to waive the parking fee for show-owned railway equipment. At a dollar per car, per day, the fee would have amounted to several thousand dollars for Conklin Shows in 1933. One show's victory helped them all.

The Conklins had expanded the show slightly for the 1933 season. They carried two more rides, a Flyer and a Twister. The sideshows were largely the same, with the addition of Ernie and his parasitic twin, Len, who Patty had found two years before. Halfway through the season, John Ogden, who had a sideshow with Clark & Conklin Shows back in 1918, replaced Al Salvail, who ran the World's Museum. They had water performers for a free act at the still dates. When girls in skimpy bathing suits became acceptable in certain public arenas, aquatic shows became popular, and the Conklins carried one for many years. As with much of the show's profiteering from loosening social restrictions, the water show played to both curiosity and prurience. Many men in the towns the show visited would never have seen a woman in a bathing suit.

Patty won the annual Showmen's League membership drive in 1933, signing up 12 new members, all from his show. At a meeting in October, five of his crew were present and they were all called on to speak. The league's reporter described one evening as "Conklin night at the League rooms."[22] The Century of Progress world's fair in Chicago, a big event for showmen across the continent, was one reason so many Conklin employees were at the league's Chicago clubhouse, the rising profile of the show another. Patty visited the Century of Progress fair and booked attractions from it for the following season.

Patty had become adept at working with organizations like the Showman's League, the fair boards, and the benevolent societies. These were business clubs with voluntary boards accountable to a small membership of modestly successful men that often filled their executive positions through an informal but conventional combination of seniority, engagement, and rotation. An actively involved member gets nominated to the lowest rung of the executive, then each year moves up a rung until the member becomes president. Through backroom deals and the bending of bylaws, this progression can be thwarted, but such coups disturb the aura of friendly co-operation and demonstrate an unseemly ambition. The manipulation of political structures was more transparent back then. In the spring of 1933, Lyndon Johnson, future president of the United States who went on to steal elections, stole the presidency of the Little Congress, an organization of congressional secretaries modelled on the House of Representatives. A few months later, Patty Conklin helped orchestrate a similar coup in the Showman's League, in this case for economic rather than political gain.

The establishment ticket for the league executive was nominated in late October, with "slim likelihood of a second ticket being put in the field."[23] But two weeks later a second ticket was filed, with Patty, on the board of governors since 1930, nominated as first vice-president. This led to "the most stirring election campaign the Showmen's League of America has experienced in many, many years," as "the second ticket, jokingly dubbed the 'bolshevik ticket,' was victorious."[24] Despite the joking, the upset would have caused tension among members. Nevertheless, barring a countercoup, Patty was next in line for the league's presidency.

At the league banquet, "Paddy Conklin was at the height of glory — not trying to get dates, but playing host to nearly everybody in his suite of rooms — where the charming Mrs. Paddy and Paddy Jr. reigned supreme."[25] Freed from the burden of Mrs. Conklin Sr. and the spectre of Speed, his show having turned the corner and now having an heir, Patty was ready to occupy the centre of the outdoor amusement world. He had come a long way from the mean streets of Paterson, a self-made patriarch gaining the heights of an industry that was just becoming professionalized.

THE SHOWMEN'S PRESIDENT

The Showmen's League clubroom is smoky and loud, jammed full of men, strung with green bunting, a buffet set up on a pool table in the middle. At this dinner in his honour, Patty sits in a large carved chair at a table raised on a low dais. Men bring him drinks and he chain smokes as he gestures and tells stories to all within hearing.

With no apparent reason, the uproar periodically explodes. Sometimes Patty stands and raises his glass to the crowd. Frank and Neil are close by, Frank watching the proceedings with a quiet smile and narrowed eyes.

A new commotion begins behind the bar as a team brings out a huge crystal punch bowl, half-filled with whiskey. They try to carry it to the head table but are interrupted in their passage by men with glasses scooping at the contents. They push through the crowd, spilling liquor over everyone, until one of them trips. The whole crew keels over and the bowl shatters.

Patty jumps to his feet and cheers. He calls out the men by name and roars his approval. He falls back in his chair, laughing and shaking his head. He has loosened his tie, but his waistcoat remains buttoned. He looks over at Frank, who is leaning back, thumbs in his suspenders, light reflecting off his head and glasses.

★　★　★

In 1931 the Showmen's League and the International Association of Fairs and Expositions (IAFE) had planned to hold their annual conventions for the first time in Toronto. The management of the CNE, long the biggest fair in the association, requested the change. By the season's end, the economy and the need to keep expenses in check had caused sentiment to mount against the move and it was cancelled. In early 1934, the Showmen's League and the IAFE again decided they would meet in Toronto later that year. Patty was named chairman of the league's banquet and ball committee for this second attempt. Busier than usual that winter, he delegated some of the work to two old hands, naming Wright his assistant and publicity agent, and Frank Bickford his general agent. Frank Conklin, now vice-president, ran the company during his brother's frequent absences.

Patty and family had made his usual trip to New York and Paterson that fall, and in the winter he circulated on his own among Chicago, Winnipeg, Toronto, and Hamilton. He worked closely with Dr. H.W. Waters, general manager of the CNE, to set the dates for the league and IAFE event. Interest from the National Association of Amusement Parks (NAAP) in joining the conclave complicated the arrangements. Amusement parks had become a thriving industry throughout North America, the NAAP representing their interests. The park owners wanted to join their brethren in Toronto and see the CNE.

By the end of March, Patty could announce plans for the meeting. It would be held the last week of November 1934 at the Royal York Hotel and would include the Showmen's League, the IAFE, the NAAP, and the Canadian Association of Fairs and Exhibitions. In its April 7 issue, *Billboard* reported, "Credit for bringing about this happy arrangement goes largely to Paddy Conklin. For weeks he has worked unceasingly, conferring with representatives of the associations, the railways and hotel, and attending to numerous necessary details." He had gotten reduced rates from the Royal York and was negotiating special rates with the railways. His accomplishment was "the outstanding personal achievement in the outdoor show world this year so far, and, make no mistake, everybody will be at Toronto."[26]

Season of 1934

Patty still had a show to oversee. He did not bid on the western B circuit for 1934. The circuit had been cut to eight fairs, covering just four weeks in July. The Alberta government had eliminated its grants for fairs. Nevertheless, on February 24 a *Billboard* commentator remarked with shock that the "Class B Canadian fairs did not have ONE show to bid for their dates at the Winnipeg meeting." These fairs might have made do with a local company that year, Moyer Amusements from Assiniboia, Saskatchewan, for instance, which had four rides and a few concessions but no shows. Conklin Shows would only work in the East in 1934. His Quebec Elks contacts gave Patty events in Valleyfield and Sherbrooke that had been World of Mirth fairs, and he renewed contracts for three Ontario fairs.

In the midst of discussions with Waters in March about the Toronto convention, Patty surprised the industry. He delivered "perhaps the most striking news in the outdoor show world" for the week, the announcement that the Conklins' Bazaars Ltd. had been awarded the contract by the City of Toronto for its centennial celebration, three days at the beginning of July.[27] The event, predicted by Patty to draw a million people, would be held on the exhibition grounds, the midway in the usual place. It was not the CNE, but it was close.

After a successful opening at the end of April 1934, the show left Hamilton on seven steel rail cars, the all-steel train that had been Patty's ambition since 1928. They had 10 shows, seven rides, and an aerial attraction for a free act. Three new shows attracted attention. Building on the Unborn show, the Life show, another Lou Dufour production, used models, preserved specimens, and pickled embryos to illustrate evolution and the reproductive functions, with an emphasis on the mechanics of the latter. The Believe It or Not show featured people who did strange and torturous things with their bodies, based on the Robert Ripley column then reaching the peak of its popularity. Patty had visited both shows during their premier engagements at the Chicago Century of Progress in 1933. He had encountered the third, Eric the Robot, in England. Eric was a six-foot, one-ton contraption that could answer 875 questions. Its owner brought it from England to tour Canada as an independent act, booking with Conklin's All-Canadian before it went on to the fairs.

The show played still dates in Guelph, Kitchener, Kingston, and Ottawa, then trolled the lucrative wilds of northern Ontario and Quebec, before taking aim at the Toronto centennial. A series of still dates in Ontario and Quebec followed, including two more weeks in Ottawa. The aimless route, the lack of advance announcement of dates, and the three weeks in Ottawa point to a route booked week by week. The show's fair season did not begin in earnest until mid-August in Valleyfield and Patty did not announce its last fair date until the middle of July, the Exposition Provinciale de Québec at Quebec City, opening in just over a month. Begun in 1911, Emery Boucher had taken over as general manager of the provincial fair in 1920. It had grown to be the largest in eastern Canada with an attendance of over 150,000. The Quebec circuit was second in the country only to the western A circuit and, with Quebec City, became an important part of the Conklin season.

The Toronto Centennial Celebration, the pearl at the centre of this patchwork, turned out well, although attendance was one-fifth Patty's estimate of a million. It was an "ambitious undertaking for a carnival to follow in the footsteps of the major shows" and Conklin's All-Canadian "made a splendid showing."[28] After closing in Timmins on Saturday, the show reached Toronto by Sunday midnight and by six o'clock the next morning was ready for the nine o'clock opening. "Rides played to capacity and every show did a land-office business." Food stands ran out of supplies. The first day was "the biggest date of their career" and the event would be "remembered as one of the highlights" of the show's history.[29]

After that, anything would be a letdown, but they were let down hard. Following Toronto, they "had three weeks of the poorest business in our entire show career."[30] When they returned to Ottawa, they were back in the money. Patty took a break. Leaving the show to Frank, he, wife, and child spent a few days at a small resort in Norway Bay, a popular summer destination on the Quebec side of the Ottawa River, 70 miles from the capital. He was likely a guest of one of his new Quebec friends.

The fairs in Quebec all had occasional heavy rain, but not enough to spoil attendance. In Valleyfield, "the shows were lauded by the local press."[31] The midway grossed more money for the fair board than it had in five years and the board invited the show back. Verdun, a working-class suburb of Montreal, had

Showmen's League members and Conklin staff, Verdun, 1935. Will Wright, Patty, an unknown promoter, and Frank are in the front row. Neil Webb is standing in the second row, far left.

been closed to carnivals for five years, but welcomed Conklin's All-Canadian. The Sherbrooke fair had a record attendance, and the *Daily Record* printed an editorial that praised the "clean show … so different from the midways we have had."[32] From Quebec City, the show returned to the fall fairs of southern Ontario and ended the season with five more days in Hamilton in October.

The Convention

His show in winter quarters, Patty turned his attention to the Toronto convention, six weeks away. Waters had resigned after 12 years as general manager of the CNE in protest against interference from its board of directors. He later wrote a book about fairs and exhibitions that promoted midways as necessary to their financial success.[33] He also managed an international industrial exhibition in Atlantic City in 1947. He would have been a good partner for Patty for the Toronto event.

Waters's replacement, Elwood Hughes, the CNE secretary since 1930, had also worked with Patty before. Captain of Canada's first Olympic team in 1906, Hughes had joined the exhibition as director of sporting events in 1909. Patty first met Hughes at the Showmen's League banquet in 1927. Diminutive and debonair, he had been sports director for William Wrigley, of chewing gum fame, from 1927 to 1929 organizing a swimming competition in Chicago that drew the largest paid attendance for any sporting event up to that time. Hughes and Charles Ross, director of amusements for the CNE, had visited Patty in May and were prominent on the midway during the Toronto Centennial Celebration.

By the end of July, Patty had appointed committees to organize the convention and sent out letters of invitation. The affable Frank was on the reception committee. Wright would see to the program. Arthur Kirk, agent for Canadian National Railway, was on the transportation committee. The railway's headquarters were in Montreal and soon after Kirk was guest of the show at Verdun, he sent in reservations for 10 for the banquet. Patty met with Rubin Gruberg, owner of Rubin & Cherry Shows, at the CNE and took away reservations for 30. In October, Patty confirmed that special trains with group rates would leave from Chicago and New York City, the train from the latter city a Canadian National.

Curiosity about the program spread around the Showmen's League clubhouse in Chicago. Patty "doesn't give us any outline of what to expect, holding this back for the surprise. But with Patty at the head we will keep plugging, for we know his capabilities for doing things just a little better than the other fellow."[34] So great was the faith of the league that it published his estimate of an attendance of 1,500 for the banquet and ball.

Late in October, presiding at his first meeting since being elected league vice-president, Patty presented a glowing report on the coming banquet. He brought Hughes as his guest of honour, and Hughes joined the club. At the same meeting, Frank's total in the membership drive reached 30, ensuring him the recruitment award. The nominating committee submitted its ticket for 1935 with Patty heading it. *Billboard* kept his name before other showmen throughout November, each issue featuring articles on the expected sellout of the banquet as reservations from the "moguls of outdoor showdom" poured in.[35]

On November 20, the day before the week-long NAAP portion of the event was to begin, the *Toronto Star* announced that 2,000 showmen were expected for the convention. A miniature midway was installed in the Royal York's lobby. The Showmen's League train arrived from Chicago Saturday night. Hughes and Patty conducted a memorial service for the league on Sunday. The meetings of the IAFE and the Canadian Association of Fairs and Exhibitions began Monday.

Everyone was fired up for the Showmen's League banquet. Canon Henry Cody, president of the University of Toronto, gave the keynote address, telling the showfolk: "You are apostles of education, pure entertainment and relaxation. Keep your standards high."[36] His speech was written up as eloquent, well-informed, and humorous, the latter derived partly from his claim to be a scion of the same family as Buffalo Bill Cody, the league's first president.

Hughes was toastmaster, introducing the guests at the head table. They included the presidents of the associations, the CNE, and the Royal Winter Fair; the mayor of Toronto; the Ontario minister of agriculture; and Bertram Mills, who since 1920 had been reviving the circus in England with his annual Christmas show at London's Olympia Theatre. Patty had met Mills, who was in Toronto for the Royal Winter Fair, in England.

Hughes and Charlie Ross organized the entertainment, paid for by Patty, the Showmen's League, and George Hamid. Hamid's booking agency was the largest for free acts, selling the CNE a contract worth $62,000 in 1932, for instance. The entertainment included musicians, dancers, acrobats, comedians, impressionists, roller skaters, and the Moose Jaw Hillbillies, comedy musicians who had travelled with the Conklin show. Some acts were cancelled as the evening drew on too long.

Patty had 60 guests, the largest party, with Hamid's 50 the next. Rubin & Cherry, Royal American, Beckmann & Gerety, and United Shows of America, the latest incarnation of Morris & Castle Shows, hosted 20 guests each. Patty had 15 staff in attendance, the rest of his guests being fair board and railway officials. Everyone visited the headquarters of Conklin's All-Canadian, presided over by Edythe, in the Royal York.

The banquet attendance of 546 proved Patty's estimate of 1,500 a wild exaggeration. Nonetheless, the event was deemed "a huge success" and "one of the most brilliant and colourful affairs the league has ever staged."[37] The *Billboard* reporter was reminded of "the gala balls of a decade or more ago when show business was in its heyday." The comparison puts the event in perspective. After five years of economic depression, the shows that had struggled to survive were finally seeing daylight, and the ball was a sign for its guests that they had come through. Patty had inextricably associated himself with that sign and portent.

Conklin personnel shared in the glow emanating from their boss. Wright was praised for his work on the program, then returned to Los Angeles to help with the Pacific Coast Showmen's Association banquet. Webb, "the hustling secretary of Conklin's All-Canadian Shows," was described as "one of the busiest boys in Toronto."[38] Frank returned the prize money for the Showmen's League membership drive back to the league for their fundraising. Hughes, Patty's new associate, was elected president of the IAFE on his own merits.

During the convention, the *Toronto Star* interviewed Patty for the first time in what became a long and usually happy relationship with the local press. According to an article printed on November 26, he was to be elected president of the Showmen's League at its next meeting, the first Canadian and the youngest man ever to hold the position. Patty or the newspaper got some facts wrong: "Conklin owns the largest carnival show in Canada and has his own 20-car train. He is 40. His show, sixth largest in the world, is in winter quarters at Vancouver." He probably did have the largest carnival company in Canada by then, but nothing else in this statement is correct.

Patty's final accomplishment for 1934 was headlined in *Billboard* on December 1. He had convinced the two Canadian railways to double their allowance for "scrip." Railways issued scrip, or credit, to showmen as a percentage of the fees for moving show-owned railway equipment. Scrip was supposed to be used by advance agents travelling in passenger service with the show, but showmen hoarded it, using it to attend winter social and business engagements. Although the new allowance benefitted only those few shows travelling the rails in Canada, it made the headlines because Patty was behind it.

After presiding in Chicago in December over his first meeting as president of the Showmen's League, Patty left for the West Coast. In Los Angeles in late January and February 1935, he attended meetings of the Pacific Coast Showmen's Association. He cancelled a vacation to Hawaii and returned to Chicago in February so he could officiate at some of the league's weekly meetings.

Season of 1935

For the first time in 13 years, Patty missed the Western Canada Fairs Association meeting. Frank filled in for him to glad hand, not to bid on either circuit. During February, Frank renewed contracts with two Quebec and seven Ontario fairs. The brothers met in Chicago in early March. Floating on their show's rise in stature, by the end of April 1935 Frank had booked the season, signing up what was becoming the usual round of late-summer, early-fall Ontario fairs. They would begin with a few still dates in southern Ontario, then travel north for stills in the mining towns. During July and early August, they would visit the Maritimes for the first and only time, playing five stills in New Brunswick and one in Halifax, Nova Scotia.

Patty brightened up his midway for 1935. He bought four searchlights, an innovation first used by Royal American in 1933. The rides were fitted with neon lights. A new calliope graced the front gate to pipe the crowds in. Combined with the public address systems for the sideshows, the noise level climbed several decibels. While not an innovator, the show shared in the carnival industry's discovery of the drawing power of sound and light.

The railway stock also sparkled. The new steel train was painted in the show's orange and blue colours. Patty purchased a steel private car and had Edythe decorate it. According to a visitor, "the new private car of Paddy and the missus is the most elaborate and complete I have ever entered. Its appointments are splendid (finished in ivory and gold) with drapes and decorations conceived and created by none other than Mrs. Conklin."[39] "James Franklin" was painted on it in gold letters. Intended to make Edythe and her son at home on the road, it functioned more effectively as a venue for entertaining guests.

Conklin's All-Canadian expanded its attractions. The show had dropped the old Merry Mix-Up and Whip. Patty had bought a miniature railway from a mine in Timmins and turned it into a kiddie ride. In Germany he had seen a swinging gondola that, with men hauling on ropes, did a complete revolution in the air. His mechanics had spent three years experimenting with this idea in the National Steel Car shop, finally perfecting a mechanically powered version. It had cost $9,000 to build. Patty and the vice-president of National Steel were the first riders, christening it the Rocket Plane.

Some of the shows were changed up. Wright's guillotine show was gone. They had a motordrome again for the first time in three years. There was a new mind-reading act and a crime show. George Weeks was running the Monkey Circus for the fourth year and his wife managed a new Mickey Mouse show. Beyond monkeys and mice, the company owned a snake show and a trained animal show and had booked an independent wild animal show. Another independent brought in a deep-sea diver show. Ernie and Len remained the star freak attraction.

The Life show was back, now with a manager who would stay with Patty for many years. Maxie Herman had worked with Rubin & Cherry in 1927 and 1928, and then as an independent concessionaire. In 1930 he had become Lou Dufour's general agent for the Unborn franchise. While working for Dufour at the Century of Progress world's fair in Chicago in 1933–34, he was a fixture at the Showmen's League clubrooms. In 1935 he had the Life show on the Conklin midway for Dufour but was soon working directly for Patty.

The Century of Progress fair had brought strippers to a mass market. Sally Rand, repeatedly arrested at the fair for her fan dance, created a rage for girl shows. The past president of the Showmen's League, Ernie Young, reported that men at the fair only wanted skin: "I opened at Chicago with a beautiful show, and lost $7,000 in eight days. All they went for was sex, so I gave it to them and made money."[40] Other showmen remarked that the Chicago fair damaged the outdoor amusement industry by boosting demand for nude girl shows. Patty brought out a strip show in 1935 to satisfy the demand. Bob

Randall, who had worked for the office since 1927, for a time as lot manager, ran the show.

Conklin's All-Canadian opened well in Hamilton in early May. The show played under auspices during the spring in southern Ontario and the northern mining towns, gathering other acts as they went on. They worked for the first time in Windsor. The site of Canadian factories for the big three American automobile makers, Windsor was the "Auto Capital of the British Empire" with a population of over 100,000. Cold, wet weather hurt them throughout the spring, but Windsor and Timmins were exceptional. After the Sherbrooke fair, moved up to the beginning of July, they headed for the Maritimes.

There, the show introduced a pay gate, a subject of controversy in the industry. When street fairs had flourished, they had charged admission, as had fairs since then, although many dropped the charge during the Depression. Some argued that an admission fee at still dates could replace revenue lost by the elimination of grift. That shows in the Maritimes could use such a replacement is evident from the scandal in 1928 surrounding Bill Lynch Shows, the dominant carnival in the region, when "the wild activities of grifters on the midway at the Halifax Exposition" led to "a campaign to chase every crooked show and showman out of Nova Scotia."[41] When Conklin's All-Canadian charged admission in St. John, New Brunswick, they had difficulty "in maintaining a tight gate, as the grounds contained many loopholes."[42] At their biggest day in Halifax, however, they collected over 11,000 paid admissions.

"While some of the spots hardly came up to expectations," Wright reported in *Billboard* on August 24, "taken as a whole the five weeks spent in the maritimes were profitable to the show." Appearing in the region for the first time, the Life show surprised everyone by leading receipts, its frank approach to human reproduction providing the draw. The company stayed a week longer in the Maritimes to fill in a gap caused when the Montreal exhibition fell through. After the Ontario fall fairs, the show reporter said only that "the average of business done at the fairs has been satisfactory to the management."[43]

A more positive report travelled through the grapevine and appeared in *Billboard* on October 19: "J.W. and Frank Conklin made some money this year.... Their season was much better than any since 1931." Soon after closing the season at the beginning of October, Patty announced that he planned "to enlarge the show to several additional cars proportion" and add "at least two" new rides.[44]

Patty and family took a vacation in Hot Springs, while Frank and Billie went to South America. The brothers were back in Chicago by November 1935, where Webb joined them. A testimonial dinner for Patty was scheduled for a few days before the Showmen's League banquet. With typical hyperbole, *Billboard* reported on December 7 that it had been "the biggest thing of its kind the league has ever staged." It was at this event that Patty was given the punch bowl that was dropped and broken during the presentation. The organizers printed a newspaper, the *Conklinville Blatter*. Some 300 attended.

Many members coming to Chicago for the league's banquet had come early to attend Patty's party. Banquet attendance the following week reached 900, the greatest since the mid-1920s. The IAFE convention, where Patty and Hughes each gave speeches, was the best attended since 1929. The carnival industry was reviving with the rest of the economy.

On the flyer for his party, Patty was caricatured sitting on a throne with a crown and sceptre. His coronation had already occurred. The league's nominating committee had submitted as the ticket for 1936 the entire list of officers from the year before, a unique occurrence. While professing reluctance to break with custom, Patty accepted the call to preside once more, the first Showmen's League president to serve two consecutive terms.

THE BIGGEST FAIR IN THE WORLD

This Barnum business is not the sweet lark it is cracked up to be. And boy, do we have our headaches. Bothersome little things like an animal breaking loose and chewing somebody's leg off, or all of a sudden your trapeze goes blooey, or maybe one of your lorries smashes up the pavement.

Then there's your ladies' local sewing circle to put up with. They'll pan a show without ever seeing it.

Now speaking of women and robots, I don't like either of 'em. Certain kinds, I mean. A robot named Eric — I thought he was a sure thing at first — but no, sir, the public didn't like him. So I just looked him in the eye and said "Eric, you've got the sack."

Now, as for women, there's just no end to this sex problem. But I'm kind of a Puritan m'self so I just rule 'em out, bingo. No hot stuff in my shows, says I. Should have been the son of a clergyman maybe. Instead, my father was a circus fixer, he used to fix it up when a bear got loose and ate up somebody's garden or something.

Barnum was wrong. There's a lot more suckers born than one every second. Except they're smarter now. If they don't get something for their money they squawk.

Interview with Patty Conklin, Daily Express *(London), March 25, 1937, p. 3*

★　★　★

Patty had earned his re-election as president of the Showmen's League. Although he missed many meetings, he was the league's best ambassador, vigorously promoting it on the road. Building on the spirit of the 1934 convention in Toronto, he infused in his fellow owners and managers the conviction that the league was important to them. Through it they could support each other without compromising their independence. This spirit — or at least the extent to which it was shared — was new to the organization. More concretely, Patty energized the membership drive and promoted new ideas for the league's cemetery fundraising campaign, one of its most important activities.

Burying them was one of the main services the showmen's associations provided their members. Without insurance, pensions, or the means of putting money away for their end, many a carnie has been saved from a pauper's grave by his club. Patty contributed liberally to the cemetery fund of the Pacific Coast Showmen's Association and, as he told the IAFE meeting, in the association's 14 years they had buried "many showmen who, at the time of their passing, were in difficult circumstances."[45] He identified Showmen's Rest, the Showmen's League cemetery, as its "main philanthropy": "We consider it a major part of our organization that we not only honor but provide for our less fortunate members in this fashion." He might have been mouthing conventional pieties, but he also acted on them.

Patty had staff in Showmen's Rest. On a hot Sunday afternoon in 1935 in Peterborough, to cool off after the overnight jump from Cornwall, some Conklin employees went for a swim in the Otonabee River. One of them, Don McCaffery, dove in, collided with a submerged log, and drowned. Don had been the show's poorly paid watchman for 12 years. Patty bought a casket and tombstone and paid for flowers and the service for McCaffery's burial. He had everyone from the show driven to the funeral, where a tear was seen to "drop from the eyes of Patty Conklin."[46] Next season, a member of the Four Queens, an aerial act booked with the show, fell to her death during a performance in Kitchener. All but eight of the show's 286 staff attended the funeral and the act's owner "paid high tribute to Patty Conklin for his remarkable kindness."[47]

Patty had used the Showmen's League cemetery fund campaign of 1935 to rally his peers. The campaign began when the league's secretary visited Conklin's All-Canadian in May. By the end of August, Patty had met with Max Linderman of the World of Mirth Shows, Jimmy Sullivan of Wallace Brothers' Shows, and Theo Forestall, his former accountant, now with Al G. Barnes Circus, all of them playing Canada, to enlist their aid. Scores of employees on Patty's own show, including all senior staff, contributed. One of the successes of his first year as president of the league, the campaign was an even greater success in his second year, when all the major shows held benefit performances for the cemetery fund. The benefits were not a new idea, but through example and the pressure Patty exerted he helped ensure they succeeded.

The fundraising campaigns relied on personal contacts, and the ability to nurture those contacts was one of Patty's pleasures in playing Ontario. When his company worked in the western provinces, he had visited other shows, but with nothing like the ease and frequency possible in the more densely settled East. A sociable man, Patty enjoyed the company of other showmen above all else, which contributed to his charisma. As his chauffeur drove him between spots, he could not pass another midway without paying a visit to look it over. Whatever the state of the other show, he would drop a complimentary remark to the owner.

Genial and popular are the words applied to Patty by other showmen, and with his staff he was friendly and personable. He would exchange a joke or pleasantry with the lowest man on the lot. Passing a ride, a greasy mechanic sprawled underneath, he would stop to ask, "Is it okay under there, kid?" If any of his staff needed a disciplinary touch, he left that to Frank. No wonder then, that in 1935, when *Billboard* began publishing the results of its poll of All-Time Favorites in the outdoor amusement business, Patty was one of three carnival owners tied for first place.[48] Throughout the life of the poll, he remained in the top 10.

The "Conklin Method," the title of a *Billboard* article in the July 6, 1935, issue, began to attract attention. Order and efficiency were the main components. The show always closed promptly at midnight. Other shows stayed open as long as the crowd warranted or closed early when it did not. Even if his midway had died with the setting sun, Patty kept it open, both to ensure that the expectations of midway patrons were always met and to instill habits of regularity in his carnies and prevent them from invading the local bars for a night of carousing. Occasionally left standing on empty midways for hours on end, this practice would have caused considerable chagrin among frontline staff. They had ways to entertain themselves, the odd resourceful concessionaire, for instance, setting up a bar beneath the counter of his canvas joint.

The arrival of the carnival train in a community was a significant event that could attract crowds of spectators. Among the carnival's many failings, the poor display some shows made for the locals who came out to watch them set up or tear down was recognized as a special public relations problem. The Conklin performance drew favourable comment. Teardown, the process of dismantling, packing, and loading the components of a carnival after a long day open, could be a rough, dirty, chaotic operation, especially in wet weather. Not on Patty's show. As described in *Billboard* on July 6, 1935, "There is no profane language, no commotion and everybody goes to work"; "No one is allowed to make noise at any time…. No yelling for this fellow or that fellow." The Conklin brothers' policy of never yelling at anyone, at least in front of witnesses, was "so different and refreshing" that in a May 25, 1935, article, a *Billboard* reporter urged "every carnival manager" to visit the show. The Conklin method was a benchmark for the industry.

By 1935 Royal American's huge investment in equipment made it the paramount show in the industry; by the end of his second term as Showmen's League president, Patty's energy and improvisations had made him the industry's foremost showman. After the family's vacation in Hot Springs, where Patty had met with Hughes and other fair officials, they went to Miami, where his movements were closely followed by the carnival press and the associations. He went to the western Canada fairs meeting in Winnipeg and planned to attend the Ontario Association of Agricultural Societies convention in Toronto, but Edythe reportedly fell ill, and he had to return to Miami. In February 1936, he was photographed with a group of fair and carnival men at the Florida State Fair in Tampa, a popular event for showmen wintering in the state. In early March, he attended a Showmen's League meeting in Chicago with Frank before they returned to Hamilton.

Season of 1936

The Conklins bid on the B circuit at the western fairs meeting for the first time in three years and won it. Frank handled the rest of the booking for the 1936 season. On February 22, he announced in *Billboard* that the show had contracted 23 fairs, "considered a record for one midway organization." The show played 21 fairs that season. The Ontario and Quebec fairs were largely the same as the previous year. They did not return to the Maritimes.

Office staff changed. Will Wright, with Patty for more than 10 years, decided to stay in California where he had always wintered and had found a slot managing a small show. Dave Picard, who had joined the show the year before as superintendent of concessions, picked up Wright's role as assistant to the Conklins. Merrick Nutting, a special agent when Picard started, moved up to general agent and was joined by his wife on promotions.

Travelling on 20 cars, the show lineup changed for 1936. The World's Fair Freaks, owned by the office, had a new 160-foot top and a 16-foot banner — a painted canvas front — with new attractions inside. Ernie and Len had their own front. Independents had joined with Public Enemies and Night in a Lumber Camp. The deep-sea diver, snake, and Mickey Mouse shows were gone, the last to copyright challenges from Disney. Despite the death of a member of the Four Queens in Kitchener, the show carried the aerial performers as a free act through to the end of the western fairs. They had sold the Tilt-A-Whirl,

Caterpillar, and Lindy Loop, but still had eight rides. They had a Swooper and Chair-O-Plane again and had added a Ridee-O and a Loop-O-Plane. The brothers had spent $3,000 on the neon lights for all the shows and rides.

The Eyerly Aircraft Loop-O-Plane, an improved version of Patty's Rocket Plane, was an exciting departure in rides. Up until then, the Ferris wheel, graceful but slow, had been the only vertical ride. The Loop-O-Plane whipped riders through the air using vertically applied centrifugal force. Its two pods attached to the ends of rotating spokes broke free of the horizontal plane of flat rides, taking speed into the air. It had a low capacity, but Patty had no problem selling tickets for it at three times the regular price. It was also easy to set up and loaded on one wagon.

The show opened in Windsor in mid-April and ended the season there 25 weeks and 7,600 rail miles later. That summer was the hottest on record up to that time. They played in five provinces, travelling west as far as Red Deer, Alberta, and as far east as Quebec City. They saw Members of Parliament in Ottawa one week in May and snow in Kirkland Lake the next. The mining district provided them "more gold than ever before."[49] Moose Jaw, holding its first exhibition in 10 years, set the B circuit record with over 36,000 paid admissions in three days. The show then split for the first time in its history, Frank managing the main unit through two weeks of B circuit fairs, while Patty took a smaller unit back to a fair in Carman, Manitoba, and Old Home Week in Kenora, Ontario. Frank's fairs were in southern Saskatchewan and Manitoba during a heat wave when temperatures hit the high 30s and the extreme weather churned up several blowdowns. Cold, dirty weather in the spring and fall in Ontario and summer drought on the Prairies hurt them, but the season was profitable. On receipts of $294,000 — over two-thirds of which came from the games — the Conklins cleared $13,500.[50] The show closed with a list of over 300 employees and Patty felt compelled to say they had "the best co-operation from a wonderful staff."[51]

Patty was credited with taking the Showmen's League through "the greatest 12-month period in the history of the organization."[52] The league had gained 325 new members, over 100 coming from Harry Ross, a Conklin concessionaire who won the membership drive award. The work of Neil Webb and Maxie Herman for the league was acknowledged, and Edythe was praised as one of the busiest hostesses at the banquet and ball. The benefit performances for the cemetery fund had seen great success. At another testimonial dinner, the league gave Patty a large bronze statue of its mascot, an elephant, and a studio photo of him made up as Bill Cody. Having re-created himself as an heir to Buffalo Bill, he would soon reap the full rewards of his performance.

Winning the CNE

Long considered the annual equivalent of a world's fair, the CNE first broke the two-million mark for attendance in 1928, but numbers had declined like everything else in the 1930s. Since his appointment in 1934 as the general manager, Elwood Hughes had talked about making changes. After the 1935 exhibition, he hatched a three-year plan, to culminate in the CNE's jubilee year of 1938. "Traveling carnival companies," he said, "will be replaced by independent amusement features of similar nature to be housed in semi-permanent buildings."[53] He quelled rumours about an independent midway for 1936 as premature, booking Rubin & Cherry again. He nonetheless remarked that what Rubin Gruberg brought to Toronto that year would "govern his identification with the midway in 1937," adding that "two or three first-rate carnival showmen might be in charge" of an independent midway in the future.[54]

During much of 1936, Hughes pursued his goal of making "the event Toronto's music center," a part of his overall plan.[55] In 1934 CNE management had presented the Guy Lombardo and Duke Ellington bands, and the following year they had signed Rudy Vallée, a radio, musical stage, and movie star at the height of his fame. He had been guaranteed $35,000, plus 50 percent of the matinee take in the biggest music deal ever made by a fair. Hughes brought Vallée back for 1936, adding radio broadcasts of the event. Hughes toured famous North American bandshells earlier in the year and had a state-of-the-art facility built. He had five rotary stages constructed to accommodate musical reviews produced by George Hamid.

Hughes had dealt frequently with Patty over the past three years, seeing him at the top of his form, as chair of the 1934 banquet in Toronto where he had invited Hughes to be toastmaster, as president of the Showmen's League, and as director of his midway at the Toronto Centennial Celebration and elsewhere. They had been conferring together at the league's meetings and events in Chicago, in such far-flung locales as Hot Springs and Tampa, and closer to home in Toronto and Hamilton.

Since the early 1930s, Patty had lusted after the CNE. In 1931 he told Frank that "World's Fairs ... may come and go. But the CNE goes on forever."[56] In 1933, after his European tour had renewed his commitment to the carnival industry, Patty decided to talk with the CNE directors. His spiel was impressive, but Waters turned him down because he did not have the equipment. He staged a repeat performance for Hughes in 1936, but Hughes gave him the same reason for refusal. They flew together to the Texas Centennial Exposition in November, after which Patty went to Vancouver.

Three weeks later, Hughes wired Patty, asking for a meeting in Toronto. Hughes was also entertaining owners of some big American shows and Patty got to see him last. After they talked until three in the morning, Hughes gave in, but he had to know what Patty could offer that was unique. Patty said he would try to get the Dionne quintuplets. Born in 1934, they were the only quintuplets on record to survive. Showmen immediately recognized they would be "an ace drawing card," if exhibited.[57] Their father contracted them to a showman for the Century of Progress world's fair in Chicago and other promoters tried to book them, until in March 1935 the Ontario government stepped in, made them wards of the Crown, and forbade their exhibition except under its sponsorship. In 1936 the "Quintland" tourist attraction was at the peak of its popularity and their name and image were licensed to a range of commercial products. Patty had cooked up a scheme the previous year to take them on an exclusive tour of the leading cities of the world. That attempt had failed and so did the current one.

Later in life, Patty provided his version of the story of getting his first contract for the CNE. In his version, as relayed in *Amusement Business* on November 16, 1968, he was waiting out a thunderstorm when he received a telegram: "I get the news that I land the contract as I lean against a tent pole at Melfort, Sask., one of the smallest agricultural exhibitions in the country. I am to do the biggest thing of its kind. As a showman, I know there isn't anything too big for the CNE. So I say, we go to Europe to find something exclusive for the CNE!" This version demonstrates Patty's storytelling prowess and ability to play with facts to satisfy dramatic truth.

At the IAFE meeting in Chicago in early December 1936, Hughes announced that he had engaged Patty "to direct the CNE midway in 1937"; on December 12, *Billboard* reported,

> This will be the first time in many years that the CNE has not had an organized carnival on the midway and it will be in the nature of an experiment. Hughes, however, says he is certain that it will prove successful. The midway in '37 will be made up of attractions independently bought and will be under the personal direction of Conklin.
>
> Conklin is much elated over his selection to direct the midway of the largest fair on the American continent. His friends, too, are exceedingly pleased, and Patty was the recipient of hearty congratulations thruout the week.

Hughes was not dissatisfied with Rubin & Cherry, he said, but wanted to experiment. Patty was to be the manager of an independent midway, with which "the title of his show will not be connected in any way."[58] Yet showmen received the news as the announcement of Patty's de facto rise to command of the midway for the largest fair in the world.

What was perception in 1937 became fact in subsequent years as Patty renegotiated his arrangement with the CNE into an exclusive for Conklin Shows. In the meantime, Patty and Hughes acted as managerial partners trying to fill up the CNE amusement area — no longer called a midway — with the finest attractions from around the world. While on a "special mission" to Los Angeles in January, Patty revealed that "he had been working on some ideas along this line for several years."[59] Hughes and many other showmen knew that Patty's takeover of the CNE midway was "by no means an impromptu invasion."

Patty had opened one campaign in his assault on the CNE the previous summer, when he consulted with Guy Weadick, an American cowboy turned showman. Weadick had promoted Wild West shows in Canada in the early part of the century and had been a prime mover behind the stampede part of the Calgary Stampede and Exhibition. He had introduced rodeo events to a number of prairie exhibitions in the early 1930s. He and Patty were rumoured to be "discussing plans for something new in the carnival and rodeo line on a big scale."[60] Patty saw possibilities for exploiting Wild West bunkum in the urban East. Tom Mix, before and after his career as a cowboy movie star, directed and performed with Wild West shows. While the CNE did not have a Weadick rodeo, it did get a Tom Mix three-ring circus, replete with a Wild West show.

Patty began discussions with Mix's manager in January 1937 in Los Angeles, where he also met with representatives of other attractions. He and Frank then went to New York to look over more shows, and Patty made a quick side trip to Philadelphia to visit ride manufacturers. He met Hughes back in New York. Together, they returned to Toronto for the Ontario Association of Agricultural Societies meeting and met again in Chicago to sign the deal with the Mix organization. In March, they sailed from New York for an extended European booking tour.

Frank was left to look after the mundane duties of running the show. For 1937 he won the contract for the western Canadian B fairs, now back up to 15, and booked the usual Ontario and Quebec fairs. In New York in January, Frank and Patty met with Art Lewis, who had a show based in the eastern United States. They made a deal for Lewis to supply the midway for three Quebec fairs that Conklin's All-Canadian had booked, but which occurred during the CNE. Frank would assist Lewis with whatever Conklin attractions were not needed in Toronto. Here was the first gambit toward what became a well laid-out routine — contracting fairs that other shows would play — and the CNE had provided the motive and the template.

Fully recovered from tuberculosis, Frank had become an active partner in the show and chief of operations, while Patty was the international midway impresario. In the words of Patty's son, they were "a perfect team": "Patty was the outgoing charmer, storyteller and optimist. Patty handled the back end, rides and shows, laid out the show and booked most of the major dates. He was the boss. Frank was seemingly serious, quiet and blunted Patty's enthusiasm. Frank handled the front end games, food and novelties."[61] Frank developed close friendships and ties with his connections, while Patty was a friend to all, tied to none.

A *Billboard* correspondent who visited Frank in winter quarters wrote at length in the May 8, 1937, issue of how impressed he was by the Conklin method, by now a mantra in the business. The Conklin suite of offices in Hamilton "compares favourably with big theatrical offices in New York." Six days a week, the office "opens promptly at 8:30" to "a beehive of activity." The brothers "apply the same strict methods in their office as they do when their show is on the road." At the shop, the reporter "never saw as much work turned out in so short a time." Frank explained that this was because the show paid regular salaries. The writer had never before "experienced full road salaries paid for winter-quarters work." He noted that the brothers "love to entertain and be entertained" and "are fortunate in having wives who are equally wonderful hostesses."

Meanwhile, Patty strolled London's streets in a blue serge suit, Stetson, and cane, Edythe on his arm, and sent home British newspapers with headlines on the "Canadian Barnum."[62] He told reporters that he was in London to find "a bit of zip for the Canadian National Exhibition." With his long experience playing to nationalist sentiment, he continued: "Every year the amusements have been run by Americans. Last year they did 95 per cent of the business. There's £80,000 to be made in 14 days. I'm going to see that most of it goes to British performers this time.... some folks think we can't do it. I'll show 'em."

Hughes, whose wife had died the previous summer, vacationed with Patty and Edythe on the Riviera before they all visited the construction site of the Paris International Exposition, where they met a British amusement park owner and an American ride builder. The Conklins returned to Canada, while the anglophile Hughes stayed on for the coronation of George VI. This event was hoped to restore confidence in the monarchy after Edward VIII's abdication due to his marriage to American divorcée Wallis Simpson. Hughes came home with the coronation as the theme for the 1937 CNE; Patty was already playing up his own ascension to the CNE crown.

Patty had booked three features while in England, but never came close to ensuring the majority of the take went to British or even Canadian performers. The Globe of Death was a motordrome within which two motorcyclists dodged each other and defied gravity. Another was a speedway, for which only the cars came from England. The owner of the cars used the trip to North America to buy a new steel enclosure and track from Spillman Engineering. The third British show was the oddly named Hollywood Chimps.

Other new shows were American. At the Texas Centennial Exposition, Patty contracted Harry Seber to present the World's Fair Dancers, a girl show, and Jean DeKreko to bring his Flaming Youth Revue, a variety show that also had a large complement of scantily clad dancing girls. As the impresario of the Ex, Patty could sign his pick of what he thought were good shows.

Perhaps his best catch was Harry Lewiston, who would present a freak show and a snake show. Lewiston came from Ringling Brothers and Barnum & Bailey and had been producing sideshows for circuses since 1914. After being an independent, he joined Conklin Shows in 1937: "I decided I would be better off with Patty. Besides his personality and abilities, there was the fact that his show was scheduled to play the great Canadian National Exposition," where Lewiston expected to "make a full season's profit right at that one stand."[63] He would produce shows, including girl shows, for Patty for many years.

At the Century of Progress world's fair in 1933–34, Lewiston had partnered with Lou Dufour to present Darkest Africa, an example of an ethnographic "educational" exhibit common at the time. The natives in Darkest Africa were from New York and Chicago. To Conklin's All-Canadian, Lewiston contributed his "Iturian Pygmies," four Black microcephalic children from Memphis, with him since 1929. He exhibited them as "African Oddities," their small, empty heads, so went the spiel, suiting them for living in the jungle with other primates. Such racism was socially accepted at the time and certainly not out of place on midways. Lewiston also brought Melvin Burkhart from his Ringling sideshow. Burkhart was an "anatomical wonder" who, beyond being a contortionist, invented the "human blockhead" act of pounding a huge spike up his nose into his sinus cavity. He was at the CNE in 1937 and kept his skull under construction well into the 1980s.

Season of 1937

Patty was back five days before opening the show in Hamilton at the end of April. After a week of rain, the lot was a mudhole, and no one expected the show to open. Making it up as they went along, the Conklins arranged with a wrecking company for 80,000 feet of planking, laying it down over 15 loads of cinders and 200 bales of sawdust. The show opened, the mayor once more performing the honours, several Members of Parliament his guests. Later in the week, Sally Rand, appearing at a local theatre with her famed fan dance, visited the midway. In a photo of Patty and Sally, he beams a wide-open grin at the camera, pleased to be in the presence of the woman who had brought the naked female body to the masses, while she looks off at one of his attractions.[64] The Speedway was the big ride for the week and the Lewiston sideshow the top grossing show. The Lions Club sponsors of the date made almost $2,500 on the nine-day event.

Frank took the show north and west, while Patty headed south and east to New York, Boston, Cleveland, and Chicago on "a 'flying scouting trip' in quest of attractions for the CNE."[65] With other showmen he took in the boxing match in Chicago where Joe Louis won the world heavyweight championship for the first time.

Lewiston left the show before it went into the northern mining towns, rejoining it in the West. A small indoor rodeo hooked up with the show in Timmins. At Winnipeg, two new rides debuted: a Tilt-A-Whirl to replace the one sold the previous year and an Octopus. The Octopus, invented in 1936 by Eyerly Aircraft, makers of the Loop-O-Plane, was the first to operate in Canada. Patty rejoined the show during the second week in Winnipeg, in time to experience the vagaries of thunderstorms, dust storms, and severe heat. The highest temperature ever to hit Canada to that date — 45°C — was recorded in southern Saskatchewan while the show was there.

While Frank was finishing off the final fairs in the West, Patty headed to Toronto in early August to assume oversight of a construction crew of 40 tradesmen at the CNE. Promotional literature was already out: "All-new amusement area.... Complete and daring departure from accepted ideas of so-called 'midways.'... Recreational and educational innovations and novelties....

Startling array of European and Asiatic features."[66] After tentatively calling the new non-midway "Playland," Hughes and Patty settled on Frolexland, a name Patty coined to play on the CNE's nickname, "the Ex." The Toronto newspaper ads proclaimed: "Good-By, Midway; Hello, FROLEXLAND, presented by J.W. Conklin."

Patty had let out to the carnival industry that Frolexland would have 35 rides, 15 of which had never before appeared in Toronto. The program lists 20 major rides, half of them repeats. Only a handful, like the Octopus and the Speedway, were really new. Ten kiddie rides were separately listed, although they were part of the total. Because Frolexland was not supposed to be Conklin land, Patty identified only a Chair-O-Plane, a funhouse, and a triple Ferris wheel as belonging to the show. Whoever owned them, the Speedway, Octopus, Loop-O-Plane, Hey-Dey, Tilt-A-Whirl, and Ridee-O had been travelling with Conklin's All-Canadian all season.

The promotional material stated that Toronto had never seen 20 of the 25 shows. Perhaps technically true, since shows often formed and dissolved, but the lineup was standard North American midway fare. Playing the patriotic card, Patty emphasized in a *Toronto Star* article on August 21 that the attractions were "65 per cent ... British and Canadian. Outside of Tom Mix and his circus, we are bringing over only about 90 persons from the United States" and there would be 1,000 performers. Eskimoland, produced by a Winnipeg man, seemed a Canadian touch, except the Eskimo village idea had been presented as far back as 1903 at Coney Island. Hughes told the press he had seen the unicorn in the Noah's Ark collection of exotic animals in England, but an American had run Noah's Ark in the United States that spring.

When Frank brought the show east, 1,800 miles from Prince Albert, Saskatchewan, to Brantford, Ontario, Patty thought this "would mark a record in the history of long jumps for carnivals."[67] Frank spent two weeks in Ontario before the CNE absorbed most of his show and he dragged the remnants on to Quebec. Art Lewis Shows had been in Canada since the end of July, playing Quebec fairs and stills, all of which Conklin's All-Canadian had played some time during the previous five years and for which the show still had the bookings. The week before Frank joined him in Quebec, Lewis had a blowdown that knocked over the Ferris wheel. By the time Frank and

Dave Picard arrived in Trois-Rivières with a merry-go-round, two shows, and some concessions, the weather was finally giving Lewis a break. Friends and business partners, Frank and Lewis travelled back to Toronto to be with Patty for the CNE opening. They returned to play Sherbrooke and Quebec City before Frank rejoined Conklin's All-Canadian and Lewis went back to the United States.

Hughes and Patty predicted an attendance of two million, but a local public health problem thwarted them. By the middle of August, an outbreak of polio was getting extensive coverage in the newspapers. Before the development of effective vaccines in the early 1950s, outbreaks of polio, which could be fatal, occurred regularly. This epidemic does not seem to have been particularly severe, although it spread quickly in the two weeks before the opening of the CNE, reaching slightly over 200 reported cases and then doubling by closing day. It was front-page news in the *Star* on August 31, the Tuesday following the opening. Concentrations of children were believed to encourage the spread of the disease and, although measures were taken to allay their fears, concerned parents kept their children away from the Ex. Heat and humidity during the first half of the stand also hurt attendance. Numbers for the 1937 CNE, Patty's first, were the lowest in 18 years.

The polio epidemic particularly damaged Patty's plan, since one of his innovations was to group kids' rides in one area — "Playland" — the name at one time intended for the whole midway. Children's rides had been developing along with thrill rides. Since the mid-1920s, amusement parks had been locating children's rides in their own area, but Patty was the first to set up a carnival kiddieland. Being at the CNE, it attracted attention, some critical since it was designed to collect a lot of kids in one place.

The show attracted other critical attention from the Toronto press, which carried stories on two incidents arising from bally shows. The CNE authorities dismissed for profanity two talkers for the girl show, one of whom had been spieling about the "dance of the roses."[68] Hughes said the Exhibition did not "want that sort of thing" and was "watching the spielers." The other story came from the snake show, when an alligator slipped off the bally platform and into the crowd, "hissing and snapping its jaws in a threatening manner."[69] Given the ease with which an attendant brought the animal under control, this was likely another example of the common bally ploy, losing control of a "wild" animal to cause a panic. Usually, it was a lethargic python that was let slip into the crowd. A gale that struck the exhibition on its closing Saturday also made the news, although only minor damage was inflicted to the midway.

The city lost money on the CNE that year, no surprise since its attendance had dropped by over 300,000. Of all the exhibitions in Canada in 1937, only the CNE and the London fair were down, but Hughes put the best face on it. As far as the midway was concerned, he was "more than satisfied with the results of Patty's work."[70] He credited Frolexland with reversing the public's poor opinion of midways and with gaining abundant publicity in the Toronto press. In various later claims, Patty gave figures from $24,000 to $50,000 as the show's cost for the privilege of playing the CNE that first year. The company's profit and loss statement for 1937 records a loss of $10,059 on the Ex. It could not recoup that money from the five southwestern Ontario fairs played after the exhibition. On the season's receipts of over $266,000, the show had a net loss of slightly more than $4,000.[71]

His actions after the season's close suggest that Patty was willing to bank on the future and confirmed the broad lineaments of what that future would be. The industry press had faith in him as well, speculating that he would buy "a big flat-car carnival at an early date."[72] Instead, he purchased property and buildings in Brantford, Ontario, for the show's winter quarters. Two days after the show closed down for the season, Hughes signed the formal letter inviting Patty to renew his contract as the CNE's midway director for 1938. Patty had repeatedly turned down this offer since leaving Toronto, but finally capitulated. Brantford and the CNE, in reasonable proximity to each other, would be the twin capitals of the Conklin kingdom for the rest of Patty's life.

The War Years

(1937–1946)

When Patty Conklin took over the Canadian National Exhibition midway, he became a force in the carnival industry and got his chance to prove his worth. No one could know how long he would keep the Ex, although the CNE had a record of backing winners and Patty had only begun to make his mark. His fame spread beyond the midway and the showmen's clubrooms. He rose as a luminary in the Canadian press, starting with a cover story, simply titled "Carnival King," for the July 15, 1941, issue of *Maclean's*, a magazine with national circulation. Other magazine features and press coverage followed. Toronto's Press Club welcomed him, and the city newspapers began to take notice. With his well-honed business sense and well-developed personal vanity, Patty appreciated the good press, but would suffer when it went bad.

THE KING AND HIS KINGDOM

They come to Patty as a delegation and are ushered into his presence in the office above the cow palace. Frank, his factotum, pours them all drinks. They light cigarettes and lounge wherever they can find a seat. Patty starts to talk about the crowds flooding his midway.

"You would not believe it," he says. "It is actually beyond anyone's wildest imagination or belief. They can't get through the gates and onto that midway fast enough. Just look out there, from here to Lake Ontario and back again. They're jammed up like it's a world's fair." He pauses. "You boys can learn something up here all right, just you keep your eyes open."

The men, some his senior, laugh and ask him who is grossing highest. "It's between Maxie's pickled punks, Seber's peelers, and the Wild West show. Depends on the day. I got twenty shows and we can't keep up with 'em, we still got lineups. Everybody's doing fire sale business from the minute they open."

Noise drifts in from outside. The late afternoon sun cuts through the haze of cigarette smoke. It is hot and close, the smell of livestock overpowering. "How 'bout the joints?" someone asks.

"Hand over fist, they got tips ten deep and they're all live ones. The lucky boys are only stopped by how fast they can take it in. They're absolutely letting money go. The marks can't help themselves from spending everything they got. You don't even have to ask 'em for it and they're emptying their pockets."

★   ★   ★

Patty had secured his reputation as a carnival king, the CNE his personal fiefdom. But since leaving his father's house more than 30 years before, he had seldom stayed in one place more than a month. The home he had bought for his wife and son was a railway car. Edythe and Jimmy spent much of the off-season with her relatives in Vancouver and Seattle, while Patty criss-crossed the continent. In her loneliness, she became an alcoholic, an early sign of which might have been her sudden "illness" in the winter of 1936 that brought Patty back to Miami. Many showmen in the first half of the century never owned a home and even the successful ones often waited until middle age to do so. John Ringling spent two-thirds of his life in railway cars, hotels, and apartments before buying his first home at the age of 45. Patty may have tired of his ceaseless wandering and wanted someplace to settle, where he could be closer to his wife and son. He chose the thriving Ontario town of Brantford as the seat of his power.

As the economic revival gained traction, the National Steel Car Company expanded its activities, and in the spring of 1937 the Conklin equipment was squeezed out of the National Steel buildings in Hamilton. When the show played Brantford for the first time that summer, at an old-home-week celebration just before the CNE, Patty scouted the city for a winter quarters. The show train left its last fair of the season and pulled into Brantford early in October. A week later, it moved to 1,700 feet of track, freshly laid by the Canadian National Railway at the show's new quarters, not far from downtown Brantford.

The Conklins had bought five acres of land, a three-story main building of over 12,000 square feet, and another building of 3,000 square feet. They built two new steel buildings, adding another 8,000 square feet, into which ran double tracks to house the train. Sixty miles southwest of Toronto on a bend in the Grand River, Brantford was a city of 30,000, the distribution centre for a rich agricultural area where the main industries centred on farm machinery and equipment. Conklin Shows became a significant local operation, spending hundreds of thousands of dollars on labour, materials, and services. Within a few years, Patty had built a "palatial home" two miles outside of Brantford and "its appointment, acreage and location" put him in "the squire class."[1] His estate had to have a name, so he called it Sky Acres.

Other Carnival Kingdoms

The carnival world had other carnie kings with larger kingdoms, but while Patty was staking his turf some of the American shows that had dominated the industry partly through their Canadian dominions were coming undone.[2] Johnny Jones, in the business since 1901, died in 1930. As head of the biggest show in the early 1920s, Jones had owned the western Canadian A circuit and the CNE but lost both before his death. Run by his wife and son, the Jones show lost $34,000 in 1931 and could not play a full season in 1932. It was taken over and reorganized under the same name, but never recovered its former glory and eventually sputtered out in 1950.

Begun in 1917 by Rubin Gruberg, Rubin & Cherry Shows had grown fast, taking the A circuit from Jones in 1925, but only for that year. Gruberg split the show into two units in 1928 and tried carrying no games on one. He snatched up the CNE that year — with games — keeping it as the linchpin of his show's route for nearly a decade, until Patty took it from him. In 1934 Gruberg declared bankruptcy, but through legal manoeuvring managed to keep Rubin & Cherry on the road, trimmed down to one unit. He died of a heart attack in 1942 and his show was sold.

Morris & Castle Shows entered the big league in 1922, buying equipment from C.A. Wortham, owner of the first major carnival, when he got out of the business. Morris & Castle picked up the A circuit the year Johnny Jones died. John Castle bought out his partner in 1931 but lost the show to the bank. He found new partners and came back out with the Castle-Erlich-Hirsch Shows, retaining the A circuit, only to lose it to Royal American in 1934. Castle reorganized again as United Shows of America, which he kept alive for two years more.

Beckmann & Gerety grew stronger during the Depression. After long experience in the industry, Fred Beckmann and Barney Gerety also bought Wortham equipment in 1922. Their outfit expanded throughout the 1920s and '30s. Although they never played Canadian dates, they took Pete Kortes and his World's Museum sideshow from Conklin's All-Canadian in 1931 and grabbed other acts in the 1930s. Beckmann & Gerety remained one of the top shows throughout the decade. When Beckmann died in 1941, his show faltered and was sold off in 1945.

Carl Sedlmayr toured his first carnival in 1922 and named it Royal American Shows the following year.[3] Curtis and Elmer Velare, beginning as circus performers, became carnival concessionaires, bought rides and railway stock, and partnered with Sedlmayr in 1924. As Patty was trying to grow his northern route, Sedlmayr was making his first incursions. A turf war that would span decades began. Royal American started bidding on the western Canadian B circuit in 1928, split it with Conklin & Garrett in 1929 and grabbed it all in 1930. The Conklins got the circuit back in 1931. After an unsuccessful bid on the A circuit in 1933, Royal American won it again in 1934 and kept it until the war put limits on American show equipment coming into Canada.

Sedlmayr and the Velares were innovators, adding searchlights and light towers, and twin and ultimately quadruple Ferris wheels. When Royal American returned to the western Canadian A circuit in 1946 it was the undisputed superpower among North American carnivals. The show retained the title for 30 years, the length of time it dominated Canada's West. It was the only other major carnival company besides Conklin Shows to survive the century's first half and grow stronger in its second.

After a visit to Royal American, Patty went on record in the August 29, 1936, issue of *Billboard*: "It is by far the most gigantic piece of show equipment that I have ever seen in my entire show career. The lighting effects are so beautiful that they are really astounding, and their attractions are superior to most anything that I have had the pleasure of seeing heretofore." Never one to shy away from superlatives, Patty even applied them to rivals. His envy is also apparent.

Personalities with the Show

Patty gathered to his Brantford capital most of the principal lieutenants and functionaries who would see him through the next phase of his reign, some remaining with him for life. Brother Frank and Neil Webb were his right- and left-hand men. Since 1932, Frank had been getting semiannual checkups for tuberculosis at the Mountain Sanatorium in Hamilton, just down the road from Brantford. His disease had remained in remission, but after the 1937 season he returned to Monrovia, where Billie had family and the sanatorium in which he met her was located, to recuperate from a relapse. Back on the road the following season, he often looked after the show on his own, especially in Quebec. He liked to entertain and had a reputation as a hard drinker. In 1941 Frank took his turn as president of the Showmen's League.

Webb's accounting system was crucial to the show's growing success. He worked out of a small tent, the front half used for the office, while "the back was used to entertain fair boards, politicians and visiting dignitaries. A few folding chairs, a table and a beer trunk were the only amenities. In the office part, two cash windows, one for the front end and one to check in the ride tickets, two stools, one large counter and a strong box ... were the décor. A gun was a permanent fixture on the counter — always empty."[4]

Dave Picard remained the show's assistant manager, Jockey Custock the lot boss, and Bob Randall the ride superintendent. Picard lived in Rochester, New York, while Randall kept roots in Vancouver. In the mid-1940s, Randall and Joe Palmer, a Conklin concessionaire also from Vancouver, joined Henry Meyerhoff's Crescent Shows based in Penticton, B.C., which had taken over Conklin & Garrett's western circuit. Merrick Nutting, the general agent and advance man Patty had picked up in Quebec City, helped coordinate the arrangements between Conklin Shows and Art Lewis and Jimmy Sullivan, and also worked for Garden Brothers' Circus and Harry Lewiston. Herman Larsen from Hamilton had been the show trainmaster since 1933, managing concessions between jumps and chauffeuring for Patty between seasons. Albert "Red" Cohn joined the show with his bingo in 1935 and made good money into the 1940s, when he left to play fairs in California and Texas, closer to his home in Los Angeles.

Maxie Herman became a midway favourite, running several shows and games in the late 1930s. In the cookhouse with a reporter who remarked on the fire-eater cooling her soup, Maxie showed the quick wit for which he was known: "I'm sorry, old boy. That's where you're wrong. She is heating it."[5] Maxie left the show when his health began to fail in the mid-1940s.

Randall, Custock, and Palmer had been with Patty from his beginning in British Columbia, along with Frank Bickford, Peter Fay, Alex Lobban, and Les Sturgeon. Some of these old hands remained stuck as concessionaires, without office positions, and began leaving the show in the late 1930s. Custock left to work in the hotel industry. Picard, Nutting, Larsen, Herman, and Cohn all joined the show in the mid-1930s, as it expanded in Ontario. They came on in senior positions and got better opportunities from the office. Herman and Cohn were Chicago natives, but as they prospered they bought winter homes in Miami and Los Angeles, respectively. Norma Nutting, Margie Palmer, Betty Herman, and Isabel Cohn were working wives with the show, Betty and Isabel bearing children on the road.

It was customary for sideshow producers to jump from show to show. Johnny Branson was one consistent Conklin impresario, running various animal acts for over 20 years before moving to Sullivan's Wallace Brothers' Shows in 1948 with other Conklin showmen. For many years a vaudevillian, Jack Halligan had become a carnie in the early 1930s and joined Patty at the CNE in 1938 with a freak show, travelling with the show until his death five years later. In 1937 the DeKreko brothers, Charles and Jean, legends who had been with the carnival since the beginning of the century, brought a sideshow out with Conklin Shows, and later contributed funhouses as well. When Charles fell ill while with the show in Regina in 1942, Patty put him up in a hospital and threw a party for him. He died in early December and Jean a month later.

Harry Seber had known Patty for years and became president of the Pacific Coast Showmen's Association in 1938. Seber had been a magician and a manager of a movie theatre in Los Angeles, and brought out his first girl show in 1917, when he was 24. He hit the big time with girl shows at Chicago's Century of Progress in 1933. A "rotund, Sultan-like gent," he told the *Maclean's* reporter that Patty would not keep anyone around who didn't make money: "He puts everybody except the mechanical workers on a percentage basis.... So they can go ahead and make as much as they like — for themselves and for him." The two girl shows Seber and his wife, Frances, had at the CNE for five years were consistently top grossing and occasionally controversial.

Jack Ray was one of Patty's most interesting hires and contributed substantially to his boss's success. Ray and his family emigrated from England in 1924 when he was 13, settling in Edmonton, where two years later he began assisting theatre artists. After three more years he formed his own business designing displays for exhibitions. He worked in succession for an American theatre circuit, a Broadway producer, Warner Brothers, and the Minskys of burlesque fame. Patty met him working as a bellhop in a Calgary hotel in the mid-1930s and hired him as a sign painter, giving him his big opportunity with the CNE of 1937.

Ray learned through experience "not only the difficulties of tear-down, setting up, and maintenance, but the tastes and habits of people — what compelled their attention, how they moved around a midway, etc."[6] He discarded the traditional midway garishness and bright, primary colours, and used new materials and a full palette to create fronts that appeared modern — clean

lines, chrome and glass, sleek pillars and buttresses — and showed the influence of art deco architecture. He produced permanent show fronts for the
CNE, putting on exhibits for the carnival owners, park operators, and world's
fair directors who visited to pick up tips. He redesigned a number of amusement parks through the 1940s and by 1949 was recognized as "having done as
much, if not more, than any other in his field to modernize the lure and height-
en the money-earning potential of midway shows." When not designing, Ray
sweetened his income by managing girl shows for Patty. During the winter he
worked for a time as a staff artist for the *Toronto Star*.

Largely through their association with Patty, Jack Ray and many other
Conklin staff became well-known industry personalities. He, however, remained the head of state. After the end of the 1938 season, he and Elwood
Hughes together took a tour of the American South and Southwest, one befit-
ting statesmen of the outdoor entertainment industry. Along the way they were
guests of George Hamid, and of the Johnny J. Jones, Rubin & Cherry, Beckmann
& Gerety, Hennies Brothers, and Royal American shows, among others.

Alfred Phillips was a celebrity in Canada before he joined Conklin
Shows. He was the Canadian champion springboard and platform diver from
1926 to 1934, retiring undefeated. He won gold in both events at the inaugural British Empire Games in 1930. He represented Canada at two Olympic
games, placing fourth in the springboard event in 1932. In 1937 Patty contracted Phillips and Sam Snyder, an American diver, to stage the CNE's first
water show, complete with Olympic diving champions and a comedy act.
Phillips took a leave from the CNE in 1939 and 1940 to manage the Aquacade
for Billy Rose at the New York World's Fair. Johnny Weissmuller, Eleanor
Holm, and Esther Williams — all big names in the entertainment industry — were among the Aquacade stars and in the fair's two seasons it grossed
nearly five million dollars. After the world's fair, Phillips took a water show on
the road with Patty. Rose, one of the biggest producers of the day, had coined
the name Aquacade, and when Patty and Phillips used it at the CNE, Rose
sued them, dropping the suit when they dropped the name. They settled on
"Aqua Frolics" and Phillips produced the show for Patty for another 14 years.
Their sons became close friends and partners, Alfie Jr. eventually becoming
president of Conklin Shows.

Collaborators with the Show

Patty retained connections that reached back to his earliest years as a car-nie. He had broken into the Canadian West with Molly Lavoie's International Amusement Company. In 1924, after the Conklins left Lavoie, International played many of the Ontario fairs that Conklin Shows would later capture. Lavoie was the first president of the Canadian chapter of the Showmen's League, formed in Montreal, his hometown, in 1928. By 1935 Lavoie had lost his show and was assistant manager on Jimmy Sullivan's Wallace Brothers' Shows, where he also had a top grossing ten-in-one. He stayed with Sullivan until forming Victory Shows in 1939. Lavoie and Patty stayed in touch, and Lavoie was a catalyst in Patty's dealings with Sullivan in the early 1930s.

Raised in Ohio, Jimmy Sullivan got into outdoor show business in 1916, when he was 18, with a fellow Irishman, John Flanagan. He bought out Flanagan, then got stuck in the army for the next two years. He first used the Wallace Brothers title in 1923, reasoning that "the Protestant towns in Pennsylvania, Ohio and West Virginia would take more kindly to Wallace Bros. than they would to names like Sullivan or Flanagan."[7] Sensitivity to the social significance of names and a willingness to change them to meet these exigencies would link the Irishman masquerading as an Anglo with the German who took cover under an Irish cognomen. They must have appreciated the ironies. Sullivan stayed in the United States until he part-nered with Larry Boyd and they moved into Ontario, playing still dates and their first fair date, the Norfolk County Fair in Simcoe in 1927. They bid on the western B circuit in 1928. Perhaps through his partnership with the Wirth brothers' circus, Boyd won the B circuit in 1932, but passed it on to Conklin Shows.

Boyd died in Sullivan's Toronto home late the next year, but Patty and Sullivan's relationship remained alive and improved once Sullivan stopped trying to thwart Conklin Shows' move into Ontario. Patty appointed Sullivan to the General Committee for the Showmen's League banquet in 1934, com-peted with him for Ontario fairs the next year, and relied on his assistance for Showmen's League fundraising. By this time, Sullivan had moved his winter quarters to the fairgrounds of the rural Ontario town of Simcoe, home of his last spot in the season, the Norfolk Fair, and had a full route of dates in Ontario and Quebec.

Patty and Jimmy decided to collaborate rather than compete. Nutting, the Conklin general agent, got the Old Boys' Reunion and Summer Carnival in London, Ontario, in 1938 for the Conklins and they gave it to Sullivan. The Conklins were not interested in the 1939 western B circuit and supported Sullivan's bid, lending him $39,000 to expand his show for the circuit. He kept the western fairs until 1943, when he forfeited his contract because the military was jamming the railways. The Conklins brought Sullivan's Wallace Brothers' Shows to the Quebec City fair in 1942. The two shows played the Canadian West in parallel in the early 1940s and Sullivan's ties to the Conklins tightened. Their companies remained joined for the next 20 years, trading staff and dates back and forth, until Conklin Shows bought Wallace Brothers in 1964 and Patty let Sullivan retire.

The Conklins also collaborated for a time with Art Lewis Shows. Lewis entered the carnival business in 1930 and by 1935 had his own show, based in New York State. In 1937, with the Conklins as intermediaries, Lewis contracted the Sherbrooke and Quebec City fairs, which Conklin Shows had worked since 1934, and fairs in St. Hyacinthe and Trois-Rivières. Lewis had also hoped to get Valleyfield. Max Gruberg's World's Exposition Shows had played these latter three fairs in 1936 and lost all but Valleyfield to the Conklins and Lewis in 1937. The Quebec fairs coincided with the CNE and with Patty absorbed in that, brother Frank and Dave Picard took a few rides, shows, and concessions to Quebec to help out Lewis.

Lewis had a similar arrangement with the Conklins in 1938, but in 1939, for reasons unknown, they handed the major Quebec fairs to Dave and Ralph Endy. Endy Brothers' Shows, formed by their father in 1909, was based in Florida and the Quebec fairs were its first Canadian dates. Along with Frank and Picard, Nutting was seconded to the Endys, Red Cohn brought in his bingo game, and other Conklin equipment augmented the lineup. The Endy–Conklin partnership lasted two years until the Valleyfield and Trois-Rivières fairs were cancelled so their grounds could become military barracks. Conklin Shows planned to take the Quebec fairs back for themselves in 1942, but that year all the Quebec fairs were cancelled, except the Exposition Provinciale in the capital. The outdoor entertainment industry had to adapt to the war, with railway restrictions and the occupation of fairgrounds having the greatest direct impact; shortage of ready money to spend on the midway was not a drawback.

The Quebec fairs presented unique opportunities and difficulties for the Conklin organization. For one thing, they could be very lucrative for carnies. The American shows had bought the Quebec fairs with bribes and Frank used the same tactics. Quebec was the only province that allowed midways to operate on Sunday, providing an extra day for money making, but putting pressure on everyone when the show had to close on a Sunday and open hundreds of miles away on a Monday. They also had to hire francophone show, ride, and games operators. Patty with his usual exaggeration claimed that French communities were only good for about half the revenue he got from English communities. Although he told Lewis that it was difficult to close deals with Quebec fair committees, Patty developed a long and friendly relationship with Emery Boucher, the general manager of the Exposition Provinciale. Frank also developed many friendships in Quebec.

It was not solely out of brotherly love that the Conklins helped Sullivan, Lewis, and the Endys, all Americans unknown to the fair boards, in booking and playing Conklin spots in Canada. The Conklins not only garnered the goodwill of show owners who were not big enough to compete with them, they also took a percentage of the net and placed their own equipment at reduced rates. They kept control of a number of fair contracts they would otherwise have had to give up to concentrate on the CNE. When the CNE closed for the war, Patty revealed that he had held on to these contracts as insurance against such an eventuality.

In cities like Vancouver and Hamilton, Patty was used to official openings by local mayors. At the CNE, politicians and entertainers from around the world toured his midway. In 1938 the concession managers for the 1939 New York World's Fair visited the Ex to get educated. The publicity director for the world's fair worked for Patty at the exhibitions of 1938 and 1939. Lord Edward Stanley, as secretary of state for Dominion affairs, opened the CNE in 1938. The lord chancellor of England opened it in 1939, the governor general of Canada performed the honours the following year, and in 1941 the Duke of Kent visited Patty's kiddieland. Attending to minor British royalty warmed his faux Irish heart.

Patty's hold on the CNE midway attracted the attention of ride manufacturers, just as the importance of their equipment was starting to be recognized. Hyla Maynes, who had built the first funhouse in 1911, was one of them. He joined Johnny J. Jones Exposition in 1915, for 15 years building the rides that were the basis for that show's success. In 1925 Maynes designed the first Caterpillar, assigning the patent to Spillman Engineering. Maynes partnered with Harry Illions in 1927, and they left Jones in 1933 and began building a reputation as independent ride manufacturers with the Century of Progress world's fair in Chicago. They took rides out with Castle-Hirsch in 1934 and by 1936 also had equipment with Beckmann & Gerety and Royal American. In 1938 they had installations at several amusement parks, including Belmont Park in Montreal. That year Illions, Maynes, and their wives visited Patty at the Ex. The next year they asked the manager of Belmont whether they could take their rides to Toronto for the CNE. After the season, they stored them at the Conklin winter quarters. Two other major ride manufacturers, Eyerly Aircraft and Allan Herschell Rides, each had several rides at the Ex in 1939. As "an acknowledged expert on rides," Patty "worked out many a new gadget" with the Herschell company and had "first crack at every new device they develop."[8] Other ride manufacturers visited Patty at the Toronto exhibition, as in 1941 did Lee Sullivan, the owner of the Eli Bridge Company, which had Ferris wheels with every major carnival in North America.

Patty used the experience, influence, and information he drew from running the CNE midway to bolster his reputation as a force within the industry. He turned the Ex into a mecca for fair committees and park and carnival operators. It became a showcase for ride manufacturers, a place where prospective buyers could see machines being ridden by thousands and get precise reports on earning power and mechanical reliability. It became a prime venue for some of the best sideshows in North America and the favourite hunting grounds for unscrupulous games agents. And it became inextricably associated with the name of Patty Conklin. The CNE midway was his.

EXPANSION

The weather in Winnipeg has been hot, sticky, and unstable. Now the clouds blacken and the wind blows up. The temperature drops, lightning flashes, the sky growls, and rain begins. The canvas tops snap and yank at their stakes, and the big banner line for the sideshow blows over. Some of the plywood fronts topple, their neon tubes crashing and sparking in the mud. The show crews flush patrons from the tents, but there is nowhere for them to go except into the rain or a scattering of beat-up cars and trucks.

The storm reaches cyclonic intensity. Roughies grab the tie ropes and secure them to whatever they can. The Ferris wheel skates unattended along the strip of broken asphalt, swaying crazily. If it slides as far as the dirt, it'll go over, so no one goes near it. A metal skirt from the Whip breaks loose and flies through the air, barely missing heads.

Clutching his hat, Patty peers through the torrent, trying to make out who and what are most at risk. He hollers into the wind for everyone to get off the midway but hopes some will stay to hold down the tents. Game joints and show tents are twisted into tangles of torn canvas and broken lumber.

The storm goes through in minutes, seeming like hours. The townies who have cars open their doors and peer up at the sky. Others emerge from what little shelter they've been able to find. Drenched carnies gather in the midway to survey the wreckage, half hysterical at their survival. Beyond a few bruises, no one is hurt. The Ferris wheel still stands.

During the winters of the late 1930s and early '40s, Patty made his usual tours through New York, Paterson, Miami, Chicago, Hot Springs, Seattle, Vancouver, Los Angeles, and points in between, attending meetings and conventions, visiting with showfolk and relatives, and planning his next season. Many of his trips were now on airlines, which had become technically and commercially viable by the mid-1930s. Frank spent much of each winter in Monrovia.

Seasons of 1938 and 1939

Patty habitually expressed optimism about the prospects for the next season. For 1938 he was "making more elaborate preparations than in any previous year and will spend at least 100 per cent more in putting our show on the road this year than in 1937."[9] For 1939 he was going to present "the largest and best show we have ever taken on the road."[10] Every year had to be better than the year before.

Conklin Shows opened the 1938 season in Hamilton in May. They had Harry Lewiston's Circus Sideshow and Darkest Africa, Maxie Herman's Life Show and Animal Oddities, Harry Seber's World's Fair Dancers, Francis "Whitey" Woods' Midget Revue, and Bob and Mildred Lee's Globe of Death. Ernie and Len, turning seven that summer, still had their own show. The free show was a high wire act. They had nine rides, of which only a Hi-De-Ho fun-house was new. The number of shows equalled the number of rides that season, the only time it ever would. After a few Ontario still dates, the show played the western B circuit for the last time before giving it up to Wallace Brothers. In 1939 and 1940, they would play a route restricted to Ontario, including northern Ontario, with a three-week jaunt to Winnipeg in 1939.

Patty focused on the CNE. For the 1938 version, he brought in his seven shows and contracted some 13 more, including E.K. Fernandez's Hawaiian show, a Wild West show, and another girl show. The rides had increased by a similar number. Attendance was up 350,000 over the previous year to 1,656,000, the highest since the record two million of 1928. Patty claimed that he lost $1,000 on the 1938 CNE, less than the previous year, but still not likely the whole truth concerning his take. He later said that he lost $51,000 on his first two years at the CNE.[11]

They blew the cobwebs off in Brantford to start the 1939 season. They were taking Ray's fronts on the road for the first time, along with six new light towers and a carload of equipment from the Tom Mix circus, which had gone bankrupt. The Conklins had a new attraction, Sally's International Dancing Show, known as the Sally Show, piggybacking on the continuing notoriety of Sally Rand. Harry Lewiston had planned to have a Sally Show with Conklin in 1938, but that had fallen through. He was no longer with the Conklins in 1939, and

Harry and Frances Seber had the Sally Show. A girl show with lots of nudity, it was consistently among the top attractions. As community strictures against strippers gradually loosened, the carnival briefly led in liberalizing standards for public sexual display, and a solidified reputation for sleaze was its reward.

During its second week in Winnipeg, Conklin Shows had a blowdown: "The show was flattened."[12] Ray was devastated by the destruction wreaked upon his show fronts. When the storm ended, a repair crew worked through the night and most of the attractions were able to open the next day. Patty estimated the damage at $10,000.

For the CNE that year, Patty boasted of "53 pay attractions," including all shows and rides.[13] The shows included Minsky's Oriental Follies, the first foray of the brothers into the carnival circuit, drawn by the visions Patty painted of a burlesque resurgence led by the outdoor amusement industry. The debut fell far short of expectations and the Minskys declined to stay on the circuit. One reason might have been that the burlesque show was up against three girl shows. Another could have been the outbreak of war in Europe.

Germany invaded Poland on Friday, September 1, at the height of the 1939 CNE, and England declared war two days later. Although Canada did not join

Jack Ray painting of a blowdown in Winnipeg, 1939. Patty is the figure at left in a cape.

the war until the day after the CNE closed, the turmoil overseas caused a dras-
tic drop in attendance during the second week. The Vancouver and Ottawa
exhibitions also saw attendance fall, and three exhibitions in New Brunswick
were cancelled.

Patty, business sense at the ready, responded quickly to news of the war.
The day Germany invaded Poland, he tore down the Cleopatra exhibit, which
had been a flop, and replaced it with war relics. He had not put on a war show
regularly since the late 1920s but, as a *Globe and Mail* article on September
4 recounted, the junk he "dragged out of his attic and dusted off some time
Friday night" drew to capacity. CNE officials closed the German state pavilion
at the same time. If not for the war, the 1939 CNE gate would have beaten the
previous year's.

Patty had the dance pavilion concession from 1938 to 1941, moving it to
the midway. For three of these four years, the main musicians were Benny
Goodman, Guy Lombardo, Tommy Dorsey, and their big bands, all stars
at the height of their dance hall fame. In 1940 Goodman and Lombardo
were replaced by Duke Ellington and Danny Kaye. Patty got 50 percent of
the net and in most of these years made a few grand, although in 1939 he
claimed he lost five thousand. Having the pavilion on the midway was a
boost to his overall operation and he liked socializing with stars from the
more accepted, although still questionable, branches of the entertainment
industry. He enjoyed having the opportunity to take well-known personalities on tours of his midway.

Patty's fame led to increased scrutiny, and some criticism of him became
public. *Billboard* magazine, at least since its campaign to clean up midways had
petered out, was usually an unqualified booster of everyone in the carnival
industry. But William Hewitt, a former carnival executive for several small
shows who wrote for the magazine under the nom de plume of Red Onion, cast
a more jaundiced eye, especially on Patty's grip on the CNE. He had expressed
skepticism about the 15 new rides Patty said he would introduce at the 1937
CNE. He lobbed another bomb at the announcement of Patty's management
of the 1938 midway in the April 16 issue:

One more bloomer for independent midways at Canadian National Exhibition, Toronto, and the management will be ready to book an organized carnival at a reasonable percentage. Seems funny that with all the big and mighty carnivals that are now in existence, this exhibition could not get at least one of them to play the date. Funny world. Organized carnivals were never bigger nor better and yet the Canadian National Exhibition midway had to go in for independent attractions.

After the 1939 CNE, Red Onion rubbed in the drop in attendance that had resulted from the start of the war. "'Three times and out!' But not for J.W. (Patty) Conklin, who will head the CNE Frolexland for the fourth consecutive year," he opined on October 12.

Seasons of 1940 and 1941

With the 1940 CNE in his pocket, Patty bought more equipment. He purchased six steel rail cars, the remains of the Hagenbeck–Wallace Circus, and two tractor-trailer units. He did not take delivery of the rail cars until 1941 but used his new trucks and three others in 1940. Among other items, they carried the show's now extensive collection of lighting equipment, with a little less breakage than on the train. Smaller shows had begun using trucks in the early 1930s, travelling the dusty roads built by Depression work crews. As the continental highway system improved, the war monopolized the rails, and transportation economics shifted when cheap petroleum became plentiful, the larger shows moved from the railways to the highways. By the 1950s, only a few major outfits travelled by rail.

Conklin Shows began to try out different means of advertising and promotion. Ray developed a series of publicity art and photo mats that could be given to newspapers to print from directly. Television was introduced to the North American public in 1939, at the New York World's Fair and the CNE, but radio remained at the height of its popularity. Having used it sporadically for many years, in 1940 for the first time the show advertised over radio in every town and city in which it played. They also began distributing ride rebate coupons through local merchants. Walter Hale, the Conklin press agent, was responsible for many of these innovations.

Although the Canadian military began to take over exhibition grounds across the country in 1940 and many fairs and exhibitions were cancelled, that year's CNE survived. Sharing its huge grounds with soldiers and sailors turned out to the advantage of Frolexland because the military men had money to spend and were in search of diversion, often with their sweethearts, before they shipped overseas. The first week was down because of rain, but attendance climbed to just under the 1938 mark and spending was way up. On the final Saturday, Frolexland scored what was claimed to be the best cash day recorded in the history of the exhibition. Patty reported an increase of $25,000 over the previous year, for a gross of nearly $170,000. The final account shows he had finally made money on an Ex, pocketing close to $5,000.[14]

The International Association of Fairs and Exhibitions held its 50th anniversary celebration at the convention in Chicago in December. On November 30, *Billboard* published a special issue with congratulatory addresses from President Roosevelt and Prime Minister Mackenzie King. One article noted that 60 million Americans gather annually at 2,200 events. The annual fair was big business and an American institution, but the United States had "no fair approaching the CNE in attendance." Conklin Shows bought a full-page spread, which works the refrain of "Faith." It begins by attributing the success of the International Association of Fairs and Expositions in its 50th year to faith, then adroitly transfers the quality to those supporting Conklin Shows: "It was FAITH ... in J. W. Conklin that rewards him with his fifth consecutive contract to assemble and produce 'FROL-EX-LAND' at the C.N.E. in 1941." This would be the year that his faith in himself would be justified.

The amusement industry in general and the carnival in particular needed the faith of the public and politicians that it had a place in life during wartime. The need for diversion was the rationale. Border regulations were one of the first war measures to hurt carnivals, as customs duties levied on American carnivals entering Canada were raised. Where once an entire carnival paid

Patty entering the Conklin office, c. 1940.

a blanket fee based on the number of railway cars or trucks it travelled on, now fees were charged against each ride, show, and concession. The new regulations had little effect on showmen coming from the United States to join Conklin Shows, since they only crossed the border once and paid the same as if they were coming with a big organization. "After carefully checking over the regulations," Patty said in the March 22 issue of *Billboard*, "I don't believe they are so bad. They will perhaps work a little hardship on a carnival or circus coming into Canada for a period of less than a month." The United States was maintaining its official neutrality toward the war in Europe, which justified Canada's change in border policy. A little jingoism in the treatment of traffic from the United States might work in Patty's favour by reducing the number of shows competing for Canadian events.

Patty's equanimity about the new regulations comes into focus with the award to Conklin Shows in January 1941 of the western Canadian A circuit, which included the Calgary Stampede and exhibitions in Edmonton, Regina, and Saskatoon. Royal American's fee of $1,000 to cover the five-week circuit, which it had played for the previous seven years, would have exploded to almost $10,000 with the new fees. There were other reasons for Royal American to bow out, including restrictions on the size of carnival trains crossing the border and the patriotic angle. The Western Canada Exhibitions Association had decided to award amusement contracts to Canadian interests whenever possible. Conklin want ads in this period specify that preference would be given to Canadian operators. Also in January, CNE officials laid aside uncertainty about the 1941 event and planned an advertising program to attract visitors from the United States. With Royal American out of the way, Conklin Shows controlled all the major Canadian exhibitions from Edmonton to Quebec City. It kept the A circuit until the war ended.

Rumours that Patty would get the A circuit had been circulating for a year and a half. Beyond his adopted Canadian colours and the border restrictions, the success of his management of Frolexland at the CNE was cited. The midway for the western fairs would be based on the same pattern as the CNE's and called Frolicland. London had planned to use the Frolicland model in 1940, but the fair had been cancelled. Now London and Ottawa, both big fairs, announced they would reopen for 1941 with Conklin midways. In a February want ad seeking staff and attractions, Conklin Shows listed Ottawa's Central Canada Exhibition as part of its route, apparently prematurely, as World of Mirth ended up playing a reduced version of it. The plans for the London fair eventually fell through as well, although not until August.

Skeptics thought Conklin Shows could never match Royal American's success in the West. Patty had an "idea carnival," a suitcase show that would turn into a nightmare. He did not own enough equipment to supply the A circuit. Patty acknowledged the skepticism and moved to address it. Want ads for the show asked for attractions of every kind. On the West Coast, he bought a new Spitfire ride, a Fly-O-Plane, and a Moon Rocket. He signed a deal with Harry

Ornamental entrance gate for Frolicland, early 1940s.

Illions to take the Maynes–Illions rides west and bought a new Caterpillar. He doubled the show train from 20 cars to 40, and had Ray design nine new show fronts, including one for a water show. The construction of attractions at the Brantford quarters continued after the show opener in Hamilton in early May, but the show consistently mounted an impressive lineup, which grew as the season gained momentum. Patty built his dream carnival and confounded all doubters, running both the A circuit and the CNE with consummate success.

Even the spring still dates in Ontario exceeded expectations. With arma-ments production and soldiers' pay, the economy was booming. The Conklins brought out five new shows, seven new rides, and other equipment for the first spot in the West, a still date in Winnipeg. Much of the equipment was only ready 20 hours before its arrival in the city. Patty was visibly relieved when he saw it all in the air for the first time. He claimed to have tripled the show's earning power. He needed 56 rail cars to carry 18 rides, 17 shows, and untold numbers of concessions. He had done a tremendous job of expanding his show in a short period to meet the demands of all the fairs and exhibitions he had booked. Without competition from any major U.S. company, for the first time Conklin Shows was by far the biggest carnival travelling in Canada.

The reaction at the Provincial Exhibition in Brandon, the next stop on the western route after Winnipeg, was overwhelmingly favourable and pre-figured Patty's ascendance at the subsequent exhibitions. Midway grosses throughout the western tour were up from 15 to 20 percent over the previous year. Various reasons were advanced for the success of Conklin Shows' debut on the A circuit, including that "the public has found the new rides and shows a decided change.... Spending, too, has been free, with military men contributing heavily. The All-Canadian angle, prominent in all advertising and publicity, was a factor in winning public support and confidence."[15] Carl Sedlmayr's bemusement during his visit to Frolicland in Regina was palpable, while Patty could laugh at the skeptics. The publication of the "Carnival King" article in *Maclean's* in July crowned his western triumph and pre-eminence over all competitors.

Returning east, Patty predicted that the CNE's 1941 grosses would exceed any seen for the past 12 years. The CNE directors predicted that attendance would top two million.[16] Opening day attendance set a record of 215,000 and the million mark was passed halfway through the run. The crowds lavishly emptied their pockets and Patty claimed that Frolexland grosses were running 50 percent over the previous year.[17] The Aquacade, with seating expanded to 2,000, was operating at capacity. He declared in the September 13 *Billboard* that "the public is joy-minded, hoping to forget the war." At the close, with an official paid gate of 1,839,000, CNE president John Miller said he "was confident that total attendance had been greatest in history, probably 2,100,000, including members of armed forces and thousands who entered in official parades."[18] Everyone agreed that business was the best since 1928, the record year. The midway gross topped $225,000, surpassing the previous year by $60,000.

The Ex's independent operators went on to other big exhibitions in the United States, and Conklin Shows finished the season with four more Ontario fairs and a return still date in Hamilton. The show's grosses for the season set records, but its net was affected by $125,000 in special war taxes, $35,000 of which came from the CNE. Although some staff members were spotted with "sizable bank rolls,"[19] Patty claimed they had been able to bank little of the money they saw:

> Our season was very good and surpassed our fondest ex-
> pectations, but in spite of the fact that we handled a tremen-
> dous amount of money, very little will stay with us, as the
> bulk will go for taxes of various kinds for war activities, and
> these we are happy to pay, as we feel the same as every other
> sane-thinking person does, that we may just as well pay our
> bill and do our bit now before it's too late.[20]

The war was turning out very well for Conklin Shows. As it drew on, the show would be forced to adapt, but Patty would continue to profit and put a patriotic spin on the fact.

IMPROVISATION

Patty berates the three men standing before him. "What is wrong with you gazoonies, anyway? Can't you steal enough from the marks on the lineup, you gotta go clip from their fucking gardens?"

"Aw, Patty, we didn't think the Clem would even notice," one of them replies. "It was just a couple of friggin' cucumbers and tomatoes."

"He said you dug up his carrots and onions, too. What do you want that junk for, you on some kind of health kick with your vegetables or you just need a celery stick for your cocktails?"

"We were hungry and the cookhouse was closed and there wasn't any place else open," the vocal one protests. The other two try to get a read on their boss. Is he giving them the gears?

"That Alvin, his two kids, their friends and cousins and nephews, his wife and sister-in-law and all her family are all gonna come down and ride the rides all day for free tomorrow," Patty says. "Who is going to make up for that kind of paper?" His conviction seems to be slipping.

"Maybe he'll bring some carrots for the horses, then we won't have to pick 'em ourselves."

"Get outta here, ya punks," Patty barks.

★ ★ ★

The fall and winter of 1941–42 passed with the usual announcements from Conklin Shows. They signed on for an eighth Exposition Provinciale, a sixth CNE, a return to the Sherbrooke Exhibition, and a renewal of the western A circuit contract. One announcement was new: Conklin Shows had won the contract for the Central Canada Exhibition in Ottawa, at that time second only to the CNE among Ontario exhibitions.

At the showmen's convention in Chicago, in a speech on wartime carnival operations delivered to the American Carnival Association six days before the attack on Pearl Harbor on December 7, 1941, Patty enumerated all the extra war taxes and expenses from which he had suffered. He made little mention of fairs shut down because of the war, except to remark that some fairs cancelled in 1941 would be revived for the next season. The Ottawa and Sherbrooke exhibitions were among those he had in mind. By the time the speech was published in *Billboard* on December 27, the United States had entered the war, a turn of global events that would affect North American carnival showmen, as well as everyone else.

In January 1942, Elwood Hughes told showmen and delegates at the convention of the western Canadian fairs and exhibitions that the CNE had the full co-operation of the Department of National Defence in putting on the Ex that year. In March, the Conklin brothers toured the country to meet with fair boards, Patty in central Canada, Frank in the West. Both reported that conditions were good, the personnel at military camps were expected to provide extensive patronage, and everyone looked forward to another banner year.

Then, on April 18, the mayor of Toronto announced that after 63 years of continuous operations the CNE was to be cancelled for the duration of the war. Patty cursed the loss in private, but in his public pronouncements recovered quickly from the blow. For the first time in five years, he reported in *Billboard* on May 2, the full show would be able to play the Sherbrooke and

Quebec City exhibitions, the dates of which had coincided with those of the CNE. It was "a tribute to the business acumen of the Conklins" to have held on to these contracts with "possible cancellation of the CNE" in mind. They would also put on a war charity show in Toronto. Patty said that "despite the cancellation of the exhibition — it will work quite a hardship on a number of people and indirectly upon a few individual showmen ... we will do just as well playing these two other exhibition dates and the charity celebration at Toronto as we would playing the CNE." The independent ride and show operators who had flocked to Frolexland and had filled in his Quebec midways would be hurt, but the Conklin operation itself would not.

Season of 1942 and First Fair for Britain

After the Ontario still dates, the show made another triumphant wartime tour of the western A circuit. In Brandon, Patty announced the appointment of Bill Green, a Detroit newspaperman, as public relations director. Green would raise the show's profile in the press, developing its press releases and ensuring they appeared verbatim as news articles in the local papers. The show began in Ontario with 13 rides, nine shows, and 34 concessions, but by the time it entered the West it had 20 rides, 15 shows, and over 50 concessions on 58 rail cars. In Edmonton, an early morning fire destroyed seven games and their contents, valued at $3,500. Patty was not a suspect. Attendance and grosses across the A circuit were up again on the 1941 figures, the increase attributed to bumper crops, good weather, and full employment due to the wartime economy.

Meanwhile, as the engagement of the United States in the war deepened, some U.S. fairs were cancelled and severe restrictions on rail travel choked the ability of American shows to travel. The once mighty Royal American Shows played in a variety of vacant lots in and around Chicago during the dates of the western Canadian fairs. Carl Sedlmayr had the consolation of being the Showmen's League president that year, so at least he was able to stay close to league headquarters. Both Royal American and Beckmann & Gerety would remain in quarters the following year.

In the Conklin publicity for 1942, Green highlighted Terrell Jacobs's Wild Animal Circus, which Patty had signed in March. The press release stated that Jacobs had headlined for several seasons with the Ringling Bros. and Barnum & Bailey and the Hagenbeck–Wallace circuses, and now had his own two-ring show. Jacobs worked with 25 lions and tigers, and his wife, Dolly, had elephants. The show also featured a menagerie, aerialists, tumblers, clowns, jugglers, and acrobats. Green made sure that the circus was amply advertised and it consistently out-grossed all other shows. The Johnny J. Jones show had begun carrying the Clyde Beatty three-ring circus in 1940 and the outdoor entertainment press noted a general trend toward circus acts joining carnivals. Circuses were suffering a long decline and it looked as though the carnival industry would absorb them.

A circus on a carnival midway was not without its perils, however, and if Patty's contract with Terrell and Dolly Jacobs incorporated a commitment to control their performers, they would soon contravene it. That summer in Calgary, Patty had to face down one of Dolly's pachyderms. On an otherwise quiet afternoon — it might have been the unexpected storm, it might have been the argument Patty had with the handler — a big bull elephant was suddenly loose on the midway, with no one to handle him. Patty confronted the animal, waving his arms in the air, trying to calm it down. In response, it kicked over show fronts. The handler was found and persuaded to return to the show and pacify his charge. With the shortage of labour, the handler and the bull elephant, both subdued, remained with the show and were soon called on to lug iron to move the rides. Although Patty planned to take the Jacobs' circus out again the next year, the deal fell through, and it went with World of Mirth.

The Calgary Stampede was a memorable spot in 1942. It started to rain Friday night and continued all night and the next day, the temperature dropping to zero. All events were cancelled for Saturday and the midway did not even open, but still grossed $79.95 from the arcade. Nevertheless, the show was ahead on business over the previous year, but when they tried to tear down Saturday night they had to give up after three men were hospitalized owing to accidents in taking apart the rides in the heavy rain.

The press material exploited several war themes, including the attack on Pearl Harbor. Publicity for Aloha Land, a Hawaiian show with music and dancing girls, credited Princess Luana and Princess Ahi with movie and Broadway experience. Many of the performers, the press releases said, had relatives in the vicinity of Pearl Harbor or had come to North America just before the Japanese attack. Green also took advantage of the Battle of Britain in 1940 and the intense air offensive against Germany in 1942: "The rides this year emphasize the airmindedness of the nation. Practically all the principal rides give their thrills to patrons in the air."[21] The western papers provided reams of coverage taken straight from Green's press book.

Green also played up the show's efforts to provide good customer service. In an article Green supplied the Regina *Leader-Post*, published on July 27, he noted that the show had begun issuing employee identification cards that had "Patty Conklin's code" printed on the back. The code consisted of injunctions to be civil to patrons: "Never show your temper. Indulge in no sarcasm.... Keep unpleasant opinions to yourself.... Always use pleasant words. Take time to be polite.... Don't try to fool your caller — he may be a smart man." While the card's practical value was probably close to nil, getting it reported on in local newspapers realized its public relations value.

Patty needed all the good press Green could get him. In May the Sherbrooke Exhibition was cancelled again, on orders from Ottawa to turn the grounds over to the troops. In July the Ottawa Central Canada Exhibition was called off because of the army's intensifying use of the grounds. The Quebec Exposition Provinciale was the only major exhibition remaining in Ontario and Quebec.

Patty had been working on a war charity fair for Toronto since before the news broke in April of the suspension of the CNE. His original plan had been for a six-day event. At the beginning of August, the show announced a two-week "Fair for Britain" to run from August 31 to September 12. An advance staff of five Conklin employees had been in the city since mid-July handling promotions. All proceeds from the 10-cent gate would go to the Toronto *Evening Telegram*'s British War Victims' Fund. Working with his friends among the Toronto press corps, especially at the *Telegram*, Patty had offered to devote his war charity fair to their fund, and together they had taken the proposal to the Business Men's Council, which sponsored the event on behalf of its 27 businessmen's associations. Patty had put together a brilliant scheme, one that would let Conklin Shows, under the cloak of patriotic support for the war, continue to operate in the vacuum left by the CNE, while further ingratiating him with the Toronto press and businessmen. He was proving himself not only as a great impresario, but as an equally impressive improviser.

The Fair for Britain was laid out on seven acres in Riverside Park, close to downtown and well-served by public transit and the city's transportation network. A 5,000-seat stadium was built for pageants, musical events, and military displays, and live radio programs were broadcast daily from the stadium. The Ontario government set up exhibits in the tent Patty had bought for the dance pavilion at the CNE, and the Ontario premier and the mayor of Toronto opened the event. Patty and the Shriners played host to 1,200 disabled and orphaned children, as they had for years at the CNE, and the Labour Day parade, another CNE tradition, was brought to the fair.

Promotion was heavy and effective. When it was over, the Fair for Britain was described as the biggest outdoor event in North America that year, with an attendance of 347,000. It brought over $42,000 to the war victims' fund, the largest contribution by a single organization, including $2,000 collected from a midnight show, for which the performers were not paid, and $2,000

View of the Fair for Britain in Riverside Park from a hill outside the park, 1941.

donated by concessionaires. Conklin Shows grossed $124,000 and netted $14,450. More importantly, Patty had kept the show in operation, making money and providing profitable carnie jobs when other shows were shut down because of the war.

The Fair for Britain was another feather in Patty's well-plumed hat. In its September 12 issue, *Billboard* called it "the greatest 'non-fair' engagement in the modern history of carnivaldom" and "the most spectacular date of its kind ever held in the Dominion." Patty was credited with "promotional genius, imagination, general skill as a carnival impresario and a deep understanding of what human nature is composed of." American showmen were "advised to give close study to this Conklin cavalcade, for therein may lie the answer to what can be done when a fair is canceled." *Greater Show World*, another publication covering the outdoor amusement industry, also presented the Fair for Britain as an example for American showmen. The Montreal *Standard*'s weekend tabloid carried a photo spread on the fair on October 31, calling it a "miniature 'Canadian National Exhibition.'" It describes Conklin Shows as "the biggest Carnival in Canada, third largest of its kind in the world and second only to Ringling's Circus in the amount of rolling stock."

The Fair for Britain was featured in a special "Cavalcade of Fairs" section of *Billboard* on November 28, published to coincide with the showmen's conventions in Chicago. Under the title "Canada's 'Planned' Fair — A Success Story with a Moral," the event was again described as "perhaps the greatest fair-date promotion of all time." In an address to the International Association of Fairs and Expositions convention, published in *Billboard* on December 26, Patty stated that the Fair for Britain proved "conclusively that it is possible to stage an event similar to an exhibition without livestock, agriculture or farm machinery."

While spinning the patriotic angle, Patty revealed a deeper motivation for staging the fair: "Regardless of what the conditions may be we should make a sincere effort to carry on and keep the public amusement-and-exhibitions minded." The public's desire for distraction should be nurtured and treated as a right, which would authorize the showman's right to profit from that desire. He also shared the unofficial news that the Toronto Business Men's Council had asked him to put on a repeat performance. For Patty and his show, it was like old times in Vancouver with the Elks, only bigger and with a better alibi.

Season of 1943 and Second Fair for Britain

After returning from a conference with federal officials in Ottawa, Patty announced the second Fair for Britain early in March 1943. The dates were moved ahead to August 13–28 so that Conklin Shows could attend to its obligations with the Exposition Provinciale in Quebec City. Although everything about the fair was touted as bigger and better, the lineup was much the same as the previous year. Ernie and Len were exhibited for the last time before they parted. As before, each day of the fair had a theme and special events. On Mary Pickford Day, a new theme this year, tickets were sold for her birthplace bungalow in downtown Toronto. A rodeo and a circus were the new feature shows, the latter not booked until the beginning of August. The lord mayor of London, keeper of the British War Victims' Fund, opened the show from Mansion House, his combined residence and office in London, via a radio hook-up. Attendance at the 1943 fair topped 410,000 and the fund received $56,000.

Patty made money from the second Fair for Britain, too, although had he not acted quickly earlier in the spring, he might have had to cancel the entire 1943 season. In February he had planned for an 18-week tour, down from the 22 weeks of 1942. His talks with federal officials had gone well and while he anticipated some difficulties with railway transportation and labour shortages, he felt "more than confident that ... we will not have too much difficulty in operating this season."[22] His opening still date in Hamilton would begin May 31, three weeks later than usual. At the beginning of May, he was still expressing optimism about the coming season. Two weeks later, the federal transportation department issued an order banning the wartime use of all special trains and cars, including show trains. Patty, blindsided by the order, began contacting fair boards and told staff not to show up at winter quarters. He declared that the show would not go on the road in 1943. The western A circuit exhibitions announced they would carry on without a midway.

Meanwhile, Patty rushed to Ottawa to negotiate with federal government transportation officials, as a result of which he proclaimed in early June that Conklin Shows would persevere. His special train was out, he could only use 12 railway cars, they would be added on to freight trains, and the show would only have a 12-week season, but at least it would be able to play. He gutted the pie car, adding three tiers of bunks sleeping two each. He cut the show down to six rides, five shows, and 200 employees. Pete Kortes rejoined him with a sideshow and Jack Ray got a posing show, featuring female models who replicated poses from well-known art works, that was slapped together at the last minute. They would open in Brantford in the middle of June, skip the rest of the spring still dates, and head west at the end of the month for the A circuit exhibitions, minus Edmonton, which had been cancelled. The deal Patty had cut with transportation officials was not available to other shows. Wallace Brothers, for one, was unable to travel and had to renege on its contracts with the western B fairs.

Despite the show's reduced size, Patty claimed the western A circuit drew on a par with the previous season. The western exhibition managers were unanimous in their praise. The Fair for Britain was up slightly and the Exposition Provinciale set records with an attendance of over 200,000. The show's gross was only 17 percent behind 1942, which had been 20 percent ahead of 1941. Because of the diminished operations, profits were equal to the previous year's. He had discovered that a lean show could make as much money for him as a bigger show.

The smaller travelling show left Patty and Frank with rides to spare, and they found a new venue in which to deploy them: amusement parks. A Fly-O-Plane and Octopus went to Belmont Park in Montreal. Crystal Beach, outside Fort Erie, Ontario, took a Roll-O-Plane and three kiddie rides. An auto speedway, merry-go-round, and Ferris wheel ended up at Burlington Beach on the west end of Lake Ontario. And Toronto's Sunnyside Park got a Caterpillar and a funhouse. All these rides were up and running before the show's opening date. Patty said they kept some of their best rides for the A circuit fairs and still had enough "mechanical devices" in winter quarters "to frame a small park of our own."[23] Conklin Shows had entered big into the amusement park industry, where it would be a player for over 40 years.

Belmont Park had been opened in 1923 by Ernest Gauvreau and three business associates on a 12-acre farm they bought in what would become a suburb of Montreal. In 1936 Conklin Shows sold its five-year-old Lindy Loop to Belmont Park for $2,700. The next year, Patty sold his year-old Loop-O-Plane to a New York ride operator who booked rides at Belmont Park. Despite its draw as a thrill ride and the ease with which it could be moved, the Loop-O-Plane had caused Patty trouble, especially with its engine. The new owner continued to have problems but could not get Patty to reduce the price. The owner tried to sell the ride and Patty contemplated booking his own Rocket Plane at Belmont in its place. He also tried to book a number of other rides there. Rex Billings had managed the park since 1935, coming from a three-year stint as manager of Coney Island's Luna Park, preceded by 10 years as manager of Idora Park in Youngstown, Ohio. Fellow Americans in the Canadian outdoor amusement business, Patty and Rex became friends, but nothing concrete came of their friendship until 1943. The following year, Conklin Shows more than tripled its equipment in Belmont Park and became the park's biggest ride operator.

As the prospect of victory for the Allies in Europe grew, the show was finding other new directions to pursue. Early in 1944, Patty began to speak to the press about his postwar planning. Because of their mutual satisfaction with each other and that season's Exposition Provinciale, he and Emery Boucher signed a 10-year contract. Despite Patty's earlier remarks about French communities, the Quebec fair, an eight-day event since 1942, had given Conklin Shows higher grosses in 1943 than any fair before, except for the CNE.

Patty praised Boucher's "creditable ideals and constructive methods," an example of which was the extended contract that Patty announced in January 1944.[24] He hinted that similar deals were in the offing and the next month announced a five-year contract with Sherbrooke. Contracts of this length were another Conklin innovation in the carnival industry, these first examples enabled by the absence of regulation over the fair industry in Quebec. The contracts gave Patty leverage, both with other shows to whom he could offer assistance and so keep within his sphere of influence, and with other fair boards that would feel more secure getting into arrangements first proven by their peers.

Seasons of 1944 and 1945

The show played much the same trimmed-down route in 1944 as the previous year, adding a nine-day still in Hamilton at the beginning of the season and switching the Lindsay fair for the Kingston fair at the end. The show's one major loss was what would have been the third annual Fair for Britain. An article in *Billboard* in the spring of 1944 had implied it would return and the reasons for its demise are unclear. With the German bombing of London all but over, Italy out of the war, and plans for an Allied counter-offensive underway, Patty and his newspaper and business partners might have felt that a charity event for British war victims would no longer be a sure sell. He was now directing his energies toward the longer term. The Sherbrooke fair, back on the circuit after a two-year hiatus, was one such long-term commitment and its dates partly overlapped with what would have been the Fair for Britain dates.

A 10-day still date in Kitchener in central southwestern Ontario filled in the rest of the gap left by the Toronto event. They located on a largely vacant street not far from downtown. Despite a profitable western tour, one night in Kitchener a few staff members, perhaps looking to economize or just because the opportunity presented itself, plundered the garden of a nearby residence. When Patty found out, he placated the homeowner with ride tickets for his entire family.

Patty's plans for the Sherbrooke and Quebec City events showed foresight and help account for the long-term contracts. Before the 1944 Exposition Provinciale, the show built four permanent buildings on the Quebec City grounds and paved the midway, a first for North America. The next spring, he enticed the management of the Sherbrooke fair with the same treatment and got five years added to the four remaining in the show's contract.

The D-Day invasion having been launched the week before the show's opening in Brantford, Patty pressed other fair boards and associations to fall in with the "big ideas" of his "post-war planning."[25] He met with the Western Canada Exhibitions Association in July and tried to sell them on paving the midways for all the A circuit events. The Winnipeg Lions Club signed a five-year contract in 1945, based on the show's agreement to "build the free attractions and exhibits so that it will be more than a mere still date, and ...

make extensive ground repairs."[26] Hughes and Patty were full of ideas for the postwar CNE, including the prospect of turning it into a year-round amusement park.

The 1944 season, the show once more on 12 rail cars, went off well, with the usual string of announcements from each fair of higher grosses than the year before. The Exposition Provinciale immediately preceded the historic meeting of Franklin Roosevelt and Winston Churchill in Quebec City to plan the Allied offensive and postwar clean-up in Europe. The show's arrival was delayed by special trains for the conference, but "towards the end of the fair great interest was manifested in the war conference and many notables on hand visited the exhibition." Patty and Boucher had come up with the theme of "post-war planning" for the fair. The paved midway was credited with saving the fair from heavy rains that fell during its dates, and midway receipts were 32 percent higher than the previous year.

The war in Europe ended in May 1945. The war in the Pacific continued, however, and Patty could make no significant changes for the coming season, so he followed the pattern of the previous two. He added an extra week to Winnipeg to fully exploit its new pavement. Edmonton, after a two-year break, was back in the fold and registered a 50 percent increase since its last exhibition. The Conklin brothers continued to run seven rides at Belmont Park, four at Crystal Beach, and two at Sunnyside Park. The optimism inspired by the imminent peace contributed to the public's willingness to increase the grosses of all the Conklin operations.

Frank shared in his brother's innovations, but also branched out on his own.[27] An inveterate gambler on the horses, while lying in his sanatorium bed one winter night in the late 1930s, he conceived of an idea to turn his habit into a business. At one of the show's dates in Winnipeg, he and Patty met R.L. "Jim" Speers, a feed and grain entrepreneur who had moved from Toronto to Winnipeg and become the dean of thoroughbred racing in the West. Speers took them to his breeding farm outside St. Boniface and Frank was struck by the possibilities.

He began visiting stables across the country, studying equine bloodlines and buying horses, or parts of them. In 1943 he bought a farmhouse and 85 acres of land outside Brantford and near Patty, and began breeding thoroughbreds, starting with three blue-blood broodmares. He bought stock during the wartime racing slump, mainly from Kentucky. Within two years he had 16 thoroughbred mares, six Belgian broodmares, and a herd of 100 Hereford cattle. Calling his operation Midway Farm, Frank brought to Canada new types of feed and other new methods developed in the United States. His horses were soon winning at Ontario tracks and competitions at the CNE, and he was raising foals for sale. He began to form friendships with other breeders and powerful businessmen outside of the carnival industry. Patty thought Frank too honest to succeed in the horse business and said he would not own anything that had to be fed in winter.

By the end of the Second World War, the Conklin brothers had diversified their interests. They had proven their ability to improvise and succeed in difficult times. They were no longer reliant on still dates and would soon jettison them altogether. They were calling the shots with fair boards that wanted to benefit from a Conklin midway and with shows that were happy to benefit from the Conklin aura. Many in the industry wondered what the brothers would do once peacetime began in earnest.

LEAVING THE BUSINESS

The Moon Rocket sits in the middle of a downtown Hamilton intersection on Dominion Day. The ride is tilted slightly at the brownstone city hall on the corner, the word "Centennial" arched around the building's main entrance. The city building with its bell and tower has dominated this corner for over 50 years while the city has grown around it. The ride landed the day before and is carrying passengers for only its second time. It backs up tight against some low commercial buildings with Tudor upper stories, British flags, and one incongruous American flag.

The glittering Moon Rocket spins its passengers at high speeds, overshadowing the sedate merry-go-round tucked underneath it. There was no other place to locate the little painted horses. A Ferris wheel occupies the next intersection, marking the spot where traffic is blocked off, with novelty stands and ticket booths scattered along the paved street.

The Hamilton store owners are closed for the holiday and will not see much trade over the coming week of the city's centennial celebrations.

The carnie ham wheels, count stores, and gaffed games, and Red Cohn's bingo are doing wonderful business. The sidewalks and narrow passages between the machines and stick joints are crowded with steel workers, local farmers, store clerks and their families, recently decommissioned soldiers still in uniform, and children running loose. Many in the crowd have money to spend.

During the day, the sun shines and women and children stroll the midway, but late in the afternoon men and teenagers begin to dominate. They collect on the steps of city hall and the courthouse lawn, smoke, ogle girls, and sip from their flasks. As the evening wears on, the crowd gets more excitable, the rides run loud and constant, the games agents become more brazen, and the women on the bally platform show more skin. The odd yell breaks through the din, as does the occasional smash of glass.

The carnie crew has only been back in action for a week. Many of them are new to working midways and they can't always control the crowd. Frank and the office staff are kept busy putting down hey rubes. Patty takes some of the city councillors back to his trailer on the other side of the market square for a drink. They enjoy his liquor and declare their support for his show against their colleagues who have already expressed outrage over the desecration of city property.

Patty will spend the coming week dealing with city officials, adjusting the location of some of the joints, watching his new equipment run, overseeing its fine tuning, and adding up the grosses. He knows they will get through the week and do well, but he also knows they have burned this town and will never play it again.

★　★　★

Another profile of Patty appeared in *Liberty*, a Canadian version of a popular American weekly, on September 22, 1945. It made much of his integrity and self-effacement and contained variations on the usual stories he told. He gave his age as 47 — five years short of the mark — and said he had been an orphan at 14. He retailed the story that his nickname came from his trait of standing pat on deals, and he relished the attribution to him of Irish wit. Explaining that the title "Carnival King of Canada" originated with his first CNE, the article said he had paid over a million dollars in taxes, charitable grants, and fees to agricultural societies over the past four years. It noted, however, that Conklin Shows' season had been reduced since the beginning of the war from seven months to four. The article ends with a return to the peanut theme threaded throughout, quoting Patty: "I started selling peanuts and I keep thinking I'd like to do it again." He had come a long way from his peanut-selling days. Would retirement from the carnival business be the next corner turned in the legend of Patty Conklin?

Rumours of Retirement

Some of the Conklin brothers' actions added substance to rumours they planned to abandon the business. Early in 1945, they advertised the sale of their entire stock of ride and show equipment. The ad lists all the rides operating in the three amusement parks, as well as the rides parked at Burlington Beach. It lists rides stored at the Exposition Provinciale and seven rides that were travelling with the show that year but would be available at the close of the season. They were selling 15 tents, including the tent used for the dance pavilion at the CNE and exhibits at the Fairs for Britain. They were selling generators, searchlights, and light towers; a complete penny arcade, an organ, and a calliope; a show front entrance, panel fronts for five sideshows, and 500 feet of miscellaneous panels; six steel rail cars and a "tremendous amount of Concession and Show Equipment."

Although the ad stated that the reason for selling the equipment was "to allow a greater scope of activity in our post-war plans," Patty immediately tried to quash rumours that they were calling it quits. "The main reason for the disposal of the equipment is that we have a large post-war plan in mind in connection with our shows and some of our other activities in the outdoor show field, but we don't want anyone to think for one minute that we are going out of the show business," he declared in the March 3 issue of *Billboard*, in which the ad appeared. He did not explain that he got a kick out of selling things off and was good at it.

The show succeeded in getting rid of some equipment and the brothers had second thoughts about selling other pieces. In total, they made $124,542 from the sale. When a shorter list was advertised in *Billboard* on May 26, Patty himself stoked the rumour mill. As soon after the war as new equipment was available, Conklin Shows would expand:

> It is too early to make a definite announcement as to our post-war plans, but you can say that we are definitely in the carnival business and intend to go ahead and develop our operations to the fullest extent after the war.
>
> I hope there will always be a Conklin Shows in Canada, and some day we might get around to building a strong unit for the United States, too.

The article mentions that American fair men were also considering "the possibilities of a more permanent type of midway in the post-war era." As early as 1934, Frank had asked the Canadian Department of National Revenue about the procedures they would have to follow to take their show into the United States.

The European war over, Emery Boucher announced that the Exposition Provinciale, in co-operation with the Conklins, would begin to operate throughout the summer, beginning in 1946. He connected the plan to the improvements made by the brothers: "This we had in mind ... when with their help, we paved all the midway zone last year at a cost of $15,000."[28] In an article in the December 1 issue of *Billboard* titled "Paved Midways Pay Off," Patty revealed that he "would like nothing better than to pave every midway area at each and every exhibition that we play." Boucher added a sidebar to the article in which his hyperbolic conclusion that a paved midway made "a big contribution to better, healthier conditions and to a better way of living" demonstrates why he and Patty got along so well. Elwood Hughes had been hinting for several years that the CNE would also become a summer-long amusement park. Enamoured with his success at existing parks, with the

reception his investments in capital works were getting, and with the five-
and 10-year contracts the show was winning, Patty must have been musing
about transforming all his major fairs into amusement parks.

Although he had wanted to pave the midways of the West, Conklin Shows
did not put in a bid for the A circuit in 1946. Patty attended the meeting of
the Western Canada Exhibitions Association, but he had tired of the gruel-
ling distances and wanted to avoid the humiliation of losing in competition
with Royal American. With the war over, Sedlmayr was coming back in force
to reclaim his old stomping grounds. Royal American took the route back
and retained it for the next 30 years, until cross-border politics returned it to
Conklin Shows.

Meanwhile, Patty's failure to bid on the A circuit fuelled speculation that
he planned to retire. He countered this by suggesting he would be back with a
tender in 1948. He pointed to the 10-year contracts he had with Leamington,
Lindsay, Belleville, and Kingston in Ontario, and Quebec City and Sherbrooke
in Quebec. The deals with the Ontario fairs had just been made at the convention in Toronto, as had an engagement to play the Hamilton centenary.
He soon had another 10-year contract, this one for the fair in Trois-Rivières,
Quebec.

The show warmed up with a still date in Brantford before opening on the
Dominion Day holiday in Hamilton. It then returned to quarters for six weeks
before beginning the short string of fairs in Ontario and Quebec. This eight-
week 1946 season was the shortest the show had ever played. They cut it to sev-
en weeks the following year, dropping the July holiday opening in Hamilton,
and continued with that length until 1954. The show kept its core route of
three Quebec and four Ontario fairs. These fairs all had paved midways or
soon would, and Patty talked about putting up permanent buildings. A concentrated season of A- and B-level fairs in Ontario and Quebec enabled the
show to travel less and make more money in a shorter period, although many
of its concessionaires, ride operators, and show producers needed a longer
season and were forced to work with other shows before and after the short
Conklin season to cover their nut.

Patty found the curtailed circuit to his liking. He could stay within a few
hours of his home, the only decent residence he had ever owned. His son was

by now a teenager who had been in boarding school most of his life and Patty wanted to spend more time with him. Edythe's drinking had become a problem, and he was forced to attend more to her. In his mid-50s, maybe he was getting a little soft, and maybe he felt he deserved a break after the hard life he had lived. Frank had his farm, his horses, and his wife to enjoy, all near Brantford, and breathing clean, country air relieved his tuberculosis-scarred lungs. The brothers could have retired, but that was not Patty's way, and he dragged Frank back into it.

Return of the King

With contracts in hand and money from the equipment sales, Patty was ready to go on a spending spree to build the show back up. He was at the top of the list for the ride manufacturers gearing up for the full production that peacetime allowed. He bought five rides from the Allan Herschell company, three from Eyerly Aircraft, and three more from other suppliers, as well as 20 new Scooter cars. Enough for an average-sized show, it was not enough. The show advertised for operators of rides, shows, and concessions to join its "post war expansion programme," entreating them to "get in on the ground floor!!!"[29] Flourishing its 10-year contracts with seven fairs, the show wanted operators to sign contracts of the same length with it.

The economy of Hamilton, that season's second spot, had boomed with its concentration of steel mills and other industries geared to the production of war material. In 1946, the flush war years over, there were serious strikes at three major plants, including one that forced employers to accept collective bargaining, but employment levels remained high. The Hamilton centennial event, synchronized with the first peacetime Dominion Day, was a big celebration. The committee booked free attractions and held a few dances with big bands. There were sporting competitions, a parade, and the first Miss Canada beauty pageant since a one-off event in 1923.

To do the centennial midway right, Patty brought in shows and rides from Bernard & Barry Shows of Toronto, for a total of 18 rides and six shows. Crowded into the main downtown streets, including the Market Square, adjacent to the city hall and the courthouse, the set-up was impressive, the bigger rides looming over the storefronts, the games and shows in the side streets. This arrangement was the show's first with Bernard & Barry, and one of the owners remarked on "a gross business that has staggered my imagination."[30] Neil Webb announced that Red Cohn's bingo topped its run at the previous year's Calgary Stampede by "more than 10 per cent." When the Hamilton event was over, Patty reported that the show would make more from it than it had at the 1945 Stampede, estimating that profits would exceed $50,000. The postwar boom had begun, and he would soon dwarf these figures.

Despite this impressive inauguration of his program to cultivate a Vancouver-of-the-East, Patty and the City of Hamilton soured on each other after the 1946 centennial. Without a paid gate, the city had no way of counting attendance or taking any money directly. Councillors felt that the show made too much, while the city got too little. Following its still date in 1945, the company had signed a 10-year contract with its auspices, the *Hamilton Spectator,* which sponsored the show to make money for its Fresh Air Fund. Such a contract for a still date was unusual and what portion of money earned would ever be spent sending kids to camp is unclear. The deal included arrangements with city officials for the use of park property to present the show.

On June 15, 1946, *Billboard* reported that during negotiations for the midway location, "There was a mild beef by some of the beauty stricken city fathers about the possibility of marring the courthouse lawn or shrubbery." Patty had been responsible for the location and layout of the midway, and used a section of the courthouse lawn. The Hamilton councillors' anxiety was borne out when the crowds flocking the midway spilled over onto city property. After the centennial event, the councillors decided that the city and its parks could do without Conklin Shows, and the *Spectator's* Fresh Air Fund would have to find another patron. Apart from damaging city property, Patty and his crew had been plying their usual routines and madly fleecing the marks. The 10-year contract was cancelled, and the show would not play the city again for 30 years.

The show continued to be warmly received throughout Quebec. It played Trois-Rivières and Sherbrooke, each the principal city in its region, with populations approaching 50,000, and the Exposition Provinciale in Quebec City.

On September 28, the Montreal *Standard*'s weekend tabloid carried a photo spread on the "Quebec Fair," claiming it drew a quarter of a million people and was "the biggest of its kind in the East." The caption to one photo notes that the "midway, with many permanent buildings, paved roads, is typical of development which is taking place in Fall Fairs as Conklins, too, become permanent." Other photos feature rides, shows, and "famed diver Alfie Phillips." The accompanying article equates the annual eastern Canadian "series of Fall Fairs" with the Conklin route, beginning in Quebec City and ending in Kingston. It concludes that "all the big eastern Canadian Fairs" boast "a Conklin Brothers midway which assures that everyone has a good time, even if they spend their last nickel getting it." The article's writer, Kenneth Johnstone, earned some ducats.

Wallace Brothers' Shows joined up with the Conklins for their seven fall fairs. Jimmy Sullivan and his crew had been playing the western B circuit while Patty and Frank relaxed, their equipment off the road and much of their staff with Sullivan to get in a longer season. Wallace Brothers travelled 2,900 miles from Prince Albert to Trois-Rivières to catch up with the Conklins. After Kingston, the Conklins' last fair at the end of September, Sullivan stayed out for another two. He claimed he had his best season ever. His show raised $2,000 for children whose carnie parents had been killed in a car accident the previous year, Patty and Frank contributing $1,500. Frank made sure the brothers' relationship with Sullivan was clear: "When James Patrick Sullivan is around his own Wallace Bros.' Shows of Canada he is the boss, but when he is around Conklin Shows he is the hi-striker operator."[31]

On September 21, two weeks after the show left Quebec in 1946, the Montreal *Standard* celebrated Patty with another "King of the Carnival" article. The author, Johnstone, would also write the effusive text for the photo spread on the Exposition Provinciale, and had written text to accompany a photo essay in July on the Hamilton centenary celebrations and one in August on Frank's horses. His feature article in the *Standard* opens on a note suitable to a legend: "It was 13 years ago that a young man rode out of the West in a shiny $5,000 Pierce Arrow to lay claim to the title of Canada's Carnival King." He points out Patty's recent domination of the western A circuit, "the top plum of the continent," and his capture of the Quebec circuit, "second richest plum," and the CNE, "topping it all like the cherry on the sundae."

Johnstone quotes "the boys" on rumours of Patty's retirement: "'He's getting soft,'" they say, "'He's smart. He's made his pile, and he's too old now to take it any longer.'" But Patty's liquidation sale was "just another spectacular move by a man whose thinking has remained consistently ten jumps ahead of the field." Having unloaded junk, he is "first on the list ... to take delivery of modern equipment just when fair officials and the public will be looking for something new and different." The public was, indeed, eager to experience the new technology that had been developed during the war and was now becoming available.

A bold red call-out in the article proclaims that Patty brought "a new slogan to fairs: 'Give the suckers a break.'" Johnstone tosses a bone to Rex Billings, manager of Montreal's Belmont Park, as one of the "pioneers in stressing the continuity of trade" to be gained through honest operations and clean grounds. Billings and Patty were partners, the article explains. Patty brought Billings's innovations to the carnival, paving midways and dealing "ruthlessly with the clipsters and petty thieves that have from earliest times made the carnie and circus their stamping grounds." He "imposes his own fanatically puritanical code of morals upon all who work for him," forbidding, for instance, any relations between carnies and townies. An employee who had taken a girl from town the year before was treated to Patty's "own system of rude and forthright justice," after which Patty "paid the hospital bill." He could impose a strict ethic on intramural sex because it did not interest him, and he could not make money from it.

Without explicitly connecting the two, Johnstone remarks that "permanent patronage ... pays off better dividends than the old scalp-'em system" and that the new riding devices require "heavy initial investment." He reveals no irony when he lauds Patty's beginnings selling bags of peanuts full of nothing but shells. How could anyone fault a conniving street kid who, becoming a successful businessman, turns to honesty as a better business principle? He concludes that, "after all, the Conklin way is usually the right way. Or how would they have Canada's lucrative country fair and exhibition business tied up in such a neat little bundle?" The Conklin way, the Conklin code, the Conklin method — Patty's practices had gained mythic proportions.

The rumour of Patty's retirement from the business persisted, but after talking to him Johnstone did not believe it: "Though at this date the announcement has not been officially made, ten will get you a hundred that after all those heavy consultations between Patty and CNE Boss Elwood Hughes this year, it will be Conklin Shows that will have the Midway responsibility for the re-opening Toronto Exhibition in 1947." He also predicted that the arrangement would be based on a 10-year contract. About the Quebec and western circuits he asserted that "Patty is not yielding an inch in the strenuous struggle to remain top man." Although Johnstone ignored the fact that the Conklins had given up the western A circuit, the prescience of his other predictions could only derive from an inside scoop.

The Ex Marks the Spot

(1946–1952)

The Conklin brothers built a comfortable routine in the first years of the post-war boom and refined it during the following decade. They gave up the West and kept rides and games at amusement parks, long-term contracts with major Ontario and Quebec fairs and, the linchpin, a lock on the midway of the CNE. Company managers operated the equipment at the parks and Frank looked after the fairs, assisted by Jimmy Sullivan, who still had a western route. Patty took the CNE under his personal purview, building permanent attractions and grosses, and sealing the reputation of the Ex as the world's largest annual outdoor exhibition and his own reputation as its presiding genie. Everyone associated with the show prospered, especially the Conklins.

THE EVOLUTION OF AMUSEMENT PARKS

A couple and their two young boys board the streetcar rolling out of town. Only the children get seats, and the older one hangs his head out the window. The streetcar travels through the Montreal suburbs, rattles under a railway bridge and through farm fields, and finally reaches the last station.

The children, stupefied by the long trip into the country, stumble from the car and are carried by the crowd purposefully moving down the road.

Their pulse quickens as they smell the diesel and the popcorn, hear the peel of tinny music, feel the low rumble of machinery, and glimpse the Ferris wheel and tall wooden struts of the roller coaster through the trees.

Their excitement grows and even the father picks up his step as they walk the block and a half to the entrance. They are funnelled with the crowd through the gates, straight into the line for the Cyclone, Belmont Park's giant roller coaster. The children are terrified as they wait in line, watching the cars being pulled up the long track and then released to plunge down the slope through the trees and toward the river.

When they get to the head of the line, they wave to their mother and cling to their father, who will chaperone them on the ride. It begins with a blur of track and noise and wind and trees, followed by panic as they drop straight down toward the water, the cars tilting precariously around the corners. Yanked through the turns, they catch their breath when the coaster climbs the hills. They beg for it to be over, and yet it is over too soon.

They go on other thrill rides with their father and he takes them one at a time on the bumper cars, until he tires of the lineups and their mother takes over on the water scooter, then the merry-go-round. She is nearly at peace under the umbrella top of the slowly turning carousel, on a bench behind her children, watching them gently rise and fall on the brightly painted wooden ponies.

The father throws some balls at a few games and lets the children play the fish pond. The boys each win a trinket and think they have done well, resigned to leaving behind the mangy stuffed animals that hang before them.

They come upon a garishly coloured plaster figure in a glass case that laughs hysterically. They hold tight to their mother's hands as they go in, but the funhouse is bewildering and disorienting. When they come out, the father has had enough and finds a bench under the trees on which to sit and smoke. The mother takes them to get ice cream.

They wander the grounds and come to rest in a picnic area at a table lined up with dozens of other tables. They eat cold hot dogs and soggy *patates frites*, and drink watery pink lemonade.

Finally, it is time to return to the city. The boys fall asleep on the streetcar as the sun lowers in a haze over the fields. The mother looks out the window. The father thinks of the money he has spent and his return to work tomorrow.

★   ★   ★

Amusement park owners had been experimenting since the 1920s, trying to identify the conditions upon which they could build an outdoor entertainment industry for the multitudes.[1] Eventually, they discovered they could make their parks exciting enough to appeal to a mass audience, while respectable enough to offend no more than a puritanical minority. To achieve this balance, they had to turn their backs on any affiliation with the male "sporting" element, their initial clientele, and promote their parks as clean entertainment for the whole family. Alcohol was not served at parks until much later in the century.

Amusement parks belonged to no particular social group or class. They were enclosed playgrounds, isolated from the demands of everyday life, and their isolation created a space within which sideshows and an array of outré amusements acquired a thin sheen of respectability. In this liminal setting, the shows drew patrons to their risqué attractions under the guise of education, the games convinced players they could buy a chance at big prizes for little money, and the rides threw sweethearts together in ways that were unseemly anywhere else.

A newly emergent urban public, largely white-collar and all white, had leisure time and money to spend. Members of this public, many of them veterans, had not had opportunities to become well educated or refined, so the parks appealed to them on an elemental level. They had gained a week or two of summer vacation and were being conditioned to do something special with this time off, something on which to spend their meagre savings, but they could not afford a trip to Europe or a cottage in the Kawarthas. Relatively cheap parks on the outskirts of the city, where the electric trolley lines would carry them, imperfectly satisfied their growing desire for release from routine. Technological marvels like huge roller coasters, Ferris wheels, and dazzling fireworks displays increased the sense of transport from the everyday, as did the exotic sideshows and even the shady games agents.

The crowd at a thriving park fed its constituents' sense of belonging to a larger social whole, a new public of pleasure seekers cutting across social divisions. This new civic space was provided by and for commercial interests, but these interests were as yet dispersed, local, and low profile. Continent-spanning conglomerates, like the future Conklin shows, were only beginning to establish their hold over the amusement park branch of the outdoor entertainment industry.

The Concept of Kiddieland

Nowhere is the appeal of amusement parks to the family trade more apparent than in the evolution of the concept of kiddieland. Children's days had been promoted at fairs since the 1930s. Carnival company and amusement park owners began developing kiddielands in the late 1940s. A 1948 *Billboard* survey revealed that amusement park operators were buying — or trying to buy — large numbers of children's rides. Park owners were told by the secretary of their association that "the child is the greatest asset" of their business and they should promote ideas to bring kids to their parks.[2] The trade papers carried extensive discussion of kiddielands, including feature articles on how to set them up and run them.

A *Billboard* article on December 6, 1947, provides the explanation for the proliferation of kiddielands: "There are millions more children in the world today than ever before and ... the child is becoming an ever-bigger factor in our economic system." The burgeoning suburban masses seeking diversion included large numbers of children, and the outdoor wing of the entertainment industry was among the first to exploit the potential of catering to children as a separate market. In retrospect obvious, this new market was recognized only with the postwar baby boom.

Kiddieland had become synonymous with the amusement park by the mid-1950s, when a Chicago couple, Arthur and Ann Fritz, tried to claim exclusive use of the term by filing an injunction against two other area parks. The Fritzes asserted that they had spent large sums over a 13-year period in advertising their park as Kiddieland. Their petition claimed that "the name has become a symbol for a children's amusement park and is identified in the minds of a substantial number of the public with the plaintiff's park."[3] On June 24, 1950, three months after reporting on the Fritzes' petition, *Billboard* printed a photo of their suburban Melrose Park site on its front page with this caption: "When Art Fritz opened Chicago's first Kiddieland 20 years ago, he did not realize the ultimate scope of the movement he was helping to pioneer. Today, kiddie parks are the fastest growing phase of outdoor showbusiness and Fritz's Kiddieland is one of Chi's largest and most popular." The term had gained too broad a currency for the Fritzes to win their suit.

Patty's Playland at the 1937 CNE might have been the first kiddieland at a fair or exhibition. In 1938 he announced in *Billboard*'s November 19 issue that next year's CNE would have "the Most Pretentious and Beautiful Kiddieland Ever Presented." He received no recognition for this innovation. When members of the International Association of Fairs and Exhibitions were told at their convention 10 years later that kiddielands were a must, the CNE was not cited as a trendsetter. Owners of the Amusement Corporation of America seem to have thought they were introducing something new when they announced that they would bring out a touring kiddieland in 1950. With interests in both the amusement park and carnival businesses, Conklin Shows was one of the pioneers of travelling kiddielands.

Under the management of Rex Billings, Belmont Park outside of Montreal became the premier amusement park for Conklin Shows' activities, which included developing the park's kiddieland. By 1945, the show's third year in the park, they had two Ferris wheels, and Caterpillar, Spitfire, Octopus, Fly-O-Plane, and Moon Rocket rides there. The following year they had eight adult rides and set up the park's first children's section with five new miniature rides. Because of postwar shortages, they had been unable to buy equipment from manufacturers, and so the Conklin winter quarters crew built their own kiddie rides. By 1947 the Conklins were the largest ride operators at Belmont, with 13 of the 25 rides in the park. In 1949 they added brand-name kiddie rides — a roller coaster and a boat ride from the Allan Herschell Company — by which time the industry was recognizing the park's kiddieland as an attraction in itself.

The Conklins' Engagement with Amusement Parks

The Conklins also helped Billings expand into adult attractions. Coney Island had established sideshows as a component of amusement parks, but the mix was never stable and it became more precarious as the parks groomed for the family trade. When Belmont Park opened in 1923, sideshows were no longer essential to amusement parks and Belmont was too small to host one. Pete Kortes, who had a sideshow with Conklin & Garrett through the latter half of the 1920s before moving on to other shows, became one of the best-known sideshow producers of his day. Kortes came back to Conklin Shows in 1943 and his sideshow played the Conklins' major exhibitions and with Wallace Brothers into the next decade. Through his connections with Patty, Kortes booked a sideshow at Belmont Park, starting in 1948, the first one to play the park. Later in the 1950s, Sam Alexander, another Conklin sideshow producer, ran one at Belmont and advertised in *Billboard* on January 5, 1959, for "Freaks — Working Acts Bally Runts and Bally Acts."

In the 1930s, another adaptation in the evolution of family amusement sites led to an emphasis on beaches, ballrooms, and picnic groves. The National Association of Amusement Parks, founded in 1918, became the National Association of Amusement Parks, Pools and Beaches. Company picnics, which could include hundreds of participants, became big business.

Belmont Park, located on Rivière des Prairies, had always had picnic grounds, a pool, and a marina. On June 23, 1945, *Billboard* reported that Belmont had "made vast strides in the last few years in the picnic business. Where a few years ago there were perhaps a half dozen picnics during the season, today the number goes far beyond 200."[4] A few months later, the Montreal *Standard* weekend magazine ran a photo essay on Belmont, titled "Summer Picnic." Kenneth Johnstone, the *Standard* writer who specialized in outdoor amusements and the Conklins, wrote the text. The following year, Johnstone attributed to Billings the innovations in honest operations and clean grounds that Patty had brought to the Quebec exhibitions.

Billings's development of Belmont included extensive beautification. Every year he repainted the equipment and in 1944 added new fronts by Jack Ray. Ray also reframed Conklin rides for the park. At the beginning of the

1945 season, Patty, commenting on how well his rides were doing, described Belmont as "one of the most beautiful parks in North America."[5] *Billboard* chimed in on June 23: "From a funspot with mud walks and poorly co-ordinated attractions, Belmont has developed year by year until today it justi-fies its title, 'Beautiful Belmont Park.' The midway has attractive, modernistic fronts; the grounds are tastefully landscaped, and buildings are painted in brilliant colors." The next year, Ray built more new fronts and four modernis-tic entrance towers for Belmont. One of the buildings burned soon after Ray finished it, but his front was saved and the towers stood.

Entrance towers and gates at amusement parks marked the separation of their "play" worlds from the "real" world, and helped visitors feel secure from undesirables. Billings also sought to assure his patrons that undesirable insects would not pester them by spraying the grounds with DDT. He con-trived a promotional campaign that offered two dollars in ride passes to any-one who found a mosquito in the park. For the 1949 season, he spent "some $150,000 ... on additions and improvements, including a new 60 by 100-foot Arcade building, a concessions building, with fronts by Ray, and the addition of asphalt paving, etc."[6] Billings saw the benefits of pavement in the Conklins' work with the Quebec fairs. They were laying down an outdoor entertainment infrastructure.

Billings's development of the park paid off. By 1946, the year Patty add-ed a kiddieland, Belmont Park had become Canada's largest and expected to substantially top the previous years' record attendance of more than a million. Patty and Billings had become close off-season friends, meeting up in Florida where Billings and his wife wintered and Patty and Edythe vacationed.

The Conklin brothers also developed a relationship with the owners of Crystal Beach, George Hall and his family from Buffalo. Begun in 1890 as part of a recreational community attached to Fort Erie, Ontario, at the head of the Niagara River, the park was bought in 1924 by the Crystal Beach Transit Company, a reminder of the days when amusement parks were set up by streetcar companies to give their passengers someplace to go. During its best years known as Buffalo's Coney Island, transit to the park for its U.S. visitors was via ferry service. George Hall, a candy concessionaire at the park since 1902, was the president of the transit company and general manager of the park, building it up by the mid-1940s to 20 rides, 30 games, a penny arcade, and a roller-skating rink. One of the company's first acts after buying the park was to build a huge dance hall, the Crystal Ballroom, with a floor that could hold 3,000 dancers. Hall's sons, Phil, Ed, and George Jr., assisted him and grew up to take over the business. The Halls would have a long association with the Conklins.

In 1943, the same year they first contributed to Belmont Park, the Conklins sent four rides to Crystal Beach. Patty commented on the park in the June 26 issue of *Billboard*: "I was very much attracted to the set-up there, particularly the picnic area. I think it is the finest I ever saw in Canada." As with Belmont Park, the picnic trade became increasingly important to Crystal Beach. Located on the shores of Lake Erie, its large beach with a bathing pavilion could accommodate 3,500. The picnic grove could seat 5,000. In 1946 Patty produced a kiddieland for the Halls: "Framed in a shaded tract with an imposing front entrance, are grouped a new Mangels' Kiddie Roto Whip, a new Allan Herschell Kiddie Ride, Aerial Swings, cage Ferris Wheel, a Kiddie Merry-Go-Round and a boat ride."[7] He added a Herschell kiddie coaster and boat ride, bought in 1949, at the same time as ones he bought for Belmont Park.

The Halls continued to improve their grounds. Once again, Ray was engaged to create his art deco fronts. George Hall claimed the park spent $675,000 for rides from 1946 to 1950. While development led to increased attendance and income at both Belmont and Crystal Beach, the latter saw greater relative growth. In the off-season, the Halls planned the construction of a new entrance to include two 40-foot glass brick towers with neon lighting effects.

Belmont Park had one advantage over Crystal Beach. Quebec provincial law permitted Sunday operations, while Ontario law did not. Since Sunday was the only day off for most retail workers, this had a significant impact on attendance. In the middle of the summer of 1948, several Ontario resorts challenged the Sunday closing law. At Port Stanley on Lake Erie and Grand Bend on Lake Huron, resort owners began to keep their amusement concessions open. The Ontario Crown attorney took action against Port Stanley early in August and the owners complained of discrimination. The following week other parks, including Crystal Beach, decided to defy the attorney general's threat to pros-ecute them. The authorities modified their warnings, saying that they would consider prosecution only where Sunday amusements went too far. The de facto permission would only be revoked if citizens complained. Here was the thin edge of the wedge prying open Sundays for commerce in staid Ontario.

The Conklins provided rides to two other parks affected by the Sunday closing laws, Sunnyside Beach Park in Toronto and Burlington Beach outside Hamilton. Swimming was always the main attraction at Sunnyside, since it was built on land reclaimed from Lake Ontario west of downtown to accom-modate water sports and the clubs and restaurants they spawned. Owned by the Toronto Harbour Commission, Sunnyside opened in 1922 with bathing pavilions, dance hall, seven rides, and 10 food concessions. Cool summers the following two years made the beach less attractive, so the commission built the Sunnyside Outdoor Natatorium for the 1925 season. Known as the "Sunnyside Tank," the heated pool was the largest outdoor pool in the world and could hold 2,000 swimmers. Sunnyside drew up to three million visitors a season, but only a portion of them patronized the midway. It went through a slump in the 1930s but revived again in the '40s. Roy Solmon's Sunnyside Amusement Company took over the lease on the midway.

When they redistributed their equipment in 1943, the Conklins booked a Caterpillar and a glasshouse into Sunnyside. They added a Hey-Dey in 1945. The next year they grouped the Caterpillar with a Spitfire, a Looper, and an Octopus in an area formerly occupied by a roller-skating rink. There was never a kiddieland at Sunnyside, but the grouping of these rides changed the com-plexion of the area in which they were located and proved to be a major at-traction. These four rides were stored in a building that burned in early 1947, for a loss estimated by Patty — perhaps inflated — of between $50,000 and $60,000. That season the park had only 10 rides.

When the Harbour Commission reclaimed the land at the lakeshore, they added an arterial road, Lake Shore Boulevard. The midway had been placed to the landward side of this road, but the pool, bathing pavilion, and dance hall were between the road and the lake. Lake Shore Boulevard was four in-creasingly busy lanes of traffic and two parking lanes. In the 1946 season, the city decided to prohibit parking on the road. Frank commented to *Billboard* on November 30: "The no-parking law, which was enforced late in the season, did not hurt the ride business, but it was tough on the food and drink fellows." The Toronto Board of Control rejected appeals to restore parking the following season.

Traffic and pedestrians at Sunnyside were a volatile mix. More and more cars made the area congested and dangerous. Patrons had to cross and re-cross two roads to get between the midway and the lakeside attractions. In 1948 a city traffic commission recommended that the parkland be turned over to a new expressway. By the early 1950s, all attractions leased through the Sunnyside Amusement Company were on a year-by-year lease. As other ride operators backed out, the Conklins took the opportunity to put in nine rides in 1950 and the next year had 12 of 17 rides in the park. Leases were not renewed after the 1955 season, and demolition of the park began late that year. Although Sunnyside Beach Park was gone in 1956, only the pool remaining, the Conklins were able to find a little patch of land amid the demolition and highway construction to set up a few rides. Managed by Patty's son, Jim, they were framed as a kiddieland, Sunnyside's one and only. An expressway would soon cover the entire area.

Burlington Beach was the last amusement park in which the Conklins planted rides in this period. Sited on a large sandbar across Hamilton Harbour at the end of Lake Ontario, it was opened by the Canada Amusement Company in 1903 with boat- and bathhouses, a playground, snack bars, and a funhouse. The area did well enough, and a Ferris wheel and carousel were added before the Great War. Another owner bought the park after the war, adding an open-air dance hall that doubled as a roller-skating rink. Other rides were added, but the park never became a substantial operation. The Conklins opened three old rides — an auto speedway, a merry-go-round, and a Ferris wheel — at Burlington Beach in the spring of 1943, taking advantage of the proximity to their winter quarters in Brantford to make a little more money from the equipment before scrapping or selling it. By 1950 the show had only two rides left in Burlington. The Conklins were not likely among the 47 concessionaires who in 1952 protested that they would be put out of business if the province supported local pressure to keep them closed on Sundays.

E.G. & J. Knapp Amusement Company was the last operator of the Burlington Beach park when it closed in 1978. Knapp had run penny arcades at Crystal Beach, Belmont Park, and other amusement parks since the 1940s. He might have taken over some of the aging Conklin equipment in the parks as the Conklins exited from the amusement park ride business. By the late 1940s, the Conklins were concentrating on games. Crystal Beach became a training ground for future Conklin executives. Jimmy Conklin, not yet out of private school, got his first midway experience running games there with friends from Ridley College. Alfie Phillips's son, Alfie Jr., got his first work with the Conklin organization running the bingo hall at Crystal Beach. The Conklins still had a ride or two in the parks until the 1980s, remaining to witness the demise of Belmont Park in 1983 and Crystal Beach in 1989.

THE POSTWAR ROAD SHOW

"Well Jimmy, what kinda season we gonna have this year?" Frank asks Sullivan.

"Well Frank, I think this is going to be a stupendous year for World's Finest. We got those new rides to bring the crowds in, and the joints and shows are all in tip-top shape. As long as we get the weather, we should do bang-up business. I think we won't go hungry next winter."

"How's your crew been behaving all spring?"

"Just the best, Frank, they've been behaving themselves very well. Ten Toes cut up a little in Sudbury, but I gave him a talking to and he's come to his senses. Marco brought in some new boys from Toronto and they're working out real well. They are becoming very accomplished thieves. We sure could've done without the weather we had though."

"Any heat scores?"

"Well, the aldermen in Kitchener didn't take well to the posing show, but that's only because they were pussy whipped. We couldn't give the miners of Noranda enough skin, we just packed 'em in. We had a hey rube in Windsor, but the boys looked after themselves, until the local constabulary showed up and cooled things down. Nothing serious, just the usual."

"That Looper going to make it through the season?"

"I don't know Frank. I gotta say, I'm sick of throwing money at it. You could've told me when I bought it that the motor was shot."

"I didn't want to spoil your fun. You only paid what it's worth."

"I guess so, Frank, since you and Patty call the shots."

"We give you a chance to make a living, what else you want?"

"A little respect maybe."

"Now Jimmy, for shanty Irish, you got a big head."

"Is Patty going to come and visit?"

"He might. He's pretty busy."

"I'd like to get down there and see what you boys got in Toronto. I heard you got a few new pieces that'll make a splash. I guess I'll have to read about it in *Billboard*, you won't cut me no slack."

"We need you down here, Jimmy."

★ ★ ★

At midcentury, a radio and newspaper reporter turned carnival press agent could assert that "the midway with its giddy rides and bedlam of noisy ballyhoo is an institution in this country. Here carnivals have outgrown the caravan stage and have become enterprises in which many millions of dollars are invested and which annually turn over millions of dollars."[8] Contrary to early predictions that it was a passing fad and despite persistent problems with its public, the carnival industry continued to thrive.

Rides Make a Midway

Before the spread of television, the midway brought the novel, the marvellous, and the bizarre to patrons who lived far from the big city. Farmers who still relied on horses as the motive force for their implements could come to the midway to experience examples of the latest technology. The Loop-O-Plane, designed by Eyerly Aircraft of Oregon in 1934, was one such wonder. Technological developments accelerated leading up to the Second World War, which saw the introduction of the Spitfire ride and various rides with "rocket" in their name.

Along with the clean family fun, postwar midway patrons of amusement parks and fairs wanted rides that reflected the new technologies developed during the war, which civilians had only glimpsed back home through newsreels. An article in *Billboard*'s "Outdoor Equipment Review" in 1947 is titled "Thrill Rides Make a Park." The article quotes an amusement park operator: "Before I invested in pig iron, I merely made a living." According to the article, park operators early on "realized that the American fun seekers wanted thrills and not stage productions." To become sites for mass entertainment, midways had to provide immediate, visceral excitement, nothing that required a contemplative or intellectual response. Ride technologies had to reflect, however distantly, the mechanical genius that had produced the atomic bomb and jet airplanes. The terrors of war were transmuted to the thrills of the midway.

What applied to amusement parks applied to travelling carnivals. Unfortunately for carnival owners, few new portable thrill rides were available immediately after the war. In the *Billboard* equipment review, another article summarized the situation in 1946: "Manufacturers couldn't begin to fill the orders, didn't have anything new to offer customers … and could only promise they'd do their best to have some new rides in 1947."[9] Although claiming that the situation had improved that year, the five new devices the article describes were, with one exception, kiddie rides or variations on existing rides. Even in 1947, few manufacturers were making immediate deliveries and many, especially the major companies, were not promising deliveries until the following year. Shortages of materials, particularly steel and aluminum, and of gas and electric motors, held manufacturers back. As materials became available, they continued to concentrate on the new and lucrative kiddie market, which they could satisfy with less risk and less capital outlay. Kiddie rides were cheaper to make and there were always buyers.

The Conklins also concentrated on kiddie rides for their park offerings but came out with one new adult ride in 1947 and helped inaugurate it at the CNE. Norman Bartlett, a respected ride builder who had gotten his start as a youngster in the 1920s designing devices in the backyard of the family home southwest of London, Ontario, produced the Hurricane, named on Edythe's suggestion. Bartlett turned over production of the smaller, portable version to the Allan Herschell Company, the biggest ride manufacturer at the time, and took charge of the larger model at his plant in Florida. The one at the CNE had to be removed for minor modifications but Patty pronounced it "the greatest thing of its kind that I have ever seen."[10] The only other Hurricane was set up at Coney Island, but it soon became a standard. Bartlett and Patty visited Belmont Park in the spring of 1948 to oversee installation of the first park model Hurricane in Canada. Patty was enhancing his reputation for picking out promising new rides.

The Conklins had indeed shown foresight after the war by selling well-used equipment and using the proceeds to buy new rides. With cash up front, they were able to take delivery of 11 new pieces in the spring of 1946 but continued to seek more. For their opening the next year at a still date in Hamilton, they were looking for additional rides. Patty inspected new rides at two manufacturers in Oregon in early 1948. For that season's opener, they were no longer trying to find independent ride operators to join them and in fact were selling more used rides. Combining their equipment with that of Wallace Brothers, they could boast 14 major and 11 children's rides for the travelling show. Because of Canadian trade protections, the Conklins had to get permission to import American rides but got it for the two major rides they managed to find for the 1949 season, as well as for the four new children's rides they added to the Belmont Park and Crystal Beach lineups.

Carnival companies accounted for two-thirds of ride purchases and amusement parks picked up the remainder. Demand remained high into 1949, but production by then could keep pace. Predictions that new thrill rides would flood the market were not being realized as manufacturers stuck with their tried-and-true models or brought out new variations of kiddie rides. Developing a new thrill ride could be expensive — the Bartlett Hurricane cost $100,000 before it reached production — and sales remained strong even without new models.

By early 1950, the ride industry had stabilized, supply meeting demand, although the children's segment continued to boom. Then the Korean War began in June and toward the end of the season manufacturers were warning of price increases of 10 percent and possible curtailment of production if the war continued. The prospect of renewed shortages stimulated buying and no new thrill rides were needed to bolster sales in 1951. The long-term outlook for ride production had dimmed once again. Two years into the Korean War, shortages were a reality, children's rides still dominated, and no new major rides appeared.

Rides were now fulfilling the function that sideshows once had, serving as attractions to bring people in to play the games. In a July 1945 article in *CIL Oval*, a chemical industry magazine, about the importance of colour to the midway, Patty says that "there are three basic elements which set the mood of the carnival customer, colour, light and music." Sideshows with their human oddities, colourful banners and lively ballys, along with the calliope, had once provided Patty's elements of attraction, but these were increasingly being supplied by rides and the marvels of technology.

The article notes that "a few of the riding devices in a carnival lack the capacity to operate at a profit, and are carried solely as attractions." The merry-go-round and Ferris wheel often did not pay for themselves, but as midway icons neither could be dispensed with. Grosses rose inexorably, usually in favour of the rides, although the serious money still came from the games. At the Calgary Stampede in 1945, the combined Conklin shows and rides grossed $59,016, while the games and food stands took $73,870.[11]

The rides were impervious to differences of language and culture, which could hurt the food stands and games. In contrast with Calgary, in Quebec City that same year the Conklin rides and shows hauled in $70,775, while the concessions only earned $49,410. Wallace Brothers had the majority of rides, shows, and concessions and had French-speaking staff. Sullivan and the Conklins hired francophone talkers for their shows in Quebec, but games agents were a special breed, staying with the show through the season, and their success depended on being able to engage in fluent, intimate conversation with the marks, which few of the Anglo agents could do.

Rides had become a significant capital investment and increasingly important on carnival company ledgers, accounting for a lot of overhead. Until 1949, ride tickets included a federal amusement tax of 15 percent, and in Quebec the show also had to collect a provincial tax. Ontario added a provincial tax when the federal tax was dropped. On the other hand, the games remained a legal liability because the agents were paid on a percentage basis and would try to get as much as they could extract, by whatever means, from their patrons. By the late 1940s, games at the parks and some of the carnivals were being forced to clean up their act.

Partnership with Sullivan

The Conklin business structure evolved to meet Patty's preferences and in response to circumstances. He increasingly devoted his energies to building up the back end of the midway, comprising the rides and shows, and Frank concentrated on the front end, especially the games. While most of the games and food concessions were managed by the show office, Frank had his own team of games agents who reported directly to him. It was this team he took to the Quebec and Ontario fairs. After the CNE reopened in 1947 and then the London Western Fair the next year, the Conklin rides and shows stayed in Ontario for these events, while Frank's agents joined Sullivan's show to play the Quebec exhibitions booked under the Conklin name. The Conklin rides and shows rejoined the travelling unit after the London fair. They named the combined Conklin–Wallace Brothers organization World's Finest Shows.

Sullivan bought equipment from the Conklins in the mid 1940s, partly to retain Frank's support in maintaining and developing his route. He bought a merry-go-round, a Loop-O-Plane, and twin Ferris wheels; two show fronts, a stage, and a number of tents; and three railway cars. Sullivan's 1946 season, when he returned to the western B circuit and played a solid route with the Conklins in Quebec and Ontario, was his biggest yet, and industry watchers observed that his show had made good money.

Sullivan became a personality in his own right. At the Showmen's League convention in December, he led the grand march at the banquet and ball, while the Conklins set an attendance record for the party in their suite afterward. Patty and Sullivan shared a railway compartment from Toronto to the meeting of the Canadian western fairs in Winnipeg in January 1947. Patty told a story in the issue of *Billboard* at the end of that month to prove that, although Sullivan was affluent enough to sign himself "J. Pierpont Sullivan," his polish was skin deep. In the stateroom they shared, a noise awoke Sullivan at 7 a.m. He yelled to Patty to "tell that donkey to cut out that 'eekee eekee' business." Patty informed his companion that it was a famous concert violinist. The title of the story, "Just Shanty Irish," was intended to apply to both him and Sullivan.

With the support of the Conklin organization, especially its investments in permanent buildings, plumbing, and pavement, Frank and Sullivan built up the Ontario fairs and Quebec exhibitions, based on their 10-year contracts with many of them. Sullivan's partnership in these events meant long-term prosperity for Wallace Brothers.

By 1948 Conklin Shows had stopped booking still dates altogether and eliminated the long layover that had stretched between their few spring stills and the fall fairs. They had sold most of their portable rides and no longer had the ability to play the larger fairs on their own, so they only kept dates for which World's Finest Shows could pitch in. Stills were not worth the bother. Unable to nail down reliable long-term contracts, Patty could not cover them with pavement, his favourite midway enhancement. He "pointed out that still dates have always been a headache in Canada as they must be played in cities that lack the population to support a major midway, and a day or two of rain can kick out any possibility of profit."[12]

Wallace Brothers took over many of the Conklin spring stills in south-western Ontario, including Brantford, Kitchener, Hamilton, and Windsor. Between the stills and the western B circuit, Wallace Brothers toured the mining towns of northern Quebec and Ontario, playing Noranda, Sault Ste. Marie, and Sudbury, territory the Conklins had played 10 years earlier. Somehow, they missed Timmins. As Sullivan discovered, Patty had cause to include weather among his reasons for giving up spring stills. Sullivan's show was often plagued with near-freezing temperatures and rain. Citing bad weather, he gave up his northern loop for the 1951 season — which Bernard & Barry promptly took over — and replaced it with stills in the West. Wallace Brothers could not escape the weather and other bad luck. The day after opening the B circuit in Lethbridge at the end of June 1951, they were covered in three inches of snow. Sullivan was convinced that a section of rail coming into

Noranda was jinxed, the show train derailing at the same spot in 1946 and 1947, wrecking railcars he had bought from the Conklins.

Wallace Brothers also took over some of the Conklins' methods and personnel. Sullivan had difficulty getting new adult rides after the war, so he started building his own kiddie attractions. In 1946, along with the Conklins' merry-go-round, he had a kiddie auto ride and pony track. The next year he added a children's boat ride and a train, and in 1948 he framed them all as a kiddieland. By 1950 Wallace Brothers had eight kiddie rides and, with a new front built by Ray, kiddieland proved to be one of its best back-end attractions.

Patty's coaching is behind the stance Sullivan took before the directors of the western Canada B circuit in 1949, relayed in the January 29 issue of *Billboard*: "His attitude was that he would be pleased to play it if granted a long-term contract; otherwise he would be forced to decline." Sullivan wrung from his B-circuit board a five-year contract for their fairs, the first time an entire western Canadian circuit had let out a contract for more than a year. The article announcing it describes it as "the most startling development." Patty "was active at the meeting, tho not a bidder," just there to back his buddy and surrogate.

Several Conklin showmen went over to the Sullivan company.[13] Jeanne and Johnny Branson had animal shows with the Conklins for 20 years up until 1946. They took them out with Wallace Brothers the next year and became Sullivan's main show producers. Eric "Alberta Slim" Edwards and his hillbilly show went with Sullivan for one year in 1946 and was back in 1950. By 1952 Slim had organized for Wallace Brothers a circus show with a baby elephant, performing bear, dog act, chimpanzee, trained horse, clown, and three cowboy singers.

Beyond Ray's services as a front designer, Sullivan got shows from him. Ray had tried his hand at producing posing shows with the Conklins on the western A circuit in 1944 and 1945. He married one of the women in his show. When the Conklins began to curtail their season, Ray's posing show and his new wildlife attraction went out with Sullivan. In 1950 he added a Hitler show, for a total of three shows with Wallace Brothers, and his girls were the top attraction in the West, although a ban on girl shows prevented him from playing them in Quebec.

Neil Webb, the Conklin secretary-treasurer, also had a presence with Wallace Brothers. He was helping Sullivan with his books when together they gave a newspaper interview in Yorkton, Saskatchewan. When Sullivan told the interviewer about a Roman sculpture of a carousel in a museum in New York, Webb remarked that "Sullivan has never been in a museum in his life, unless it was on a carnie midway."[14] Sullivan liked to put on airs, which the Conklin entourage delighted in deflating. Webb's Crystal Maze travelled with Wallace Brothers in 1948. In 1952 he had a shooting gallery and two children's rides. The operations of Ray and Webb illustrate the carnival practice of giving loyal office staff the chance to make money on the side.

Sullivan jumped at the opportunity to book the Aqua Frolics, the biggest show he got from the Conklins. Tommy McClure had managed the show in 1941 and 1942 at the CNE, with headliners Sam Howard, a champion American acrobatic diver, and Alf Phillips, the Canadian Olympic high diver. When the Conklins took it west for the A circuit, it was a top grosser and one of the few office-owned shows. After the cancellation of the CNE and the loss of the A circuit, McClure took the Aqua Frolics out with Sullivan. Phillips and McClure worked the CNE when it reopened and with Wallace Brothers until 1950, when Phillips took the show over and played only the Ex. Howard put on an independent water show on the Lake Ontario waterfront in 1947, competing with the CNE's Aqua Frolics.

The Conklins might have asked Sullivan to take some of their under-employed show producers with him when the CNE was cancelled and later when the Conklin season was shortened. By 1951 none of the Conklin side-shows were with Wallace Brothers, although the show continued to carry games owned by Conklin staff from which Frank took a cut.

The Conklins' Ontario fairs were B class, according to the prize money put up for agricultural competitions. Belleville and Kingston were small cities with populations in the 20,000 to 30,000 range, while Leamington and Lindsay were just under 10,000. These cities were centres for extensive farming or lumbering hinterlands, but by the mid-twentieth century they were in decline as economic and industrial activity concentrated in larger cities like Toronto, Windsor, Hamilton, and Oshawa.

From their beginnings, the agricultural exhibits that were the rationale for the Ontario fairs were increasingly eclipsed by the entertainment on offer. As in the West, agricultural purists persisted in seeing midways as irrelevant to their fairs and havens for shady characters, but business and industry representatives infiltrated the fair boards. They could not resist the attendance and income a large midway brought, and they yielded to Patty's pressure to sign long-term contracts.

For the first few years, the Ontario fairs occurred in September, after the Quebec exhibitions and the CNE. In 1948 Kingston and Belleville moved their dates to mid-August, overlapping with a fair in Valleyfield, Quebec, new to the Conklin route. Renfrew was also added as another World's Finest fall fair with a five-year contract in 1948. The Conklin–Wallace shows could play the fairs as the World's Finest combination if the fairs were in September. The Conklins had to play Belleville and Kingston alone when these fairs changed their dates. Kingston returned to its old spot on the calendar in 1950.

The 1950 season was typical of the arrangements between the Conklins and Sullivan. While Wallace Brothers played its still dates and the western B circuit, Conklin Shows stayed in the barn, although some Conklin agents and showmen toured with Sullivan. In mid-August, Frank took the Conklin equipment to Belleville to get the kinks worked out. After that fair, most of the Conklin rides and shows went to Toronto for the CNE, while Frank's agents and some of his equipment joined Wallace Brothers in Trois-Rivières and continued on to Sherbrooke and Quebec City. After the CNE, many of the rides, shows, and games from it returned to the United States, so the entire Conklin organization worked the London fair, which overlapped with Renfrew and Kingston. Wallace Brothers played Renfrew and Kingston — fairs booked under Conklin Shows — on its own. When the Quebec City, Toronto, and London exhibitions were over, Conklin Shows and Wallace Brothers recombined to play Lindsay and Leamington at the end of September. The Conklins then put their equipment away for the season, while Sullivan stayed out for the Simcoe fair, the buildings of which served as his winter quarters.

The take from the Ontario fairs in 1950 provides a benchmark for other years in the Conklin contracts with them. In Belleville, the shows and rides grossed $4,054 and the concessions $5,840. In Leamington and Renfrew, where Frank's three rides and two shows shared the midway with Sullivan's eight in each category, the Conklin shows and rides grossed $1,842 and $1,396, while the games made over $8,000 at each fair.[15]

Opening day in Leamington in 1950, when the rides and shows did not make the jump from Lindsay in time, illustrates the dependence of the games on the attractions. Without anything to draw marks to the midway, the games made a mere $205. The next day, a Tuesday, with the full show present, Frank's games pulled in $1,786. After expenses, Conklin Shows cleared between $4,500 and $6,500 from each of the three Ontario fairs. They paid the fair boards from $2,150 for Belleville to $3,800 for Lindsay. These figures come from the company's ledgers, but some financial transactions were not on the books.

Revenue for the Conklin & Garrett parent company from the rides and shows came after paying the fair boards their percentage, between 15 and 20 percent. The games operators paid a flat rate based on footage, as well as a premium for the right to operate controlled or gaffed games, the heat for which the office had to take. Frank booked his rides with Sullivan for 30 to 35 percent, keeping the 10 to 15 point difference between that and what the Conklins paid the fair boards. The Conklins also took percentages from Sullivan's net for his rides and shows. For the 1950 season, he gave the brothers almost $4,000 for Lindsay and over $3,000 each for Leamington and Renfrew, at the latter of which Conklin Shows was not even present. Kingston was a blank that year and Sullivan gave the Conklins $700 from his measly $2,000 take.

The Western Fair in London, which had not been held since 1939 when it had a Conklin midway, finally revived in 1948, signing the Conklins to another of their five-year contracts. Other shows had played still dates in London in the interim, including Bernard & Barry Shows in 1947. Wallace Brothers tried to book into London that year but were turned down because they followed Bernard & Barry too closely. London was not much of a carnival town, but the Western Fair could be good. Neither would Sullivan's boys get a shot at the city when the fair revived. The Conklins needed them to cover Renfrew, a fair they had actually signed to five years after London, but which overlapped with the Western Fair. While they did not get into the Western Fair, Wallace Brothers finally started getting London still dates in 1951.

Sullivan's crew got its best money when it played the Conklin exhibitions in Quebec, while all of Conklin Shows bore down on Toronto. They had to travel 2,300 miles to get from Prince Albert, Saskatchewan, to Trois-Rivières, Quebec, but it was worth their while. The pavement and buildings the Conklins had put into Quebec City and Sherbrooke paid off. According to Sullivan, the heavy rains they experienced at the provincial exhibition one week "proved the cash value of Patty Conklin's policy of paving the midways at his long-term contract stands."[16] The rain would have closed them had not "the paving drained so effectively," and they "were in action within a minute after the rain stopped." The provincial censors were one of the few drawbacks to the Quebec exhibitions, harassing the shows to ensure they were kept clean and prohibiting girl shows. They did, however, allow strong games to work.

Frank's games agents must have liked playing Quebec. In 1950 they grossed over $10,000 in both Trois-Rivières and Sherbrooke, and close to $20,000 in Quebec City. Profits for the Conklin concessions operating company were $5,657 for Trois-Rivières, $6,868 for Sherbrooke and $10,058 for Quebec City. The fair boards' net from World's Finest was $5,460, $4,575, and $12,700, respectively. From rides, shows, and games, Wallace Brothers netted roughly $25,000 for each of the two smaller fairs, and over $65,000 for the provincial exhibition. Sullivan paid the Conklins around $9,000 for the first two, and almost $25,000 for Quebec City.

Conklin Shows cultivated another significant date during this period. Winnipeg was a good city for midways, and in the early 1940s the show had played still dates there after the western A circuit. They had transferred the Winnipeg still date to Sullivan in 1946, and Royal American also played stills there in the late 1940s. Nevertheless, when the committee for Winnipeg's 75th anniversary in 1949 came to hand out the midway contract, they chose Conklin Shows. The event did not fit into anyone's route, but Patty managed to throw together a bunch of independent operators and got help from Sullivan.

The six-day anniversary event in early June proved profitable. Another Conklin–Wallace combined show, they had 16 adult and six kiddie rides and 14 shows, and as at the Hamilton centennial they were set up on the downtown streets. "Midway area," *Billboard* reported on June 25, "was so crowded at times that it was almost impossible for the Conklin org to accommodate would-be patrons despite the large array of rides and shows." They kept the midway open as late as 1:30 a.m. on some nights.

The celebration had good crowds despite the E.J. Casey Shows' midway set up outside of Winnipeg, in St. Vital, where Casey was based. Casey had become a show owner in 1935 at the age of 39, and played stills in Saskatchewan and Manitoba and parts of the C circuit. He had taken over Sullivan's B circuit route in 1943 and 1944 when Wallace Brothers had been unable to negotiate rail transportation into the West. Casey eventually had three units and spread into remote communities in northern Ontario, playing as many as 111 fairs, all of them small. In 1950 he opened an amusement park outside of Winnipeg to cut down on travel. Casey was a friend of the Conklins and Sullivan, and they were not bothered by his competition in Winnipeg.

For Winnipeg's first annual Red River Exhibition in 1952, the committee contracted independent attractions, including four Casey rides, but no major show. The exhibition ran for seven days in mid-June. Winnipeg remained the carnival mecca it had been when the Conklins first arrived there 30 years before. Wallace Brothers played a 12-day still that ended a week before the Red River Exhibition, and Royal American a 10-day still that overlapped with the end of it. Both shows reported record business at their still dates, probably because the independent midway at the exhibition was inferior.

Patty and Frank did not attend the western fairs meeting in Winnipeg early in 1952. At the meeting, Sullivan was given an expensive clock by the B circuit directors for his 14 years' association with them. Frank remained content with his route of seven or eight fairs in Ontario and Quebec and his horses, while Patty kept his eye on the CNE and the Western Fair, and went looking for the latest rides.

THE WORLD'S GREATEST FAIR REDUX

The sun shines and a light breeze blows as the athletes pose on the bally, girls in bright bathing suits surrounding men in red-and-white robes. The talker ends his spiel, the performers leave the stage, and the gathered crowd files up to the ticket booth.

Inside the arena, the talker begins by announcing the Fairbrother Sisters, four young women in matching bathing suits and caps. They dive gracefully into the pool from each of the four sides, joining up in the middle to perform their water ballet to music. It's hard for spectators in the lower bleachers to make out all their moves, but their heads arch out of the water in synchrony and their arms extend with their hands bent at odd angles. The crowd politely applauds.

As the announcer begins to introduce the divers, two clowns interrupt him with antics that take them to the lower diving platform. "Get off the platform!" he warns them. "You don't know what you're doing!"

They continue, chasing one another to the next level. One of them mocks a fall from the springboard and hangs with his arms and legs wrapped around it. The other performs a comic dive and surfaces with his hat still on. As they are chased from the deck, they manage to fall in the pool and splash patrons near the edge.

Next up, a series of male acrobatic divers. The crowd can barely follow the aerial rotations and revolutions, bodies flashing in the light before cutting cleanly into the water of the small tank. In the finale, two of them climb the paired towers to the springboards and launch into reverse two-and-a-half somersaults. Their synchronization is a little off, but no one notices and they get a huge hand.

A display of the season's swimwear fashions follows, exhibited on a bevy of bathing beauties. They demonstrate the utility of their attire by diving into the pool, climbing out to mount a dais at one side, and pulling off their bathing caps to let their tresses fall over wet shoulders glistening in the sun.

The clowns provide another interlude, as the acrobatic divers and the swimsuit models exit through the curtains to join another bally out front. After the announcer gets rid of the clowns, he begins the buildup to the star attraction. "Alfie Phillips, Olympic diver, winner ten times in a row of the British Empire high-diving championship and still undefeated, star performer with the Billy Rose Aquacade at the New York World's Fair and the Golden Gate Exhibition in San Francisco, performing a 90-foot dive into a five-foot deep tank!"

Silence falls as Alfie starts his climb to the board above. He has done this dive dozens of times, but he's tired and feels thick. He picks up energy from the crowd, the climb, the swaying ladder he can trust. He focuses on his ascent, while the spectators see him outlined against the brilliant summer sky, looking less athletic than they expected. Still, he is up there higher than the Ferris wheel and this is more about experience and daring than youth and strength.

He pauses, arms outstretched, at the end of the board. A cloud drifts by. He falls slowly over and plummets through the air. His entry into the tank is clean, yet explosive enough that no one can see what happens beneath the surface. After a suitable delay, he appears, standing on the bottom of the tank, arms outstretched to the cheering crowd.

Meanwhile, the tip has been turned once more, and the entire performance is set to begin again.

For a time, it looked like the Conklins would get in on the ground floor of two new amusement parks, one in Quebec City, the other in Toronto. Since their first contract with the Exposition Provinciale, it had grown into a fair as big as some of the western A circuit exhibitions. By the early 1950s, attendance climbed to over 300,000 for the 10-day event. A three-million-dollar sports arena was added to the grounds. Meanwhile, with its reopening in 1947, the CNE became, in effect, the Conklins' amusement park and annual world's fair wrapped up in one.

Emery Boucher's plans for an amusement park on the grounds of the Exposition Provinciale in 1946 were not fulfilled. Reiterating his intentions later that year, in the November 30 issue of *Billboard*, he said that this time "the details" had "been completed" with the Conklins. Frank reported that construction would begin after the 1947 fair to be ready for operation in 1948. They planned to build permanent structures, including a roller coaster designed by Joe McKee of Palisades Park, New Jersey, who had several others under his belt. The National Amusement Device Company was to build it under the supervision of Charles Paige. This was supposed to be part of a boom in coaster construction for which McKee and Paige already had three others underway. The coaster was never built, nor did Quebec City ever get its amusement park.

Amusement parks had always had large thrill rides built as permanent installations, but many portable rides were also first developed as stationary equipment in parks. The parks were known for their exhilarating, often dangerous, roller coasters and a good one could make a park. A 2,500-foot-long roller coaster with a 62-foot lift and a top speed of 50 miles per hour had been installed at Belmont Park for its second season.[17] Built along one edge of the park and racing through trees to the water's edge and back, it was one of the park's main attractions. In 1944 Billings had to fight rumours that nine people had been killed on it. A few years later, Jack Ray built a new front for the coaster and it was renamed the Cyclone.

Crystal Beach had a reputation for its roller coasters. After the success of two smaller ones, the Giant was built in 1916, slightly larger than Belmont's Cyclone. Another coaster, also called the Cyclone, was built in 1927 at a cost of $175,000. It was 96 feet high, 2,953 feet long, and reached a speed of 60 miles an hour. On opening day, 75,000 lined up to ride it. A man was killed on this Cyclone because of a failed lap bar in 1938. The ride was overhauled that year to try to reduce the high forces that stressed it, but maintenance eventually became too difficult and it was torn down in 1946. Timber and track from the Cyclone were incorporated in its replacement, the Comet, which opened in 1948. The Comet was the same height and reached the same speed as the Cyclone but was 4,224 feet long and had fewer tight turns and spirals. It became Crystal Beach's most popular ride, even after it too killed a man.

The CNE had a mixed run with coasters. John Miller, the first coaster builder in the United States, put one in at the CNE in 1920 and it lasted for almost 20 years, until it was damaged by a storm just before the war and had to be torn down. Planning to replace it began in 1946 in anticipation of the exhibition's reopening. In the spring, Patty told Elwood Hughes that his show wanted the franchise for a coaster and later that year Patty stepped forward to say the Conklins would build it. Other arrangements to get the midway ready got in the way of plans for a coaster. The area occupied by the Stanley Barracks was the only one suitable for a major permanent ride and city council resisted demolishing the building. The barracks became an emergency housing project in 1948. That year Patty announced that he would construct a coaster for the 1949 CNE and now had Joe McKee completing plans and Ray designing the front. The National Amusement Device Company was ready to ship the equipment. Once again, the ride was not built. Shortages of materials because of the Korean War were a factor. Only in late 1952 were the plans finally in place, with McKee and Ray as the designers. The Ex survived without a coaster for almost two decades, not unusual for an annual exhibition, but the Ex was more than that.

Rebuilding the Ex

The Conklins had better success at the Ex with permanent buildings, another tactic from their amusement park strategy. Patty and Hughes had been tossing over the future of the CNE during the years it had been closed and, as a result of concrete discussions held in April 1946, Patty submitted a proposal.[18] He offered to invest up to $250,000 for a seven-year contract with an option on five more years. The proposal stipulated 17 major rides and a kiddieland with 10 rides, and suggested a list of shows, including one that would contain "many of the things that were brought about through Scientific Discovery during the last war." Patty would construct permanent buildings for a Magic Carpet, a dark ride, a glasshouse, and a penny arcade. He wanted exclusive rights on 10 group games and would give up 25 percent of the gross receipts of the penny arcade and 20 percent from the other games. He offered 35 percent of the after-tax gross for the shows and rides, except new rides, for which he would pay 25 percent. As a final enticement, he noted that with the Sunnyside Beach Park contract soon to expire there was the "possibility of building a permanent Amusement Area in the Exhibition grounds."

Patty got most of what he asked for, except that he got it for five years with an option on a further five. The reduction to 25 percent for new rides was a change from the company's last contract with the CNE, signed in 1941. The Conklins had food and game concessions since 1941, but had now gained an exclusive on group games, which had groups of players competing against each other and could make serious money. Otherwise, the terms were the same. They would supply more adult and kiddie rides, but no more than six shows. Patty recognized that rides had become more important than shows

Patty, Elwood Hughes, and Frank Conklin on the grounds of the 1947 CNE.

and had made a convert of Hughes. When Hughes announced the contract, as reported in the November 30 issue of *Billboard,* he said he believed that "six well-framed, meritorious shows will be sufficient" and "Frank nodded his assent."

By Christmas 1946, Patty had returned from a vacation in Hot Springs to Brantford, via the Showmen's League convention in Chicago, where he talked up ride and show operators who might be interested in coming to the Ex. He made a public call for "showmen who are in a position to plan a five-year project" and "ride operators and manufacturers who are willing to install permanent or semi-permanent rides."[19]

Bookings for the shows did not start to get finalized until May 1947, when Patty signed Phillips for a water show, with McClure on the outside microphone. In June he announced contracts with Terrell Jacobs for his wild animal circus and Ray Marsh Brydon for a sideshow and exhibit. Walter Hale's Pin-Up Parade and Eddie Hollinger's Harlem Boogie Review followed in July. Patty had long worked with Phillips and had toured Jacobs's circus in 1942. Hale had been the Conklin press agent in 1941. Brydon in the late 1940s was just starting to gather steam as a show producer. He would continue to expand the offerings of his Associated Independent Midway Operators, in 1948, for instance, working as the agent for Sam Howard's water show and the Jacobs circus.[20] Hollinger's dubious show was an unknown.

These were the six major shows that would justify the Conklin and Hughes emphasis on quality, rather than quantity. They were all standard fare but produced by leaders in carnival show business. The plan was to provide these shows with enough capacity to earn as much as 20 smaller attractions. The water, girl, and Harlem shows could all seat close to 1,000, the circus over 3,000. Brydon's two grind shows, with no seating and continuous performances, were able to turn over 35,000 paying customers a day. These were enormous capacities for midway shows; on the road, they would be lucky to handle a quarter of these numbers.

An iron lung respirator, hardly a show, was the seventh attraction and placed in kiddieland. The iron lung, invented in 1928, was first used in the 1937 polio epidemic to keep patients with respiratory paralysis alive and was taken out on the midway the next year. Conklin Shows had one on display in 1947 as the only approximation to Patty's ambition to show things "brought about through Scientific Discovery."

Accommodations for the shows were part of Patty's construction work on the midway. He built a permanent pool and a huge front for the water show. He bought large tents for Jacobs and Hale, and Brydon and Hollinger brought their own new tents. Ray designed new fronts for everyone except Brydon. While the other producers had their shows organized, just weeks before the CNE began Brydon was still looking for acts to fill his tents.

Ray's plans were realized by Joe Drambour, a glasshouse builder with whom Ray had worked in redesigning the Rocky Point Park layout in Warwick, Rhode Island. Drambour was hired as the Conklin builder for the 1947 CNE and oversaw construction of the buildings Patty had proposed to Hughes, as well as buildings for a 30-car auto scooter, the group games, and a cookhouse. Ray also designed a new Laff in the Dark building for Leon Cassidy, who had invented the classic dark ride in 1928.

Counting the children's rides and the walk-through funhouses, the midway would have 35 rides, including a new Bartlett Hurricane, all owned by the Conklins, except for Cassidy's and a new ride debuted by Harry Traver called the Bird Cage. Patty first met Traver in England in 1937, when Traver was building a roller coaster and Patty and Hughes were looking for attractions. Another new ride, the Comet, set to be inaugurated at the 1947 CNE, did not materialize.

The CNE board in mid-March approved construction by Conklin Shows of permanent buildings on the exhibition grounds. The plans were for "the largest permanent construction job ever scheduled by any one showman for a fairground on the North American continent."[21] In the June 14 *Billboard*, Patty announced that the building program, with 84 men on the job, was "half way home." The construction crew was increased to 100 a month later and 140 a month after that with less than two weeks to go. He confidently reported in the August 16 *Billboard* that they would be "up and ready with everything three days before the opening gun." The same day, the Toronto *Telegram* identified it as "the first permanent midway constructed on a fair or exhibition grounds in America" and said he spent $500,000 on it, the exaggerated figure coming from Patty loosely tossing off numbers to his press club friends.

Patty had not received this much press since his last Fair for Britain in 1943 and he thrived on it. He and Frank were taking visitors on "an almost continuous inspection tour."[22] They felt they were "pioneering a new field" and took "considerable pride in their accomplishments." If not a new field, this was certainly an exhibition on a new scale. Hughes presented their work as part of the CNE's five-year expansion program, worth 10 million dollars, that would result in "the World's Fair of Tomorrow."[23] According to Hughes, the CNE board had granted the brothers a five-year contract to enable them "to erect permanent buildings to house the midway on the style of the New York and Chicago World's Fairs." Ray's "modernistic exhibition design" was crucial to their ambitions. On November 29, 1947, *Billboard* published three pages of photos of the CNE light sculptures and the Conklin buildings. After the event, one industry insider praised "the unusual fronts on many of the shows and rides, particularly the bingo building, Laugh in the Dark, Skooter, Water Show, Mirror Maze and Magic Carpet, not to mention most of the concession buildings"; the midway seemed to him to present "a new type of park architecture ... worthy of considerable praise" to all, especially Patty, "who actually merits the chief credit."[24]

The exhibition staff had even more work to do than the Conklin crew to get ready for the reopening. The federal government paid the CNE $1.3 million for the use of the grounds during the war, but exhibition officials expected to spend close to two million dollars. Refurbishing building interiors alone cost more than a million. Approximately 2,500 men were working on the grounds in mid-July. The CNE grandstand had burned down in April 1946 and by the end of the year tenders were being sought for a new one, to have a capacity of 21,500 and be built in time for the reopening. Plans had slipped by late winter and Hughes had given up on a grandstand for the coming season, although construction on it would continue, masked off by one of the Conklin concession buildings. Hughes took another hint from Patty and was having a new Hall of Science built. The sold-out commercial exhibit space would highlight technological developments, including a futuristic train and an RCA booth that televised exhibition activities.

Reopening the Ex

The preparations for the revived CNE paid off; the people of Toronto were ready to host the world. On August 22, 1947, both the city's newspapers hailed the CNE — now commonly called "the Ex," as if it were the only one — the *Star* in an editorial as "the world's greatest annual fair" and the *Telegram* in an editorial illustration as "the greatest show on earth." Prime Minister Mackenzie King gave the opening speech in person, which made the front page of the *Telegram*, describing the CNE as "the greatest exhibition of its kind in the world." On September 13, *Billboard* described it as "the greatest and largest of the annuals presented in any of the hemispheres." Supported by

Jack Ray painting of preparations for the 1947 CNE. Patty and Frank confer at right with Jim holding his uncle's arm. Elwood Hughes is second from the left.

such unremitting superlatives, predictions of attendance ranged from two to three million.

No preparations could have been sufficient to meet the pent-up demand.[25] The day after the Friday, August 22, opening saw an all-time attendance record of 272,000 jamming the 350 acres. Food concessions sold out; ride lineups stretched for blocks; shows played beyond capacity — and this was just the midway. Outside ticket sellers worked more than a mile away from the entrances and traffic jams leading into the city caused hundreds to turn back. Only one day did not break attendance records and the final tally was 2,360,500, beating the record set 20 years before by 321,500.

There were a few sour notes, like complaints about traffic and slow ticket sellers, but then Isabel Ross, chairman of the Toronto Board of Education, gained attention for her beef about the vulgarity of the evening show headliners, popular American comedy act Ole Olsen and Chick Johnson. She was given an audience with the performers, but no one took her seriously. She would repeat her complaints and get more time with the CNE board when the comedy duo returned the next year.

During their discussion, Johnson asked Mrs. Ross whether she had "been around some of the shows on the Midway and watched the kootch dancers they have there?"[26] Johnson was not surprised when she admitted she had not, but reports immediately arose that Hale's Pin-Up Parade was going to be closed. The police inspector for the exhibition denied the rumours: "Our morality officers inspect all midway shows daily. It is true that we have asked

Jack Ray at work on a three-dimensional front for a girl show at the CNE, late 1940s.

to have the show modified in a few respects, and Mr. Conklin has been co-operative in that regard."[27] The ethics and social attitudes surrounding the availability of open displays of sexuality were changing, and carnivals, especially big ones like Patty's operation at the Ex, with girl show producers ready to push limits, were part of the change.

Sitting in his now-permanent office on the grounds, Patty saw that this was, indeed, his amusement park and world's fair all rolled into one. He entertained representatives from every major ride manufacturer, almost every A circuit exhibition in Canada, most major amusement parks in the Northeast, and the New York and Texas state fairs. The latter fair, held in Dallas for two more days than the Ex, was the only annual that could approach the CNE's attendance, and the Texas vice-president was frankly surprised at the size of the Ex. The midway rides and shows grossed over $432,500, beating the annual gross of most amusement parks at the time and the combined gross of all Conklin fairs that year. The company-owned food and game concessions made over $200,000. Frank and Patty anticipated they would split $100,000 profit between them before taxes. On its own, the CNE could support any major carnival company then in existence.[28]

The CNE continued to grow throughout the Conklins' first five-year contract. Attendance climbed to 2,723,000 by 1950 before dropping by 24,000 in 1951 — blamed on rain and cold. In 1948 the new grandstand, seating 22,000, opened at a final cost of $3,400,000. With two returns by Olsen and Johnson, despite Mrs. Ross, and stands by Danny Kaye and Jimmy Durante, it played to capacity each year. The grandstand probably cut into the Conklin gross, which dropped in both 1948 and 1949, bottoming out at $350,000 before beginning to climb again. The opening days of 1951 looked so good that Patty started talking about his goal of half a million dollars. The shows and rides made $435,000 that year, a new record.

In an advertisement looking for "a real outstanding attraction" for the Ex, the Conklins claimed to have "pioneered a practice of limiting the quantity of shows" and were "going to continue with it."[29] Each year Patty looked for an outstanding attraction and each year he changed a few of the shows on the CNE midway, letting the number climb as high as 12. Only Alfie Phillips continued with the Conklins throughout this period. While the shows themselves changed, the types remained consistent. Apart from the Aqua Frolics, there was always a girl show, a freak show, an animal show, and one or more novelty acts. Pete Kortes had the freak show, beginning in 1949. Patty had Jack Ray put together a crime show for 1950, which became a snake show the next year. Herman Larsen, who had joined the show as trainmaster in 1929 and became head mechanic and ride superintendent, had a freak show called The Thing in 1951. Harry Seber, whose girl shows had been top grossers with the Conklins for the five years up to 1941, came back to the CNE in 1951 with Zorro Gardens, showcase for his feature act, Zorima, and 16 other girls. Whitey Woods's midgets had been with the Conklins at the same time as Seber, and they, too, returned in 1951. Seber and Woods were tied to no company, playing any big North American fair they could book, including the Texas State Fair after the Ex.

Patty added one or two new adult and kiddie rides each year. Though the CNE contract specified 17 adult and 10 kiddie rides, there were over 20 of each by 1951. The Conklins got a miniature roller coaster in 1951. Built at the Conklin shop in Brantford, it cost $35,000 and was 22 feet high. It was among the top grossing rides that year.

The Sky Wheel, developed by Curtis and Elmer Velare, registered the biggest ride sensation during the tenure of the contract. The Velares built their Sky Wheels, two Ferris wheels rotating on independent axles at either end of a long arm that also rotated, at a factory in California and took them on the road for the first time in 1950, including a stop at the CNE. A Sky Wheel stood 92 feet high, the tallest object on any midway. Weighing 16 tons, it was carried on two semi-trailers and sold for $20,000. The device was good flash for a fair, but to make money the ticket price had to be higher than for other rides or the percentage paid to the fair boards lower. The Conklins followed the latter practice, which caused them problems later. The *Globe and Mail* featured a picture of the Sky Wheel on the front page of the September 6 edition.

As rides became more expensive for both owners and the public, the Conklin concession business at the Ex grew. In 1948 they constructed another building for games, this one with a warehouse in back for prizes or stock. They had 42 food and game concessions in 1950 and said they had $240,000 in prizes to give away. The next year they made further improvements to their

Crowds at the 1949 CNE. Jack Ray's fronts are evident on the buildings on either side of the midway.

buildings, spending $3,000 on the food joints alone, but the food business was down that year. The effect of the new thrill rides on stomachs — or wallets — might have been a factor.

Patty continued to entertain just about every major figure associated with North American carnivals, fairs, and amusement parks. Over 65 park owners and operators visited the CNE in 1948. The executive secretary of the National Association of Amusement Parks, Pools and Beaches remarked that, since "each year more and more park men, ride operators and manufacturers are making the CNE a must on their program," the association should set a specific time when all could gather at the Ex for "a post-season meeting."[30] The Conklins and Hughes offered full co-operation and provided a location for "an informal summer meeting" at the 1949 fair.[31]

Of all the CNE grandstand headliners, Danny Kaye was the one who spent serious time with Patty. When he headlined at the Ex, Kaye had finished his career as a radio star and was beginning to be known for his recordings, movies, and live performances. Patty got a kick out of dragging him all over the midway, taking him on the rides, and having him ham it up for photographs with show personnel. In a series of photos of the two on the midway and riding rides, Kaye mugs for the camera, looking like he is enjoying himself. There are also shots with Kaye, his entourage, and key Conklin people. Ray designed the grandstand stage for Kaye. High winds blew the fronts down a few days before opening. Ray and his crew worked around the clock to get them back together for the first show.

Lord Louis Mountbatten, British naval officer, statesman, and earl, paused during his farewell world tour as the last viceroy and first governor general of India, newly independent under his oversight, to open the 1948 CNE. Patty escorted him on a tour of the midway afterward. At one point, Patty stooped to pick up a nickel. Mountbatten raised his eyebrows and said, "Mr. Conklin, I've heard a lot about you. Now I see how you got rich."[32] Patty could not recognize the lord's comment as anything other than a compliment and he often retold the story as part of his legend, concluding with the punch line that he had "friends who can get into Buckingham Palace and ... other friends who can't get out of Leavenworth."[33]

Meanwhile, the city and the exhibition association were looking for ways to expand the capacity of the Ex. Too many people were not even getting in the gates, or, with the massive crowds visitors created once inside, getting to enjoy all the attractions. Toronto's mayor, Hiram McCallum, wanted to extend the CNE to three weeks and demolish the Stanley Barracks, replacing them with a new administration building. Hughes was for taking over city parkland to the west of the grounds. He and Patty had their eye on the Stanley Barracks as the site for extending the midway and putting up a roller coaster. These conflicting plans foreshadowed the conflict that would soon erupt between, on one side, the city and the association, and on the other, the CNE management and the Conklins.

THE CNE ROLLER COASTER

Patty and Edythe sit on the deck outside their stateroom, smoking and watching the sun set over the Pacific. The SS *Alaska* of the Alaska Steamship

Line lies in Sitka Sound, having left Juneau that morning. After dinner with Edythe's mother and their son Jimmy, they wheeled the old woman back to her room and left the boy to wander the decks on his own. Edythe leans back in her chair. Patty puts down his glass and gets up to stand by the railing.

"That is one beautiful sunset, you really have to say that," he says.

"Don't you think dinner was lovely?" she asks.

"They sure are treating us right, aren't they? And they should, for what I paid."

"Is it getting cooler? The sun takes so long to go down. Get me another drink, would you?"

Patty comes back from their room to find Edythe's eyes closed and he puts her drink on the table beside her.

Twenty-five hundred miles across the continent, crickets chirp in the deep summer night. The air has cooled and the stars are bright over the rolling hills. A truck moves slowly up the road, its lights off, and pulls in past the Sky Acres sign to park on the driveway beside the darkened house.

Two men get out and hunker behind the house. They find a window, surprisingly easy to jimmy open. Inside, they take off their balaclavas and stuff them away, suppressing their exhilaration as they search for the stash they had heard they would find. They locate the kitchen with the pantry beside it and there they are — cases of booze. They slap each other on the back.

Three loads later and they have cleaned up. They check around for loose bottles, close the window, and leave. They bring a bottle into the cab of the truck and kick up gravel as they fishtail back onto the county road. They turn on their lights and open the bottle when they get to the next concession road.

At the same moment, Patty turns on the light in the stateroom and half carries, half drags Edythe to bed. Mrs. Bell loudly snores from her room within. Jimmy has returned to his berth and closed the door.

★　★　★

The roller coaster that the CNE became for the Conklins climbed for five years before hitting its first drop and when it did, they threatened to stop the ride. A glimpse of disturbances on the horizon might have prompted Patty to suggest to Hughes, in a letter he wrote on November 4, 1950, anticipating the end of the Conklin contract the next year, that they "be relieved of furnishing the amusements at the Canadian National Exhibition, and sell our permanent buildings to whomever you may decide to have succeed us." The letter was a tactic to push through speedy renewal of another five-year contract, for Patty went on to offer the exhibition association an alternative if it could not find a replacement. The Conklins would accept another contract if it were in place within a month, but it had to include improvements, especially to the midway, and licence to build more of the permanent attractions he had threatened to sell.

The first public hint of trouble arose when Hughes was reported to have suffered a bout of pneumonia early in 1951. The association board of directors granted him a three-month leave of absence. Unknown to Hughes, the board had approached Mayor McCallum to take over as general manager when his term was up at the end of 1951. The board also reported that the Danny Kaye grandstand show had lost over $17,000 because Kaye's fee had been too high, perhaps one reason for his delight when in Patty's company. Critics of Hughes on the city council were behind the report.

Hughes refuted almost all points of the story. He had high blood pressure, not pneumonia. He claimed that the association president denied that the board had approached McCallum. He corrected the amount paid to Kaye and asserted that neither the grandstand nor any other division of the past year's operation had lost money. Unfortunately or not for Hughes, the part about his three-month leave was correct, and he was heading to Florida to enjoy it. In his absence rumours continued to circulate that he was to be replaced by McCallum. The machinations of the board proceeded.

Hughes had been coming up against city hall with increasing frequency since the resumption of the CNE. He had repeatedly forced through the big-name American talent created by the film and music industries as grandstand headliners, rather than Canadian acts who lacked international reputations. He had resisted pressure to clean up the Olsen and Johnson grandstand show. He had refused to withdraw a painting to which the mayor objected. It would later be revealed that he had also taken it upon himself to interpret the contract with the Conklins as he saw fit. Hughes's justification that he knew international show business better than his critics was no doubt true, but he had begun to look like the independent emperor of the Ex and to be represented in the local press as such. Without support, his days were numbered — and Patty was his only supporter.

Despite his denials, Hughes's health was not good. He had been an Olympic athlete in his youth, but had long enjoyed his cigars and Scotch, and would turn 67 before the 1951 CNE. He kept a hectic pace and needed his annual rests in Florida. Patty and Hughes had been partners at the CNE since Hughes gave him the contract in 1937, three years into Hughes's tenure. They had been cordially working out arrangements that seemed to be for the mutual benefit of both the exhibition and the carnival company, but outside scrutiny might find irregularities in the Conklin monopoly. That scrutiny would soon come, even before Hughes was pushed out of his position.

Patty and Frank did not want trouble with any fair board, especially one in charge of such a lucrative event and as potentially powerful as the exhibition board if it had city council on its side or, more likely, pulling its strings. The Conklins liked their routine. They had to expend little effort on the parks, other than assigning crews for ride maintenance and managers to collect the money. Frank ran the short season of Ontario and Quebec fairs, letting Sullivan and his staff do most of the work. The Ex gave Patty his profile in the outdoor entertainment industry and what effort it took came as second nature. His staff were gaining experience and skill in looking after it for him, and he wanted to hire "three more key men to participate ... in improving the Amusement Area."[34]

Off-Season Activities

The Conklins had slowed down and were spending less time on their midways. From working up to 40 events and six months a year in the 1930s, they were down to eight or nine spots and two months on the road. They allowed World's Finest to miss some opening and closing days at their fairs, and not always because there was an overlap. Sometimes it was just too much effort to get from one place to another on time and the returns did not justify it. They would never have missed a day before the war, but they were making enough money now and did not need to chase every nickel, despite the Mountbatten story.

Patty preferred travel and visiting his international circle of showmen friends and competitors on their midways to hanging around on his own. He was attending to the future of the industry, which he saw in riding devices: "The mere hint of a new ride being manufactured somewhere" sent "him scurrying to the airport."[35]

He did, however, have other motives for travel. After the Winnipeg anniversary celebration in June 1949, for instance, he set off on a 32-day excursion to Alaska, largely for his wife and mother-in-law. He passed through Vancouver to pick up Edythe, Mrs. Bell, and Jimmy for the cruise. Mrs. Bell was in poor health and would die within two years. Confined on a cruise ship with her ailing mother, Edythe's drinking could be monitored. It also provided a rare chance for father and teenaged son to spend some extended time together. Patty could not leave business completely behind and took the opportunity to visit Henry Meyerhoff whose Crescent Shows was playing Anchorage. He had left the Ontario and Quebec fairs to Frank and Sullivan and returned in late July in time to settle the final arrangements for the CNE. The Brantford house, Sky Acres, was burgled while the family was away, the thieves making off with $700 in liquor. Someone had tipped them off that Patty was a good entertainer.

Down the road from Sky Acres, Frank's attention to Midway Farm was starting to pay off. He began to exhibit livestock at the exhibitions that carried his midway. At the 1947 CNE horse show, three years after starting his stable, his horses finished first and second in the express division, and first in the light draft horse division.[36] That year he helped found the Ontario chapter of the Canadian Thoroughbred Horse Society, which held its first annual yearling sale at Toronto's Woodbine Park racetrack. He left the Quebec exhibition to attend the sale in 1948. E.P. Taylor, the Toronto businessman who became Canada's most successful horse breeder, bought one of Frank's horses for a record $11,000.[37] Frank's sale of seven yearlings got him $36,000 and another sale brought him $42,000 in 1951.

Frank was an expert on breeding and handicapping horses. Major bookies called him for tips. He would only race his own horses if he could not sell them, but horses he had bred were winning at the track. He had expanded Midway Farm to 289 acres and owned 20 handpicked broodmares, which in the winter he took to Kentucky to breed. He bought a box at the Kentucky Derby to cope with being ignored by society at the track. He was also spending a month or two each winter looking after his health in Monrovia, where his wife still had family. At Midway Farm, he and Billie entertained friends from the professional sports and horse breeding worlds, like Taylor, George Gardiner, another major figure in Canadian thoroughbred horse racing, and George Drew, Ontario premier. Billie developed her talents as an amateur photographer and some of her work was published in magazines.

When it reopened in 1948, the Conklins got the Great Western Fair in London, but playing it required some effort. They ran the London midway on the same basis as the CNE, which it immediately followed, and brought roughly three-quarters of the CNE's attractions with them for the first year back. Attendance and the midway gross doubled that of the last fair, held in 1939. The Western Fair's midway continued to thrive under Patty's direction. He got another five-year contract in 1952, paved 10,000 square yards of the midway, and talked about permanent buildings. That year 387,000 attended.

There was only one major fair in Ontario and Quebec that Conklin Shows did not have wrapped up. The Central Canada Exhibition (CCE) in Ottawa was second in the country only to the CNE. Conklin Shows had come close to working the CCE in 1941 and had a contract for it in 1942, the year it was cancelled for the war. It reopened in 1947 with World of Mirth, its former midway provider and the only big American show playing Canada besides Royal American. Like all the major North American exhibitions in the postwar period, the CCE set new records year after year. Attendance climbed to 450,000 in 1950 and the rides and shows on the midway grossed over $150,000. Early in 1949, Herb McElroy, general manager of the CCE for 20 years, announced that a spring fair would supplement the August exhibition and the Conklins were to supply the midway.[38] McElroy met resistance from his board of directors and the spring fair never materialized. Conklin Shows would wait another 50 years to get into the Ottawa exhibition.

Another event that almost occurred was the show's oft-rumoured break into the United States. The American government planned to celebrate the sesquicentennial of the city of Washington in 1950 with a Freedom Fair. A commission was granted three million dollars to organize the fair. Patty partnered with Harry Batt, owner and operator of the Pontchartrain Beach amusement park in New Orleans, to submit a bid. The partners made several trips to Washington in 1949 to confer with officials and Jack Ray prepared three-dimensional models of their plans. The commission in charge of the event had difficulties in providing information and receiving bids. Patty and Batt garnered national attention when they formally withdrew their tender because of the commission's administrative delays.[39] The fair was postponed to 1951 because of a multitude of problems — land leasing and clearance, a kickback scandal, and tangles over contracts and general policy — and was finally cancelled. Patty's relationship with Batt survived, however, and he and Edythe vacationed with the Batts in New Orleans a few years later. A Conklin–Batt partnership would eventually get Patty working again in the United States.

The Conklins were also making money from shrewd investments in the stock market, but one investment that did not pay off was a loan to the Johnny J. Jones Exposition.[40] After the death of its founder in 1930, the Jones show ground to a halt before being bought by E. Lawrence Phillips, a promoter and movie theatre owner from Washington who had been an old friend of Jones. Phillips ran the show from 1934 to the end of the 1947 season. While he brought it back to moderate success, he did little to maintain or upgrade the equipment. He entered into a brief partnership with two long-time concessionaires, Morris Lipsky and Harold "Buddy" Paddock, the latter of whom had married Jones's widow. The partnership dissolved, but in 1944 Lipsky bought a half-interest in the show and three years later Paddock bought the other half.

Paddock and Lipsky spent a lot of cash trying to restore Johnny J. Jones to its former glory. Much of this money came from the sale of old equipment, but some came from a loan from Patty, who had known Paddock and Lipsky for years, and could sympathize with them in their troubles with banks. The Conklin and Jones shows played different territories, so they did not compete. With a pledge of equipment and shares in the company as collateral, in early 1948 they borrowed $28,000 at 5 percent from Patty to buy six rides. They were to make payments of $5,000 plus interest per year. The 1948 season did not justify the heavy capital outlay. They borrowed another $10,000 from Patty in September. After the 1949 season they had to renegotiate and despite good fair dates in 1950, the show lost more money. They were late with payments, but Patty continued to help them. Through Dave Russell, a Chicago associate, Patty bought nine lighting installations and leased them to the Jones show. Finally, in March 1951, the Internal Revenue Service seized the Jones equipment for back payment of taxes and forced a public sale. Patty attended the sale, describing it to Arthur Morse, a Chicago lawyer who represented him in this and other matters, as "a big fiasco."[41] He and Russell were able to recover their light plants, and Sullivan picked up 12 railway cars, but Patty lost the money still owed him; he took an ornate entrance gate and four diesel generators as recompense for a portion of it.

Trouble with the Mayor

After extricating themselves from the corpse of Johnny J. Jones, the Conklins rounded the next dark-ride corner to face another skeleton, this one from the city of Toronto and newly reanimated. In early August 1951, Patty and the CNE executive had negotiated another five-year contract, which the executive had accepted in principle. In the municipal elections that fall, Allan Lamport was elected mayor. As an alderman since 1946 and city representative on the CNE board since 1948, Lamport had been vocal in criticizing the way Hughes ran the CNE. At the executive directors' meeting in December, before his mayoral term started, he convinced the CNE board that they could not accept the Conklin contract. He assumed office in early 1952 and quickly took aim at Hughes and Patty. Complaining that his previous attacks had been unreported because the CNE board held closed meetings, he made them public through several addresses to civic groups and at the annual general meeting of the board.

"'MIDWAY MILLIONAIRES' ATTACKED BY LAMPORT," shouted the front-page headline of the Toronto *Telegram*, a paper where Patty had friends, on January 24. Lamport claimed that the contracts signed between Hughes and the Conklins had made "millionaires out of midway operators at the expense of Toronto taxpayers." The next day on the front page of the *Star*, Toronto's other major newspaper, he petitioned for the "czar-like power wielded by Mr. Hughes" to be curtailed.

A colourful mayor who craved publicity, Lamport was known for his impulsiveness, obstreperous manner, and tendency to overstate his case — a typical politician. In the January 25 *Telegram*, he pointed out that the CNE had made Patty "one of the biggest showmen on the continent." Through the CNE contract, according to Lamport, Patty had "gained a monopoly over midway concessions and shows operating in cities, towns, and villages throughout Ontario and most of Canada returning fabulous profits."

Lamport saw the larger picture, although he undersold his target. In the same issue, the *Telegram* reported that he wanted full disclosure of the "secret" contract, which would show that it "is so powerful that not one inch of midway space can be rented except through" the Conklins. While nothing Lamport said was untrue and he had the support of most councillors, Patty's critics and supporters shared the recognition that no one "else in the country other than Paddy Conklin has the organization to handle such an undertaking as the CNE every year."

Apart from the Conklin contract, Lamport attacked Hughes for his policy of hiring American talent for the grandstand show. In 1949 he had unsuccessfully called for Hughes to resign over a statement that Canadian talent was incapable of staging a performance worthy of the Ex. By bundling the debt charges on the grandstand with the CNE operating expenses, Lamport was able to contend that the Ex had cost the city over $300,000 in 1951 and to blame it on Hughes. The profits made by the Conklins were "of a size that would meet the city's deficit on last year's CNE operations," he claimed.[42] Among other demands, he wanted the show's buildings on the CNE grounds to be taxed at the commercial rate, not an unreasonable requirement, although something for which the Conklins had not budgeted.

When the Conklin five-year contract expired, Lamport, having held up approval of its renewal, hoped to get it opened for tender. In advance of a special meeting of the executive in January 1952, he promised "a bigger fireworks display than the one at the CNE" if the directors tried to push the contract through in its original form.[43]

As Lamport recognized, Patty was an international player largely because of the Ex. Conklin Shows was setting trends in kiddieland with new spectacular rides, and extending its innovations to a select roster of central Canadian fairs. Fairs across the continent were following the Conklins' lead in paving midways and granting long-term contracts to midway companies. Patty was seldom referred to as a carnival company owner anymore. He was now a "midway impresario" or the Canadian "carnival biggie." He had let oversight of most of his operations fall to others, keeping a personal hand in only when it came to the CNE and buying rides for it. He needed it as a showcase for new rides, so he had to do something about the Lamport problem. If he lost the Ex, he would lose his status in the business.

Routine

(1952–1961)

Fairs in North America attracted approximately 85 million people in 1952 and the major fairs broke attendance records year after year throughout the baby boom decade. Despite the attempts of municipal officials to gum up the works on the CNE roller coaster, the Conklins were able to maintain their routine, pinned on the Ex and their Ontario and Quebec fairs and amusement parks, all of which shared in the continent-wide attendance boom. Patty was now identified with promoting new rides and Frank with his stable. James Franklin, Patty's son, began his training on the midway and started taking over some of his uncle's duties. But before they could get on with their routine, they had to deal with Metro Toronto politicians.

FIGHTING CITY HALL

Patty sits on a bench in the marble hall outside the council chambers. Hunched over, elbows on knees, hat on his head. Light from the high, leaded windows carves shafts through the cigarette smoke curling around his head. Frank and Neil are there.

He curses under his breath. "They want to run it their own damn selves, they can go ahead, the loogans. They got no idea, they really have no idea at all." He takes a drag and spits.

"Patty, Patty, Patty," Frank intones. "They're not going to cut us loose."

"Real big man that chump mayor of fucking Hogtown. Thinks he can make me eat shit. He got Elwood, he won't get me. He'll find out. They're gonna have to beg me to take that thing on. I still got friends in there."

He continues to mutter and shake his head, as Neil and Frank say little. Finally, a council functionary comes out and tells him they will see him now. Patty stands and beats his hat against his leg. He huddles with his men for a moment, deferring his response to the summons, then enters the chambers.

When he comes out 15 minutes later, he jams his hat back on his head and growls, "Come on, let's get out of this joint."

★　★　★

The Conklins' fight with city hall had only begun. Toronto Mayor Allan Lamport was determined to expose the "network of intrigue" surrounding the CNE midway contracts.[1] He wanted to get rid of both Elwood Hughes and Patty Conklin, but he lacked a contingency plan. At a three-hour meeting on January 26, 1952, he forced the exhibition executive to make the Conklin buildings at the CNE eligible for city taxation and to revoke the Conklin bingo contract. He made them agree to remove a clause in the contract that let Hughes act as the CNE association's representative without reference to the board, and to consider the appointment of an assistant general manager as a Hughes understudy.

Successful in his campaign to curtail Hughes, Lamport could not get his way with the Conklins. Constrained by a commitment by the former president the previous August, he grudgingly stood back to let the CNE executive renew the Conklin contract for five years; otherwise, the city "would have to buy back souped-up buildings standing on public parks."[2] Despite the agreement Lamport thought he had, the executive's offer on January 28 to renew the Conklin contract still included the lucrative bingo concession, although it had the other changes Lamport had demanded.

The Conklins had not accepted the offer from the executive or signed a contract for 1952 by the middle of February. Lamport obtained a copy of the 1947 contract, compared it with the new one Hughes had drafted, and questioned the changes that had been made. In the earlier contract, Conklin Shows paid for all the electricity it used, but in the new one its electricity charges were capped at $3,000. Where the show used to pay the association 25 percent of the gross from the penny arcade, it would now pay $3,000 flat. Instead of the complete cost for ticket sellers, under the new contract the show would pay a fixed rate. According to Lamport, these changes had been made solely on Hughes's agreement "with his friend Conklin," and he was probably right.[3] He claimed the changes would cost the city $50,000. Lamport was successful in getting Hughes's changes to the contract revoked.

Lamport enlisted the support of the city board of control as he broadened his attack to include the CNE board of directors. The contest turned on whether the city would manage Exhibition Park for 12 months, with the CNE association a tenant for two weeks, or the association would manage the park throughout the year. Lamport claimed victory as the city gained more leverage over the association, but without getting year-round management of the grounds. He also alienated some of his aldermen.

Pressured about uncertainties in past payments by the Conklins to the city, the executive examined the accounts more closely. They found minor inaccuracies in the CNE management's financial statements covering the contract in previous years. There was a discrepancy between the amount recorded for electricity payments and the amount Hughes quoted. The CNE treasurer was called back from his Florida vacation and Lamport threatened to slap an injunction on the entire CNE board to keep it from touching the books. Robert Saunders, acting president of the board, termed it "a nasty situation," admitted that "heads may roll" and called a special meeting.[4]

Evidence examined at the special meeting on February 28 revealed that the incorrect information and the discrepancies were clerical errors. The executive and the mayor did, however, discover that Hughes had indeed been flexible in interpreting the Conklin contract as he saw fit. Although all rides were to pay the CNE 35 percent of the gross after their first year, Hughes had allowed the Sky Wheel to continue at 25 percent, the rate for new rides, in its second year. He had also changed the basis of payment for the penny arcade from a percentage to a flat rate. The board moved that the Conklins be ordered to pay the estimated $3,800 the city had lost as a result of the latter authorized change. It let the issue with the Sky Wheel go, since this piece of equipment was a draw that only Patty could have brought in.

After the February meeting, Bob Dixon, secretary for the association, wrote Patty to tell him his show owed the association close to $4,000 and that all changes made to the 1952 contract in response to his requests to Hughes were to revert to the terms of the old contract. Further, the show would have to pay a larger share of the insurance and the bingo concession was once more up for tender. The show would have to post a performance bond that, although stipulated in the contract, had never been collected, and the bond was raised from $10,000 to $50,000. In another concession to Lamport, who had complained that no lawyers had been involved in rewriting the contract, the deputy city solicitor was preparing the legal wording. Even though this was Lamport grandstanding, it was also good business practice.

Lamport estimated that his changes to the contract would save the city $100,000 over five years and he was convinced he could find more. "We're not finished yet," he said after the meeting.[5] He had become the taxpayer's champion. He was quoted in the February 29 *Telegram*: "Elwood Hughes has for far too long been a protector for Patty Conklin. Everything done in the past has been for the benefit of Mr. Conklin. The interest of the taxpayer has been entirely ignored." The editorial pages of the Toronto newspapers were now behind Lamport and any resisters on the CNE board had been cowed into submission. He succeeded in getting an assistant general manager to Hughes appointed. Ex-mayor Hiram McCallum, Saunders' choice, was given the job, providing substance to the rumours from the year before.

For the first time in 30 years, Patty and Frank decided to pass on the western fairs meeting, held in Winnipeg that year. They needed to keep on top of the trouble in Toronto. When called by the newspapers, Patty had no comment. He had dealt with municipal politicians and fair boards for decades, but he had never faced a challenge as severe as that now posed by Toronto's elected officials.

Lamport's next move was to propose to the CNE executive that they should hire "a well-known firm of business examiners" to go into the Ex's operations.[6] Since this was ostensibly a national fair, some aldermen called for a royal commission, but Lamport, confident that the executive and the board of directors would support him, wanted the city to solve the problem. The analysts would look for evidence of improper practice, for ways to improve the system of auditing and accounting, and for recommendations to reform the letting of contracts. Saunders, as acting president, asserted that without such an inquiry he would quit. Public confidence in the management of the CNE had to be restored.

Capitulation

The Conklins finally received a draft of the 1952 contract from the city solicitor on the second Friday in March. Over the weekend, Patty considered negotiating with Saunders, who was also chair of the midway committee. The following Monday, March 10, he prepared a letter to Saunders that, based on "the realization there is but a comparatively short time to prepare for this year's Exhibition," proposed a one-year contract under the same terms and conditions as the 1947 contract. He did not send it. The next day he prepared another letter to Saunders, this one referring to the negotiations of the past summer and his surprise "to learn, in the month of December, 1951, that you were not then in agreement with the terms of the contract approved in principal and accepted by both parties in August." He defended himself in the disagreements that had arisen and refused to sign the contract prepared by the city solicitor. He did not send this letter either. On Wednesday, he prepared a third letter, this one addressed to the CNE association as a whole, and he delivered it in person to a meeting of the executive that day. Much discussion ensued, with Patty defending his business practices and challenging the association's perception of his dealings with Hughes, but generally striking a conciliatory tone.

In the letter, Patty conceded to the terms of the 1947 contract as repeated in the 1952 contract and quibbled with the new demand that his show carry separate insurance. Raising the issue of a five-year renewal, he reiterated his inclination, which he said he had already expressed to the management and several directors, "to sever my connection with the Canadian National Exhibition without, of course, in any way harming the efficient operations of the Fair." He also said that "on the basis of the understanding made with me in the summer of last year, I have spent a considerable amount of money in capital investment." He would enter into a contract for two years for the shows and rides, and five years for the bingo and the four permanent amusement attractions the show had built. His veiled threat still hung over the board, and they knew he would be hard to replace. Patty was biding his time, looking ahead to the end of Lamport's term as mayor.

On March 13, the *Toronto Star* reported that "the meeting ... presided over what may mark the departure of J.W. 'Patty' Conklin, Midway operator, after a further two years." He "remained outside the committee room for four hours while the committee tightened up his contract." Dixon, the association secretary, relayed to Patty the committee decision and the following week wrote a letter to the city solicitor informing him that the Conklins had capitulated to the draft contract as tightened up by the committee, but would still get the bingo.

Patty got on with his business and the management consultants proceeded to produce their report on the CNE. Hughes was convinced the report would vindicate him, but in the meantime, he continued to duke it out in the press with Lamport. When the report finally came in at the beginning of July, Hughes got off lightly. It confirmed the removal of his powers to interpret contracts, but he was otherwise untouched. Its main recommendation was that the CNE association, as constituted, should have year-round responsibility for the grounds. If it did not show a profit, it would give up responsibility to the city. While the report went extensively into the Conklin contract, it touched only briefly on those aspects that Lamport had criticized. It recommended against opening the midway contracts to tender, suggesting that the association should retain its power to pick the concessions it felt were suitable.

The disagreements between Hughes and Lamport remained especially tense over the grandstand show. Lamport directly involved himself in negotiations for the grandstand entertainment. Jack Arthur, a Canadian theatrical producer, had been named by the board to replace Leon Leonidoff, an American, as the show's producer. When Hughes was in Florida, McCallum was told by Lamport to void the contract with George Hamid's New York talent agency. Admitting that a Canadian headliner could not fill the stands, Arthur looked to book an American, making overtures to Dean Martin, Jerry Lewis, Bob Hope, Jack Benny, Judy Garland, and Betty Hutton, all of whom were otherwise engaged. Less than two months before opening, Arthur finally got Tony Martin, an American singer and actor who had a string of popular songs in the late 1940s and early '50s. Arthur was able to promise a "90 per cent all-Canadian show."[7]

American commentary on the grandstand show pointed to Canadian political interference as the reason for its poor quality. Canadian reviews were more positive, but said the show could have done without the American Martin. With higher admission prices, extra seating, and a boost from the local press, the 1952 grandstand ultimately set a new record of $430,000 for gross revenue.

For his first exhibition under the new contract, Patty maintained the trajectory of growth he had followed through the previous five. Although the contract still specified 17 major rides, 10 children's rides, and six shows, the midway had 20 majors, 23 kiddie rides, and 11 shows. The Conklins owned most of the rides, but none of the shows, although Patty controlled their presentation. Using the gaudy arch taken from the defunct Johnny J. Jones show for an entrance, he set up "the largest Kiddieland ever to play any fair."[8] On children's day, a record 208,000 tickets were sold. Harry Seber's girl show, Paris after Midnite, led the back-end grosses, as it did throughout this period, followed by the freak show, with Alfie Phillips's water show in third.

On the Thursday before the last weekend, 30 newspapermen — who had got such good copy out of Patty the past winter — threw a surprise party for him, to which they also invited exhibition officials. They needed to patch things up with their pal, who could share credit for another successful CNE. Attendance for the 1952 fair reached 2,717,000, just 6,000 short of the record set two years before. Everyone was relieved, owing to concern that "the charges to which the exhibition management had been subjected by politicians

The bally for Harry Seber's Paris After Midnite girl show, designed by Jack Ray, 1952.

during the past year would be harmful."[9] The shows and rides grossed close to $400,000, of which the Conklin share was $242,000. Out of that, they had to pay everyone else.

At the closing luncheon held for the exhibition directors, Hughes "hinted that conditions under which he has been compelled to conduct the affairs of the CNE in the past year have been made so difficult that he was not inclined to continue any longer."[10] At the next director's meeting, he officially offered his resignation to the board. After 46 years with the Ex, the past 18 as general manager, it was time to leave. His health was failing and he was tired of fighting with Lamport. He said he had tried to retire in 1950 but had been convinced to remain until his replacement could be found. With McCallum in place, he could go.

With their opponent vacating the field, the directors and politicians could afford to be gracious to him. The directors voted to continue Hughes in an advisory capacity on full salary for the next year and then provide him an annual pension of $7,500. Lamport grudgingly acknowledged his contribution to the

CNE's success, while the current association president went further, perhaps with a swipe at Patty: "Mr. Hughes, more than any one individual, has been responsible for bringing the Exhibition to its present high level."[11] The day after submitting his resignation, Elwood went with Patty to New York to take in the World Series. McCallum took over as general manager and the post of assistant general manager was dropped.

Hughes continued to spend his winters in Florida and his health continued to decline. On May 1, 1956, a month before turning 72, he died from a heart condition and pneumonia. At his retirement and on his death, articles and editorials in the Toronto newspapers praised him, although none failed to mention the criticism to which he had been subjected. He was described as one of Canada's best-known showmen and named "Mr. Ex." McCallum said he "was one of the chief architects in bringing the CNE along from a small provincial fair to the national exposition it is today."[12] Hundreds attended his funeral. Patty was an honorary pallbearer, together with four former presidents of the exhibition association and eight other associates and friends.

The Conklins had begun their relationship with Hughes during the first year of his tenure as general manager and he had always been their main contact at the CNE. By the time Hughes retired, they had learned to work with McCallum. McCallum had been actively involved with the CNE during his four years as mayor, although not nearly so active as Lamport. The local media were aware of McCallum's lack of experience when he took over from Hughes but were willing to give him a chance. They thought that, given his background, he could assist in smoothing out the rocky relations between the association and city council. With seasoned staff to assist him, he grew into his role, which he occupied for the next 12 years and on which he put his own mark.

Smooth Rolling

As the controversies around the CNE settled down with the departure of Hughes, the Conklins again felt secure in their relations with the fair. They resumed discussions with CNE officials on the construction of a roller coaster. By November they had settled on a location and blueprints were ready before the end of the year. As had been planned before, Jack Ray designed the building and entrance, and Palisades Park's Joe McKee designed the structure and train. In early March 1953, McCallum and Patty announced that they had closed the contract, although details were still being worked out in June, even as construction had begun. The Conklins would pay the CNE 22.5 percent of the gross for 10 years and 35 percent for an optional further 10.

Patty was elated to finally get his big coaster, another notch in his belt as an impresario of thrill rides. Named the Flyer after the old Sunnyside Beach coaster, it was only the third to be built in North America since the war. Toronto firms were hired as architects and engineers. McKee's plans were re-engineered by engineers at the University of Toronto. The superintendent of construction at Palisades was brought up from New Jersey to oversee the work. The track was 2,612 feet long and 67 feet high. It had four cars per train, rather than the usual three. It averaged admissions worth $5,000 a day for its first season. Its gross of over $7,000 for one day in 1954 was believed to be largest ever for any roller coaster. It cost $185,000 to build and Patty was rumoured to have said it paid for itself in three years, but publicly claimed he took nine years to recover its cost.

CNE attendance was down by almost 100,000 in 1953, thanks to another polio scare, but the Conklin gross was up. The deal they had worked out three years before with the Toronto *Telegram* to print coupons that could be redeemed for ride tickets finally began to affect ticket sales. By the end of the 1953 Ex, relations between the Conklins and the CNE management and association had stabilized enough for Patty to withdraw his threat to "sever his connection" and another five-year contract for rides, shows, and concessions was sealed. Throughout the 1950s, attendance fluctuated just under the three million mark, although the show's gross climbed steadily, in some years by close to $100,000. In 1955 the show finally broke the $500,000 mark, as for five years Patty had annually boasted it would.

These years were not without controversy, although none matched the battle between Hughes and Lamport that almost took the CNE away from the Conklins. Seber's girl shows often came under attack. Jennie Lee, "the Bazoom Girl," was star of Seber's French Vani-Tease in 1954. Hearing that Canada was stuffy, she had toned down her show. Nevertheless, two city councillors found it lurid and sensual, and she was ordered to do less with more. A smile on his face, Patty personally helped cover up some of the offending billboards on his midway. The publicity did not hurt attendance. Another wonder, Marilyn Bell, put on a more wholesome show of female prowess that year when she swam across Lake Ontario during the CNE, a feat for which she was showered with money, gifts, and fame.

Despite the flack he drew, Seber and his girl shows remained welcome. He kept testing the limits of staid Toronto, calling his show Striporama in 1956. Its success that year was aided by *Flash*, a Toronto tabloid that on September 8 offered its full front page to the headline, "Public Blasts CNE Sex Wallow," the accusation that "Kids Admitted to Jungle-Raw Girlie Shows" and the

Young boys looking at posters for the French Vani-Tease girl show, early 1950s.

full-torso photo of a stripper, all a teaser for a centrefold spread on the performance. A short article accompanies photos that, as a caption points out, left "to the imagination, nothing." It describes how "a lurid spectacle of prancing naked women erupts night after night before the fascinated gaze of curious teenagers and hot-eyed adult males," or, as another heading has it, "popeyed punks" and "drooling oldsters." Accusing the CNE of taking special privilege to mount "a gigantic orgy of lust" and allow "raw sex" to be "this midway man-trap's main attraction," the spread included a photo of Mayor Nathan Phillips's membership card in the Official Jennie Lee Fan Club. Only the mayor suffered from this exposure.

The number of shows on the postwar CNE midway peaked in 1956 with 12. Along with Striporama, the Pete Kortes freak show remained a top grosser until that year, after which he had a falling out with Patty and did not return. The Alfie Phillips water show stayed in the top three for a remarkable 11 years. Phillips had a miniature circus in 1954, and a seal show and a girl in a fishbowl show in 1956. The following year was the last Ex for both Seber and Phillips. Phillips retired to curl, but Seber left because of failing health and died two years later. Patty's old friend, Lou Dufour, came back in 1957 with his Life show — which he last had with Patty in 1934 — and added a freak show in 1958. By then, Patty had reduced the number of shows to five and a girl show still got the best money. A girl revue again led the three shows of 1959.

Jack Ray continued to produce new fronts for shows and rides, and was also contracted to dress up the huge CNE grandstand. He designed a 30-foot-high birthday cake set for the 75th anniversary in 1953, with pianist Victor Borge the headliner. Jack Arthur booked Roy Rogers, the cowboy entertainer, for 1954, but a squabble between two rival entertainment unions reduced the show to a small variety package. Arthur was reported to have had a heart attack and Ray took over running rehearsals. Ed Sullivan, just becoming a television star, led the grandstand in 1955, Bob Hope in 1957, and Danny Kaye, on a return visit, in 1958. Ray designed all their sets. When Arthur tried going without a big-name American star in 1956, the results disappointed. When attendance at the George Gobel show in 1959 was also off, the local papers began clamouring for a change from celebrity acts. The Ex had the Ringling Bros. & Barnum & Bailey Circus for matinees in 1957 and while attendance

Portrait photo of Jack Ray, c. 1955.

was less than hoped for, a locally produced circus appeared in 1959 and for several years after. The Conklins were not directly connected to entertainment the Ex provided, but their midway benefitted from every boost in star power and the opportunity to rub shoulders with celebrities boosted Patty's ego.

The CNE's continued success encouraged discussions of ways to expand it. Attendance of over 300,000 on big days became expected and pushed capacity to the limit, especially on the midway. There was debate about adding a week and moving the dates back so that it ended with the Labour Day holiday, rather than running through it. Two days were added in 1958. There was talk about bringing in a Major League Baseball franchise and developing the grandstand to accommodate one. In 1959 the Toronto Argonauts Canadian Football League franchise signed an arrangement to use the grandstand and pay for its expansion. The grounds were enlarged by reclaiming 50 acres of land from the lake. The Conklins were eager to take part in upgrading Exhibition Park.

Before they would invest more money, the Conklins wanted more security. Three years into their five-year contract, they negotiated a new one, this time for eight years, beginning with the 1957 exhibition. They could now proceed with their plans to spend a quarter of a million dollars on the midway. They paved a 1,250-foot go-kart track that took up most of the space under the Flyer and for which they bought 12 cars at $1,800 a piece. They constructed a 10,000-square-foot concrete block building to house a 56-horse Derby Racer, and another permanent building to house 20 photo booths. They imported a mechanical band, a mechanical village, and rides from Germany. They also hiked the price of all children's rides from a nickel to a dime. No wonder that, although the 1957 CNE attendance was the lowest since 1953, the Conklin ride and show gross beat that year's by over $200,000. Not coincidentally, the Conklins had also tied the success of the CNE more tightly to their company. There would be no more attacks mounted against the Conklin CNE midway monopoly for over a decade.

BUSINESS BEYOND THE EX

Jim leans against the fence at the end of the midway, watches the sparse crowd move from ride to ride, notes which rides get them on and off fastest. He writes down his tallies. His father, there earlier, told him to make sure the ride gazoonies behaved themselves and paid attention to what they were doing. He had identified one or two who might give Jim trouble. So far, they are working the best he could expect. He continues to time them.

The dozen or so rides set up before him are as much as Jim wants to manage without more reliable help. With a couple of grab joints and some hanky panks thrown in, he's earning his pay. His father will deal with beefs from the city and leave the midway to Jim. Patty has had enough of hanging out with roughies he's paying little to do less.

Where the midway pavement ends, the ditch for the road begins, a flimsy snow fence dividing them. Most of the roadwork is done and both lanes are open to traffic, but there are still machines sitting in the dust. Traffic is heavy at the edge of the city and the drop-off for midway patrons adds to the congestion. People are still getting used to the increasing number of cars, the faster speeds. A midway in the middle of a highway becomes part of their acclimatization.

On that midway, mothers and their children ride a merry-go-round with buses, cars, and fire engines instead of horses. Mini cars with mini drivers circle a track. Kids on tiny motorbikes at another ride wave to the motorists driving by on the expressway. Some of the motorists wave back. Accidents are avoided.

Jim surveys the scene where his summer will play out. He's working on a deal with a grocery chain that will start in a month, just as school lets out. That will prove he has some ideas of his own.

He thinks of Norma, back in Kirkland Lake for the summer after finishing nursing school. If things go well over the next few months and before she gets serious about a career of her own, he will ask her to marry him. He had shown his seriousness by giving her his fraternity pin, but it will not be as an architect that he will ask for her hand. He hopes she can accept him as a carnie, albeit a carnie prince who will inherit a carnie empire.

★　★　★

By the time his father had settled with the CNE association in 1952, Jim Conklin had graduated from Ridley College, a private school in St. Catharines, and gone on to study architecture at McGill University in Montreal. During his senior years at Ridley, he had hosted his birthdays at Crystal Beach, his guests given free rein to the rides. He had begun working on a midway when he was 16, later than many carnival scions, running a game at Crystal Beach.

Other than crossing paths on the midway, Patty had not spent much time with Jim. During the few months when Patty was not travelling, Jim was away at school. Edythe, left alone much of the year, had a confirmed alcohol use disorder by the time Jim was a teenager. He grew up reserved and introverted, but with the quiet confidence that wealth and private schooling provide. He would find his own place on the midway under the tutelage of his father and uncle, and Neil Webb.

Amusement Park Developments

Patty was ambivalent about his son following him in the carnival business. He wanted him to join a profession, but Jim never completed his certification as an architect. After he'd had a few years' experience at Crystal Beach, his father gave him the midway at Sunnyside Beach to manage in 1954 when he turned 21. He had 13 rides to look after and was paid $75 a week, plus the profits from four new kiddie rides installed that year. The next year they moved the operation across the road from the main Sunnyside midway; in the new location Jim had 10 rides, plus novelty and food stands. When the park was torn down in 1956 for the expressway, the Conklins negotiated with the Toronto Harbour Commission to operate a few rides. City council and the media were incensed, but this time the Conklins were only the indirect targets of their outrage.

On March 15 the *Telegram* reported that, as the old park was being demolished, "Canada's Mr. Midway, Patty Conklin, announced ... that a new $200,000 Kiddieland, the most modern of its kind in the world, will open at Sunnyside April 18." The Metropolitan Toronto chairman immediately declared the decision "a retrograde step beyond all common sense." Upon further reflection, he added, "It looks like planning is to be returned to the dark ages. ... We just got rid of one amusement centre. How can anyone contemplate this?"[13]

The old park had been between Lake Shore Boulevard and Lake Shore Drive; the Conklin kiddieland had already moved south of both, closer to the lake. These two roads were transformed into east- and west-bound arteries, with speed limits raised to 40 miles per hour, while an expressway was built. The Metro chairman raised aesthetic considerations, describing the Conklin kiddieland as a return to "the Coney Island, hurdy-gurdy amusement development" that had been a "disgrace" to the western approach to the city during the Sunnyside years.[14]

The Harbour Commission, taking the position that it had jurisdiction over the land and was immune to city zoning, had not consulted the city or metropolitan regional planning and traffic authorities when negotiating with the Conklins. Mayor Phillips called the Harbour Commission chairman before the Board of Control to explain why the contract had been let. The *Globe and Mail* published a series of editorials demanding that the city seek an injunction and solicit the provincial and federal governments to start proceedings to dispossess the Harbour Commission of the land. The newspaper deplored the secrecy that surrounded the deal. One editorial was accompanied by a cartoon depicting a child sitting in the middle of heavy traffic under a sign pointing "To Kiddieland." Patty kept his sense of humour, annotating a clipping of the cartoon with a label pointing at the child: "Jim."[15]

After almost 20 years of talking about it, the Conklins had their own stand-alone, season-long kiddieland and Jim was the manager. It was, however, on public land, saving the Conklins overhead, but keeping control of its tenure out of their hands. The company paved an 800-by-300-foot plot, erected an eight-foot fence, and set up 16 rides, including a new German carousel with buses, cars, and fire engines in the place of horses. The city and Metro governments took consolation in the fact that the licence was only for one year and would expire in time for the rides to be moved to the CNE. The licence was not renewed for 1957.

Complaints about Sunnyside often identified Exhibition Park as an alternative location. In negotiations, the Conklins attempted to keep the CNE association committed to giving them first consideration if it decided to establish an amusement park on the grounds. The building of the Flyer in 1953 implied a summer-long stand, since an annual fair of a few weeks could not afford such an expensive structure. When it was built, Patty "declined to discuss the possibility that the CNE midway may be converted into a year-around operation."[16] The construction of four permanent juice stands the next year led to further speculation that "Conklin apparently is moving in the direction of readying for the possible operation of a permanent amusement park operation on the CNE grounds."[17]

Sunnyside temporarily satisfied Patty's desire for a Toronto amusement park. When he could not renew the licence with the Harbour Commission, in his 1957 negotiations with the CNE association for a longer contract and an increased number of permanent installations, he also asked for a summer-long kiddieland. He got the rights to establish one on the exhibition grounds from mid-May to the CNE opening. It was set up near the Flyer, then would be moved to its usual location for the run of the Ex. It used the 14 rides formerly at Sunnyside and Jim was the manager. It had a refreshment stand, an arcade, and a picnic area, although they only booked one company picnic that year. Once again on public land, the Conklin kiddieland's existence and makeup still depended on the whims of city politicians and bureaucrats.

Patty reported that in its first year the CNE kiddieland doubled the business it had at the Sunnyside location. However, in a letter to Dixon, the association secretary, on November 8, 1957, he wrote that "the venture was not too profitable to ourselves or the Exhibition." Nevertheless, "the experiment was worthwhile" and he wanted to try it again. He thought that they could do just as well with 10 rides instead of 14, but he wanted to add a Ferris wheel, for flash and to provide adults at least one ride to share with their children. Dixon took the request to the board but replied on November 22 that "it was the firm decision of our Directors that this must remain strictly a Kiddieland operation" and they turned down the Ferris wheel.

After decades of trying to get an amusement park at the CNE, the Conklins let it go after two years. No adult rides, no profit. They turned to the London fair association and did not meet the same resistance. In May 1959, they opened Frolicland on the London fairground, the very name signalling that they had more than children in mind. Under Jim's oversight, the park had 18 rides, three for adults. None of the children's rides grossed more than $500 a month, while the three adult rides always broke $1,000 and sometimes came close to $2,000. But the Conklins had to close the park during the CNE, take the rides to Toronto, and then bring them back for the London fair. This arrangement, satisfactory to no one, was not repeated.

The Conklins continued to expand at their more profitable Belmont Park and Crystal Beach operations. In 1952 they produced a water show for Belmont, Phillips managing the 35 performers. With the addition of seven rides, that year at Belmont they had a total of 15, plus a funhouse. By mid-decade they were up to 11 children's rides, nine major rides, and two funhouses. At Crystal Beach, they had 12 out of 20 rides in 1952, including the only new device they put in the parks that year, a Kiddie Tumblebug. Three years later they had 13 kiddie devices and two majors. Their game concessions ran at both parks.

They maintained social ties with their amusement park partners. In the spring of 1952, Frank spent a week off the Florida coast fishing on the cruiser of George Hall, owner of Crystal Beach. Each winter, Patty and Edythe visited with Rex Billings, Belmont's manager, and his wife in Miami. Hall, Billings, and their sons visited Patty at the CNE every year.

Belmont Park staged its 35th anniversary in 1958 as a promotional opportunity. The park had won first prize for outdoor attractions in Montreal's beautification campaign three years earlier. Its annual attendance had grown from 40,000 to nudge a million. It had hosted two picnics its first year and now had over 400 annually. A popular radio program broadcast from the park each Saturday, and live television programs and a National Film Board movie had been produced on site.

The Conklins, booking rides in the park for 15 years, were responsible for the currency of the riding devices the park offered. In 1957 they brought in Dufour's sideshow to replace Kortes's. Kenneth Johnstone, who as a reporter for the Montreal *Standard* had written so extensively about the Conklins, the Exposition Provinciale, and Belmont, was by then in charge of the park's press relations. The park remained in the Gauvreau family. Charles Trudeau, a successful businessman, retained an interest and his son, Pierre, was a director. Already known in Quebec for his opposition to the repressive regime of Maurice Duplessis, by the time of Belmont's 45th anniversary Trudeau would be prime minister.

The Conklins had also become involved with an American amusement park, Riverside, near Springfield, Massachusetts. Patty's acquaintance with Ed Carroll, the owner and manager, went back to the Fair for Britain, during the 1943 version of which Carroll visited Patty to attempt to interest him in midway passenger trains. Carroll was associated with the Eastern States Exposition at Springfield, which during the war expressed an interest in getting a Conklin midway. Frank visited Carroll's park in 1947. The Conklins put seven rides into Riverside in 1951. Patty and Edythe visited Carroll that year, when he was president of the National Association of Amusement Parks, Pools and Beaches, and Carroll reciprocated with a visit to the CNE. Patty later served as a broker between Riverside and a European ride importer.

Patty also brokered rides for Jack and Irving Rosenthal, owners of Palisades Park in New Jersey. The Conklins and the Rosenthals exchanged team members. Joe McKee, the Palisades ride superintendent, helped the Conklins out with their roller coaster. Jack Ray, when not busy with his own company or his work for the Conklins and Jimmy Sullivan, worked on designs for Palisades. In line with a trend in the outdoor amusement industry to provide themed attractions, Irving Rosenthal got a licensing agreement with DC Comics in 1956. Palisades took out advertisements in comic books and Ray devised a Superman Village for the park. He also designed fronts for new rides at Palisades.

Given his experience and connections, it was natural for Ray to get into the park business himself. In the March 27, 1954, issue of *Billboard*, he said he had "always wanted an experimental workshop where new park ideas and operations may be carried out." After opening a California office for his design business in 1953, he moved to La Jolla, California. In 1954 he and a partner leased Mission Beach Amusement Park from the City of San Diego. They changed the name to Belmont Park, and augmented the Giant Dipper coaster, built in 1928, with a new kiddie coaster, a $60,000 kiddieland, and a picnic area.

For the time being, amusement parks remained profitable. In 1953 the *Wall Street Journal* published an article detailing just how good a business an amusement park or kiddieland could be.[18] Patty had been with kiddielands from the beginning and was finally getting some recognition for his pioneering role. He was invited to speak on the subject at the International Association of Fairs and Exhibitions (IAFE) convention in 1952.

Kiddieland and Other Innovations

In his address to the IAFE, Patty said that his ideas about kiddielands went back as far as 1933, when he first took a shot at the CNE midway. He had "realized that more efforts would have to be put forth to attract the children to exhibitions on a mass scale."[19] In his proposal to Elwood Hughes in 1946, he had pointed out, based on his five years of experience at the CNE, that the children's area was not profitable, but "is a means of attracting children who bring along adults who spend money in many other places around the Exhibition grounds." But recent experience at the CNE had partly changed Patty's mind about the profitability of rides in general and kiddie rides in particular. To the IAFE, he pointed out that gross receipts for the CNE kiddieland had increased 14-fold between 1937 and 1952. He produced similar figures for the London fair and the Exposition Provinciale.

Patty had not forgotten the original motivation behind kiddielands. Referring to children's days at fairs and amusement parks when the ride price was reduced by half, he said, "Our reason for these cheap prices is that we have found, from various surveys, that on the average, every three children who come to the exhibition grounds bring along at least one adult; and, as a result, we receive some patronage from the accompanying adults."[20] He was also trying to encourage the development of rides targeted at 10- to 14-year-olds.

The impetus behind Patty's other innovations was also not wholly altruistic. Automatic timers on rides compelled "operators to be on the job to take care of the children when the ride has been completed."[21] They also ensured that rides ran to consistent set times, usually short. Selling strips of six children's tickets for the price of five increased volume and reduced the need for ticket sellers. Although introduced in 1942, Patty was still touting ticket strips as an innovation in an April 7, 1956, *Billboard* article that cited the show business adage that "fast dimes are better than slow quarters" as the reason behind the show's price policies.

In the early 1950s, Patty found yet another way to collect fast dimes. Coin-operated mechanical children's rides had been invented in 1931, but only became popular in the late 1940s when sales mushroomed. The beauty of these devices was that they ran themselves and parents provided all the necessary supervision. In 1951 Patty began putting coin-operated children's rides in Eaton's department stores and had some at the CNE. For the 1952 Ex, he capitalized on the popularity of Roy Rogers, King of the Cowboys, by setting up a Roy Rogers Ranch, probably unlicensed, with 18 coin-operated horses. He had 12 in a corral the next year, but without the Roy Rogers branding.

Bally Manufacturing, the pinball and slot machine manufacturer founded in Chicago in 1932, was one of the main companies producing coin-operated children's rides. Patty wanted to be the Canadian distributor for Bally but needed someone to handle the American end. The Conklins had known Dave Russell, a Chicago businessman, for five years. Patty and Edythe socialized with Russell and his wife during their annual trips to Hot Springs. Russell had 10 coin-operated crane machines with Wallace Brothers' Shows in 1950, as well as an installation at Belmont Park. It was with Russell in Hot Springs in 1951 that Patty cooked up the scheme to buy nine light plants and lease them to Johnny J. Jones Exposition.

In January 1953, Bally announced that Russ-Con, a new company formed by Russell and Conklin and based in Montreal, would be their Canadian distributor. Their first deal was with Patty himself, who in February closed negotiations to put 34 mechanical horses and two spaceships in 36 stores in the Loblaws supermarket chain. Russ-Con also had coin rides at Belmont. The fad was fading quickly, however, and by 1954, according to the *Billboard* ride survey in the April 10 issue, coin-operated rides were "on the wane." Russ-Con folded soon after.

The Conklins followed this foray into supermarkets with another marketing deal. In the summer of 1954, the Dominion supermarket chain hired them to put together two units of four kiddie rides each and tour them around 13 of its stores, from Windsor to Montreal. The units stayed for two weeks at each store. Dominion tried selling tickets, but then switched to letting children ride free with any purchase by their parents. According to Dominion's advertising manager, "Mr. Conklin planned this promotion with Dominion Stores ... and organized the crews to operate the rides."[22] He made the arrangements for power and permits, and Conklin Shows received good exposure. Dominion revealed that the promotion increased sales by 25 percent and used it again the next year.

Carnie Prince

In 1956, Jim's third year managing the Sunnyside operation and its last, the Dominion promotion was turned into a promotion for the Conklins. Jim was given credit for working out this innovation. Dominion would exchange one wrapper from its bread for a ride in the travelling kiddielands in the stores' parking lots. It would trade five wrappers for a Sunnyside ride ticket. The rides at the stores were now promoting both Dominion and Sunnyside. Full-page colour newspaper advertisements for Dominion described the Sunnyside rides. While Jim would pick up other deals with supermarkets, Dominion did not stay with the Conklins when they moved their kiddieland to the CNE the next year.

By that time, Jim was married to Norma Woodruff from Kirkland Lake. When Jim met her in 1955, she was at the McGill School of Nursing, training to become a registered nurse. Spinning a tale in his father's manner, he claimed to have seen "a beautiful girl walking by one night" at Sunnyside and "asked her if she'd like a ride on the Ferris wheel. She said yes."[23] He gave her his fraternity pin on Christmas Day. She received her nursing certificate in the spring of 1956 and in the fall they were engaged. Jim introduced her to the outdoor amusement world at the Showmen's League of America banquet in Chicago in December. They were married three days before that Christmas in the chapel of Ridley College in St. Catharines. Well-wishers from his father's past included Aunt Catherine Brocco from New Jersey and Theo Forestall. None of Patty's other brothers or sisters sent regards. The newlyweds honeymooned in Montreal, Quebec City, and Monaco. They were looked after in Quebec City by the chief of police, who was a friend of Uncle Frank's, and they were taken on a skiing trip. Their first child, Patricia, named in honour of Jim's father, was born the following November. Norma recovered in time to attend her second Showmen's League banquet.

During the first years of their marriage, the amusement park business declined, forcing Jim to spend an increasing amount of time on the Ontario circuit of Conklin Shows, picking up from his uncle, whose health was failing. What can be seen in retrospect as the harbinger of the amusement parks' recession at first seemed to signal their rejuvenation. In April 1954, Walt Disney Productions and the ABC television network announced a deal to invest 10 million dollars in the most imaginative and costly amusement park the world had seen. As early as 1950, Walt Disney was said to have "held conference after conference with such amusement experts ... as Patty Conklin ... during the International Assn. of Fairs & Expositions (IAFE) convention in December. Walt got a great kick out of his new friends and made a great hit as speaker at the SLA President's Party."[24] But unlike his new friends, when Disney visited existing parks, he was disturbed by their carnie atmosphere and what he saw as their aura of danger and disorder. His park would be cleansed of these flaws. It would also be inaccessible by mass transit and would eventually adopt an expensive one-price admission policy, means by which the park's clientele could be culled and managed.

Disneyland in Anaheim opened in July 1955, at a final cost of 17 million dollars. It set a new standard that few existing parks, which were mainly small family businesses, could meet. Disney agents bought the vintage merry-go-round at Sunnyside through Patty in 1954 and completely refurbished it for their park. Other than the minor-league kiddielands the Conklins ran after the demise of Sunnyside, the city of Toronto would never have its own permanent amusement park and never on the Disney scale. Canada's Wonderland, opened in 1980 well outside the city to keep away the riff raff, is a theme park built by a consortium on the Disneyland model. Belmont Park and Crystal Beach were able to survive as long as they did only because of the expensive new rides Patty was constantly finding for them through the later 1950s and '60s.

NEW RIDE TECHNOLOGIES

That's how Patty did business. He always had a roll in his pocket.... One day we were in Germany. We were at a table with all these big shots, rich people. He had bought three or four rides. I think he spent a million and a half on new equipment.... We're sitting there, and this one rich guy brought out a roll with one, two, three thousand-mark bills. Everybody looks. This other guy says, "What are you talking about, what about this roll?" Patty had a roll with thousand-dollar bills. A thousand dollars was four thousand marks. He had 200-, 300-, 400,000 dollars.

If you bought a ride for $40,000, you'd pay $10,000 cash under the table. The ride would then be priced for $30,000 and you'd only pay duty on $30,000. This was how the Germans worked and they'd pay less sales tax. So, Patty always had a roll like that. Patty would be careful. He'd tell me to go ten feet behind him, in case somebody had a gun.

He carried a lot of money, but never got robbed. One day we came from Stuttgart to Munich late at night and he got sick. We went from one factory to the next factory; there was five, six big factories in Germany.... He said, "Heinz, I don't feel good." We stopped, went in a restaurant and I phoned a doctor. Then he gets better and he says, "It's two in the morning, Heinz, let's go. I'm all right." I said, "No, no, I phoned a doctor. I got him out of bed at two in the morning. We're lucky to get him. He's coming to this restaurant out on the autobahn. No, no, we're staying here." Then he got really sick. I dropped him off in the hotel. He said, "Get me up at eight." I said, "It's two in the morning now." Then I couldn't find a hotel room, so I slept in the car. He stayed in a first-class hotel there, Four Seasons. They kept his room for sure. We had a big Mercedes and I slept in there all night.

I wake up, the sun is out. It's eight o'clock, nine o'clock. I came a half-hour late. He's walking up and down the lobby of the hotel, "Where have you been? Where've you been? Have you been shopping?" I says, "No, I couldn't get a room, because I came late, at two in the morning, they rented the room to somebody else." He said, "Why didn't you come up? I have a couch in there, you could have slept on the couch." He wasn't that sick. The doctor gave him a couple of pills and he was down in the lobby waiting for me. I was half-dead from sleeping in the car all night.

He said, "I got a lot of money in my coat. I've got a fake pocket in my night coat." There was some 30-, 40,000 dollars in there. He said, "If anything happens to me, the first thing you take is the money. Give it to my son, Jim. Don't give it to Mr. Webb," the financer for the company. "You got a lot of nerve," I said. "You're dead, you think I'm going to go in there and take the money? ... No way, I won't do this; that would be stupid.... What happens if I come back to Brantford and Mr. Webb said he gave you four hundred thousand and that I stole it?"

That's how the business worked in those days. Everybody did this. Usually in those days, when we bought a ride in Germany for, let's say, 40,000 marks, by the time he brought it over here, he sold it for $40,000 and the dollar was four-to-one on the mark. He made good money then. Some rides, we bought five at one shot. He'd just write a cheque in Germany and take a cheque here. We'd have nothing to do with the ride. The only guy who was involved was me. I went there and put it up wherever it went. The buyer had to pay my wages, my meal allowance, my hotel, not Conklin Shows.

Interview with Heinz Schlichthorn, April 26, 2006

★ ★ ★

Patty became convinced the sideshow would die out as quickly as the small-time amusement park. The reason, as he told *Billboard* in the January 9, 1961, issue, was much the same: huge media conglomerates "have boosted the price of talent for midway shows to a point where it is almost impossible to give the public a real value for its money." Since taking over the CNE, he had left the risk of mounting shows up to independent producers. The one exception was the Alfie Phillips water show in which he had an investment.

The money he and Frank put back into the company went mostly toward rides. Rides could cover their own overhead, but more importantly they now drew the crowds from which the show skimmed its profit through the games. Patty knew that his public increasingly demanded the mechanical thrills they imagined as potential in the technology burgeoning around them. But in the early 1950s, the North American ride industry lacked the new ideas that show-men were looking for to satisfy their patrons' demands. The miles showmen like Patty once covered looking for new freaks like Ernie and Len they now travelled in search of novel rides.

Shortages of material, steel especially, limited ride production in the United States from the start of the Korean War until after its end in 1953. Some ride manufacturers gained toeholds in the defence industries. Children's rides continued to be in heavy demand, sustaining companies that could supply them. No new major devices were developed as long as manufacturers needed all the materials they could get to build kiddie rides. Irving Rosenthal of Palisades Park blamed operators reluctant to invest in anything other than juvenile units for the shortsighted neglect of new major rides.[25] The amusement parks association considered offering a cash prize for the first company to produce a significant new device. By early 1953, even manufacturers were acknowledging "the need for one or more major riding devices to stimulate new interest and buying."[26]

A German Invasion

Park owners began to look further afield for new equipment. A new device at the Munich Oktoberfest in 1949 immediately attracted attention. The Rotor was an upright hollow cylinder, 12 feet in diameter, that spun at 15 miles an hour, creating sufficient centrifugal force to pin passengers to the inside of its walls. When top speed was reached, the floor dropped away and riders stayed stuck on the walls. The Rotor got international exposure, including a photo essay in *Life* in October 1949 and an article in *Popular Mechanics* in December 1950. It drew big crowds at fairs throughout Germany in 1950 and London's Festival of Britain in 1951.

The Rotor's German inventor, Ernst Hoffmeister, had taken out patents in his homeland and other European countries in the 1940s and applied for the U.S. patent in September 1949. He granted limited rights to a partner, Mickey Hughes, who through John Ringling North, president and director of Ringling Bros. and Barnum & Bailey Circus, brought a Rotor to Palisades Park in 1951. The version at Palisades did not follow Hoffmeister's specifications and did poor business. Hoffmeister got entangled in a legal battle with his erstwhile partner, suing him for spoiling the Rotor's reputation in the United States. The proprietors of a Rotor company formed in England for the Festival of Britain brought versions to amusement parks in Chicago, Long Beach, and San Francisco in 1952. According to Hoffmeister, they too were inferior and he threatened legal action against these parks.

Hoffmeister's American patent had not yet been granted and whoever had a Rotor up and running in the United States could contest it. In mid-1951 Patty contacted him. To protect his patent in Canada, Hoffmeister was willing to give Patty exclusive Canadian rights. Patty recommended that Hoffmeister retain Arthur Morse, Patty's Chicago lawyer, to look after his legal wrangling with the American parks. Morse and Patty formed a company to recover control of the American rights for Hoffmeister. Morse worked out a deal with the parks whereby Hoffmeister — and Patty and Morse — got a small percentage of the proceeds from the rides.

Patty's reluctance to become involved with Hoffmeister's legal problems was tempered by his conviction that the Rotor was going to have an impact on North American midways. He wanted two for use at Belmont, Crystal Beach, and the CNE. As Morse was looking after the rides that had already slipped into the States, Patty was trying to acquire two still in Europe, one in London, the other in Rome. Hoffmeister's importers promised Patty the London Rotor for Belmont's 1952 season. The London operator claimed he had problems getting the ride ready to ship and it did not make it to Belmont, although it ended up later that summer at Riverview Park in Chicago.

Patty and Hoffmeister met for the first time in June 1952, when the German came to North America. He signed Patty up as his sole agent in Canada and negotiated with Patty to bring a Rotor set up in Hamburg to Canada. He wanted Patty to advance him $100,000 to pay off debts he had contracted to build it and the one in Rome, and to pay for dismantling and shipping one of them. Patty and Morse discussed financing the move, but Patty broke with Morse and turned Hoffmeister down, explaining to him in a letter on February 13, 1953, that "we have never ... made financial advances to anyone with whom we do business; and, we are going to strictly adhere to this policy." Morse might have provided financing, but however he managed it Hoffmeister got his Rotor from Rome on a ship for Canada at the end of February.

Hoffmeister was on hand at Belmont to supervise his Rotor's installation, the first time he had this privilege in North America. His version included an elaborate gallery for spectators to view the riders' contortions. This enabled him to register the Rotor with customs as a show rather than a ride, reducing the bond from $200 to $100 a month. The distinction made by Canadian customs red tape reflects how the drawing power once held by shows had been transferred to rides.

The Rotor headed the list of new attractions at Belmont in 1953, along with a new Rock-O-Plane, a ride invented by Eyerly Aircraft in 1948. When moved to Toronto for the CNE, the Rotor was the second-highest grossing ride, after the Flyer. Hoffmeister still owned the ride and Patty had to strike a new deal with him to use it the next year. By then, Hoffmeister had set up a Toronto office. He stuck close to the version he leased to the Conklins until 1959. The Rotor remained a powerhouse at Belmont and on the midways of the CNE and the London fair.

The rights to manufacture portable Rotors in the United States were transferred to a partnership of the Velare brothers, the California amusement park owners, with the British Rotor company. The Velares announced they would have two out, costing $70,000 each, for the major 1953 fairs.[27] Continued legal problems delayed their release until the next spring.[28] Royal American finally got a Rotor in 1958. It became a standard attraction on North American midways.

The Rotor's reputation enabled Hoffmeister to sell another invention. In 1938 he had built a new type of mirror show, the Varioscop, operating it in Germany and Sweden. It consisted of a series of distorting mirrors mounted on an oval revolving track. He had set one up at the 1939 New York World's Fair and taken out the patent but had done nothing with it since. Hoffmeister granted Patty North American rights to the ride, then called the Mirrors, in late 1952. Nothing came of the arrangement until early 1955, when Patty announced that he had acquired the device, now called Flex-O-Rama, through Eric Wedemeyer, Hoffmeister's new import agent. He had also acquired a German flying car ride through Wedemeyer. In the spring, Wedemeyer reported that Ed Carroll and Irving Rosenthal had each bought the mirror units outright for their parks. The device was now called the Laff-O-Rama and Patty had been instrumental in arranging the deals. No matter what it was called, the device was not well received and did not fulfill his prediction that it would "revolutionize the Funhouse business."[29]

Patty had negotiated his first deal with Wedemeyer in the summer of 1954, this one for a Roto-Jet built by the German firm of Kaspar Klaus.[30] Tubular capsules at the end of long sweeps, the Roto-Jet's innovation was that it allowed riders to control the elevation of the sweeps, up to 20 feet in the air. By the time Patty got his, Wedemeyer had placed units with Riverside Park, Palisades Park, Coney Island, and a kiddieland in New York. Patty's Roto-Jet was the first in Canada. He ran it for four weeks at Belmont Park before moving it to the CNE and then the London fair. At the CNE it had the third-highest gross among portable rides, with the Rotor in first. It ran well enough at the 1955 CNE, but in subsequent years Patty let it stay at Belmont for the season. Wedemeyer's big success as an importer of German rides was yet to come.

An American Response

Spurred by the encroachments of German ride manufacturers, American companies were finally moving to meet the demand for new major rides. Frank Hrubetz and Company in Oregon came out with the Round-Up for the 1954 season. An open circular cage on a spinning platform with curved enclosures for passengers, the Round-Up, like the Rotor, relied on centrifugal force to pin riders in place. As it achieved top speed, the platform was raised to a 75-degree angle. It came in sizes for 24 and 30 passengers, selling for $16,000 and $19,500. The installation at the 1954 CNE grossed second among portable rides. Twenty-two Round-Ups were in operation by the end of 1955 and Hrubetz was soon producing and selling a dozen or more a year.

The Eli Bridge Company had been making Ferris wheels in all sizes for half a century. In the fall of 1953, they tested the Scrambler, their first foray into other rides. The Scrambler was invented in the late 1930s and Eli Bridge acquired the patent in the early '40s, but because of war shortages and the fact that their full production capacity was taken up with Ferris wheels, 10 years elapsed before they built one. Their production of five Scramblers for 1954 was spoken for, as were 20 the next year, and although they reached an annual production of 25 in 1956, they could not clear their waiting list for the ride until into the next decade. Selling for $16,900, the Scrambler featured rotating pods of four buckets hung from sweeps that also rotated.

The Allan Herschell Company, the largest U.S. manufacturer of riding devices, finally brought out a new ride in 1955. The Twister had rotating four-seat tubs that were attached to sweeps rolled on a tilted track. Priced at $16,000, it also sold out the year it was introduced and the following year. It, the Scrambler, and the Round-Up all became midway standards. Patty had a Scrambler and a Twister on the CNE and London fair midways in 1955. He added a second Scrambler and a Round-Up the following year. But by that time, he had begun his own trips to Germany to look for rides.

With new major rides finally appearing, manufacturers still could not meet the pent-up demand. By the middle of the decade, there were signs that the growth of kiddielands was declining and some existing kiddielands were starting to include major rides. No new amusement parks had opened, with the exception of Disneyland, which raised the cost to enter the industry to a level only large corporations could meet. Patrons were starting to identify their midway experience with rides such as Disneyland provided, and rides across the midways of America were earning record grosses. Their soaring popularity was expected to continue. That same year, however, one ride operator lamented in the April 24 *Billboard* that "we need more thrill rides.... Teen-agers today are speed and thrill-minded ... we know that the few new thrill rides introduced in recent years have received big business."

In 1958 some U.S. manufacturers saw their sales decrease for the first time in years. Prices of major rides had been climbing 5 to 6 percent. The economy was in recession and the kiddieland market for children's rides was failing. By the end of the decade, operators were again complaining that American manufacturers were not inventing new major rides to keep their customers interested, but the economy was now part of the reason. Carnival and park men in search of novel devices had by then become accustomed to turning to Europe, especially Germany.

The Wild Mouse

Patty retained his perambulatory habits, constantly covering the continent — Chicago, Seattle, New York, Miami, Los Angeles, Hot Springs, New Orleans, Vancouver, Toronto. He seldom spent more than three months in a year at his home in Brantford. His planned 1951 trip to the Mediterranean with Edythe, cancelled because of political disturbances in Egypt, was back on in 1954. Their first stop was England where they visited the owners of the Blackpool and Battersea amusement parks. When he returned to North America two and a half months later, his report was sought by fellow carnival owners because of his "reputation for astute and novel showmanship."[31] While he described Blackpool as "out of this world," he had found "no lessons to be learned and no ideas to be brought back." Germany was not on his itinerary for this trip.

Patty regaled the Toronto press with tales of his adventures abroad. In Israel, he told the *Telegram* on April 20, "an Arab sniper's bullet whined past him as he photographed wooded hills on the Arab side of the no man's land which separates Israel from its neighbors." He had been warned not to take photographs. He introduced himself to the Aga Khan at a casino in Cairo and in Monaco to the former King Farouk of Egypt, who had been deposed two years before by a military coup. He also had his pockets picked in Cairo, an event that disturbed him because "Patty Conklin, for the first time in his life had had his pocket picked and he hadn't felt a thing." The *Billboard* and *Telegram* publishers were happy to report that he had their papers air mailed to him wherever he went, at a price as high as $6.50 an issue.

In early 1955, Patty, Edythe, and Jim embarked from New York on a three-month cruise around the world, another trip that kept him from touring the European ride manufacturers, although when he arrived back in Los Angeles he visited the site of Disneyland, then nearing completion. Other showmen went to the German Oktoberfest that year and reported on a new ride that promised to be a North American sensation. Patty and Jim finally took a trip to Munich in October 1956 to see for themselves. Jim was becoming his father's travelling companion at the expense of his studies, while for Patty this first visit to Oktoberfest marked the beginning of an era. It was there that he witnessed the future of midway technology.

A Munich showman had registered the plans for the Teufelskutsche, or Devil's Coach, in 1953. It had been renamed the Wilde Mause to reflect its skittish motion and was an innovation in roller coasters. Instead of trains, it used two-seater cars, which allowed riders to be yanked through tight, hairpin corners. Most importantly, it was a portable coaster that could replicate the thrills of the big stationary installations. It became the midway sensation that its early witnesses thought it would be. Four were set up at the 1956 Oktoberfest and after seeing them in operation, Patty immediately arranged to buy one. The day he returned from Munich he announced that Conklin Shows would have the first Wild Mouse in North America.[32]

Patty and Jim board a plane home from Munich, 1956.

Patty soon revised his announcement to say that he would have the first of the original portable German versions of the Wild Mouse. Joe McKee was building a stationary version at Rosenthal's Palisades Park with a front designed by Jack Ray. Rosenthal was importing the cars through Eric Wedemeyer, but they did not arrive in time for his park's opening in the spring. Patty returned to Germany in December 1956 to oversee shipment of his Mouse ride. McKee accompanied him and Patty lent Rosenthal cars until Palisades' were delivered in June. In the meantime, Patty spoke enthusiastic- ally about the Wild Mouse and Oktoberfest in general whenever he had an opportunity, playing up his reputation as the "Canadian ride tycoon."[33]

The German Wild Mouse manufacturers had not sought patent protection in North America. Patty bought plans for the Wild Mouse and sold them to at least one U.S. amusement park owner. American manufacturers developed their own copies. B.A. Schiff and Associates listed the Wild Mouse in its promotional material in 1956 and sold as many as 30 to parks by the end of the decade. In 1958 the Allan Herschell Company began selling its Mad Mouse ride and the next year introduced a Mite Mouse for kiddielands. Less well-established companies were also trying to sell versions of the ride. Wedemeyer failed once more to cash in on his connection with the homeland and stopped advertising imported mouse rides in 1959.

Flush with the success of his Wild Mouse at the 1957 CNE — it almost paid for itself by grossing over $38,000 — Patty returned to Germany and bought two more early in 1958.[34] He moved his original unit to Belmont, used one of the new ones on his own show, and sold the other to Playland, an amusement park in Rye, New York. He set up Fun Cars Ltd. and bought five more later in the year.[35] He sold three, including one to Crystal Beach, but had trouble getting rid of the other two. His colleagues were buying the cheaper, more available American versions and he had to stress that his were the "ORIGINAL ride built in Germany."[36] While the Schiff and Herschell companies were selling dozens a year, Patty could not unload his last two until 1961. By that time, the Wild Mouse in its many versions was an established attraction on the midways of all major North American amusement parks and fairs. It had consolidated a new category of rides, that of the spectacular, or "spec." Big, flashy, terrifying rides that offer dramatic light, sound, and spectacle, impressive specs would become a Conklin Shows trademark.

Patty had become thoroughly enamoured with European rides, while retaining his critical edge. In February 1958, he travelled to Brussels, site of the upcoming world's fair, "to note what progress has been made in erecting the fun zone at the big expo and to keep his eye out for possible new attractions he might import to Canada."[37] He returned to Europe in April, spending "four days in England, four at the Brussels Fair and two days in Germany."[38] He attended the opening of the world's fair with CNE general manager McCallum. "Both were unimpressed by the midway area," and while McCallum liked the buildings and thought the cable cars could be adapted to the CNE, Patty found "concessionaires ... bemoaning bad business."[39] Nonetheless, members of the National Association of Amusement Parks, Pools and Beaches held their annual late summer meeting there. Patty bought one ride in Brussels, a new type of funhouse.

Conklin Shows' support of American manufacturers grew tepid. The CNE had featured a Twister, a Scrambler, and a Round-Up as soon as they were available. Norman Bartlett had debuted his Hurricane there in 1947 and his Rodeo in 1952. In 1958 Bartlett brought his Flying Coaster out for trials at the CNE. It had cars on sweeps that flew over a ramp 30 feet in the air. Despite the American rides at the Ex, after a midway tour from Patty, a reporter had the impression that Germany was "where most amusement rides are manufactured."[40] The intended effects of the Marshall Plan were manifest in the amusement ride industry with money being made on both sides of the Atlantic from the revival of German manufacturing.

Throughout the 1950s, the Conklins were again selling off surplus equipment, all of it American. The reason, they said in an advertisement in *Billboard* on March 16, 1959, was that they were "importing new Rides from Europe." For the 1961 season, they had eliminated "all of our old ride equipment" and imported "rides from Switzerland, France, Germany, Denmark and the United States," until they had "a product that is different — a product that has greater earning power."[41] As the business practices of carnival companies evolved, "earning power" and how to calibrate it, especially for rides, were becoming significant considerations on midways.

PREPARING FOR A NEW DECADE

Jimmy Sullivan invites the interviewer, Fred Davis, to sit down and they talk about changes in the carnival business over the years. Davis is working for the National Film Board of Canada on an ethnographic television documentary. They sit at a small table behind the cookhouse, beside the office trailer.

"Oh yes, yes indeed, plenty of changes," Sullivan says. He sports a grizzled moustache, a battered hat, a suit jacket and tie, and he squints into the bright afternoon. "In the olden days it was all shows and very few rides.

Today it's all new riding devices and the shows are really big productions now." Sullivan is compact but wizened, with a mild Midwest twang that alternates between whines and assertions.

"Yes, the public has changed to a certain extent," he continues. "They want something for their money now. And they're kinda thrill crazy. In other words, they like thrilling rides, the bigger and the more dangerous they look, the better they seem to like 'em."

Asked whether he thinks the carnival can survive competition from other types of entertainment, Sullivan replies, "Well, Fred, I think it'll always survive. I'll tell you why.

"People are caged up all winter long, and ours is partly, you know, an outdoor business. People been caged up looking at televisions and radios, moving pictures, and all that stuff. Well, it, it gets boresome. They get tired of it too. So, we come along, and they come outside and like to get the fresh air and see what's new. That's why I think our business will outlast even movies.

"You take the West, for instance, out around the Prairies, as we call 'em, out around Manitoba and Alberta and Saskatchewan. The towns are so far apart, they don't even get to see the things like they do in the East. We're a big thing out there in the West. When we go out there with our show, why, they make an event out of it."

Davis asks him about getting a job as a lion tamer. Sullivan says that is not his line of business and sends him to Terrell Jacobs, "down at the other end of the grounds."

From Carnival, *National Film Board of Canada, 1955*

The CNE remained the largest outdoor exhibition in North America, even continuing to mark impressive attendance figures during the recession of 1958 to 1962. When the fair was extended by two days to 15 in 1958, attendance was predicted to surpass three million, but that took five years to happen. In 1959 McCallum warned that the CNE faced "three difficult years because of construction on all sides of its grounds."[42] The Gardiner Expressway was being built to the north, 50 acres of lakefront were being reclaimed to the south, and new buildings were being constructed throughout the grounds.

Improvements to the CNE Midway

After their quarter-million-dollar investment of 1957, the Conklins' improvements to the CNE midway became more incremental, largely the addition of a few new rides and changes in the shows. Dufour stayed on with his Life show and varying sideshows. Chick Schloss, a Chicago booking agent, brought in a girl show in 1958 to replace Seber's and stuck with the Conklins at the CNE and the fall fairs for several years.

Patty bought more German rides, mainly kiddie devices. In 1959 he bought a French ride, the Himalaya, similar to the Cortina Bobs brought out by a German company two years before. It had mechanical problems and he replaced it with a Cortina Bobs. He had two Wild Mouse rides on the CNE midway in 1960. The Velare brothers had sold the patent for their Sky Wheel to Allan Herschell and Patty made a deal with Herschell to run one of the first fully portable Sky Wheels at the CNE and the London fair for four years starting in 1961. The deal included Ed Carroll's Riverside Park in Massachusetts, where Patty's Cortina Bobs and the Sky Wheel played throughout the spring and summer before being brought north for the Ex. These expensive machines needed to be kept in operation for as much of the season as possible.

The CNE midway grosses, after some big leaps, also became more incremental, although always ahead of inflation. The rides and shows broke $600,000 in 1957 and $700,000 in 1958, and the Conklins planned for $800,000 in 1959, but settled for $750,000. They upped the gross by $25,000 in 1960.[43] When Patty announced during the 1961 CNE that he was aiming for $900,000, he pointed out that, "if reached, it would give the CNE midway in two weeks more than any carnival's entire season revenue, except … the Royal American Shows."[44] The Conklin gross that year of $794,000, while short of his goal, still surpassed the annual revenue of all but the largest midway companies.[45]

An *Amusement Business* article on "Canada's Big Show" observed that in "every aspect of fairdom it is the largest."[46] The Texas State Fair in Dallas was the only other fair on the continent that came close, approaching to within 100,000 of the CNE's attendance in some years. It had an independent midway, so no single show reaped the benefit of its crowds. Other American fairs reached a million in attendance during these years.

In Canada, the Calgary Stampede was the next biggest fair after the CNE. The Stampede first passed the half million barrier in 1955 but could not break through the next 100,000 mark. Ottawa's Central Canada Exhibition made 500,000 by 1958. Ottawa was the anchor to the World of Mirth's route and kept that show among the top carnivals. Calgary and the other western Canada class A fairs ensured that as long as Royal American held the circuit it would remain the world's largest midway company.

The CNE was their premier exhibition, but the Conklins still had other fairs in Ontario and Quebec. Patty treated the Western Fair as an extension of the CNE, persuading as many as possible of the independent ride and show owners he booked for Toronto to follow him down the road to London. About half the rides and concessions that made the trip were show-owned. In 1955 Patty signed a contract extension for 12 more years at the Western Fair. The gate stayed around 350,000, although the midway gross always rose. In 1960 the fair extended to two weekends, but the first of these overlapped with the CNE, so it opened without the full Conklin midway. The overlap was rectified the next year when the CNE moved its dates to a week earlier and 43 of the 62 rides and shows at Toronto went on to London.

World's Finest Shows

Frank's road show had a season of little more than two months, often not starting until August and ending by early October. Many eastern carnival owners complained about the rain, muddy lots, and small crowds they suffered at spring still dates, but despite resolutions to the contrary most continued to open in late April. Conklin Shows led a trend — to which the disappearance of vacant lots from cities was contributing — of opening late. On April 20, 1959,

Billboard announced "Eastern Future Dim for Still Dates" because of "more touring shows and fewer lots." The shopping centres that had been paving over the lots offered an opportunity to work a few rides before opening up full-scale operations. The Conklins were leading in this trend too, and it went along with the greater concentration on riding devices as the core of the midway. While not on the road, they kept their rides running at the Toronto and London Froliclands, Montreal's Belmont Park, Riverside Park in Massachusetts, and other parks.

While the Conklins were able to employ ride operators in the spring, they had trouble holding on to games agents and sideshow producers. Early in July one year, in an advertisement listing 10 fairs, the first of which began in August, Frank sought "legitimate Game Concessions. Have real attractive propositions for worthwhile Shows."[47] Game concessionaires and showmen at loose ends this late in the season were not likely legitimate or worthwhile.

When Frank took his crew out in the middle of the summer, it was usually to an opener at the Leamington fair. They worked the Belleville fair consistently throughout the decade and added the Peterborough Industrial Exhibition in 1954. Frank got a five-year contract with Peterborough the following year and a 10-year contract for Leamington in 1958. They played the Kitchener centennial as a street celebration at the end of June in 1954, one of their only still dates in the decade, then signed up the Kitchener Industrial Exhibition, a fall fair, the next year. They got a five-year contract with Kitchener in 1956, but only completed three years of it. In 1955 Frank attended the first of the five years he contracted with the Sudbury fair and then let Sullivan have the rest of them on his own.

The Ontario fairs counted their attendance in the low tens of thousands, but the Quebec City Exposition Provinciale remained among the top five in the country. Attendance there rose to 400,000 in 1958, and Trois-Rivières and Sherbrooke both continued to grow. These three fairs remained Conklin–Wallace Brothers combinations, with Frank in charge and Sullivan assisting. In the mid-1950s, Frank renewed long-term contracts with Sherbrooke and Trois-Rivières. By 1957 the combination was carrying as many as 15 major rides, 11 kiddie rides, 13 shows, and scores of concessions into Quebec.

Frank and Sullivan continued to work the Ontario fall fairs, which always included Renfrew and Lindsay. They played Kingston for five years starting in 1957, Kitchener for several years in the middle of the decade, and Chatham, Sudbury, Picton, and Oshawa for one year each. Sullivan, as he had for over 30 years, finished his season without the Conklins at the Norfolk County Fair in Simcoe in October.

Wallace Brothers not only finished late, it started early, typically opening in Brantford or Windsor in April, then playing still dates in western Ontario before heading through Sault St. Marie to a still in Winnipeg that kicked off the western B circuit. After the B circuit, Sullivan dragged his crew back across the continent to Trois-Rivières and reunion with their Conklin brethren.

Because of the length of his route, studded with some of Canada's best fairs, Sullivan was able to keep a consistent office lineup. Phil Cronin, owner of kiddie rides and bingo games, had been with him since 1921; William "Tiny" Jamieson, transportation superintendent, since 1934; Pat Marco, concession manager, since 1939; brother Mike, secretary of concessions, since 1942; and Hank Blade, lot boss, since 1946. Many of Sullivan's games and ride men were also long term and many were francophone, having joined him when he first entered Quebec in the late 1930s and stayed on to work over their linguistic compatriots in all parts of the country.

Sullivan gained a reputation in the outdoor amusement business. While playing an Edmonton still date in 1952, he hosted a dinner for government officials, leading businessmen, the Edmonton chief of police and the mayor, the president of the Edmonton exhibition, and the manager of the Red Deer exhibition. Officials from fairs and exhibitions and staff from rival companies regularly visited Wallace Brothers and the show received thorough coverage in the trade publications. He was the Showmen's League president for 1952–53. At the end of his term, 600 attended the president's party at the convention, where Patty presented him with a tape recorder. (Four days later at the banquet, Patty crowned Miss Outdoor Show Business.)

Sullivan had a feature article on him published in the February 27, 1954, issue of *Billboard*. In Renfrew in 1955, the National Film Board produced a half-hour television special, titled *Carnival*, on his show in which he was interviewed, but Frank was not; it aired nationally on the CBC in December.

Weekend magazine, circulation one and a half million, did an illustrated article, and he even got an article in *Railway Progress* in October 1955. The Wallace Brothers' thank you pages in *Billboard*'s annual "Cavalcade of Fairs" special were larger than Conklin Shows', but never neglected to thank Patty and Frank for their support.

Sullivan's road to fame and fortune was not without its bumps. "Johnny Denton's Gold Medal Shows registered a thumping surprise," stated *Billboard* on January 30, 1954, "when the Dothan, Ala.-based aggregation snared the midway contract for the 1954 Western Canadian B Fair Circuit." The contract award was made after "a spirited nine-hour session" and "provoked considerable debate." It took several ballots for Gold Medal to edge out Wallace Brothers "by a slim margin." Wallace Brothers had been on the circuit since 1939, with a gap of four years because of the war, and had just finished a five-year contract. Those fair delegates who voted against Wallace Brothers felt "the time was ripe for a change." Sullivan drastically revamped his route, settling for a series of still dates in the West. The change to Gold Medal did not go well and Sullivan took the 14-fair circuit back the next year.

During Sullivan's year off from the B circuit, Patty drafted him to assist in one of the periodic skirmishes in the Conklin campaign against Royal American Shows. Winnipeg, a good city for still dates, did not have a major fair. Royal American and Wallace Brothers typically began their seasons on the A and B circuits, respectively, with stills in Winnipeg. In 1953 the Canadian government raised the fees charged on carnivals coming into Canada from the United States if they were coming for stills and not fairs. To avoid the fees, Carl Sedlmayr of Royal American talked Ed Casey, a local operator who had picked up the B circuit from Sullivan during the war, into giving up his 17-year tenure at a small fair in St. Vital, a Winnipeg suburb. As the fair's business manager, Casey expanded it to a full week for 1954, moved it from a 10-acre tract to a 90-acre site, renamed it the Greater Winnipeg Exhibition and cultivated ambitions to join the A circuit. It would have a Royal American midway.

After the war, Patty had not competed with Sedlmayr for the West, although he kept hinting he might come back. He saw his opportunity in early 1954, signing for the third annual Red River Exhibition in Winnipeg. For its first two years, this exhibition had not had much of a midway, but Patty encouraged its Kinsmen Club sponsors to develop "high hopes of building it into a full-scaled exhibition."[48] The Conklin takeover of the event enabled "them to predate the mighty Royal American Shows, with which there exists something of a rivalry, to say the least." Wallace Brothers would also predate Royal American with two still dates and then join Conklin Shows for the exhibition. Together they hoped to empty the pockets of Winnipeggers before Sedlmayr got to town.

Their scheme was only partly successful. "Two Winnipeg Fairs Battle for Dominance" shouted the *Billboard* headline on August 7, 1954, and the organizers of the two events fought for attention on local billboards. The Red River midway had all the Wallace Brothers' equipment, some Conklin units, and some independent rides for a total of 18 major rides, 12 kiddie rides, and nine shows: "The Conklin aggregation of rides, shows and concessions offered ample earning capacity, but did not get sufficient play to come up to its profit expectations."

The Red River Exhibition closed on a Saturday and the Greater Winnipeg Exhibition opened the following Monday. While the former managed to break even, the latter had a strong run. Patty and Sullivan could not dethrone Sedlmayr. The next year Wallace Brothers kept to its still dates in Winnipeg, Conklin Shows stayed in the East, and Royal American enjoyed an attendance of 150,000 at the Greater Winnipeg Exhibition. A few years later the two Winnipeg exhibitions merged under the Red River title, joined the A circuit, and continued to thrive with a Royal American midway.

Sullivan was having increasing difficulty on his western route, with its long jumps to and from the East, and between spots. The number of rail cars and the railway fees kept increasing. In 1955, the year he returned to the B circuit and renamed his show World's Finest, he anticipated a railway bill of $140,000. In 1957 Lethbridge and Moose Jaw left the B circuit, so Sullivan's travel was reduced the next year. He still expected to pay $150,000 to cover 15,000 miles, but in the middle of the summer of 1958 the railways imposed an immediate 10 percent increase on moves. By the end of the season the Board of Transport was considering another 20 percent increase. That was enough for Sullivan, almost 70, who had been hospitalized briefly the year before. He decided not to bid on the B circuit for 1959 and it went to Thomas Shows of Lennox, South Dakota. Sullivan and his crew would never play the West again.

New Competition

The only other bidder for the B circuit in 1959 was Bernard & Barry Shows. Bernard Arent had founded the show with equipment bought from the Conklins in 1946 when he joined them at the Hamilton centennial. He had shadowed World's Finest, working many of the same still dates and taking over dates that Sullivan gave up. Arent competed with World's Finest for the 1957 B circuit, but when he did not get it, he sold his show to Jerry Bonder, one of his concessionaires, and Bonder's brother Bill. The Bonders moved the show from Toronto to Windsor. Molly Lavoie reappeared as the Bernard & Barry transportation manager. Meanwhile, the Bonders' Bernard & Barry Shows aggressively went after Conklin–Sullivan dates.

Even as he gave up the B circuit, Sullivan knew he had another gap in his 1959 season: the Conklins had lost the Exposition Provinciale in Quebec City to Racine Greater Shows, a company based there that played still dates around the city but had no other fairs. In the mid-1950s, Jules Racine, a general contractor who specialized in paving, had begun placing rides at the exposition, and had a Ferris wheel and a merry-go-round at the 1957 fair. He also tried to get permission to set up a carnival on the grounds before the exposition. The Conklin five-year contract was to end in 1958 and when the exposition called for tenders in late 1957, Racine Greater Shows put one in, competing with bids by Conklin and Bernard & Barry shows.

The city, which ran the fair, set up an exposition commission to assess the bids. Frank and Webb wrote to Emery Boucher to protest the special treatment given to Racine by the Quebec City council. Council was allowing Racine to resubmit his tender and to avoid naming the specific rides and shows he would bring. The commission submitted two reports, both of which recommended giving the contract to the Conklins. For political or other reasons, city council overruled the commission and favoured the local outfit. The mayor considered exercising his veto but refrained. Racine Greater Shows was signed in March

1958 and the announcement made at the end of the 1958 event.[49] After 25 years the Conklins lost one of their best fairs to the company that paved its midway for them a few years before.

World's Finest carried a large contingent of shows, but the Conklins had not been able to spare any of the spectacular European rides they had at the CNE for Quebec. Rides were costly and sideshows continued to draw well in Quebec and the farming communities in the West. One sideshow operator in the United States believed that the "best Sideshow towns are those which either have many 'good solid working people' or one that draws farmers."[50] The urbanization of Quebec and changing tastes to which the Conklins might have been insensitive could have been a factor in the loss of the Conklin–Sullivan bid for the Exposition Provinciale.

Racine promised a Wild Mouse and other spectacular rides. No one — perhaps not even Jules Racine — knew where his show was going to get all the rides and shows he promised. As it turned out, the Quebec show split the midway at the Exposition Provinciale with the other bidder, Bernard & Barry, and they jointly invested in a Wild Mouse. Frank learned a lesson and took a Herschell Mad Mouse and Mite Mouse out on the road in 1959. Nevertheless, when the Trois-Rivières contract came up for renewal in 1961, and Racine and Bernard & Barry once more competed with Conklin, the fair committee gave the contract to Bernard & Barry.

The World's Finest route, its western extremity cut off, was much tighter. Sullivan and crew played their usual spring still dates in southern Ontario and then spent three weeks at a couple of lots in Toronto. He could use trucks for these shorter moves, and he cut the show's overall mileage from 15,000 to 10,000. He then worked some still dates in northern Ontario and southern Quebec, including Quebec City. The longest jump was over 700 miles from Quebec City to Leamington to join the Conklins. Frank did not need World's Finest for the Peterborough and Belleville fairs after Leamington, so Sullivan went to Montreal for another still, followed by the rest of the Conklin fairs. When Sullivan bid for the 1961 B circuit, it was given again to Thomas Shows. Although Frank let Sullivan join him for Peterborough and Belleville the next year, the 1959 route was the template that Frank followed until he retired.

Frank had been attached to the Exposition Provinciale and kept in touch with Boucher, who would retire in 1966 after 46 years as manager. After the loss of Trois-Rivières, Frank negotiated a 10-year renewal contract for the Sherbrooke fair in 1961, but with his own health in decline he otherwise reduced his involvement with the Quebec and Ontario fairs. After the failure of the London Frolicland amusement park, Jim Conklin was free in 1960 to assist his uncle on the road.

Frank continued to spend the off-season working with horses. In 1954 the *Thoroughbred of Canada* published an article on his Midway Farm. By 1956 he had $250,000 invested in horses and they had earned him $500,000 through sales and stud fees. His ambition was to raise "a really great horse, one capable of winning the Kentucky Derby or the Preakness."[51] In 1957 he became the first Canadian breeder to consign stock to a U.S. sales ring. The next year he bought a horse in Kentucky that had won the Preakness and placed third in the derby, and syndicated it for stud duty in Canada. By 1960 he had bred two of only 13 Canadian horses that had earned over $100,000 in prize money. His stable was the second largest in Canada and the Canadian Horse of the Year for 1962 was his.[52]

As Frank was being forced out of the Quebec fairs, he and Patty were deliberately withdrawing from Montreal's Belmont Park. The Conklins' long association with Rex Billings had given the park the benefit of the spectaculars they acquired, many of which were first tested in Belmont. At the end of the 1959 season, Billings was telling friends that, after 25 years managing the park, he was retiring to become a ride concessionaire, lining up a select group of larger amusement parks where he hoped to operate new rides. He was actually partnering with the Conklins. They had sold their Wild Mouse to the park, but with Billings continued to operate four other rides. The Conklins on their own ran seven different rides at Belmont in 1960.

In the fall of 1959, Patty and Billings visited several parks in the northeastern United States and the next summer they went to another dozen in New York, New Jersey, Pennsylvania, and Ohio. These trips were to see whether they could book rides with the parks. They got some rides into Riverside in Massachusetts and Palisades in New Jersey. In 1960 the Conklins had 13 kiddie rides, two major rides, and a half-interest in the Wild Mouse at Crystal

Beach. They sold all their rides at Belmont to the park owners in 1961. The partnership languished, so Billings retired completely and moved to Florida, where he died, destitute, in 1981 at the age of 93.

The Conklin brothers had let their travelling midway operation decline to the point that they were losing major fairs, and they could only play the fairs they held on to with the help of Sullivan's World's Finest Shows. They had also started backing out of their involvement in amusement parks. As they entered the 1960s, they seemed headed for retirement like Billings, although better off. Frank had invested his time and money in expensive horses and Patty in the carnie equivalent, expensive riding devices. Frank, forced by his health, would continue on the path he had laid out in the 1950s. Patty would continue to be involved in meeting the demand for thrilling midway rides, but had one last surprise for the outdoor amusement world.

Return

....

(1961–1965)

....

As the 1960s began, fairs and exhibitions in North America were an eagerly anticipated part of the yearly round of festivities. Over 1,200 annual events were served by more than 540 carnival companies, and 100 million patrons across the continent now looked to them for the latest thrill machines. But as the decade progressed, the physical thrills midways offered young people were being replaced by the psychotropic thrills they found on the streets. In between, the Conklins, with their show in the top 3 percent of North American carnivals, grabbed a good chunk of the over $100 million that carnivals annually grossed. Patty won further fame and fortune from an outdoor amusement venue not known to be congenial to carnies, forging the deal that finally returned him to operating in the United States and gave him one last opportunity to bask in the glow of international attention.

PATTY'S WORLD'S FAIR

"Some unflattering stories have been told about carnivals, some of them telling, for instance, of dishonest methods. How true is this?" the interviewer asks.

"Well, Joe, I'm happy to tell you it's very untrue. I believe that 90 percent of the people in the world are honest and that also applies to people in the carnival business. We find dishonest people in all walks of life." Patty paces back and forth in the mid-distance, glancing at the camera occasionally, speaking to an invisible microphone. "And I'm very, very happy that there are so many honest people in this world and I'm very pleased to count the carnival people among them. I find them very honest, Joe."

"Where in the world do they all come from, Patty?"

"Well, that's the strange thing about show business, Joe. We have a lot of old-timers with us and it seems that they just come around from the four winds of the heavens. When we need them, they're on the job."

"And you've played in all kinds of weather, Patty?"

He smiles under his hat as he replies. "You bet I have, Joe. I've been in cyclones, tornados, Chinook winds, all kinds of storms. Been blown down many times. But, uh, we were happy sometimes to see these things happen, Joe."

"Yeah?"

"Primarily for the fact it was a lot of fun wondering what the next thing was gonna come at us."

"Always a little excitement, eh?"

"You bet there is. This is one business there's a lot of excitement. But we take every precaution and every care to see that these kiddies are well looked after. We try to give them a real good time, primarily for the fact that these kids, we know, are going to be the customers of Patty Conklin and his carnival in the future, when they grow up."

Interview from "Life and Times of Patty Conklin," CBC Telescope, 1971

★　★　★

Unlike the appetite for county fairs and regional exhibitions, the taste for world's fairs took time to recover after the Second World War. There had been 10 world's fairs in the United States in the first half of the century, four of them sanctioned by the Bureau International des Expositions in Paris. The last was the New York World's Fair of 1939–40, at which the shift to corporate dominance of these events began. Then came the war. In the next 20 years there were no world's fairs in North America and only one Category 1 General Exhibition anywhere, the Brussels Exposition Universelle et Internationale in 1958. The Belgium fair saw over 40 million visitors in three months and renewed commercial interest in world's fairs. American showmen crossed the ocean to check it out and were impressed by the possibilities it suggested.

Preparations for a World's Fair

Organizers for a world's fair in Seattle started planning in 1955 and got the commitment of municipal and state funds during the next two years. By 1959 the Washington World's Fair Commission had a name for its fair, a theme, and the sanction of the Bureau International des Expositions for a Category 2 event: the Century 21 Exposition, Man in the Space Age, would be held in 1962. The intensifying Cold War and the beginning of the space race fed into the Seattle location, with the Boeing aerospace company, a central participant in both, there to attract federal support for the fair. The competing New York committee put its fair off until 1964.

Unlike most world's fair commissions, the Seattle organization planned from the start to provide the masses a midway to complement the genteel attractions of the art shows, concerts, and theatrical productions, early on conducting a survey "to assist in planning a fun zone."[1] Midways would feature at world's fairs to come, but none as successfully as Seattle's.

In the spring of 1960, the commission hired a consultant for the Seattle midway. George Whitney had been the director of rides and concessions for Disneyland and the deputy director of the U.S. pavilion in Brussels, and was then the owner and manager of a San Francisco amusement park. Five months after starting as a consultant, he was appointed the Seattle fair's director, concessions and amusements division. Two other former Disneyland executives were brought in to assist him. Whitney was planning a "midway themed to the good old days" to contrast with the world of tomorrow theme of the fair, and began accepting bids for rides, shows, and concessions, intending to book "standard" units.[2] Eight months into his appointment and with less than a year until opening, Whitney made his most significant decision: he awarded the contract for the midway to Patty Conklin and Harry Batt.

The news blindsided the outdoor amusement world. Batt, of Pontchartrain Park in New Orleans, and Conklin, partnered as Gayway 21, were the first sole operating group to get complete control over a world's fair midway. They had a two-million-dollar contract to present "the most expansive gayway ever assembled for a world's fair," as a front-page article on June 14, 1961, in the *Seattle Daily Times* described it. The partners ditched Whitney's nostalgia theme and proposed to introduce 12 new rides, nine from Europe, among the 16 rides on the midway. They had already contracted 11 devices and would include only two kiddie rides. They eventually brought in 19 rides, none of them new in concept, although some were new versions of older rides and some had only been introduced at the CNE in recent years. More proof of the success of the Marshall Plan, 11 had been manufactured in Germany.

The partners also put up buildings for 40 or so games and concessions. Jack Ray designed the midway and dressed up the fronts, updating the designs he had been developing for over 20 years to fit the vision of the future embodied in Century 21's iconic Space Needle, being built as the fair's Eiffel Tower. Gayway 21 had no sideshows. Because they included nudity, even in a puppet act, the few shows at the fair were relegated to a dark alley well away from the family midway and lost money.

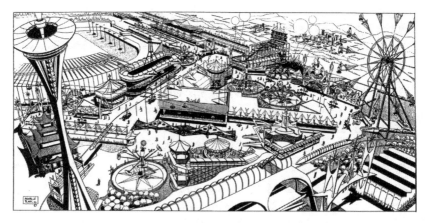

Drawing by Jack Ray of his layout for the Seattle World's Fair, 1961.

Whitney's deal with Conklin and Batt had been developing since he was taken on as a consultant and began asking them for advice. He first approached Batt, who in turn approached Patty. "We kept asking questions," Whitney said, "and they kept answering. I don't know who suggested what, but it was only a short time before it was obvious that we were talking to the people who should be the operators and that's the way it worked out."[3] Ray assisted in developing the proposal with mock-ups and drawings.

Jim Conklin told a version of how the deal began: "My uncle and I tried to talk my father out of this venture. The logic behind our thoughts was — why risk a reputation at age 70 on an amusement venture at a World's Fair? World's Fairs up till then had been losers for outdoor amusements. My father's answer was swift — if you guys don't want to join, I'll do it on my own! From then on we were very supportive."[4] Others also wondered why Patty and Harry would risk reputation and money, when they needed more of neither. The answer was "two words — challenge and ego. Both men have thrived on a sense of accomplishment and this, undoubtedly, has contributed greatly to their success."[5]

Conklin and Batt had been friends for years and had tried to partner on the aborted Freedom Fair in Washington, D.C., in 1949. Batt and his sons visited the CNE and Conklin and his family reciprocated with trips to New Orleans in the off-season. Their mutual friends included Ray, Jimmy Sullivan, and Rex Billings. Batt's main business being the Pontchartrain Beach amusement park in New Orleans, which he had run for his family since 1934 with great success, he had a good reputation in the outdoor amusement world. He was a past president of the National Association of Amusement Parks, Pools and Beaches (NAAPPB) and in 1958 was the advance man for the trip by its members to the Brussels world's fair. Patty hosted the NAAPPB's late summer meeting at the CNE in 1959, at which Batt invited the association to New Orleans for the next year, vowing to beat Patty's hospitality. He bought components for a Wild Mouse from Patty and, like him, began making regular trips to Europe to look for new attractions. They both spoke on European rides at the NAAPPB convention in December 1960, at which time the negotiations between them and Whitney were well underway.

They were ideal partners: Batt, a Southern gentleman, flamboyant and dapper, always impeccably dressed and groomed, down to his pencil moustache;

and Conklin, a midway roughie, 11 years Batt's senior, dishevelled and often in need of a haircut. Batt worked the inside, handling the paperwork and the telephones to get the equipment and staff in place, the arrangements with the fair commission and contractors secured. His was the easy job. Patty worked the outside, ensuring that the rides were located where he wanted them, erected properly, and well maintained. Soon after they secured the contract, they went to Europe to look for attractions and "purchased or booked more than a million dollars' worth of rides."[6] They had "negotiated for a new and better location for the fun zone than was originally offered" and with Ray "created a plan and design favorable to the compact five acres allotted them."

Conklin and Batt had another partner, this one unofficial, but essential to getting the equipment they wanted. Morgan "Mickey" Hughes, an Irishman, spent 12 years in the British army and ended his service as a major stationed in Germany, being honourably discharged in 1949 at the age of 30. He married a German woman and through his connections got partial rights to a Rotor, setting it up in an amusement park in Manchester, where John Ringling North ran across it. Through North he promoted the Rotor in the United States, making a deal with Irving Rosenthal in 1951 to book it at Palisades Park. He formed Hot Rods Inc. to import cars for Palisades the next year and, having met Patty there, brought hot rods to the CNE for 1955 and Belmont Park for 1957. In both locations this new ride technology did very well. Patty bought cars from Hughes for the hot rod track set up under the Flyer coaster at the CNE in 1957. One of Hughes's first imports beyond hot rods was a Satellite Jet at Palisades and the CNE in 1958. The German Wild Mouse rides he advertised in late 1959 were the rides Patty had imported the year before.

By 1960 Hughes was importing over a million dollars a year worth of mainly German rides to parks and carnivals across North America. Hughes made deals with Patty and Rosenthal to showcase new European rides exclusively at the CNE in Canada and Palisades Park in the United States. Of the sought-after pieces — the Calypsos, Himalayas, Cortina Bobs, carousels, dark rides, and kiddie rides — some he sold and others he operated on commission. Batt and Conklin naturally looked to Hughes to assist them in getting equipment for their world's fair midway. He went with them to Europe, half their million-dollar order of equipment went through his company, and he

Jack Ray, Curtis Velare, Harry Batt, Elmer Velare, and Patty at the Seattle World's Fair, 1962.

returned on his own to Europe to supervise shipments to Seattle. Patty even advised the public relations director for the fair to try to get some mileage out of Hughes, who was personable, articulate, and amusing, and a great promoter of the technology he imported.

Gayway 21 took a percentage on all rides and games at Seattle, but owner-ship, management, and profits were spread around. Conklin and Batt split on five rides, and Conklin and Hughes on two. World's Finest Shows — a company set up by Frank that had nothing to do with Sullivan's carnival — owned two, Hughes one, and Batt's sons one. Manufacturers had several, including Curtis and Elmer Velare with a funhouse and a Rotor.

The Velare brothers were supposed to have a Giant Wheel worth a quarter of a million dollars at the fair, but their shop could not get it built in time. Since this was to be a showpiece and the midway could not open without a Ferris wheel, Conklin and Batt were in a panic to fill the gap. Patty called Al Kunz, owner of Heth Shows in Alabama, to ask him for his Sky Wheel, built by the Herschell Company from the Velare patent. With five days to go, Kunz loaded it, transported it 3,200 miles, and set it up in time for the opening on April 21. The 110-foot high Velare Giant Wheel made it to Seattle for the beginning of June, replacing the Sky Wheel. To maintain all the rides on the midway, Patty brought trusted, experienced staff from Brantford, including mechanic Herman Larsen, construction superintendent John MacDonald, and electrician Grant Sinclair. Harry "Centre Pole" Shore ran the conces-sions for him.

Response to the World's Fair

The six-month fair was a success from every angle, beating the forecast attendance of nine million by over 600,000. Celebrities and politicians visited, including John Glenn, who had just become the first American astronaut to orbit Earth, Prince Philip, who turned down a request to speak to the crowd, Elvis Presley, who filmed a movie there, and Attorney General Robert Kennedy, who rode the Wild Mouse with his children. Patty thrived on showing his midway off to them all, he and Batt entertaining over 3,000 visitors between them.

President Dwight Eisenhower had begun the countdown to the fair in 1958 and President John F. Kennedy was scheduled to attend the closing ceremonies in October, but bowed out, pleading a cold. He was actually in the middle of dealing with the Cuban missile crisis. Apart from the narrowly missed nuclear apocalypse, the fair was the news story of the year, appearing on the cover of *Life*, as well as in hundreds of other magazine, television, and radio features. Unlike most world's fairs, it ended in the black, making a profit of almost $100,000. It also revitalized the city, leaving behind the 600-foot-high Space Needle and the Seattle Center, a fairground, park, and entertainment complex.

When mentioned at all in the deluge of publicity, the Gayway drew favourable comments. It was small by most standards, but Conklin, Batt, Ray, and Hughes made sure it met expectations and complemented the fair's theme. Larson, MacDonald, Sinclair, and crew ensured that it all ran smoothly. To outdoor showmen, it was a landmark to equal the Space Needle, especially when it turned a profit, something no other world's fair midway had done before or has done since. It grossed well over the two million dollars invested in it and more than the partners had expected. The Concessions and Amusement Division, including food, turned over $600,000 to the fair, more income than any other area except admissions. Conklin and Batt, having talked the fair commission into accepting just 15 percent of the rides gross, added significantly to their own fortunes, netting $190,000 between them. After the close of the fair, Patty said that he was "tired of making money."[7]

Patty had made a triumphant return to the United States and it raised him to a new level of fame. He could fancy himself a peer of the world's top celebrities. A 14-member delegation from Seattle came to see his CNE mid-way in 1961. The trade publications closely followed his movements through-out the months leading up to the Seattle event and in the *Amusement Business* special "Report from Seattle," he and Batt featured prominently in several articles, with one feature devoted exclusively to them. A half-dozen conces-sionaires who had worked the Seattle midway took out ads to congratulate and thank them, and one ad sponsored by four carnie associations offered best wishes to Patty alone. His gamble had paid off and taken him to the pinnacle of his career.

A LIVING LEGEND

I went out on my own with them on the fair season, with Conklin Shows. I used to see Patty the odd time. His brother Frank was the one who used to look after the circuit on those fairs. Patty was busy getting ready for the Exhibition, then after the Exhibition he used to play the Western Fair in London.

So, I really didn't see much of Patty.... Patty was a very amiable guy. He always ... stopped and shot the breeze with you. Didn't matter who you were. He liked everybody in the business; he loved the business. Frank was a little different. He had his horses that he loved more than anything. I worked with him out on the road at the fairs. Then I used to go into the Western Fair, which Patty was involved in after the Exhibition was all over....

I operated these digger machines down in Quebec out on the road. Conklin had the Sherbrooke Fair, the Three Rivers Exhibition. I was down in Quebec playing some still dates with some shows, then I went and played those spots with Conklin. After that was over, I used to come back and play London. London was where you used to see Patty a little bit more.

So, when I made up my mind to buy a Dodgem ride, I got ahold of Patty and told him what my idea was and that I'd like to book it with them on these fairs. Now, no one has got a portable bumper car ride at that time around this part of the world, so we would have no trouble booking it in whatsoever. We got the ride and got it over to Canada, and I had enough money to handle the deal. We booked it in with him for the fairs and then I booked it wherever I could.

So, it worked out pretty good for a few years. Conklin Shows would be lucky if they had one or two rides, that's all they had. In the meantime, I was buying other rides and every time I'd get another ride, I'd get a three-year contract with Conklin. The result is that we started to get a few rides around us at this time and it was new equipment, too.

Patty was a hell of a smoker and he bummed more than he ever bought. "You got a cigarette, kid?" I don't think he was much of a drinker, either. I never seen him drunk. Frank was a good drinker. Over at the shop where they are now, he used to have the odd party that Patty would put on himself. I remember one time he had an oompah-pah band with the German shorts. Patty loved the business and everybody in the business, so that's why he'd get 'em all together to shoot the breeze. He was a great storyteller.

One time Frank kicked me off the show. I was down in Quebec playing with Sullivan at a couple of still dates that he had down there, after they lost those fairs. Sullivan still used to go down, I think he still had Sherbrooke. I was down in eastern Canada, playing with King Reid Shows. So, I used to boot it back and I'd play a couple of still dates with Jimmy Sullivan and the Leamington Fair for Conklin. Anyway, I'm playing with Jimmy Sullivan. So, I put my trailer on his train to bring it into Leamington because he had to open up in Leamington, too, with Frank. I asked Jimmy, "What are you going to charge me to put my unit on one of your flat cars?" I don't know what it was, a hundred bucks, maybe a hundred and fifty. I said, "Jeez, that's great." Now the train got, not derailed, but sidetracked and it didn't make it in for the first day. So, Frank Conklin just blew his top at me. He says, "Jesus Christ, Campbell, you better find yourself a new show."

Frank was a Jew and Patty wasn't. I don't know what he was. He could have been a Scotsman. Little Jimmy Sullivan, he was a Scotsman or Irishman. I used to do business with him, too. Him and Patty used to get along good, but not him and Frank.

Patty was a different guy altogether, he was very amiable, but Frank was different. Not too many guys liked Frank. The horse people liked him, I guess, because he was a breeder. But as far as other people around the show, not too many liked him. One time the gateman challenged him because you've got to have a ticket to get in. Frank said, "I'm Frank Conklin," and the gateman said, "I don't give a fuck who you are, you haven't got a ticket or a pass." Bang, he just laid the guy right out. He was bad. He was a pretty big man. In later years, when he had his affliction come back on him, he settled down.

Interview with Don Campbell, April 25, 2006

★　★　★

In the years immediately after the world's fair, articles on Patty were published in *Canadian Weekly, Executive,* and the *Financial Post.* But he probably felt that one world's fair was enough. When the organizers of the New York World's Fair of 1964–65 and of Montreal's Expo 67 sought him out to produce their midways, he turned them down, ostensibly because they were not willing to give him complete control. The midways at both fairs lost money.

Canada's centennial exhibition in 1967 would have turned out differently had Ottawa supported Toronto's plans to hold the event. As far back as 1958, CNE management began mulling over the idea of hosting a world's fair for Canada's centennial, but they were not aggressive enough or quick enough. In 1960 three orders of government — the Montreal municipal council, the Quebec provincial assembly, and the federal government in Ottawa — pooled their resources to put in a bid to the Bureau International des Expositions. They won recognition a few years later for a fair in Montreal and the Toronto bid was dropped.

Patty negotiated with the Montreal officials for some time before turning them down. Written partly to quell Hogtown anxiety about the challenge to its status from Canada's more cosmopolitan other major city, an article printed on August 28, 1965, in the Toronto *Telegram* on "The Ex and the Spectre of Expo" contrasts the reality of the Conklin CNE midway with the idealistic plans for Expo's La Ronde. Expo's prospective "orchestration of rides" is met by Patty's "horse laugh … from the north-east corner of the CNE Horse Pavilion," and the reporter, mimicking the master, concludes you can't "tell these keen naive nuts from Montreal that a midway will always be a midway, that it's just hokum, salesmanship and sex, that a ride is something you pay 35 cents for so you can get your arms around the blonde when the car goes over the hump and she squeals — eeeeeek! — like she just saw Ringo Starr."

The article reports that Patty is refusing to acknowledge La Ronde's latest call for proposals, and he conveys his annoyance with the Expo officials:

> "They're bothering hell out of me," Conklin says. "I don't like their.... They have been fooling around here. Last Thursday, Friday, Saturday we had two big boys down from Montreal. Just picking brains. You can't get any answers out of 'em. They didn't get any answers out of me.... As far as Expo — I'm going to stay and do a better job here than they are there."

In the same article, Toronto's mayor expresses confidence that the CNE midway will meet the challenge of La Ronde's permanent "thematic amusement area" with "a bigger and better mousetrap," saying that "Patty came through for the CNE a long time ago when nobody else would. His heart is here. He's getting older but he's still got the vigor and drive to come up with great ideas."

Patty was now a bastion of proven and practical success against the winds of change and innovation.

Back to the Ex

Patty had continued to run his personal annual world's fair even as the one in Seattle was underway. The summer of 1962 the CNE finally topped the three-million-attendance mark it had been skirting for the past few years and the 57 rides and four shows on the Conklin midway grossed over $886,000. The Conklins got to keep more of the gross that year because the Conservative government of Ontario had gotten rid of the provincial amusement tax.

For the 1963 CNE and London fair, Patty brought two rides from Seattle, signed Hughes for three hot rod rides, a giant Ferris wheel, and a new airborne ride, and contracted the new European Trabant ride from its owner and another new ride from the Hrubetz company. He cut the sideshows to two, a fat show and a freak show, both run by Lou Dufour. On August 31 *Amusement Business* reported that the other shows were "eliminated to make room for more rides which, Conklin says, will gross more money and please the public better." Son Jim's hand can be detected in renewed efforts to increase the earning capacity of rides, but little could be done to improve the earnings of shows except increasing ticket prices.

On the first Saturday of the 1963 CNE, Patty had his first $100,000 day, when attendance made it to over 343,000: both figures would have been respectable for the entire run of all but the largest exhibitions. He had publicly stated that he aimed to gross $935,000 that year, and he got just shy of $960,000. Before the 1963 event, he began projecting a one-million-dollar gross, to be achieved "in the next couple of years."[8] But in 1964, for the first time in 25 years, the ride and show gross fell, by almost $6,000.

The CNE had long been experiencing the problems attendant on excessive growth, the worst of them being traffic congestion and crowding. After the 1963 fair, general manager McCallum said that "about 3.2 million people is all the CNE can hope to handle, with present facilities," only 125,000 more than it had just seen.[9] There were various ideas about how to relieve the problem, including expanding the grounds, building piers on the waterfront for the midway, and adding days to the fair's run.

When Bert Powell replaced McCallum as general manager, one of his first ideas was to make the event "truly national" with "a national board of directors composed of top businessmen from each of Canada's 10 provinces."[10] Instead, the Metropolitan Toronto Council took over from the City of Toronto and the board was broadened to include "representatives from the suburbs."[11] No solutions for the problems of capacity were forthcoming.

With the exhibition grounds bursting at the seams and constraining growth in attendance, Patty had to figure out how to get more money from the crowds who squeezed in. Starting in the early 1950s, outdoor amusement business pundits began to talk about increasing per capita spending as an alternative to simple increases in attendance. Patty might not have been familiar with the technicalities of the concept, but he knew how to implement it. To increase volume sales, he kept ride prices low and ensured that the games gave out at least 30 percent of their gross in prizes. He optimized ride throughput by minimizing the length of the experience and expediting the loading and unloading processes, but stopped short of the point where these measures would reduce ride appeal. One of his favourite innovations was "good house-keeping — excellent sanitary facilities, cleanliness of the park and restful places for patrons to relax."[12] His insight was that by making people comfort-able, he could keep them on the midway longer, and the longer they stayed, the more money they spent.

In the early 1960s, spending on North American midways averaged little more than one dollar per head, but it was much lower at the CNE because of all the other attractions, some like the grandstand requiring substantial ex-penditures on their own. While Patty thought he was getting something from 65 percent of the people who attended the CNE, he was not getting much, but the one figure he was consistently increasing was per capita spending. In 1950 the midway "per cap" was 12.5 cents. Ten years later it was 27.5 cents and by 1969 it was 53.5 cents, a more than four-fold increase in less than 20 years. Even taking inflation into account, this is a testament to Patty's acumen in designing and operating his midway.

The Million-Dollar Midway

The Conklin CNE midway passed another milestone in 1965: the first million-dollar midway anywhere, the kind of first that attracted attention in an industry that aspired to mass-market appeal. Overall attendance was down for a second year, but per capita spending was up 5 percent, which Patty attributed "to the powerful line-up of 61 attractions and the fact that the public appeared to have more money and was in a spending mood."[13] News of the milestone made the front page of the *Toronto Star* on September 7. Patty had two $100,000 days and the Flyer coaster grossed over $110,000, followed by the Wild Mouse, a new ski lift ride, and Hughes's new Go Kart Rally. There was only one show, a Dufour sideshow, which Patty said he kept only because of his friendship with Dufour. In the September 18 issue, the editor of *Amusement Business* was effusive in his praise: "The magic

million-dollar midway gross figure, talked about for years, has finally top-
pled.... The record gross ... came about because Conklin astutely planned,
revised and refined his attractions from year to year to achieve the greatest
possible capacity."

On December 4, the *Globe and Mail*, the national newspaper, featured
Patty in an article in its Business and Finance section on how "the growing
spending power of young people will prompt Canadian fairs to drop girlie
shows in favor of more teenage attractions." The article quotes his address to
the Canadian Association of Fairs and Exhibitions: "As far as I'm concerned,
midway shows are on their way out and fairs will switch to amusements that
give teen-agers an opportunity to participate and have fun themselves." The
Globe demurely identified him as "a veteran showman," but his local paper,
the Brantford *Expositor*, printing the article on the front page of its second
section the same day, added with pride that he was "known as Canada's outdoor carnival king" and his company was based in Brantford. While he had no
trouble self-fulfilling his prophecy about shows, Patty would prove less adept
at matching in practice his prescience about teenage attractions.

Patty was living up to the assessment of him as "a living legend to North
American showmen" that *Executive* magazine had published in April 1965,
before the CNE that broke the million-dollar gross. The writer described
him as "King of the Carnival, greatest outdoors showman on earth, maker of
millions on midways, a unique Canadian asset" and the "Great White Chief
of the Great White Way." He was too old and had gone through too much
to let such language swell his head, and he retained his mock humility and
self-deprecating ways. He could afford to take his financial worth lightly: "I'm
supposed to be a millionaire or something." He knew well how much he was
worth and that he was at the peak of his career.

During the early 1960s, four Conklin companies were paying Patty and
Frank each a salary of just over $70,000 in total and they were earning annual
dividends from their company shares in the $40,000 to $50,000 range.[14] The
companies were Conklin & Garrett Ltd. for rides, Bazaars Ltd. for concessions, Flyer Coaster Ltd. for their CNE coaster, and Fun Cars Ltd. for the
imported rides booked at parks. This income is what Patty reported, but his
was a cash business and tens of thousands of dollars of tax-free income did not

show up on the books. Nevertheless, he did not live a particularly opulent life, although he did not stint when it came to travel and entertaining. He liked a good game of bridge or gin rummy and he still liked fishing — at least in theory, since he did not get out much.

HEIR APPARENT

Mid-afternoon on a cool November Monday, pallbearers emerge from the brick church near downtown Brantford to carry their burden to the waiting hearse. The Central Presbyterian Church had been full and the mourners file slowly through the narthex, collecting their hats and coats to protect against the late fall wind.

They descend the shallow steps to the sidewalk under the dull sky. Their cars are scattered for blocks, the luckiest parked in the lot of the Carnegie library next to the church. Most have to walk a fair distance under the leafless trees or through the park across the street, and for some it is a struggle.

Few of the mourners are younger than the 60 years Frank laboured to attain. Some had arrived the day before for the visitation at the stately funeral home a mile away from the church. Many are not familiar with the small city, and some lose their sense of direction and have trouble finding their vehicles.

A provincial police car leads the hearse through the city. Businesses have been closed for the remainder of the day to keep the downtown streets clear for the procession. Over 120 cars gather behind the hearse before another police car closes off the rear.

The mourners have come from across North America, not as many showmen as Patty thought would have been respectable, but Frank had withdrawn from that world. A few show owners and local politicians are there mainly for the older brother. Some of Frank's rich and powerful friends have come. Sportswriters and journalists who had got good copy from him rub shoulders with the horsemen attending to pay their respects to a fallen leader of Canadian thoroughbred breeding.

The procession winds south and west out of town, through a suburban neighbourhood, picking up speed as the farmland opens up. The road skirts the escarpment falling away to the Grand River. Parking problems recur at the cemetery and some of the elder showmen and their wives are unable to witness the burial. Patty stays with Billie, Edythe, and Jim until the first shovels of dirt are thrown in the grave, then circulates among the mourners, making sure he sees all his friends and many of Frank's. He invites them to Sky Acres, just down the road.

It is growing dark as they begin to disperse. The trees are bare, the fields brown, the horses are in their stables. In a few weeks snow will cover the cemetery, the surrounding fields, and the countryside around Midway Farm, the glitter of ice crystals under the beaver moon wiping out all memory of summer.

★　★　★

Patty returned to earth after the heady apogee to his career at the Seattle Man in the Space Age world's fair, but he did not slow down. Visitors and interviewers always noted his energy, and he was said to look 10 years younger than he was and to run around his midway like a much younger man. He still chain smoked and could enjoy a drink. Edythe's drinking, on the other hand, remained a burden to him and he stopped taking her on his annual off-season pilgrimages. He still took her on cruises, where he could monitor her behaviour and confine her to their cabin, if necessary. Frank's health was another concern.

The Death of Frank

Despite a robust appearance, Frank's health had never been good since his long struggle with tuberculosis, something few people beyond his brother, wife, and nephew knew. He had smoked cigars and drunk with the boys when he was younger, but he gave up any excesses and he did not keep his brother's hours or level of activity. A two-month season on the road was about all he could manage, and the loss of the Quebec City and Trois-Rivières fairs was a blessing. He became more involved in local affairs. In 1950 he joined the board of directors of a sanatorium in Brantford that provided residential care for tuberculosis patients, becoming president of the board in 1960.

But it wasn't tuberculosis that killed Frank. In early 1961 he had gone to the Henry Ford Hospital in Detroit, reportedly for surgery. The hospital had specialists in multiple sclerosis, with which he had been diagnosed. Given the difficulty in identifying the disease and its episodic nature, he had likely had it for some time. When Patty returned from Seattle in 1962 with all the money he had made for them, Frank commented that, instead of the money, he would rather have his health back. A few months later, he sold his thoroughbred stock and let it be known that he was entering "temporary retirement from the breeding and amusement ranks due to illness."[15] Billie, drawing on her nursing background, cared for him at home over the winter, but he was back in the Ford Hospital the next spring. Patty, putting on a good front, told *Amusement Business* in May 1963 that Frank was making "excellent progress" and would soon be back home. He died at the Ford Hospital on November 8, 1963, at the age of 60.

Frank was better known as the Master of Midway Farm than as a carnival potentate. Many Canadian sporting columns and publications, as well as outdoor amusement business publications, carried obituary articles about him, noting his contributions to raising the status of the sport of kings in Canada. With remarkable consistency, they also noted that, although he had horses come close, he had never had one win the Queen's Plate, the oldest continuously run race in North America and Canada's most prestigious. His best chance to take this honour occurred the spring before his death, but the horse that might have achieved it was ruled ineligible to run because its nomination papers failed to establish that it was foaled in Canada.

Showmen, horsemen, and leading sports columnists from across North America attended Frank's funeral on November 11. His nephew Jim, Herman Larsen, and Evan McGugan, manager of the London fair, were among the active pallbearers, and Hiram McCallum and Jimmy Sullivan among the honorary ones. Billie received hundreds of letters, cards, and telegrams of condolence, many of which praised her husband as a good friend and host, kind to everyone and a true gentleman.

Although they had been partners since they transformed themselves from Renkers to Conklins over 40 years before, Frank and Patty had been seeing less of each other as one settled on his farm and the other remained in constant motion. Frank had not accompanied Patty on his European tours looking for rides and Patty had not been involved with Frank's horses and trips to Kentucky. Patty was presiding over a meeting of the Showmen's League of America in Chicago when Frank was dying. The meeting heard the news of his death at two o'clock in the morning, a half hour after it had occurred. The Showmen's League sent a delegation of six, five of whom were past presidents, to his funeral and 50 members of the Ontario chapter of the league attended.

Frank's estate was valued at $1.85 million in stocks, bonds, real estate, and shares in the various Conklin companies. Patty, Neil Webb, and the Canada Permanent Trust Company were named the executors. Frank left everything to Billie and made provisions to set up a trust to provide her an annual income of $20,000. His will also set up trusts for his sister Catherine, who was 64 and still in Paterson, New Jersey, and brother Charles, 77 and living in New York City. They were the only Renker siblings with whom he and Patty had kept in touch, and each was to receive $1,000 a year in four equal payments.

Frank had been slipping away from the Conklin carnival enterprises for several years and his death did not cause them to falter. He had last been involved in contract negotiations in the summer of 1961. The Sullivan office staff had been assisting him more and more on the Ontario and Quebec road show and, other than dealing with the fair boards, could easily run the show without him. Patty had Webb to look after the financial side of things and son Jim had been increasingly responsible for operations outside of the CNE.

The Rise of Jim

Jim Conklin, 30 and a father of three when his uncle died, was ready to step into the breach. A month after Frank's death, Jim became president of the Showmen's League of America and two weeks after that president of the

Ontario chapter of the league. His father had been one of the prime organizers of the new chapter in 1959. Pat Marco had been the acting first president, but when the chapter became officially recognized Patty was the president and Marco the vice-president. One of Patty's first acts as president was to buy 100 gravesites. Marco became president and was succeeded by Sullivan and then the younger Conklin, at which point membership had grown to over 500. Jim was noted as the youngest-ever president of the Chicago club and the only man to be president of both clubs at the same time. In 1969 Webb would be the president of the Chicago club, confirming the high regard accorded him by the industry.

Jim was following in the footsteps of his father and uncle in other ways. *Amusement Business* published an annual industry forecast, as had *Billboard* before it. For many years, Patty had been one of the featured contributors to the forecast, commenting on either the prospects for Canada or for carnivals in general. James F. Conklin, as he signed himself, provided the forecast for carnivals for 1964, published on January 11. In the accompanying photograph, he looks young and he's holding a cigarette, his father's trademark. Patty had focused on rides, but Jim followed his uncle's interest in games, noting that they had not shared in the steady increase in revenues that rides had gained. He predicted that concession receipts would remain static until they were "modernized, with new and different merchandising methods introduced." He would focus on games, which the Conklin office had long left to independent operators.

In his emphasis on modernizing games and treating them as mere merchandisers, Jim was taking a different direction than his elders. Younger carnies, including many of Jim's peers who had inherited carnival businesses, increasingly saw games not as gambling propositions with the odds stacked wildly in favour of the house, but as merchandise operations, in principle no different from department stores that sold their goods to the public for a certain percentage in profit. The older operators had largely left the games agents to themselves, and the agents had been able to make outrageous sums without reporting them because there was no way of measuring the take. By regulating games and monitoring what they gave out in prizes, the younger concession managers further cleaned up the midways of their fathers, protecting their capital tied up in rides. They developed techniques for estimating the take and controlled the amount of money made by agents by keeping an exact inventory of stuffed animals and flooding the midway with them.

Patty made his son an instant millionaire at a dinner before the CNE in 1964 when he officially announced that 50 percent of his amusement interests, including the midway at the CNE, now belonged to Jim. CNE general manager McCallum quipped, "You may have 50 per cent of the business, but I'll bet your dad still has 60 per cent of the say-so."[16] Jim had replaced Frank as his father's partner, but it would be years before he would have the kind of control he wanted over the Conklin midway.

CHANGING OF THE GUARD

When Patty Conklin was 14, he was selling peanuts in front of Madison Square Garden. When his son Jimmie was 14, he was enrolled at Ridley College, one of the most expensive boys' schools in Canada.

Two years ago Patty announced Jimmie, college-educated in architecture and business, was being made a full partner in Conklin shows, the biggest midway operation in the world.

Great, said the experts, because Patty, an old-timer who operates entirely on instincts and handshakes, needs a bright young business school grad with slide rules and charts and graphs and maybe even a computer.

But it hasn't worked out that way. Jimmie, the college boy, doesn't spend much more time in the office than Patty. And Patty's never there.

His black Cadillac with walnut trim is a roving command post these days. It glides to a stop beside the ferris wheels and arms and noises come out the window.

It's left stopped with the front doors open in front of the Magic Carpet — just for a few minutes — then the doors are slammed shut and it's away again, headed for the Wild Mouse.

Then the Sky Diver. Then the Sprungschanz. And the Alpine Way. Then all the other rides on the Exhibition Midway, until he's been to all 62 of them. Somewhere along the way the big black Cadillac meets Jimmie's long dark-blue Buick station wagon. When he leans out his window and Patty leans out of the Cadillac, you can see they're father and son.

"I can't make any money in the office," says Patty. "Business is out here."

Although Jimmie spends almost as much time away from the office as Patty, he seems to get joed for most of the desk work. Behind Jimmie's desk sit two briefcases, open and bulging with papers.

"They belong to The Boss," says Jimmie, as if he doesn't know what's in them. But Patty says he doesn't know either.

Neither Patty nor Jimmie uses a pencil. They zip up and down the midway all day, ordering painting and wiring and carpentry and writing down nothing.

They can tell you what each ride brought in last year — "327,000 rode the Flyer Coaster last year" — plus other little bits of information — "there's 7,354 light bulbs on that Sprungschanz ride" — that only people in love with their work bother about....

"The key to success in this business is keeping your eye on everything that you've got, get right in there where it's being done."

Excerpt from "For the Midway: New Rides and a New Generation," Toronto Star, *Saturday, Aug. 20, 1966, p. 33*

★ ★ ★

The guard was changing on midways across North America. Men who had been in the business since its emergence early in the century were now passing their shows on to their sons, their long-time associates, or outside buyers. Newer shows like the Deggeller brothers' Magic Midway and the Vivona brothers' Amusements of America were on the rise. Royal American Shows and Conklin Shows were among the few carnival companies that continued on trajectories set before the Second World War, even as the younger generation took over. While Patty shared his show with his son in 1964 and managed to survive, Carl Sedlmayr passed his show on to his son in 1965 and then passed away.

Endings

Frank's death and Jim's rise to partner were just two changes happening on the Conklin midway. After the breakup of his crew during the war and with his subsequent focus on rides and the CNE, Patty had never regrouped his loyal band of games agents and show producers, although he had kept his core office staff, mainly Frank and Webb, and his ride men, Herman Larsen, John MacDonald, Grant Sinclair, and Bill Davis. Harry Shore, his one constant among concessionaires, supervised games at the parks and the CNE. Maxie Herman had retired to Miami, Lou Leonard and bingo operator Al Cohn had left to work shows in the West, and Bill Levinsky, Al Kaufman, Johnny Branson, and others had joined World's Finest. Patty squeezed out most show producers from the CNE, Alfie Phillips left the business, and Lou Dufour was the lone showman he allowed to stay on, mainly to keep him company in his old age. Jim would rebuild his team of front-end staff, although it would be years before he established a consistent roster of sideshow operators.

While known for his common touch and for palling around with all his staff, Patty's closest friendships were with park owners, who were his peers in responsibility and financial status, but not direct competitors. Rex Billings, George Hall, Ed Carroll, Irving Rosenthal, Harry Batt, Mickey Hughes, and Jack Ray were among the companions he sought in the off-season. Dufour, who had employed him in the 1920s, was one of his closest friends at the CNE for the 16 years that Dufour stayed there with him. Each night after closing, the two men, both in their late 70s, would sit up until three in the morning exchanging stories of the past. According to Jim, "Dufour is good medicine for my father. They cut up jackpots and each one tries to top the other."[17] E.K. Fernandez, with whom Patty and Edythe stayed for 10 days during their tour of the South Pacific in 1965 and who visited Patty the next year, was another old friend. Fernandez was seven years older than Patty and still in the business, although also not a competitor since he stuck to his territory in Hawaii.

Along with Frank's passing, the deaths during these years of many of the concessionaires who had been with him in the 1920s and '30s must have shaken Patty. Alex Lobban died in 1958, Al Cohn in 1960, Bill Levinsky in 1962, Maxie Herman in 1967, and Al Kaufman in 1968. Al Brown and Ed Sopenar, both of whom had helped found the Ontario chapter of the Showmen's League and had been with World's Finest Shows, died in 1962. Henry Meyerhoff, whose Crescent Shows had succeeded Conklin & Garrett on the C circuit in the west and whom Patty had visited at his showing in Alaska, also died that year.

A shock to the show world at large and Patty especially was the death of Jack Ray on December 29, 1963, of a heart attack following surgery. He was only 52. His obituary appeared in the same issue of *Amusement Business* as Jim's first industry forecast and noted: "Until 1959 he created and designed for Conklin on a regular basis, and designed the Seattle World's Fair Gayway. Parks with Ray-designed features include the Nu-Pike, Long Beach, Calif., Palisades (N.J.) Amusement Park, and Pontchartrain Beach Park, New Orleans, to name just a few." His former showgirl and widow, Eleanor, and son, Robert, continued to manage the San Diego Belmont Park under a lease from the city. In 1969 they finally gave up the park to a local hotel owner. Jack was posthumously inducted into the International Association of Amusement Parks and Attractions Hall of Fame in 2000.

One old associate of the show died in a strange and tragic manner. Robert Restall and his wife, Mildred, came from England when he was 31 to present, under their stage names, Bob and Mildred Lee, an English-style Globe of Death for Conklin Shows. A thrill show, it featured the two of them riding motorcycles around the inside of a steel mesh globe. The attraction was one of Patty's few good finds on his first foray to Europe. The Restalls stayed with the Conklins for nine years, during which the Globe of Death was one of the top grossing shows, and for two years they also had a Frozen Alive girl show. They left Conklin Shows after it lost the western A circuit in 1946, reappearing as operators of an old motordrome in a New Jersey amusement park, which they brought to the CNE for one season in 1949.

Ten years later, Bob and his two sons became treasure hunters. Oak Island, a tiny island off the coast of Nova Scotia where underground tunnels had been discovered in the early nineteenth century, was reputed to be the site of buried treasure, the loot attributed to various pirates. The Restalls searched the island and its tunnels for six years. In the summer of 1965, the shaft they were working in filled with carbon monoxide and the three Restalls and another man suffocated. Had Bob ever asked, Patty would surely have advised him that riding a motorcycle in a motordrome was a safer occupation than hunting for treasure.

Other endings in the outdoor amusement business affected Conklin Shows more directly. As World of Mirth Shows, one of the great shows of the 1940s and '50s, came to an end, Patty and Jim had the opportunity to expand their road show route with the only large Ontario fair that had eluded them.[18] World of Mirth had been in decline for several years, but the Central Canada Exhibition in Ottawa kept it afloat. In the 1962 and 1963 seasons, there were several bad ride accidents there, including one fatality, and these, plus the run-down World of Mirth midway and the agents on it who still played strong, drew intense criticism from local newspapers and politicians. The fair set an attendance record of over 600,000 in 1963, but this did not cool the heat directed at the show.

Under fierce pressure from local media and city officials, including the firebrand mayor, Charlotte Whitton, the executive of the board of directors cancelled the World of Mirth contract, with three of its five years yet to run. Having played Ottawa since 1933, the cancellation of its contract signalled the end for World of Mirth, which went into receivership at its last date of the season. The contract was thrown open for bids at the beginning of October and within a week Patty was asking Jack Clarke, general manager of the exhibition, for details. In mid-November 1963, the Central Canada Exhibition contract was awarded to Amusements of America, a 10-year-old show that had gotten its first fair contracts in 1959 and would expand quickly based on its success at the Ottawa exhibition, which it would keep for more than 30 years. In 1968 Amusements of America took the Trois-Rivières and Quebec City exhibitions from the Racine–Bernard & Barry combination that had taken them from the Conklins.

The deadline for bids for Ottawa had been the end of October, but, despite having wanted this fair for years, the Conklins did not submit one. Frank's health would have been an inhibiting factor, as were questions about the future of Sullivan's show. The Conklins would have had to use World's Finest to play Ottawa, since it occurred during the CNE. Hank Blade, identified in the

Ottawa Journal on October 22 as a "former National Hockey League star, now general manager and part owner of The World's Finest Show," had also called on Clarke. World's Finest did not put in a bid either. The new arrangements between Conklin and World's Finest did not congeal in time for either to take advantage of the opportunity.

Jim's Road Show

Sullivan had been talking about retiring and selling the show to his staff at the end of his 1963 season, and, perhaps confirmed in his decision by the death of Frank, he made the official announcement early in the new year. Blade could not come up with the cash to buy Sullivan out and soon after, Conklin & Garrett Ltd. bought the entire show. Sullivan helped manage the World's Finest route for two more years and kicked around the Showmen's League clubrooms in Toronto and Chicago until he had a stroke early in 1967. He spent his remaining years an invalid until his death in May 1971 at the age of 79.

World's Finest would continue to end its season in Simcoe, but would no longer keep winter quarters there. The show's Pullmans, boxcars, and flats, up to 50 in total, had been parking on the CNR tracks and at the fairgrounds for three decades. When Jim talked to the *Simcoe Reformer* about the sale, for an article that appeared on the front page of the February 3, 1964, edition, he said they would winter "somewhere else." The main change would be "a lot of new rides"; they would "concentrate on rides of all kinds, rather than shows." They would be playing the fair with Conklin equipment, as they dissolved Sullivan's show and got rid of his equipment.

Sullivan had declined to sell off individual rides, wanting to sell the show as a package, but the Conklins immediately put the World's Finest pieces up for sale. There were a dozen each of major and kiddie rides, and 10 shows; the rides sold and the shows were retired. Jules Racine, the Quebec competitor of the Conklins and Sullivan, was a big buyer, picking up an Auto Skooter, a dark ride, a funhouse, a train, some hot rods, and some concession and electrical equipment. King Shows in Toronto, which had recently been bought by its manager, Howard Jones, took three major rides and four kiddie rides. Two other small Ontario shows bought a few rides and Phil Cronin, Sullivan's kiddieland manager, bought a Tilt-A-Whirl for his new company, Kiddie-Lands. Blade apparently could not afford to take anything. By the spring, the Conklins had sold $160,000 worth of World's Finest equipment. They kept the name, the route, and the show train.

Conklin & Garrett also bought the London-based Gray Shows from Clifford Gray in June 1964. Having inherited the show from his father, Gray claimed to have the oldest carnival title in Ontario, in operation since 1927. His show had once been big enough to bid on the western B circuit, but when he dissolved it he only had five minor rides, and some transformers and trucks for sale, and the Conklins got it all for just over $20,000. Patty's plan was again to sell the equipment to other shows. As the older and younger Conklins and their wives played tag team on trips to Europe that spring, Patty "disclosed that his family is still as much on the move as ever searching for new equipment and ideas."[19] As Patty had done after the war, they were once more doing their best to saddle other Canadian shows with old rides from defunct operations, while they accumulated capital to buy new European equipment.

The Conklins had no interest in Sullivan's spring stills, 10 of which went to King Shows, but they continued to play the fairs, which, although contracted under their name, had been World's Finest dates. Despite the loss of Frank and Sullivan, the route over which Jim took the World's Finest crew during August and September remained remarkably consistent with what it had been for the previous decade, apart from the absence of Quebec City and Trois-Rivières. The only difference for Jim was that he stayed out into early October to work the Markham and Simcoe fairs.

Remarking in an article on him in the April 1965 issue of *Executive* that Conklin Shows still played dates it had been meeting for over 30 years, Patty said, "These smaller fairs stuck by us when things were thin.... Now we'll stick by them even though they are not quite so profitable." He added, "There is more loyalty and honesty in this business than in any other." He might have noted that without those small fairs, his son would have nothing to do except butt heads with him at the CNE, where Jim was relegated to managing the

60 or so game concessions. Other than the Ex and a few rides in amusement parks, the small fairs were all that Conklin Shows had. These fairs had kept Frank and Sullivan in the game. Now that they were both gone, the fairs provided an internship for Jim.

Jim was loyal to and depended on many of Sullivan's old, reliable crew. When Jim took over the Conklin road show in 1964, Sullivan came out to help him manage it. They kept Pat Marco as concession manager and lot boss, as well as Marco's wife, Dottie, who had come from World of Mirth in 1957, and Frank Eastman, who had run several concessions for Sullivan for years. Tiny Jamieson, Sullivan's ride superintendent of long standing, left the business, as did other old office staff who were ready to retire. But many of Sullivan's games agents stayed under the new owner. Jim was different from his father, his uncle, or Sullivan, all of whom were showmen of the old school, from an era when shows got away with robbery, and it would take time before the World's Finest carnies accepted him as one of their own. Some old carnies never did. Marco was the first to befriend the new boss, sitting for hours with him and sharing his experience and wisdom, while Jim shared his own ideas.

Having sold most of the World's Finest rides, when Jim went out to the fairs, he needed help from independents. He had half a dozen owners of a few rides each with him for the dates before the CNE. Phil Cronin, from World's Finest, was the largest of these with three major and four kiddie rides. The independents abandoned Jim to make serious money with Patty in Toronto and London, while Jim dragged the remnants of the show down the road to Sherbrooke, where Florian Vallée and his Beauce Carnaval joined him. Vallée had eight or nine major rides and five or six kiddie rides and stayed with Jim for the remainder of the season. Founded in 1953, Beauce would later get the Exposition Provinciale in Quebec City on its own.

The Conklins still owned the contracts and exacted substantial tribute from sub-contractors for the privilege of playing their fairs. Don Campbell began with the show in the early 1960s with Digger games. He bought a bumper car ride one year and gradually built up his ride holdings. In 1968 Campbell brought six major rides out for the entire season of 11 fairs. Jim took 44 percent of Campbell's ride gross, out of which he paid the fairs their 35 percent and covered his overhead, keeping the rest as net profit. That year the Campbell rides grossed $134,300, but after advances to cover expenses, Campbell received a cheque for $30,900 and still had to pay off his staff.[20] Jim added more than $35,000 to the Conklin coffers from the proceeds of Campbell's rides alone. Tired of his profits going to someone else, Campbell would leave the Conklins after the 1972 season to establish his own route. Other independents also found the Conklin take exorbitant.

In 1964, his first year in charge of the road show, Jim managed to increase the season's gross from rides and shows by $22,000.[21] The Sherbrooke exhibition climbed by $7,000 and Markham, a new fair Jim contracted on his own, added over $8,000. The Norfolk County Fair in Simcoe, which had been Sullivan's alone, dropped by almost $6,000. Other fairs brought in around the same as previous years or climbed slightly. For 10 weeks on the road, Jim's operation grossed $185,700. For 15 days in Toronto, his father's operation grossed $953,900. Jim's road show figures were closer to the reality of most carnival companies, while the CNE figures provided the financial foundation for Patty's stature in the business.

Jim began to put his mark on the Conklin road show route in the second half of the decade. Since the loss of the Quebec City exhibition, there had been a gap of a week between the end of the Sherbrooke fair and the beginning of the Ontario fairs. There was also a week off before Sherbrooke. In 1966 Jim picked up fairs in Prescott and Perth to fill in the gaps. Neither provided enough money even to fill holes in the route and they were gone the next year. That year the Kitchener fair, which Jim had taken back two years before, was moved to fall between Sherbrooke and Renfrew. He also added three Ontario still dates, the Oshawa fair in July, and the Barrie fair in the fall.

The 1967 season was the longest Conklin Shows had been out continuously since 1945, when they last played the A circuit in the West. They headed out on the road at the end of June and, after 16 events with only a few weeks off in between, did not go back in the barn until the second week of October. Jim's first experiment with still dates did not go well. The rides and shows only brought in around $3,000 at each spot and he dropped the new stills the following year.[22] For 16 weeks on the road, Jim's rides and shows grossed $325,100, while for 15 days in Toronto, his father grossed $1,351,200. It would be some time before Jim would permanently alter the show's travelling schedule in any significant way, but his ambition to expand the season was already evident. He wanted to make his show a true travelling carnival and not just an adjunct to the big fair in Toronto.

Never His Like Again

(1965–1970)

Although Patty put on a brave front and tried to deny it, by the middle of the decade he finally began to slow down. He did not stop making money or cutting a figure in public. Some of his public appearances, however, cast him in a light more critical than that to which he had become accustomed. He would never retire or find any real leisure, and in his last years he would have to defend his reputation, but he would make it to the grave before his powers were depleted, his fiction exposed, or his legend anything worse than a little frayed around the edges.

ANOTHER INVESTMENT AND NEW QUESTIONS

On their own for the first time in a big city, the two young teenagers ride the streetcar, joining the multitudes flowing from all over Toronto and beyond to converge on the lakefront park. No need to consult the route written out for them by the one boy's aunt as everyone is going the same way. They are among the 200,000 people who that day pour into the exhibition.

The boys, unnerved by the throng funnelling into the gate, are processed with no need for them to engage, their money taken, their hands stamped. Once through, they collect themselves to the side of the crowd. They check their money and look at the map of the grounds to figure out where they are. They spot the Automotive Building on the map and look up to see its classical pillars before them. They had talked about visiting it, although maybe not as their first stop, but it's right there and it's starting to drizzle.

The huge hall is unlike anywhere they've ever been, full of a mass of humanity unlike anything they've ever encountered. Apart from the numbers, the diversity unsettles them as they have only ever been among people who look like them. They try to see the exhibits, but the crowd frustrates and distracts them. They leave the building, unsure about what they have just been through.

After a few more exhibit buildings, the boys end up at the terminus of the Alpine Way. The 50 cents they pay to take the ride is their first contribution to the Conklin coffers. The ride is spectacular; they see the entire grounds awash in people. But the air is stuffy and humid, so they open the gondola's windows to let the breeze flow through.

Back on the ground, they find the Food Building, where their movement is again bound by the press of bodies. The smells, the lineups, the array of unfamiliar food — they feel accomplished just to get a hot dog, fries, and Coke, but they can't find ketchup and have to sit on the curb to eat as no tables are free. Gulls gorge on leftovers, barely acknowledging the little children lunging at them.

Grease settling in their stomachs, the boys discuss whether to see a free performance by Don Messer and his Islanders in the bandshell or to head to the midway. With a mix of apprehension and excitement, they choose the latter. Consulting the map for the best route, they set off, struggling to stay together.

As they near the midway, they see a golf cart with a wizened old man hunched over its steering wheel, forcing the crowds to part to let him through. Their bemusement turns to a thrill of recognition as they see the dapper gentleman sitting beside the driver. "That's Art Linkletter!" they exclaim. Art waves and smiles to his fans, while Patty scowls ahead, taking it all in but seeing no one. The boys have had a brush with a television star and feel satisfied that they are really experiencing the world. They had hardly noticed the driver and now they enter his midway.

The sensory assault intensifies. Diesel fumes are the dominant smell, with undertones of fried onions, burnt sugar, salty popcorn, and sticky people. In the still air an oily mist settles on skin, mixing with personal and general sweat, as people bump and jostle. The cacophony of tinny music, the rattle of the rides, the laughs and screams of thousands jammed into a narrow road bordered by brightly coloured tents interspersed with huge pieces of careening equipment. Vision is flooded with garish hues, glittering machines, faces in perpetual motion.

All interactions fall to the favour of the minority who are not there for the fun of it. The boys know about carnies, a subset of the city slickers and other degenerates they have vowed will not take advantage of them. They don't play the games and they look away from the offers thrust at them. They are, however, held by the bally at the girl show.

The lines are long at the major rides and the prospect of that much idle waiting in the service of amusement offends them, so they settle for a sedate spin on the Ferris wheel. They go into one show, a Life show with salacious displays about reproduction and a collection of deformed rubber dolls in jars. It is stifling in the tent and one of the boys starts to feel queasy. He thinks it's a bad hot dog, but his friend thinks he's squeamish. He feels faint and needs air.

Back out on the midway, the sick boy has had enough, even though they both have change in their pockets from the $20 they each started with. His friend can dump his money however he likes, but he's heading for the streetcar. The outflux is less overwhelming, the energy of the crowd gone with its money. After the boys gain a seat on the streetcar, relief takes over. They have survived a trip to the world's largest fair without incident.

As Patty entered his 24th season at the CNE in 1965 — the last 15 posting consecutive record grosses — its directors were at a loss about how to continue breaking their records or even how to maintain their run of success. Changeable weather was on the horizon for the Canadian National Exhibition. The Metropolitan Toronto Council's members, when they considered taking over the Ex, assessed the 87-year-old grounds as "'rundown and deteriorated' and feared the CNE could be wrecked by competition from Montreal's 1967 exposition during Canada's centennial year."[1]

The Alpine Way

The CNE board had been fretting over the threat of Expo 67 for several years, appointing Hiram McCallum the managing director for the 1967 Ex upon his retirement in 1964 as general manager. The directors voted to develop plans for expanding the CNE facilities and in 1965 commissioned a $108,000 study. The report released 10 months later called for expansion, new buildings, and rearrangement. It recommended complete co-operation among municipal, provincial, and federal governments, as well as substantial spending by them. Few of the recommendations were implemented, although the report provided direction for years. While damning all around, it did find that, despite its critics, the midway remained the most popular attraction at the Ex.

Since early in the decade, however, the CNE midway had been drawing unfavourable comparisons with Disneyland. Many blamed Patty for an outdated carnie-style production and even suggested that Walt Disney be contracted to reform it. When consulted, Disney "confessed he didn't know anything about the exhibition business," but did not think that Toronto could support a Disneyland-like park.[2] In begging off making any recommendations, he might, on the one hand, have been identifying an obvious flaw in some of the ambitions for the CNE. On the other, he might have been thinking of a friend's reputation.

Patty claimed an acquaintance with Disney from having sold him the rundown but vintage merry-go-round from Sunnyside Park, which in the later retellings became a rare and perfect find. In an article published on August 23, 1960, he told the *Toronto Star* that he had coached Disney before Disney built his amusement park and countered adverse comparisons by saying he would invest in a "Toronto Disneyland" on the CNE grounds if it could stay open Sundays. Patty and Walt had a reunion in Calgary at a memorial dinner in 1965 that McCallum also attended. The happiest moment for Patty, reported by the Calgary *Albertan* on July 8, came when "'Walt got to meet the grand-children ... and sign his autograph for them.'"

Back at the CNE, how to transport millions of people around the 350 acres of Exhibition Park was a crucial problem, and here Patty could draw on the Disneyland example. Disneyland had an Alpine Skyway cable car ride, there was one at the New York World's Fair, and Patty had been enthralled by the monorail at the Seattle fair. He introduced the idea to the CNE board as a solution to the transportation problem, but for him it was another ride. The directors considered installing "a skyride costing between $750,000 and $1 million" to replace the trains on wheels that shuttled people around the grounds.[3]

When, in 1965, Patty had his contract extended to 1972, part of the deal was that Conklin Shows would have the "Sky Ride pact ... to run 20 years."[4] About the contract renewal, general manager Bert Powell said that the management did not "bother having anyone else bid," adding that "no one can touch Patty for capital or experience. He's got a million dollars in permanent buildings alone."[5] Patty was about to almost double his investment and Powell's words would come back to haunt him.

While making plans for his own cable cars, Patty contracted a small ski lift. Discussions for an overhead monorail like the one in Seattle also began in 1965, but those discussions would continue for 10 years without result. Once he had the board's blessing for the cable cars, Patty solicited proposals from a number of manufacturers, four from Germany, not surprisingly, as well as several from Canada. By the end of 1965, he had made his selection and signed a $600,000 contract with the Breco Aerial Tramway Division of the Bridge and Tank Company of Canada. Bridge and Tank, founded in 1863 in Hamilton, had built steel works of all kinds across Canada and around the world.

According to the president of Bridge and Tank, the *Globe and Mail* reported on December 15, 1965, "Once the aerial tramway at the World's Fair in New York is dismantled, the Toronto installation will be the only major twin aerial tramway system in the world." There were one-way cable car rides at several fairs in the United States, including the Texas State Fair. The Ex's ride would run both ways over 2,100 feet, suspended 100 feet above the ground on five towers with 80 four-passenger enclosed cars. It had a projected capacity of 750,000 for the 15-day fair, but Patty "would be satisfied if 500,000 persons took the ride in the first year of operation."

In March 1966, work began on footings for the towers for what Patty would christen the Alpine Way. In June he reported that it would be ready for the CNE that year. When the Ex opened "after a siege of high-pressure worry, crisis and criticism," the cost of the Alpine Way had risen to $710,000 and because of minor hitches it did not open.[6] The hitches included the insistence of provincial safety inspectors on "testing each car to ensure it will carry the specified 700 pounds safely." After beginning full operation on the first Monday, it rode about 400,000 passengers over the length of the fair. Like the Flyer, Patty ran the Alpine Way as a company separate from the rest of his midway; it grossed almost $200,000 in its first year. He and his successors would have another 19 years to make good on his initial investment. Once again, he had added significantly to the permanent attractions at Exhibition Park. He told the Toronto *Telegram* that he had plans to make the Alpine Way "a year-round tourist attraction."

Doubts About the Ex

The exhibition's opening day coverage in the *Telegram* on August 19, 1966, noted that "Paddy Conklin's still there" and "has become a CNE attraction on his own." The next day, the first Saturday, the front page of the *Star* carried a full-colour photograph of the Round-Up, covering a third of the page and captioned in 32-point capital letters, "CHEERS ... IN 'PATTY CONKLIN'S CHAMPAGNE.'" The front page of the entertainment section had a similar-sized colour photo of "Patty Conklin's Ferris wheel," while the back page had a three-quarter page colour shot of the midway. Sharing the page with the Ferris wheel, a long article described "the father–son team that runs the biggest midway in the world ... a $3,000,000 layout with an annual insurance bill of $100,000."

The other article on the entertainment section's front page asked, "Is the Ex outdated?" The first paragraph in this piece by the *Star*'s drama critic answered his rhetorical question in the affirmative: "What is wrong with the Canadian National Exhibition in the first place is that it isn't particularly Canadian, it certainly isn't national, and anyway it has lost the reason for its existence." With the contradictoriness attendant on a free press, the writer criticized newspapers — notably his own, it would seem — for treating the CNE "as if it were still a major occasion in people's lives." He spread the criticism around by identifying "a sense of futility and spreading dry rot" pervading all annual exhibitions and fairs, and even the world's fairs: "The spectre which haunts Expo '67 is the dismal experiences of Brussels and Seattle, and the colossal calamity of New York." The critic singled out Disneyland as "the one truly successful contemporary exhibition of our age."

Patty no doubt read this article while laughing on his way to the bank after closing that first Saturday, but son Jim might have caught an unsettling glimpse of his future. On the last Saturday of the event, the *Star* published a survey of "people in exhibitions or allied fields" who answered the question, "What should we do about the Ex?" That the *Star* thought it important to ask the question suggests the significance of the Ex, at least to the people of Toronto. Most of the opinions offered called for an extreme makeover, although none quite as extreme as that of the Toronto alderman who responded with his own question: "How big a bulldozer do we have?" When the bulldozer eventually came, it would be very big.

Patty and Jim Conklin on the midway of the CNE, 1966.

Fixing fair attendance numbers was not unknown, and the *Star*'s drama critic wondered whether "3,000,000 men, women and children *really* turn out for it? How reliable are the attendance figures anyway?" The consultants' report issued that summer had noted that "rising attendance figures concealed a real loss of popularity" and claimed that the "State Fair of Texas and four other State Fairs in the U.S. are more popular than the CNE."[7] It would take the Texas fair two more years to become the first U.S. event to draw over three million people. Despite the Ex having the largest attendance of any fair in the world, "in 10 years, total attendance has increased only 0.6 per cent, while Ontario's population has hiked 2.6 per cent."[8] While everyone assumed it would, the 1966 CNE failed to reach the three-million mark it had hit before. The 62 rides and Dufour's two shows took in only $7,000 more than in 1965, not counting the Alpine Way's earnings. Mickey Hughes's three new rides did well. The results did nothing to abate criticism of the CNE and the Conklin midway.

The concessions' take continued to be a company secret, but the means through which Bazaars Ltd. obtained that take came under scrutiny that year. Toronto detectives tested the rings of a Hoop-La game and found that 45 percent of them would not fit over the boxes. Charges were originally laid against Conklin & Garrett, Patty, Jim, and Cy Hardy, their concessions manager. Hardy would have been barred from working the midway had he been convicted. But Louis Herman, Maxie Herman's nephew and the company lawyer, managed to have those charges dropped, and Stanley Galuska and another operator took the fall. They were convicted of cheating at play through what the magistrate characterized as "underhanded and despicable deceit."[9] Crown council called it "a scheme to cheat the public," most of whom were children. The case ended Galuska's midway career, but Patty showed his gratitude by keeping him on as a full-time shop employee. Galuska's son eventually brought the family name back to the midway's games.

Bazaars Ltd. and the operators were fined a total of $5,000, but the incident drew heat from the mayor and other city officials. Detectives related how they had given countless warnings to operators, and CNE directors admitted the issue of cheating had arisen before at board meetings, but no one could recall any discussion of how contracts were let to concession owners. Herman said that in his 30 years of representing the show, this was the first time such charges had been laid, which might have been true on a technicality. The press for the moment ignored Patty's involvement.

The Western Fair in London did much better in 1966 in relative terms. It had 52 of the CNE's 64 attractions and, with an attendance approaching 400,000 for 10 days, the midway gross was up 27 percent. This year was the last in an 11-year contract, which, shortly after the end of the fair, general manager Evan McGugan announced would not be renewed. Conklin Shows had been playing the London fair for as long as it had the CNE, but, as sort of a sequel to the Ex, Patty's troubles in Toronto might have been spilling over into the city down the road. As reported in the December 10 issue of *Amusement Business*, McGugan still considered "Conklin to be one of the best midway operators in the business," but he had visited the Texas State Fair in Dallas, liked the way it operated with an independent midway, and wanted to take his fair in that direction. Although McGugan considered this a trend, the Western Fair remains one of the few big fairs ever to run its own midway successfully, largely on the basis of McGugan's abilities. The London event was the third-largest fair in Ontario, after Toronto and Ottawa, and its loss hurt Conklin Shows and their contractors.

REPUTATIONS AT RISK

The bellowing can be heard across the whole second floor of the Horse Palace. "Who is this fuckin' loogan? Who does he think he is? Does he think I'm going to take this bullshit?" Patty storms into the outer office, veins bulging on his forehead and glasses askew. "Have you read this piece of shit?" he yells at no one in particular as he crumples the newspaper and throws it at the floor.

His staff had all read the article and had been dreading the moment when the boss got to it. None of them had been able to muster the courage to bring it to him and try to mollify him ahead of time. Now, they sit with their heads down, staring at their desks.

Still muttering and cursing, he picks the newspaper up again, his abused incredulity persistent. "I don't have to take this lying down."

Finally, one of his managers approaches him and tries to soothe him. "Patty, it's just some punk.... Don't take it seriously ..."

"Don't take it seriously? It's on the front page of the city's biggest fuckin' newspaper! He's calling me a thief in public! How am I supposed to take it?"

"It's all just speculation, he doesn't have anything on you ..."

"Those shithead independents sure were ready to talk to him — he got lots of bullshit out of them. Who else has been talking to him? How'd he come up with all this garbage?" He has not calmed down, but he is no longer shouting. "Get Jim over here," he commands and returns to his office.

He picks up the phone and dials. "Bob, you read this piece of crap in the *Telegram*? Who's at the club? What are they saying? Is Coleman there?... Get him on the phone.

"Coleman, you seen this bullshit story on the front page of the *Telegram*? Who is this punk that wrote this? Do you know him? Who's his boss?... Yeah? Well, you can let him know I don't appreciate his paper saying these kinds of things about me.... Yeah, and you can tell him I'll be talking to my lawyer about this and we'll just see who gets away with what. I don't hafta let some hack think he can take me down.... Sure, sure, I appreciate your sympathy and I'm glad to hear the boys are saying the same.... Never mind, never mind, this thing isn't over." He slams down the phone.

★   ★   ★

The ambitions manifest in Expo 67 and the expectations they raised in the public were one of the main ways its existence, even in concept, had been impinging on the CNE. Ontario's premier, John Robarts, had opened a $175,000 exhibit on Expo at the 1966 Ex that, paradoxically, made "Expo '67 ... one of the CNE's finest attractions."[10] The exhibit, sponsored by the Ontario government and the Canadian Corporation for the 1967 World Exhibition, was "designed to get 3,000,000 Ontario residents to Montreal's Expo '67." That was the number the City of Toronto had hoped to see at its own exhibition that year.

The Rival Ex

Patty downplayed the Expo threat, at least in immediate terms. He visited the grounds in May 1966 with E.K. Fernandez and reported "much work in progress but a staggering amount remaining."[11] A year later, he and Jim attended the fair shortly after it opened at the end of April but did not go on record with their opinion. Patty would have been comparing it with what he had achieved in Seattle and chewing over how he might have been involved, but his pronouncements were not sought by reporters.

Others were not so reticent. *Amusement Business*, on June 3, claimed unanimity among "fun industry" professionals that "the Montreal world's fair is by far the best ever staged and that it is unlikely that its equal will be seen again in the foreseeable future." The amusement area, La Ronde, with two dozen rides and 46 games, was "one of the best fun sectors of this century's world exhibitions." Unlike in Seattle, there were no colourful amusement business personalities to play up, although Montreal mayor Jean Drapeau, a driving force behind the fair, was a remarkable personality in his own right. Expo 67 would go on to record over 50 million paid admissions, five times what Seattle had seen.

To help the CNE compete, Patty announced that he was "bringing in five or six new rides and giving the midway a $200,000 refurbishing to produce an 1867 look."[12] By the time it opened, his investment had been reduced to "about $85,000 to theme" the midway "to resemble a western pioneer town."[13] With Jack Ray no longer around and his modernist aesthetic on the wane, Patty turned his back on art deco fronts and pulled out the old-time look he had rejected for the Seattle midway.

The faux frontier theme might have been appropriate for the Canadian centennial and distinguished the CNE midway from the futuristic Montreal fair, but Patty was also starting to graft in a vague, make-believe Bavarian theme, with rides like the Matterhorn and Zugspitz, and names like the Alpine Way for his cable cars and the Bavarian Gardens for a restaurant and bar he would open in 1968. Patty Conklin–Joe Renker was producing a hybrid of the imagined heritage of his adopted country by splicing his suppressed ancestry onto the kitschy facades of his midway. The colonial past was modelled in the pioneer dress-up worn by the concessions and concessionaires, while the Teutonic spirit was summoned through heavy metal machinery and beer. Midways have always been mongrels, but Patty's more than most. It reflected strains in the society around it and in its producer.

The big new German ride for the 1967 Toronto fair was to be an enlarged, figure-eight version of the Wild Mouse style of coaster, the Wild Cat, built by Anton Schwarzkopf and imported by Mickey Hughes, who also brought one to Palisades Park. As with the Alpine Way the year before, Patty had problems getting the Wild Cat ready for opening. It was delayed in New York because of a dockworkers' strike and finally loaded on nine trucks with only a few days to go. Conklin and Hughes used their influence to get an escort of New York state police dispatched to expedite the trip to the border, where Canadian Forces personnel met the trucks and rushed them on to Toronto, an enormous production on both sides of the border just to move an amusement device. After the Wild Cat components arrived late on Wednesday, the Ex set to open in two days, Patty personally supervised two German factory representatives and his own ride men as they worked overtime unloading and erecting the massive ride. Because the midway was already laid out and they could not get the trucks close to the ride's location, they lugged the huge components by hand, taking almost five days to get it in place and set up. Missing the first weekend, the ride opened on Monday.

Patty paid $100,000 for the Wild Cat, having put a third down in January with the commitment to pay it off by October. But Hughes had promised it for July and Patty had expected it to be delivered down the St. Lawrence Seaway directly to Toronto. It cost almost $10,000 to ship and another $5,500 to transport from New York. Handling and brokerage fees amounted to a further $2,000. Labour costs and a crane rental added over $4,000.

Patty wrote Hughes a four-page letter on September 21 itemizing his complaints about the extra expenses. He wanted an adjustment for the shipping, handling, brokerage, labour, and crane expenses. He would not pay the transportation and insurance from New York. "The most important factor that I really have something to complain about is that we lost the opening day ... and the biggest gross day of the exhibition," he wrote. "I would say that we lost at least $14,000.00 in revenue," he continued, "and, technically, in view of you missing the July delivery date, we should be compensated by Schwarzkopf and yourself for a big portion of this $14,000.00." He also wanted payment for two telephone calls Schwarzkopf had made from his Toronto office to Germany. Hughes did not settle to Patty's satisfaction, and further tension developed over Hughes competing with Patty as a ride importer. Hughes was not asked to return with his rides to the CNE, although after he wrote a formal apology three years later, Patty let him come back.

Canadians and visitors to the country were fair-minded in the centennial year and the 50 million people drawn by Expo 67 did not hurt CNE attendance, which reached the second best in its history, only 50,000 short of the record of 3,075,500 set in 1963. The midway grossed $1.35 million, another record. But Expo did cause the Ex problems. The Toronto mayor, William Dennison, had early on objected to a proposal to preserve some of the Expo 67 buildings for permanent use, arguing that they would compete with Canada's rightful national fair, hosted in his city. The Ex continued to be publicly criticized as outmoded in comparison with Expo. Premier Robarts visited the world's fair four times and pressured the federal government for financial support to enable him to rebuild the Ex in the image of Expo.

"Should Paddy Conklin be allowed to continue operating the midway or should the job be handled directly by the exhibition?" was one of the first questions that arose as the provincial government pressed forward with its planning.[14] A ruling against coin table games at La Ronde led to their ban at the CNE. Patty had a question of his own: "If something can run for 35 years without a complaint, why does it have to be stopped now?"[15] The indirect answer to both questions was that Expo 67 was setting precedents.

Mayor Drapeau came to the CNE in 1968 to reassure Toronto that the Man and His World permanent exhibition on the Expo grounds was "a cultural and educational exhibition" that would not compete with the Ex.[16] Man and His World would die, but in the longer run, La Ronde, the amusement park Expo spawned, would become the real threat to the Conklin enterprises. In the middle of Expo 67 and despite any parochial objections from Toronto, the municipal, provincial, and federal government partners "announced a two-year extension as a trial period for the amusement park," with "strong possibilities it will become a permanent fixture."[17] There was immediate speculation as to whether Montreal could support "another major amusement park, and whether La Ronde, which is controlled by three governmental structures, could justifiably be considered unfair competition to privately owned Belmont Park."[18] La Ronde, a corporate theme park on the Disney model, went on to draw as many as five million people a season, while family-owned Belmont's attendance never exceeded 800,000.

The owners renovated Belmont to try to keep it competitive and the Conklins, who had sold their rides to the park in 1961 when Rex Billings retired, came back with five major rides in 1969. They continued to have rides and concessions in the park until the late 1970s, by which time Belmont had begun to deteriorate. There was an accident on the Wild Mouse in 1976 and injuries to two riders on a Paratrooper in 1979 led to the ride being closed. The municipal and provincial governments continued to run La Ronde and pressured Belmont around alleged illegal activities. The park was sold in 1980, but limped on for a few more years, finally failing in 1983. A subdivision was eventually built on its land. Among the many economic and social factors that contributed to Belmont's demise, the legacy of Expo 67 was significant.

Good Press and Bad

On the strength of his perpetually rising grosses at the CNE, Patty remained an elder statesman of the carnival industry and took advantage of opportunities to revel in his reputation, all of which received ample press. In January 1966, he "acted as toastmaster at showmen's club banquets in Seattle, Los Angeles, Chicago and Toronto" and turned down invitations from two other clubs.[19] In October, the Ontario chapter of the Showmen's League of America celebrated the grand opening of its new clubrooms and the burning of the mortgage by hosting a "lavish testimonial dinner" to honour him as "the prime mover in the establishment and good fortune of the still young club," naming the general meeting chamber the "Patty Room."[20] All of the major ride designers and manufacturers in the United States and many from Europe persisted in showcasing their wares at the CNE and posing for photo opportunities with Patty.

His reputation continued to spread beyond the carnival industry. In the spring of 1966, he was flown by helicopter from Brantford to Toronto to be the guest speaker at the Toronto Sales and Advertising Club. On October 7, 1967, *Amusement Business* reported that he was the guest at a "Toronto Variety Club luncheon honouring him as a charter member and outstanding contributor." It was attended by 300 "local business, city and provincial government officials, all of whom heaped praise on Conklin for his charities." One speech was given by the Honourable Ross Macdonald, lieutenant governor of Ontario, who had at one time been the Speaker in the federal House of Commons and the majority leader in the Senate.

Patty and Jim also sought to ensure their show achieved a type of recognition and longevity beyond that built on spectacular riding devices and huge grosses. Patty hired Chris Yaneff's design and advertising firm to create a logo for Conklin & Garrett Ltd., his ride operating firm. Yaneff, an award-winning designer based in Toronto, was responsible for some of the country's most well-known logos, including those for Canada Trust, Air Canada, Canadian National Railway, and Via Rail. The resulting logo won first place in 1966 in an annual competition sponsored by *Communication Arts* magazine, and Patty saw its potential for raising brand recognition for all the Conklin companies.

Called Conko, the stylized round clown head in red, white, and black, with plus signs for eyes, has become one of the most recognizable logos in North America, exceeding anything associated with any other carnival company. Replacing Patty's grizzled mug as the face of his show, Conko has been embedded in the minds of a generation of midway patrons across the continent. The icon became an integral part of the Conklin Shows' identity and the show threatened to prosecute anybody who considered borrowing it.

Beyond adding the Conko branding to the game concessions for the first time, Patty developed a new colour scheme with fluorescent paint for the 1968 CNE. The CNE management, despite its handwringing during recent years, only brought in two innovations in 1968, although they were significant, especially for the midway. The first concerned the timing of the exhibition. Its run was extended by four days to 19, opening on a Thursday instead of a Friday, and operating on Sundays. The *Globe and Mail* reported on the front page of its September 6 edition that, at the grandstand ceremonies closing the 1966

CNE, the president had announced that the board would give "top priority consideration" to "open Sundays" to compete with the seven-day-a-week operation allowed in Quebec for Expo 67. People who visit Expo were "not going to be impressed by an exhibition that shuts its gates in their faces on the one day that offers the most people the most leisure," he had said, "to wild applause." The board had been unable to get around Ontario's blue laws for the centennial, but a bill to amend the provincial Lord's Day Act was finally introduced in April 1968 and its provisions allowed the Toronto fair to operate on Sundays for the first time.

The second innovation was the partial relocation and expansion of the midway, enabling Conklin Shows to add eight rides for a total of 71. While this would boost the show's gross, it would also bring grief to Patty. With the extra days and extra earning power, he modestly predicted a 15 percent increase over his 1967 gross to $1.7 million. Four days of rain kept him $60,000 short of his goal. The press rained even more heavily on Patty's parade.

Perhaps a faction in the Toronto press had become jaded with the midway king and decided it was time to dethrone him. Perhaps it needed a scapegoat on which to pin the public's perception of the increasing tawdriness of the CNE. Perhaps a zealous young reporter owing no dues to the Toronto establishment found a bone to pick and his editor let him off his leash. Whatever the case, on August 30, 1968, the last Friday of the Ex, the Toronto *Telegram* published the first part of a two-part special report on "Conklin's CNE Sweetheart Contracts." In the home edition, it appeared at the bottom of the front page, but in the final edition, it was moved to banner position.

Not since Mayor Lamport had gone after Elwood Hughes and Patty had the exhibition management's arrangement with Conklin Shows come under such scathing attack. The article alleged that bribery and graft were occurring under a veil of secrecy and threats. Because of this secrecy, however, the reporter could provide few facts and argued by innuendo. He questioned the "Sweetheart contracts with James Wesley (Patty) Conklin, feudal lord of the Midway," and suggested the changes to the layout that year had been exclusively for the benefit of his midway monopoly and to the detriment of the few small independent operators who impinged on that monopoly. He implied that Patty had hidden interests in other concessions, such as Bert Murray's nine food joints, beyond those openly contracted to his companies. He claimed that the Conklins were making exorbitant profits off public land, while paying no taxes on that land and short-changing the CNE. In response to the excuse that the Ex needed an expert to run the midway, the reporter pointed to La Ronde, run by a retired navy officer; the Western Fair, where Conklin Shows had been replaced by independents and the midway was run by the fair board; and the Quebec City fair, where when open bidding was allowed, the show had lost the contract.

The first part of the special report drew responses from general manager Bert Powell, Metro chairman William Allen, and a number of other civic politicians, who defended their relations with the show. Surprisingly, controller and ex-mayor Allan Lamport provided a defence of Patty, however lukewarm, saying that he paid to the exhibition as much as or more than other concessionaires. The other respondents claimed that everything was done above board, but proved the reporter's contention that they really did not know what was in the contracts or the extent of the Conklin interests.

Patty fought back by going to the rival *Toronto Star* the next day with the claim that "he loses by CNE change." He said that he had tried with the other concessionaires to prevent the reorganization of the midway. The *Star* reporter found three independent concession operators to attest that the changes could not have been made to help Patty, although their own receipts were all down substantially. The *Star* story concluded by describing the midway where "the rides, sideshows and booths of Patty Conklin were jammed with people spending money."

In the second part of the special report in the *Telegram*, the reporter extrapolated from Patty's invention of a rigged basket game in his youth to his rigged game with the CNE, suggesting that they existed on a continuum with no change in the underlying morality. He recalled the convictions for cheating two years before and dismissed Patty's contention that you could make more money on an honestly run midway. He substantiated the dismal fate of the independent concessionaires who had lost their locations at the top of the midway for locations in less-travelled areas but could not prove that these changes had been made at Patty's behest. Everyone the reporter asked supported the explanation that they had been made to improve traffic flow.

The *Telegram* articles hurt and angered Patty. He clipped and saved dozens of copies. Habituated to consistently effusive press, he could not imagine how anyone could see him in any other light. He had come to believe in the image the press had created, even though he knew it was false. He compromised his credibility, however, when he told reporters that he, too, would lose by the changes to the CNE midway layout. The *Telegram* exposé, coming at the end of the exhibition, fizzled out as the fall drew on. Conklin Shows had too many people beholden to it to draw any sustained fire, at least in the press. Besides, it was unseemly to beat up on an old man. Still, the articles were a dark cloud over the otherwise warm glow of Patty's sunset years and there would be others.

NEW CHALLENGES

These are Patty's last days on the midway, captured by a Canadian Broadcasting Corporation documentary crew, who did not know how exclusive the footage they were getting would be. They begin with him sitting at a food stand during set-up for the CNE. He finishes the contents of two soft drink cups. "What do ya say we go out and start makin' a buck, fellas?" he says, and stands up. He gets in the passenger side of his Cadillac, parked just feet from the counter. The driver starts the car as Patty closes the door.

Next, he's on the midway, measuring out the location for a ride. Then, jacket and glasses on, he peers at ride plans, held in gnarled hands with a huge showman's ring on one finger, and looks up at the crew throwing steel in the background. "What's your tight measurement on that?" he asks, walking up to the foreman. After a brief exchange, Patty says, "Well then, you're all right, you're set now?" and the man confirms they are. Cut to Patty in shirt sleeves later, talking to the same crew: "That's one thing I couldn't understand, a man manufactures a ride and didn't know the amount of space it takes."

"Well, they swing out, the legs they swing out quite a bit," one of them explains.

"Yeah, right, I know."

Another man mentions a ride down the midway with only two inches' clearance. "I've seen it, I know. That's all I need," insists Patty. "Two inches is as good as a mile." He clears up some other details and they ask his advice. He tells them they can make up their mind and let his office know. "Right, see you," he snaps, as he gets back in his car.

"Nice meeting you, sir," someone says off-camera.

He stops to deal with Polish contractors refurbishing the gondolas of the Alpine Way. His manner is familiar and jovial, but down to business. As he takes one of them in the car to the shop to get paint, the man, in stained overalls, points to the midway and says it looks nice now. Patty responds, "Everything looks nice with a coat of paint, even you look nice, after you got some paint on you." The man is unsure about the joke.

Now he talks vociferously to a concessionaire, following the man, punctuating his speech with his hands: "We'll get you set up, you'll find that we'll give you all the co-operation we can, anything we can help you with, in the mechanical department or any one of our departments, that's what we're here for. Because the only way we can make a buck, is if you make a buck."

"That's what we came here for," the concessionaire manages to get in.

We are in the car, driving down the unfinished midway under heavy rain. "If we have rain like this, this hour of the morning tomorrow, why, you wouldn't have, uh … a hundred thousand people intend to come, you wouldn't have five thousand. First time we've had rain like this the day before we open since I've been here, 1937."

Cue vintage midway footage, young Patty, suit and tie, cigarette in hand, coming down the exit ramp of one of his rides, walking into the camera. He transforms to old Patty, slouch hat and raincoat wrapped around him, making the short trip in the rain from the car to his office. We follow him through the outer offices, the few staff busy with their work as he walks past them to his windowless private room. He throws his coat and hat on the couch, takes out his glasses, and sits at his desk. He dials the phone. "Hello, honey … hello, it's me. How you feeling? How was your trip home? How was the dentist?… You didn't go?" He reads memos as he speaks.

The documentary cuts in stills of a young Patty at his desk, and Patty and Edythe. "Anyhow, I just come back from the hospital, I'll tell you about my own problems." He repeats himself and she interrupts him. "If you gimme a chance, I'll let you know," he says, raising his eyebrows. The sound of voices from the outer offices, typewriters.

"First of all, when I was there yesterday, they wanted to put me in the hospital, and I may have to go tomorrow.... So I just come from the hospital, just now, they took some blood again, eight vials of blood away from me, and after they analyze this blood, why, we'll make a decision as to what's going to happen, what I'm going to do. So that's about it, yeah."

Patty pauses, as he gets a response, then describes how he has gone from eight pills a day to three. "He's putting me back to where I first was when I come back from Germany, you know, on that, just on that medicine after I got out of the hospital in Long Beach, California.... Yeah, so anyhow, I'll give you a report tomorrow.... No, no, but I'll be seeing him tomorrow. I may have to go to the hospital tomorrow."

Patty is out on the midway, looking concerned as someone says, "There's water coming up out of this. Right out of this plug or whatever, some kind of fitting or connection down in there. I've already, I went over and talked to MacDonald and he got a hold of the plumbing people." Patty examines the problem and goes back in, to the phone. "You're going to have to do something, yeah, because you can't sell people tickets and ask them to walk through two or three inches of water, you know."

We see him next directing a bunch of big men installing large, illuminated signs on a ride. They get one up and Patty tells them, "Now let's give him that one, fellas, hump it up to him right the way it is." He walks spryly among them, encouraging them, "Get all your hooks turned, so it'll drop right in. Don't try it by yourself, Lorne, let's all get together." He follows their every move. Someone asks him about a brace and he gives him precise instructions, "Because anything can happen on this corner." He walks around the installation, examining it critically and, satisfied, returns to his car.

Back at the food stand, someone asks him how he is feeling. "No good," he says. "I'm going to my doctor's today; I can't hardly breathe. Short of

breath, pains in the side," — his voice drops to a whisper — "Jesus Christ."
He is wide-eyed, looking blankly around. "It's my sickness, my blood. The
old machine is starting to wear out, you know, I'm 78 years old."

Telling someone else he's been on this midway for 43 years, he adds,
"Too long ... I think I've got another year to go." He supervises the placement
of more equipment, but as work goes on around him, the camera cuts away
and we hear him retching, then see him leaning against the side of a ride,
head down. He turns, pulls a large handkerchief from his pocket, wipes his
face, and casts a watery gaze up at the structure looming above him.

Telescope, *Canadian Broadcasting Corporation, Jan. 26, 1971*

⋆　★　⋆

As if to atone for a young reporter's faux pas, in the fall of 1968 the industry
press memorialized Patty. On November 16, *Amusement Business* published
a special 22-page tribute to the "Life and Times" of the "Master Showman."
According to the front-page notice for the section, "he is acknowledged as
the midway industry's dominant personality." The section is preceded by a
raft of paid tributes, including a "salute" from the board and management
of the CNE. Most of the text comes from Jim McHugh, the magazine's publishing director, supplemented by an article by Jim Coleman, a syndicated
sports columnist from Toronto and friend of the Conklins. Coleman asserts
that "probably no other Canadian ... enjoys warmer rapport with the news
media." He refers to the "feeble" exposé in the *Telegram* and its repercussions
in the Toronto Men's Press Club: "To a man, the old-timers in the Press Club
were miffed by this display of journalistic nitpicking. There was a good deal
of muttering about 'some punk trying to put the zing on our old pal, Patty.'"
Regardless of his status, Patty was still a mere mortal who was growing old.
Apart from the attack on his CNE contract, a host of other afflictions plagued
him and his business.

Regulations and Expenses

Delays in getting them open were not the only difficulties Patty had with new rides at the Ex. The German Trabant had debuted in 1963. Two-seater cars on a circular platform that spins and tilts, the Trabant was a hit and is still found on many midways. At the 1966 CNE, the Trabant's hydraulic system failed and it fell 10 feet to the ground from its tilt. Fully loaded, 23 passengers were injured, two of them seriously. At a press conference, Patty stressed that the crash was the worst since he had taken over the midway. According to him, the rides were inspected every day by city and provincial officials, but a Metro inspector said that only cursory checks were made daily. The accident made the front page of all three newspapers published in Toronto, but reports the next day said that it had not deterred patrons from going on other rides. An editorial in the *Globe and Mail* on August 30, while noting that "the accident rate is remarkably low," called for "more rigorous inspection and supervision."

The Toronto Board of Control looked into the accident and confronted the fact that, as with the midway contracts generally, the city had no effective control over ride operations. After the accidents at the Ottawa fair in 1962 and 1963, with the fatality in 1962, city officials there had discovered that they had no way to regulate rides. There had been other accidents in recent years at North American fairs. In 1965 two people were killed and 45 injured at the Nebraska State Fair and a young boy was killed and eight injured at an amusement park near Amherstburg, Ontario. In 1968 one person was killed and 48 injured in a monorail crash at the HemisFair in San Antonio, Texas.

Midway riding devices had become more extreme and dangerous, but regulations had not kept up. There had, in fact, been little regulation. The Ontario Council of Women demanded in 1965 that the provincial government pass legislation to regulate riding devices. The Toronto Board of Control made the same request after the CNE accident. These demands were paired with strong recommendations that carnivals should be required to carry more liability insurance.

While provincial and state governments studied the issue, some jurisdictions would not see legislation for years. Michigan was the first state to get ride laws on the books, in 1966 passing the Carnival-Amusement Safety Act. This

act was taken as a model by other jurisdictions, providing the basis for legislation in Saskatchewan in 1968, for example. In 1970, however, the Canadian
Association of Fairs and Exhibitions still found it necessary to propose a national midway safety code. The Ontario Amusement Device Act was not passed
until 1986. Many American states do not have ride regulations to this day.

As far back as 1935, Harry Illions, one of the first major ride designers,
insisted that ride safety was essential to the viability of the carnival business. Ride accidents hurt all carnivals, and carnival owners have, for the most
part, been careful to ensure the safety of their devices. But no one likes to be
regulated and carnival owners have always resisted ride regulations. They
are concerned that regulations are made and enforced by people who have
no understanding of the business or the mechanics involved. Nevertheless,
with the development of more thrilling rides and the attendant increase in
the risks of riding them, safety legislation has been passed in more states and
provinces. As the 1960s wore on, safety legislation and requirements for more
liability insurance were among factors raising the overhead for carnivals.

Labour costs were also rising generally, although carnies had no organization to advocate for them. In 1952 a labour organizer had tried to start a
carnival workers' union under a local charter of the American Federation of
Labor (AFL). The AFL had opposed organization because of the transience
and instability of carnival work. The same organizer was more successful in
1955 under a charter with the International Brotherhood of Teamsters and
signed an agreement with Carl Sedlmayr of Royal American Shows. No other
shows followed suit. Before the 1965 CNE, work was briefly halted by a picket
line around the grounds thrown up by the United Brotherhood of Carpenters
and Joiners against exhibitors using non-union labour.

Carnies never would successfully unionize because of the conditions of
their employment, but owners took no chances. In 1965 a group of owners
organized the Outdoor Amusement Business Association, largely to resist
organized labour. Its first victory was in lobbying Washington to keep carnivals out of minimum-wage legislation in 1966 and the association became
an effective organization for show owners. Nevertheless, carnies were part of
the North American labour force, however marginally, and shared in some of
the gains made by labour in the 1960s. Carnival owners have long complained

about the difficulty of finding good help, and these gains worsened their difficulties, as did high employment. The independents bore the brunt of labour relations within the Conklin organization, but the show still had to deal with higher labour costs.

Fair and exhibition boards further added to overhead with expectations for larger percentages or flat fees from midways. This was partly the result of a new breed of more competitive carnival owners offering higher percentages to take dates from their rivals. The boards became savvy and started pushing on their own. Where 20 percent of the gross had been the average in the 1940s, by the '60s the percentage had risen to 35. This came straight off the top, before any other expenses were covered. Still dates were also becoming more expensive, as well as harder to book in decent lots. Mall parking lots relieved some of the latter problem.

Increasing Competition

The carnival industry began to face increasingly effective competition in the 1960s. Television had become a mass medium, satisfying much of the appetite for the spectacular and exotic that the midway once had an almost exclusive claim on feeding. Horror movies humoured the hankering for the grotesque and the ghoulish that freak shows, almost banned under the pressure of public morality by the end of the decade, once had gratified.

Amusement parks had always competed with travelling carnivals, but beginning with Disneyland, tremendous amounts of money were being invested in parks. Portable rides could only compete for so long with park rides that could be larger, faster, and more thrilling because they did not have to be moved. The Conklins tried to meet this challenge with imported European rides, their own amusement park rides, and stationary installations on the CNE grounds, but the challenge would not go away and the travelling companies — even Patty's CNE midway — eventually could not effectively counter it.

Rock concerts and festivals attracted the same demographic that midways targeted, but with thrills more in tune with the evolving tastes of that population. In June 1967, the Monterey International Pop Festival ushered in the era of big festivals with performances by major rock stars before over 200,000 people. Two years later, Woodstock doubled that attendance. The idealism of the decade would fade and rock music, including the festival circuit, would be commercialized, but the proportion of youth who spent their money on music rather than midways grew. As the decade unfurled, Patty felt increasingly bemused and out of touch with the kids he had always been able to entertain.

But he still had a few tricks up his sleeve. In 1968 he got a concession for a 250-seat Bavarian Gardens unlicensed dining room under the western terminus of the Alpine Way. Passengers disembarked in front of the Conklin wax museum at the other end. The 1966 report had recommended rezoning parts of the midway from their parkland status to enable liquor licensing. The city made the change for 1969 and the Bavarian Gardens was one of the first beneficiaries. Now a real beer garden, it did extremely well, with lineups during peak periods. It set a record for draft beer pumped in one day. So many plastic beer mugs were stolen the first year that Patty decided to sell them as souvenirs.

Patty called up Jockey Custock to help him get the Bavarian Gardens running. Since leaving Conklin & Garrett in the early 1940s, Custock had had a successful career as a hotelier. He had been president of the British Columbia Hotel Association in 1957–59 and president of the Hotel Association of Canada in 1960. Most recently, he had owned the Astor Hotel in Burnaby, B.C. This kind of experience in an old and trusted friend would have been invaluable to Patty in getting the beer garden off the ground. But with Patty's vigour waning, Custock had to deal more often with Jim, who had his own ideas about how to run the establishment. Custock left before the end of the fair.

Ontario was gradually relaxing some of its liquor laws and more straitlaced regulations and in 1970 allowed gambling wheels to operate at the CNE. A day after opening, there were complaints that the agents running the wheels were not respecting the 50-cent maximum bet. These lucrative additions to the company's food and game concessions were accompanied by the routine annual acquisition of new rides.

THE LAST OF HIS KIND

The second half of the CBC documentary opens with Patty in the car, his driver asking him if he knows how long he'll be in the hospital. "He says from three days to a week. Maybe longer."

"And when you come back, will you take it easy or what?"

"Oh, sure!" he chuckles. "That's been one of my biggest problems, I don't take it easy when I'm supposed to, you know. I bang away too … too hard, you know." He raises his voice, "If I told this doctor everything, just everything I did this morning, he'd go through the ceiling, you know. I don't let him know, I just told him I'm just relaxing, nod my head." The car drives through city streets. "I feel pretty weak at times. When I got out of the car there, you may have noticed me caving in on my legs a little, you know." He continues, "We want to find Concession Road. We'll ask up here at a gas station where the Henderson Hospital is."

Switch to Jim, talking on the phone about his father's health. Scenes of the midway in full swing. Jim on the Flyer with his young son. Patty in a hospital bed says to his nurse, "I got my Scotch and soda, my cookies, you girls are improving." He drinks from a glass of milk.

A little later he says to the interviewer, "I think I'll be out of the hospital before the Exhibition's over. I definitely think so. If I don't, I'm going to sneak out some night and come back and say I took a look at it anyhow." He talks about Jim managing the CNE on his own, speaking over scenes of Jim looking calm and competent. Patty is sorry he's sick, but happy to let Jim see what he can do by himself.

"So, one day I call him up, I says, 'You know, Jim, if more people in our line of business could read and write English, no telling how the hell many cards I would have received.'" He and his visitors laugh. The film cuts back and forth between Patty in the hospital and Jim on the midway. "So long," Patty says to his visitors. Jim drives the Cadillac himself and sits at his father's desk.

Jim introduces the *Amusement Business* special issue on his father. Patty has a copy with him in his hospital bed. Jim notes that his father's career peaked with "doing the biggest thing in the industry, which is the Canadian National Exhibition."

"I've increased the gross receipts from 1937 from $113,000 to last year, in nineteen hundred and sixty-nine, to $1,780,000, I think, or $728,000," Patty says. Jim talks about his own late start in the industry and Patty comments, "He's really doing a much bigger job than I anticipated he had the ability to do." Jim is shown yawning over the books.

Patty uses the magazine special issue with its "any number of wonderful photos" to tell the stories he has told so often, telling them possibly for the last time, this time in front of a camera. Lord Mountbatten and the nickel, Conklin Shows' first CNE, trying to borrow $400,000 from the bank, Lou Dufour's sideshow at the Exhibition. Dufour and others are interviewed to testify to Patty's stature and influence, his stamina, and to express their faith or doubt that he will return. Back at the hospital, Patty instructs Jim to keep visitors away. "They can just pick up the phone and call me, instead of visiting." He is clearly feeble.

"I got married when I was 38 years old. I played the field pretty good. I was an eligible bachelor for years. In public school, I went to the sixth grade, that's all.

"That's another thing, my son went to Ridley and McGill. He never was on the show grounds, only for a birthday party. I'd visit him at school. He had a dollar a week spending money, and I'd hide a two-dollar bill in his shirt or five-dollar bill someplace. My wife never knew it. He's never mentioned it to me. I've never mentioned it to him to this day. But he always found it somewhere. And while I was sick here, I could have got to the phone, you know, someway or other. Phone him, give him advice, but I just let him carry on."

Telescope, *CBC, Jan. 26, 1971*

Jim Conklin continued to look after the fair circuit. The London fair had been an addendum to the CNE, so its loss had not affected the road show. Sherbrooke was the only remaining Conklin fair outside of Ontario. Once a flourishing event in this regional centre, grosses at the Sherbrooke fair had fallen almost every year during the 1960s. The fair board complained about the midway in 1967 and got a commitment for at least eight new rides in 1968. On August 26, the president made his complaints public in the Sherbrooke *Daily Record*: "Jimmy Conklin promised us something better but it's the same thing. In fact it's worse than last year's because there are less rides." The show played the fair for the last time in 1968, but Jim likely welcomed the loss. The rising overhead for transportation had squeezed the net from the falling gross to almost nothing. He filled the hole in his road show route with a still date in St. Catharines and by getting some Ontario fairs to shuffle their dates.

In May of 1968, Jim visited Gorky Park, an amusement park in Moscow, but saw nothing to inspire him. The next month his father did an inspection tour of parks in eastern North America. That year, the Conklins put concessions under the management of Harry Shore into Bob-Lo Park on an island in the Detroit River. Six rides were included in the show's return to Belmont Park in 1969, when they also put new rides into Crystal Beach. Jim did not pick up any new fairs for the time being. He was successfully developing fairs already on the circuit. Bringing new rides into Markham, some of them from the CNE, helped him boost his receipts for that fair by 30 percent. He added the Kitchener Oktoberfest, the largest event of its kind in Canada, for one year in 1970. All the Conklin fairs averaged a 30 percent increase in 1970. He was also expanding and rejuvenating the parks business.

Patty Slows Down

While Patty's walking pace on the CNE midway had slowed and he began to use an electric golf cart, he did not cut back on his international travel. In early 1967, he accompanied a delegation of showmen on a trip to a riding device trade fair in Hanover, Germany. Upon his return, he went to California, where he was joined by Edythe, who had been in Palm Springs. They planned to leave for Hawaii to visit E.K. Fernandez, who they had visited two years before. On February 26, while at the home of Elmer and Curtis Velare in Long Beach, Patty collapsed. The Velares rushed him unconscious to the hospital where he was found to be suffering from internal bleeding and was placed on the critical list. He required blood transfusions and was hospitalized for over a month, but eventually recovered. He and Edythe began their return home at the end of March, travelling by easy stages through Seattle and Vancouver to visit her family. They took the train, rather than flying, to avoid any recurrence of blood loss because of altitude. Patty credited the Velares with saving his life.

His standing within the outdoor amusement industry was demonstrated again during his stay in hospital. In a note to *Amusement Business*, published on April 22, he said he had "received 57 floral pieces, 68 letters, 15 telegrams, more than 150 cards, and at least 250 long-distance telephone calls." Given that more than one person signed many of the cards and letters, he estimated that "at least 1,000 responded." By late June he was well enough to visit Expo 67.

It was fortunate that he did not make it to Hawaii. E.K. Fernandez, who was 83, suffered a severe heart attack in mid-May. That fall, Romeo Gauvreau, president of the Belmont Park Company, died. Louis Herman, the Conklin & Garrett attorney, would die in September 1969.

While the ranks of his peers thinned, Patty returned to business for the 1968 CNE. The following winter, he travelled to Las Vegas; San Francisco;

Patty in 1969.

Los Angeles, where he visited the Velares again; Honolulu, to see Fernandez; Tampa; and Palm Springs. He reported that his health continued to improve, but a photo of him at a clubhouse in Gibsonton, Florida, published in the March 9 issue of *Amusement Business*, clearly shows a weary man.

Few carnies had pensions to retire on and those among Patty's old associates who were still alive remained in action. The Velare brothers continued to manufacture and operate rides. In 1968 Rip Weinkle, the principal in the hey rube incident in Kindersley, Saskatchewan, in 1930, was still running a game at American fairs at 73. Theo Forstall stayed working in the Royal American office, although sickness kept him out of action for the 1969 season and he died on the road in 1973 at the age of 80. Pete Kortes kept his sideshow out until retiring in 1972; he died in 1974 at 86. Lou Dufour, who had vowed to live to 100, continued as Patty's sidekick on the CNE midway, even adding two more attractions to his sideshow in 1969. He would live to be a month short of 82, dying in June of 1977.

Going into the 1969 event, an article in the *Toronto Star* on August 16 asked whether Patty's success would cost him the Ex. "Ten years ago it would have been inconceivable to think" of a CNE without Patty running the midway, it began. "But now with Conklin's soaring grosses and the CNE's mounting deficit," the contract was to be examined and an Ex without Patty suddenly became possible. Metro council openly declared the city should "take a bigger cut of his revenue" or someone else should get the job. The show kept over one million dollars of the previous year's gross, but Patty would not divulge his profit, other than to boast that he "makes more than the rest of the 26 amusement park operators in Canada put together."

The article went on to describe how Patty owned the midway with four and a half million dollars in equipment on it and it would be difficult for Metro to come up with the capital to buy him out. It also noted that he would be safe from the politicians for three more years, until his contract ran out in 1972. The politicians and the press were pandering to taxpayers at Patty's expense, but they would be rid of him sooner than they expected.

Patty presided over the ride lineup at the 1969 Ex and took his golf cart down the concessions line occasionally, but he left the concessions up to Jim and his staff. Patty vowed to break two million dollars that year but had to settle with the $1.7 million mark he had missed the year before. Attendance remained in the area of 3.2 million, although down by 55,000 from 1968. After the CNE and the end of the fair circuit in Simcoe in October 1969, the Conklins began preparations to move to a new winter quarters in Brantford. It was a modern, purpose-built facility, some buildings rising to three stories. The preparations involved advertising the usual "Disposal Sale" of equipment, including 12 major rides, in *Amusement Business* in November.

The CNE board was now envisioning its event as a permanent world exposition and once again making plans for expansion. The board of directors approved a preliminary plan early in 1970 and asked the Metro council to authorize $2,235,000 for repair work and immediate improvements. A final plan, ready at the end of the year, recommended reorienting the midway on a north–south axis to integrate the grounds with the provincial Ontario Place pavilions being built on reclaimed land in Lake Ontario.

While Jim was supervising the building of the new winter quarters and the move, Patty had been asked by Jim McHugh to chair a committee to put together the 75th anniversary souvenir issue of *Amusement Business*. He assembled a committee of 75, which included all the old-timers who were still able to function, as well as younger representatives like Harry Batt Jr., Carl Sedlmayr Jr., and his own son.[21] Patty claimed to have devoted 90 percent of his time during the two months required to prepare the issue. His main job and that of the committee was to sell advertising pages for the issue to individuals and companies. *Amusement Business* staff, past and present, put together the editorial content.

Sickness continued to sweep through Patty's family and associates in the spring of 1970. Curtis Velare became seriously ill early in the year and died in April. That month Edythe was hospitalized in Brantford for a few weeks. Neil Webb suffered a series of heart seizures and spent several weeks prior to the CNE in the hospital. Webb was able to work reduced hours at the Ex and kept tabs on the early fairs, announcing that Oshawa, Leamington, and Peterborough "were way ahead, the best they ever did."[22] One newsworthy event occurred at the Peterborough fair and was reported in *Amusement Business* on August 29. A woman phoned the police to report that a bomb had been planted in the bingo. No bomb was found. It turned out that the woman's husband considered her addicted to bingo and had threatened to bomb the concession if she returned, which she had. The domestic drama was lost in the title of the article: "Bingo bomb threat doesn't faze Patty."[23]

Patty's Last Ex

Patty said the show spent $350,000 on six new rides for the 1970 Ex and again he expected a two-million-dollar gross. After the first six days, Webb reported that "we'll coast into the $2 million if we get the continuing good weather that brings the crowds."[24] The second Saturday, they grossed a one-day industry record of $157,968. The next day, a Sunday that could have been big, business was wiped out by intermittent showers all day followed by a severe thunderstorm in the evening. The blowdown tore off sideshow fronts and closed the midway. No one was hurt and replacement fronts for the sideshows were brought in from Brantford. By the end of the fair, overall attendance had dipped slightly for a second year and the midway take had only increased by $12,000. Patty would never see his two-million-dollar midway gross.

Although the press continued to refer to Patty Conklin's midway throughout the 1970 CNE, everyone knew that for the first time since 1937 he was not on it. He had been there for opening day, August 20, handing out ride tickets to four Toronto boys who were the first ones in the gate. Later that day, however, his driver took him to Hamilton's Henderson Hospital, a regional facility on the Niagara Escarpment, with "a blood disease and a possible heart condition."[25] He was diagnosed with aplastic anemia. It was now clear that his collapse three years before had been owing to it and this was a relapse.

Aplastic anemia, a rare and serious disorder, results from the failure of bone marrow to produce all three types of blood cells, red, white, and platelets. Symptoms can appear sporadically over years and it is difficult to diagnose. Treatment involves blood transfusions, as well as antibiotics and isolation to prevent infections. Stem cell transplants and drug therapies have been developed, but these were not available in 1970 and might not have worked on someone Patty's age. While the condition sometimes cures itself, it can become chronic and be fatal. It is often not possible to discover the cause of the disease, but it is associated with exposure to benzene, an industrial chemical once widely used in gasoline, paint removers, and some glues and household cleaners. It is also a component of cigarette smoke. The hours and days and months that Patty spent in poorly ventilated winter quarter maintenance shops over 45 years, a cigarette constantly in his hand, provided him with a prolonged and concentrated exposure to benzene that could have triggered aplastic anemia.

Reports from Henderson Hospital, delivered by Conklin Shows staff, continued to be encouraging during the Ex and after, always noting that he was convalescing. He had hoped to get out before the fair was over, but throughout September and October he remained in the hospital, with one brief visit home. He died on Sunday night, November 8, age 78, seven years to the day after brother Frank. Among his siblings, he was survived by Charles, five years his senior, who would die in 1973, and Catherine, six years his junior, who would die in 1982. His youngest brother, Henri, had changed his name to Harry Ryan and would die in 1978.

After two and a half days of visitation using all three viewing rooms of the A.W. Miles Funeral Home, Patty's funeral service on Thursday taxed the capacity of Grace Church on the Hill in Toronto with some 600 mourners. More than 150 cars were in the procession over the 17 miles to his burial plot in Showmen's Rest at the Glendale Memorial Gardens. An exception was made to the provincial ban on funeral processions over freeways and Patty's procession used the Queen Elizabeth Way. Eight motorcycle policemen escorted the cortège and there were squad cars at busy intersections.

The coffin was carried by members of Conklin Shows' permanent staff. The 18 honorary pallbearers included Lieutenant Governor Ross Macdonald; showmen Harry Batt and Lou Dufour; journalists Jim Coleman and Jim McHugh; hotelier Jockey Custock; E.K. Fernandez's son, Kane; the current and past presidents of the CNE; showmen from Sydney, Australia, and Seattle, Washington; representatives of the Showmen's League of America and the Sherman House in Chicago; a well-known Toronto radio personality; and the owner of the Brantford *Expositor*. Lou Leonard and Theo Forstall, who, along with Dufour and Custock, were colleagues of Patty from his first years in the carnival, were present, too, as were hundreds of showmen from across North America. As many again would have been there but for their own frailties and ailments.

The Toronto, national, and outdoor entertainment business press published scores of articles about the passing of Patty Conklin and his funeral. News of his death reached the front page of the *Globe and Mail*. The articles surveyed his career, repeating the myths he had forged, including that he was Irish, that he was born a Conklin, and that his nickname arose because he always stood pat on every deal. His very identity remained an accepted fiction unto his death. The November 21 issue of *Amusement Business* described him as "an almost legendary figure in his own time in the world of outdoor show business."

The *Toronto Star*, an enthusiastic contributor to his legend over the decades, said on November 9 that he was "admitted even by his competitors to have been the most successful operator of outdoor shows on the continent." Acknowledging the material facts of his success, a notice on the newspaper's editorial page ventured to conclude on a touching note: "For all of us who visited his domain, the smile may have lasted but a moment, the thrill for a second, but the memory will linger forever. For that we remember Patty Conklin and mourn his passing."

Summing up his friendship with Patty and Frank in his column in the *Niagara Review* on November 13, Jim Coleman concluded that "it's even money that we won't see their like again." Coleman was accurate in ways beyond which he intended. Patty's career began during a time when some people were able to fabricate their personas from whole cloth and on the strength of those personas amass huge fortunes in the burgeoning entertainment industries. Almost 30 years later, in 1999, Patty was among the inaugural inductees to the Amusement Business Hall of Fame, along with other self-made luminaries like Buffalo Bill Cody, the Ringling Brothers, Colonel Tom Parker, and Walt Disney. By the end of Patty's career, the entertainment industries had evolved into massive, diversified corporations, like the Walt Disney Company. Corporations, not promoters, were now making the stars, the hits, the successful shows. At Patty's death, Conklin Shows was on its way to becoming one such corporation.

Patty Conklin was a showman, the star attraction of his own personal show, a hands-on impresario. Jim Conklin, with his privileged youth and private school education, his university experience and world travels, his detached demeanour and willingness to delegate, was the ideal corporate man. He was the right person at the right time to take over the show. In a letter published in the November 21 issue of *Amusement Business* in which he memorialized his friend, Lou Dufour claimed that "Patty rejoiced to see his son take over Conklin Enterprises and help bring it to its period of greatest expansion." Dufour, too, was prescient beyond what he could know: reorganized by Jim without his father's interference, the Conklin enterprises entered a period of expansion beyond Patty's wildest dreams.

A Carnival Empire

....

(1970–1979)

....

Patty Conklin ascended to carnival royalty through his personality and his rule over the midway of the Canadian National Exhibition. While he played Canadian fairs and exhibitions coast to coast, big and small, for almost 50 years, and had put on the show at a world's fair, he reigned as emperor of the Ex. Other business radiated from his Toronto fiefdom and it made his offhand attention to the road show inconsequential. Lacking Patty's charm and bluster, and his deep bond with the CNE, his heir inherited the kingdom, not the crown. But as perpetual prince regent, Jim Conklin would expand his patrimony by rebuilding the road show, retaking major Canadian exhibitions his father had given up, and penetrating the U.S. market for the first time.

CARNIVAL SCIENCE

That's where I met Patty Conklin, was here, at the Ex, when I was 12, 13. Patty and my dad were good friends. Patty used to come to our house and play cards with my dad, before the Exhibition opened. He was always here in town before the Ex opened and he would come up there a few evenings.

Patty used to love to play bridge. My dad was a good card player, too, and my mother, so they had a good time....

I guess it was in '53, Patty asked me if I wanted to run a game. I said, sure, so I was running a game for him in the Silver Dollar building. It housed about 20 games. I was involved with summer camp, Camp Pine Crest, a YMCA camp, as a counsellor. I was involved with the water program because I was a swimmer. I wasn't a diver, my father was a diver. Then I'd come down here and work the Exhibition, and go back to school with a little money in my pocket.... They don't pay you very well at a YMCA camp, but it was a good place to be for a kid who was 15 or 16. Spending your time up there in Muskoka, which is a wonderful place to be in the summer, and then come here for three weeks and make some money. It worked out very well for a number of years.

Then we got involved in the bingo at Crystal Beach. Conklin also had the kiddieland and a couple of major rides in that park. Patty used to come down there and visit, once a week. The Hall brothers ran it. They were there when I was there, and they were there when I left. Then they sold it and now it's a housing development. We were involved with the Halls for a long time. That would take up most of my summer, then I'd come here to the Exhibition. We normally opened on May 24th, the holiday weekend, and carried on until Labour Day. Those were fun summers, when you're young. We didn't have any games, we just had the bingo.

Then, it started to expand unto itself. When I was 21, I got a job as a manager in a curling club that had just opened. I was more of a curling instructor; they didn't have pros then. So, I used to work there in the winter and come and work for Conklin in the summer.

In '69, Jim Conklin hired me. He had been taking over the game operations before then. He hired me full time in '69 and I started in the office in the Horse Palace. For 30 years we had that office, '69 to '99. We had always used it during the Ex, but that was the only time we used it until '69. During the '70s, we had as many as a dozen people working in that office. Jim was expanding the company and he had design people, a photographer, and marketing people, and they were all working out of that office. They all came over from the office on Front Street. They all wound up in the Horse Palace.

Then we were just playing Ontario and the CNE. We didn't play outside the province until 1976 when we went West. Before then, Jim was expanding in the parks.... We were still in Belmont Park in Montreal. Patty had got involved in Belmont. The Gauvreau family still owned the park, but eventually it closed.... La Ronde was the new park and it kind of buried Belmont.

We were in Hemmingford for a while, too, not many years, but we were down there with some rides. We had an arcade down there. One day in Hemmingford we had to get the arcade ready for the season and the guy from the park came around and said, "You better stay inside, the tigers are loose." So we stayed inside. That made the headlines in the *Montreal Star*: "Tigers Loose in Hemmingford." I wondered to myself if they did that every year, just to get the season started. We got on the front page of the *Montreal Star*. I thought it was quite a ploy, if they were doing that intentionally. I never knew for sure.

Patty died in '70 and Jim took over and tried to do many things, some of which worked and some of which didn't. He never stopped trying. He's still messing around today. He was in here this morning. He's an early riser and he usually gets here before anybody's here. Consequently, he never sees anybody and then he leaves. This morning he happened to hang around long enough to see me. It was nice to see him. I don't see him that often anymore.

Interview with Alfie Phillips Jr., Sept. 1, 2005

The new president of Conklin Shows created positions for executives with whom he wanted to work. Jim appointed J. Sergei Sawchyn, former manager of the Winnipeg Ballet, as special assistant for promotion and development in 1972, and the next year hired the manager of the Peterborough Exhibition, Colin Forbes, to serve as liaison with the Ontario fairs. After the president of the CNE association finished his stint, Jim hired him to supervise the parks operation. Some of the people brought in under aspirations of empire, such as Sawchyn, did not stay long. Jim made Neil Webb a vice-president, an honorary position as Webb retired a year later. At his testimonial dinner, 500 showed up and Jim gave him and his wife a trip around the world. Jim hired Al Ross, a former car salesman, as secretary-treasurer to replace Webb, and John Drummey to assist Ross. John MacDonald, an old hand, became head of ride maintenance and operations. Pat Marco, a mentor to Jim, ran the road show, with Ray Coffing his ride superintendent.

The son of Patty's water show producer, Alfie Phillips Jr., who had worked summers with his friend Jim since 1954, was hired on full-time in 1969. He took over game concessions at the CNE, was made a vice-president in 1972, and grew into a role similar to the one Jim's Uncle Frank had played for Patty. A big, cigar-smoking man six years Jim's junior, Alfie became the face of the office on the midway, especially for the concessions, letting the boss concentrate on the show's ride investments.

Breaking the Mould

Jim's plans to expand required breaking out of "the old carnival mould." As he said in *Amusement Business* in the September 23, 1972, issue, he had his sights on "some big activities in the future and outside financing may be required — so our entire operation is being upgraded, streamlined and re-structured." He countered the unspoken comparisons with his father: "I can't accomplish these objectives on a personality basis because it's not my style — but a sound corporation can do some of the talking for me." His intention was to create "a modern growth organization to take advantage of any possibility that comes along … no longer limited to carnival operations."

The changes the public saw, beginning with the 1972 season, were largely matters of branding and derived from an "identity program" launched that spring. The Conko icon spread from merchandise tags to everywhere it would fit — staff watches and uniforms, ticket boxes and boxer shorts, ride flash and game fronts, midway flags and garbage pails, vehicles and equipment — and Conko the Clown made his first personal appearance as a suited mascot on the midway. Liberal coats of paint were applied to every exposed surface. Jim told the *Telegram* on August 10, 1971, that they were "trying to get rid of the old look which dates back to the mid-40s." Jack Ray was being erased.

The new staff began to modernize office practices and equipment. Until then, payroll had been handled manually — cheques for 1,400 staff at the CNE written by hand. They introduced an automated system in 1972, along with mechanical coin sorters and money counters, and walkie-talkies for communications over the vast grounds. They switched to a system where ride tickets were weighed, not counted. Ticket weighing became an industry standard.

While Patty had theories about rider preferences, Jim sought facts through a survey of riders. "We want to prove or disprove our theories," he told the *Telegram*. "We think, for example, that our riders like the thrill rides best. With this survey we'll find out for sure."

Unlike Patty, who measured success by the gross number of dollars, Jim counted the number of riders. He focused on these figures as a more reliable basis for improving results. Patty had prided himself on keeping ride prices at 25 and 50 cents, pointing this out to anyone who might care. Once the universal ticket system was implemented in 1972, the show could begin adjusting ride prices according to demand, without the public being fully aware when they were paying more. All rides were priced in multiples of 10 cents and strips of tickets bought at any booth could be used at any ride. Instead of touring Europe for new rides, Jim bought used equipment and refurbished it, revealing another change from his father's priorities. For the time being, Don Campbell's rides still made up the bulk of the 16 major rides and eight kiddie rides on the road show, but the office dictated the price of admission.

Jim tried diversifying into the trade show business by signing on as producer of the annual Christmas carnival at the CNE grounds for 1971. In previous years, Conklin Shows had a few rides in for a Christmas Fairyland run by the *Telegram* and a public relations firm, but now it would take care of space rentals and all details, and provide more rides, its own game concessions, and live entertainment. This attempt failed because the show was not "properly geared for it," but Jim took steps to ensure that his show was "no longer limited to carnival operations" and would not fail again.[1]

He expanded the company's amusement park operations. Bazaars Ltd., the Conklin concessions company, took over all games, including the bingo, at Belmont Park from the park's administration, promising to change 95 percent of them for the 1971 season. Adding sound to the lightshow, he equipped the four major Conklin & Garrett rides at the park with loudspeakers and added two more rides in 1973. He put equipment into Riverside Park in Agawam, Massachusetts; Kennywood Park in Pittsburgh, Pennsylvania; Sportsworld in Kitchener, Ontario; two new African Lion Safaris — one in Hemmingford, Quebec, five miles from the U.S. border, the other in Rockton, 20 miles from Brantford, both planned by Gordon Dailley, a retired army colonel; and the new Lake Ontario Park in Kingston. Ontario Place, built on land reclaimed from Lake Ontario and extending from the CNE grounds, opened in 1971 and within two years the Conklin interests had Dainty Dora's, an Ontario Place restaurant with a sideshow theme, named after a performer in a show run by Sam Alexander.

The 1971 road show season started in July with company picnics before launching into the fairs with Oshawa at the end of the month. After 12 weeks of fairs, the season ended in early October with the Norfolk County Fair in Simcoe, basically the same route they had played for the previous three years. The following year, Jim began to substantially lengthen the road show season by adding a series of spring still dates to the roster of fairs. By 1975 the show's season began in mid-April, playing 10 weeks of stills before the fairs began.

In the meantime, and on his own for the first time, Jim had to plan the midway for the 1971 CNE. Articles without fail mentioned the inheritance from his father. In a piece in the *Toronto Star* on opening day, August 19, he was introduced as "Mr. Midway, Jimmy Conklin, the handsome son of the late Patty Conklin, CNE Carny King." Not only did the article deny him his father's sobriquet, but it focused on a "private toy" he had added to his "extensive amusement empire." The "toy" was a railway car he had bought to take to the Ontario fairs and brought to the CNE to house himself, Norma, and their children, Trish, Frank (named after Jim's uncle), and Melissa.

Jim planned the 1971 midway as "a memorial" to his father: "It's going to be just the way he would have done it."[2] He brought in 66 rides and shows, and tried to bring in one new ride that his father would have loved. The Super Loops is a 60-foot high, enclosed vertical loop that hurls a train around a 360-degree track. A reporter for the *Telegram* on August 10 found that the advertising copy for the ride evoked "shades of Patty." Jim had lined up one of the first through an independent, but it had to go back to the factory for servicing. It was replaced by Don Campbell's Rock-O-Plane.

One "new" attraction was very old indeed. Lou Dufour produced a mechanical dinosaur show that he had last booked at the New York World's Fair in 1940. He had it set up beneath the Alpine Way loading platform where he had been spotting shows for five years. Dufour had a second show, Alexander's freak show was back, and there were four other shows. Most of Patty's associates came back with their rides. Attendance at the 1971 CNE was up slightly, as was the Conklin gross. The only incident was the recurrence of Webb's heart troubles.

Jim and Norma were also dealing with his mother. Soon after Patty's death, they moved Edythe to a home for seniors in Brantford. Her son, daughter-in-law, and grandchildren visited, but the full, exciting life she had known with Patty had ended with his death, and she died a few years later. When Webb and Dufour went, the avatars of his father's generation had all departed. Norma was a support for her husband and, with his mother gone, encouraged and guided him in branching out into other interests.

Although it was the first CNE midway Jim had planned on his own, a CNE official, describing it as the best anywhere, saw it as "the ultimate tribute to Patty."[3] Jim had kept it "old-fashioned and corny" because, he explained, that was "part of the peculiar attraction that a place like this has and I intend to keep it that way." But he revealed a contradictory attitude to his father's legacy: "I may run things a little more scientifically than my father did, but until his old way is proved to be less than the best, I'll stick to it."

At the Showmen's League of America convention that December, Jim opened a workshop on game concessions. As reported by *Amusement Business* on December 21, he stated "that a system of controls must be instituted in every facility, in order to cut down on profit loss due to employee theft." He recommended controls on cash and stock, and "an espionage system which locates marked currency in the booth in order to see 'who is honest and who isn't.'" This system was part of his "scientific" approach and he had used it effectively at the CNE to catch employees stealing from him.

Jim continued to hope that an opportunity for a large, permanent amusement park in the Toronto area would come his way, but municipal and provincial regulations and licensing continued to obstruct him. He was ready to invest heavily in any park with the right location and he was also scouting opportunities in the West. He had plans to make his own opportunities by expanding the road show, "moving into larger cities, notably in Western Canada," he told the *Financial Post* in an article on August 5, 1972. Nothing concrete would arise from this ambition for several years. Meanwhile, the CNE was studying the feasibility of a new midway, on a 12-acre lakefront site south-east of the main grounds, that would be open five months a year.

Renewing the CNE

With politicians once more discussing changes to the CNE and its midway, Jim was uncertain about the future of his show after the end of its contract in 1972. Before the contract ended, however, he got it renewed, according to the *Globe and Mail* on July 11, "for an indefinite period, with cancellation subject to two years' notice," although he had to give the board a further 5 percent on ticket sales and accept an increase in rent. Weather was perfect for the 1972 event, attendance passed three and a half million, and the Conklin midway, with 47 major rides, 22 kiddie rides, and nine shows, reached Patty's elusive goal of a two-million-dollar gross. In reaching "the magic figure," an article in the *Star* on September 16 still presented Jim as "carrying on in the footsteps of his late father," while he told the reporter that "all it took was a proper combination of the breaks."

While modernizing his operations at the 1972 CNE, Jim showed his appreciation of carnival history and tradition. He kept his father's ritual of holding a pre-opening banquet and party for the press, midway officials, and other notables, but expanded it to include children. He brought in a 60-year-old German swing ride that he had bought at the Munich Oktoberfest and restored. He also brought home a hand-carved miniature German mechanical village. The ride was better suited to the more sedate atmosphere of Belmont Park, where he took it the following season. He began planning for an antique carnival, at first hoping to unveil it in 1973 as part of a 50th anniversary celebration of the company, but the plan was delayed.

Jim played up the continuity with carnival tradition embodied in his private rail car, the Sir James, named after its first owner, Sir James Whitney, an Ontario premier, noting that his father's private car had been called the James Franklin. The name also reflected his own status. In November 1972, he took the car on its first trip outside of Toronto since he bought it, riding with eight guests to London for the fairs association meeting. There, he picked up fellow directors of Mott Manufacturing, a firm specializing in kitchen, industrial, and laboratory cabinets, and they had their board meeting travelling the Canadian National Railway's main line to Brantford, location of the company's head office. Much was made of the outing in the business press in articles that barely mentioned the carnival connection.

Independent ride operators continued to debut new rides at the CNE, while Jim focused on remodelling the midway. For 1973, he reduced the kiddieland rides by a third and added potted trees, shrubs and flowers, and benches to the area. He bought three new kiddie rides from Danny Glosser, who had become Mickey Hughes's competitor for importing European rides. Hughes had never made it back into the Conklin good graces and Glosser became an important associate of the company. Jim also bought a Polar Express from Glosser and took it on the road after the CNE. Kiddieland was adjacent to one terminal of the Alpine Way and Jim replaced the usual Dufour show there with an arcade supplied by E.G. & J. Knapp Company. For the Knapp brothers, who had long languished in the dusty arcades of Crystal Beach and Belmont Park, this was their first Ex.

The 1973 CNE midway experienced a few hitches. The Alpine Way jammed when unruly riders rocked one cabin until the cable jumped the track and 39 persons spent almost seven hours stranded 100 feet over the midway. The fire department was called in to rescue passengers. Their cherry picker was 10 feet short of the highest cabin and the last two passengers had to climb down a ladder to the bucket. They were from Scotland and said they enjoyed the experience.

In another incident, a child in the Dufour and Alexander freak show was found to be five years old, rather than the 18 her birth certificate claimed. Under Ontario law, it was illegal to exhibit children. The girl, only ever identified as Pookie, was exhibited as "The Monkey Girl" for one day only. Her age and condition were exposed in newspaper articles.[4] There was a brief public outcry and the CNE directors forbid freak shows for the future. This was the public sign of a significant industry trend. When he cancelled the freak show the following year, Jim brushed off the offence. "Some people got uptight about the show last year," he told the *Star* on August 14. But big sideshows were fading away, and Alexander's show was one of only four playing in 1973. He had been operating a sideshow at Belmont Park for over 30 years. His freak show at the 1973 CNE would be the last to play the Ex.

The main attraction in 1974 was a water thrill show, the first since Alfie Phillips Sr. last put one on in 1956. A Toronto transit strike kept attendance down, but the midway gross was still up. The universal ticket system had not performed as expected and had been retired in 1973 for rethinking but was brought back in 1974 with tickets at a quarter a piece. The ticket system was another way for the office to monitor and enforce employee honesty.

The economy was slumping by the mid-1970s, especially in the United States. Inflation was up; employment numbers and pay scales fell. A recession was in the air and some carnival and amusement park owners were having difficulty with credit. The demand for new riding devices was flat and used equipment was all they were buying. The prices of some new rides were climbing to a million dollars. The federal government reclassified amusement rides for tax purposes and owners in Canada were finally able to buy them without paying a heavy import duty, but according to Glosser, identified by *Amusement Business* in a January 4, 1975, article as "a leading ride importer into Canada," the change "would help importers in the quality of rides sold rather than quantity."

The Canadian economy was not as bad and Conklin & Garrett had no trouble borrowing money. Jim had been quietly taking advantage of the show's financial clout and changing the way he ran its midways. He had been buying rides and placing them temporarily at the eight amusement parks with which he dealt. He began rotating the rides into the CNE, replacing equipment provided by independent operators. At the 1975 Ex, "The business-oriented showman supplied 70–80 percent of the equipment himself," *Amusement Business* reported on September 20, implying that some old-time carnies were feeling squeezed by these new practices. By analyzing ride capacity, part of his "scientific" approach, he was able to reach 60,000 rides per hour at the CNE, an increase of 10,000. He could now cash in on the universal ticket system, using it to implement an across-the-board 10 percent increase in ride prices. He would continue to find ways to increase profits through smart, sometimes ruthless, business practices.

GEARING UP

The hotel opened not long after the CNE closed and I moved everything into the hotel. My first job was to sell everything off in the hotel. We worked with a guy who was a junk sale dealer. This guy came out and priced everything and took all the old furniture out. Then we started renovating. The basement used to be the old Place Pigalle, which was one of the best-known bars in Toronto in the '60s and early '70s.

Just seeing that take shape and working through the whole hotel was really great. I was 21, 22, and this was exciting. There was the two of us. We had to hire staff and get everything ready. It was a pricey, big chore. We had a lot of fun doing it, but a lot of hours. You worked from the time you got up to the time you went to bed at night. A lot of the reconstruction was done during the summer after it was purchased, so basically the dining room and the basement were the last to be done. That was when that whole area was still a hippy haven. It was just starting to become the posh area. Some of the regulars would come and tell me that they were buying up houses for hundreds of thousands because they were going to be worth millions.

That hotel itself was very remarkable. All the carnies stayed there for the CNE the first year we had it opened. I think they took over the top three floors.... Hans was the only management that stayed there ... with the guys. Everybody else was at the CNE or in the train. By the time they got back at midnight or one o'clock, it was party central. We kept the other guests on the second and third floor. That was the first time that I met all these guys. They were the carnie carnies. They kind of got in my face one day and they said, "Well what are you going to do about it?" I said, "You guys can just leave." After that, we got along great. It was very memorable.

Then there was the opening of the Penny Arcade. This was just after the big press conference. I'm walking around and there was a bunch of guys standing at the bar who looked older. I walked by and I could smell some pot. I'm like, "Jeez, who's smoking in here?" I walked back and the older guys were chuckling. So, I walked over and, sure enough, I saw one of the older guys taking a puff.... I said, "Guys, come on. Go outside or do something." They said, "Well, Mr. Hotel, we're carnies and Jim Conklin owns the hotel." I said, "He's also my boss and I'm here to do a job."

When I first took over the hotel ... we had three grand pianos. I put them in the paper and sold them the next day, cash, bang, bang, bang, and I deposited it. I'm going through the paperwork the next day and my jaw dropped because I realized that they were rented. The money was in the bank and they were gone. Nobody from the leasing company ever came back to look for the pianos. They were from one of the original deeds that were done in the hotel. Maybe the person had passed away or just wasn't there anymore. I never heard a word. The boss knew and Stan Doerling knew, but that was all. They just kind of laughed and said, "We'll see what happens."

Interview with Dave Vance, April 25, 2006

★ ★ ★

"Expansion of the Conklin midway empire could mean end of the small-time carnies," read the title of an article in the *Globe and Mail* on September 27, 1974. The writer was Linda McQuaig, a journalist who had exposed Sam Alexander the year before and would go on to write a series of bestselling books critical of economic policies and developments. She had found two Ontario carnival owners who were, in fact, feeling squeezed out by Jim's departure from his father's laissez-faire attitude toward the road show. They had lost fairs to Conklin Shows and blamed their loss on the show's grip on the CNE, which enabled "the Conklin enterprise to invest its capital in new equipment with a guaranteed high rate of return." Other shows, McQuaig speculated, might soon be facing competition from Conklin Shows. She admitted it might be "just that Mr. Conklin is a better businessman who offers a better deal."

Relations with Smaller Shows

The advantages of scale enabled the show to be mercenary. The fall fairs and shopping centres that it was picking up were, McQuaig said, "bread and butter to the small operators," but mere "icing on the cake for Mr. Conklin." Beyond two "embittered" owners, McQuaig spoke to the publicity director of the Canadian chapter of the Showmen's League who contrasted Jim with his father. Patty "didn't hesitate to push people around," but would never "move in on the fairs that the small operators really counted on." Patty was "a fellow carnie who ... remained a showman at heart," but "Jim Conklin ... has never quite fit the old-style carnie mould." Patty's "suave, well-dressed ... son rarely showed up" at the league's clubhouse and had little "in common with the unsophisticated small midway operators."

Alfie Phillips explained to McQuaig that "the company doesn't go looking for small fairs; the fairs just come to them. 'We just got tired of saying no.'" Spokesmen at the new Conklin fairs gave varied explanations for switching carnivals, but Alfie claimed Conklin Shows had turned down requests to play dates held by other operators. The article points out "that Patty Conklin even used to help smaller operators," implying that Jim was responsible for the decline of small carnivals to "a handful, roughly half of what it was 10 years ago."

But Jim helped smaller operators, too, giving many a start in the business, and many who worked for him spun off their own shows. He gave the contract for Lake Ontario Park to Webb Vivian, a concessionaire just starting out, and Don Campbell, John Homeniuk, Robert Gable, and other Conklin contractors used the decades of experience they gained with the show to go out on their own. They usually booked their equipment back with Jim, as did other Canadian shows like Big A Amusements, Beauce Carnaval, and West Coast Amusements. He managed to support them and, at the same time, through their dependence on his favour, prevent them from becoming rivals. For much of its existence, Conklin Shows had been a source of used equipment for smaller carnivals, generating the capital it needed to buy new equipment.

The Canadian carnival concession supply industry, especially the Ganz Brothers, developed largely through its dependence on Conklin Shows. In the United States, many more and larger shows would be supported by the kind of dates Conklin Shows had in Canada. Although the show dominated the Canadian carnival industry, and Jim's style, inherited position, and business tactics provoked resentment among his father's colleagues, years later Homeniuk could still describe his relationship with Conklin Shows in collegial terms: "We all work together.... Whoever needs a piece or more, we go back and forth. It works well."[5] Campbell thought Jim took too much off the top, but even after he cut his ties, he could still say "the association was always amicable on both sides."[6]

Expansion

Operations under the Conklin & Garrett parent company were also expanding. In 1974 the show instituted an annual awards dinner for the Ontario fair committees and started a recruitment program to line up summer staff. By 1975 the carnival company, Canada's Conklin Shows, was only a part of "a multi-faceted conglomerate." A direct sales operation begun in 1976 expanded to eight units selling jewellery, hats, patches, T-shirts, and silk flowers on Conklin midways. Conklin & Garrett bought Graffiko, a graphic design firm, and enhanced the marketing arm with new staff. The *Jackpot* newsletter and Jackpot Books, Jim's first foray into publishing, began during this period. Permanent staff grew from 30 in 1974 to 100 in 1978, while several thousand temporary employees were hired during the fair season. Offices were added and shuffled back and forth among several locations in Toronto. The show had three winter quarters shops in Brantford. As business activities spread in all directions, keeping track of the money was becoming a problem and the accounting department expanded. A board of directors was instituted in 1979.

As McQuaig's *Globe and Mail* article observed, even the Conklin travelling carnival business was expanding. The 1975 spring still dates began in snow in mid-April in Woodstock and they picked up the fair route in late July in Kingston. The road show travelled with 24 rides and 40 to 50 concessions, splitting into two, sometimes three units to handle smaller stills and fairs that ran concurrently. In September, it covered four engagements at once. Only one

Portrait photo of Jim, 1987.

fair reached an attendance over 100,000, but Jim had a rationale that echoed
Patty's. He told *Amusement Business* on September 20: "My father started with
small fairs and I feel we have a responsibility to continue providing them with
the finest midways we can." He also wanted to keep the travelling show small
so that he could use it to groom staff members for positions in other Conklin
enterprises.

Jim characterized the 1975 season as the best his company had ever seen.
He noted further room for expansion in Ontario and told *Amusement Business*
it was "quite conceivable Canadian shows could handle the Western dates."
The Canadian government had become stricter in granting work permits to
American carnies coming into Canada, but he thought that this change had
been blown out of proportion: "There is presently a great trend of nationalism
in Canada, but it is not restricted to the carnival industry." Rumours continued to circulate that fairs and exhibitions would be forced to give priority
to Canadian companies. While Jim professed to believe that a show should
be judged on its quality, not its nationality, he had nevertheless renamed his
carnival Canada's Conklin Shows.

Jim was becoming known around Toronto as a businessman who took his social responsibilities seriously. He had been a trustee of the Brantford Art Gallery and in late 1974 joined the board of Toronto Arts Productions, which handled events at the St. Lawrence Centre for the Arts. In February, he organized a mammoth bingo as a fundraiser, volunteering half a dozen of his staff to set it up and run it. Some 7,000 players attended to play for $35,000 in cash, with draws for four cars. The *Toronto Star* reported on February 17 that while looking after the event he resided in "his luxuriously furnished home-away-from home, a private railway car ... tethered at Exhibition Park." The press had stopped calling it his "private toy."

Jim made another mark on Toronto when he opened his Penny Arcade tavern in the National Motor Inn on Avenue Road. He had formed a partnership in the hotel, as well as partnerships in a golf course in London and a ski lodge in Collingwood. The 400-seat bar in the hotel had been well known in the 1960s and early '70s. Under Dave Vance's management, it was fully renovated and reopened as the Penny Arcade in March 1976. The Toronto press was now making much of Jim's appreciation of theatre, classical music, and ballet, amazed that these tastes could coexist with his carnival pursuits. They were also surprised that "the son of Canada's king of carnie hyperbole" could be so reserved: "Sure, I'm shy and introvertish," he said in the *Toronto Star* on March 16, 1976. "I'm not a flamboyant character like my father." But he wanted to ensure they knew he was "still proud to be a carnie.... And I'm continuing my dad's tradition as a carnie buff, with this difference — I'm toning down the old-fashioned hype hoopla." The Penny Arcade, decorated with "more than 150 nostalgia artefacts and museum pieces" and "intriguing curios," was judged to be "wonderfully charming." Perhaps this carnie scion could be rehabilitated for the Toronto establishment.

Jim had his sights set beyond Toronto, beyond Ontario, beyond Canada even. He had "upgraded, streamlined and re-structured" his corporation. He had sought out and taken advantage of a multitude of opportunities, not all of which would succeed. Although Conklin & Garrett had been primed and readied for it, the chance to explode into the next major phase of its expansion came through circumstances for which Jim could not have planned.

BOOM

Out West one year Alfie used to lay out the joints, and I'd lay out the rides. So, we'd always fight for the corners, who was going to get the corners. In Calgary, I win, and Alfie was pissed, and he said, "Well, we'll call Jim, and let him be the decision-maker." I wasn't going to give up the corners. I had two corners in Calgary, and he had two corners. But he wanted more corners. He wanted them all, for the joints.

I had a Tidal Wave on one corner, and a Monster on the other corner, 'cause they used to ride the shit out of the Monster in Calgary, they used to love it, and they'd ride the boat. I wasn't giving up the corners. So, Alf says, "Well, I'll phone Jim and let him decide." So, he phones Jim and Jim says, "Well, I'm with you, Barry, you can keep the corners." So, I kept the corners.

I had that strong corner, because it was strong, I put a ticket box there. So now … Joe Staten and a couple of other jointies take the ticket seller out and put a mannequin in, with a T-shirt and a wig. People come up there to buy tickets, and a mannequin would be sitting there. So, Jimmy Glover, he comes over to me, he said, "Barry, you have one dummy in that ticket box, and I mean dummy!" So, I go over to the ticket box, and I look in there, and son of a bitch, there's a dummy in there. I open the door and throw the dummy out, get in there, and start selling tickets myself.

Now, they get a piece of cardboard put across the front of the ticket box: "Closed." And I'm in the ticket box. Then they lock me in the ticket box. Now, after all this is going on, they wanna take and move the ticket box, figuring that I'll give in to them. They get it moved, too, and I get it back and I get a big chain and I chain it to the base of the Tidal Wave. They had some fun with that.

Because they were messing with the ticket box, that night I took a PC [percentage] joint with the crane and set it right on top of a joint trailer. Then we got into their fish joint, and we got a case of that Mr. Bubble. We didn't say a word and they come in there the next morning and put the pumps on, open the awnings up. Well, you couldn't see the joint for bubbles, bubbles all over the midway.

Another time, Alfie and I got in a grab joint, kicked the staff out, and started serving the public ourselves. There was a big run on drinks. There must have been a lot of garlic in them hamburgers. I don't know if much of the take ended up in the count that night.

This is what we would do, you know, we would have a little fun, have a little humour. We had a really good time out West, and made a lot of money.

Interview with Barry Jamieson, Aug. 23, 2005

★　★　★

A major shake-up in the North American carnival industry was in the works.[7] The RCMP had begun investigating carnival operations in Saskatchewan in 1974. The focus initially was on games that contravened the Criminal Code or at which operators were cheating, but with the involvement of the Department of National Revenue it expanded to include income tax offences and skimming from gambling games. Over the winter, analysis of the evidence led to plans for a more concentrated effort the following season, one that would target Royal American Shows as the principal carnival working in western Canada. The investigation would look for evidence of income tax evasion, illegal games, cheating, customs violations, drug offences, skimming from casinos, frauds against fair boards, and corruption of exhibition officials.

Crackdown on Royal American

Two authorizations for wiretapping were in place by the time Royal American reached Calgary. Several games were closed and charges laid at the Stampede and after the opening of Klondike Days in Edmonton. Then, on Thursday, July 24, 1975, at two o'clock in the morning, a force of more than 130 RCMP and Edmonton city police officers converged on the Royal American midway. Acting on a search warrant, they seized from Royal American and a number of its independent midway operators several thousand documents, mostly accounting records, and an estimated $750,000 in cash, jewellery, and merchandise. During the five-hour raid, locked trailers were entered with crowbars, and workers attempting to leave the grounds were stopped and searched. Three members of Royal American, including owner Carl Sedlmayr Jr., were immediately charged with possessing illegal firearms. Despite reports that the Klondike Days midway would be cancelled, the show somehow opened later that morning, only 30 minutes behind schedule.

Royal American finished up that weekend and moved on to Regina. On Friday, August 1, Sedlmayr and a staff member were arrested and taken back to Edmonton on corruption charges related to allegations that over the past 18 years Sedlmayr had been bribing Albert Anderson, the Edmonton general manager. Anderson's home had been raided on the same night as the Royal American midway and he was also charged. Sedlmayr and his employee pleaded not guilty on Saturday and were released on $5,000 bail each. The corruption charges would be heard in November.

When the show tried to leave Regina to return to the United States, $400,000 worth of equipment was seized as a jeopardy assessment for back taxes. Most of the assessment was against independents, whose equipment remained locked up, but after posting a $13,000 bond Sedlmayr was allowed to take his equipment across the border. Royal American played the rest of the season with a sadly depleted midway. The provincial and federal tax arrears for 1974 and 1975 were assessed at $2.2 million, of which Royal's share was said to be close to $700,000.

A Royal American spokesman still could characterize the show's Canadian tour as a success, with all spots up between 10 and 25 percent. He had no explanation for the sudden crackdown, although management had smelt something in the wind when a concessionaire had equipment and money seized on a fraud charge at the Calgary Stampede. The show was in the first year of a five-year contract with Winnipeg, Calgary, and Edmonton, and planned to return the next year, "if the exhibitions want us," the spokesman said in *Amusement Business* on August 23. "But if it isn't economically feasible we might take another look at it." At the end of September, six counts of defrauding the Edmonton exhibition association of a total of $52,000 were laid against Sedlmayr and two staff members.

At the International Association of Amusement Parks and Attractions convention in Atlanta on November 21, in what the December 6 issue of

Amusement Business termed "the biggest bombshell in decades," Sedlmayr released a statement announcing that his show would not return to Canada for the 1976 season. He cited the Edmonton board's unreasonable demand for a one-million-dollar performance bond. Calgary also required a large performance bond. He apologized to Winnipeg and Regina for not playing their fairs. Royal American had given up six weeks of the top fairs in North America, worth a combined gross on the books of over two million dollars. Royal had played the western A circuit since 1946, when it had taken it from Conklin Shows. Sedlmayr took a parting shot while backing out of Canada, filing a damage claim against the solicitor general for unlawful interception of private communications.

The contest to claim the old A circuit gold mine began immediately. At the International Association of Fairs and Exhibitions convention in Las Vegas the week after the Atlanta event, Bill Pratt, spokesman for the western exhibitions, set a deadline of December 5 for tenders to be submitted. The bond demanded by the Edmonton board was dropped. The decision would be made by December 12. Six American and five Canadian shows bid. Jules Racine, the Conklin Quebec competitor, entered into a combination with Lawrence Carr to put in a bid, and Florian Vallée, who had helped Conklin Shows with its Quebec dates, reorganized his operation for a shot at the contract, but none of the Canadian shows other than Conklin had a realistic chance.

The deadline for the announcement passed with no decision. Although each of the fairs had identified their top three companies, Pratt said that the "tougher political situation" Edmonton faced forced them to hesitate.[8] The final decision came down to a contest among two American shows and Canada's Conklin Shows.

At a press conference in Calgary on December 19 the announcement was finally made: Conklin Shows won the contract. The American press, including *Amusement Business* in its January 3, 1976, issue, unequivocally attributed the decision to "a wave of Canadian Nationalism." Jim admitted that nationalism might have helped, "but it was not the No. 1 consideration." Pratt, the circuit spokesman, said that "Canadians would prefer to deal with Canadians if they could," but "the Conklin bid was as good as any and better, in some ways."[9] In practical terms, the fairs would no longer have to be concerned about difficulties American suppliers might experience, through their actions or inadvertence, with Canadian immigration, labour and tax laws, and regulations.

Conklin Shows had offered more than its American competitors. For Calgary and Edmonton, it gave up 32.5 percent of the first $300,000 gross from the rides, 35 percent on the next $100,000, 37.5 percent on the next $100,000, and 40 percent on anything over $500,000. Ride grosses in Calgary and Edmonton ensured that those boards would get into the 35 percent bracket and probably higher. They would pay $80,000 as a flat fee on the regular games, plus 25 percent of the gross from games that gave money prizes. In 1973 in Calgary, Royal American had paid only $40,000 as a flat fee. Noting that "Conklin was extremely delighted. He really wanted the Western Circuit," Pratt continued: "I think he has given us a tremendously good contract."[10] He would also be required to bring in guest relations and commercial sponsors. The performance bond for Calgary was only $200,000.

That year, the CNE association also extracted increases from Conklin Shows. It upped its percentage from the games five points to 45 and got the ride percentage converted to a sliding scale that worked in favour of the association. This deal prompted one industry commentator to predict that "the CNE is dangerously close" to "the breaking point in fair–carnival contracts."[11]

Commenting on the industry in general, the president of the Outdoor Amusement Business Association said it was "in serious trouble" because fair board demands were forcing carnival companies "beyond reasonable bounds."[12] Conklin Shows was contributing to the problem by offering sweet deals to get or keep the large exhibitions, which tempted smaller fairs to follow suit. But the grosses were not high enough at the latter to bear these fees and leave anything for the carnivals. By the end of the decade, Jim himself was complaining that the fair boards took too much.

With the loss of its Canadian fairs, Royal American entered a long, slow decline.[13] For the next 20 years it slouched along as an attenuated shadow of its former self. It filled in its route with still dates and smaller fairs, all in the United States. It lost more of its bigger fairs, including the spring opener in Tampa. The show began to look shabby and cut its railway cars each year until it converted wholly to a truck show in 1982. A shrunken version of Royal American achieved some stability in the 1980s, but it shrank further in the 1990s until, after several poor seasons, it finally expired in 1997.

After three years, all charges against Royal American and the Edmonton general manager were dropped because of infighting among the investigating authorities and problems with the evidence they had collected. Sedlmayr brought countersuits that were also eventually dropped. The same year the Canadian charges were dropped, he was charged in the United States for filing false tax returns. A nine-month, half-million-dollar Canadian inquiry was called under Justice James Laycraft. It found fault all around and suggested that Royal American had been guilty as charged, although it had done little more than was common practice on other shows in the United States. The inquiry also heard testimony from Royal American staff that Conklin Shows had bribed an RCMP officer to focus the investigation on their show to open the western circuit for Conklin. Laycraft dismissed these rumours as without foundation, but for years they sullied the Conklin reputation in the industry as evidence of its cutthroat practices.

Conklin Shows had learned from Royal American the importance of keeping its books in order and above board, even as those books grew fatter and more complex. In the dust left in the West by Royal, Conklin grew to replace its rival as the largest carnival company in the world. With the western exhibitions occurring in July and August, the circuit led from Calgary to Winnipeg and straight into Toronto. Major rides that were only profitable to run at the CNE could now be taken on the road and operate for two full months, rather than three weeks. With the western contracts in hand, the show bought three new major rides, including a Super Loops, and had to bring back some of the independents it had squeezed out of the Ex. Even before his first season playing the West, Jim began talking about a western winter quarters and undertaking a feasibility study for a permanent amusement park in Edmonton. He only went as far as opening an office in Calgary.

Back on the Western Circuit

Conklin Shows' first season back in the West exceeded all expectations and stretched it to the limit. The economy in the Canadian West had been growing with the increase in oil prices following the Arab oil embargo in 1973. Midway grosses were up 30 percent in Winnipeg and 60 percent in Calgary. At the Stampede, where attendance broke one million for the first time, ride capacity was 25 percent higher than Royal American's and the show planned to expand capacity more for 1977. The show was also up at Edmonton and Regina, but weather almost ruined the move between the two. The rain started midnight Saturday, as the show closed in Edmonton, and continued all night until a foot of water covered the midway in places. They had 36 hours to tear down, move 700 miles to Regina, and set up for opening at noon on Monday. No one with the show had ever made such a jump, but they did it. The CNE also broke attendance records that year and its midway was up 30 percent.

Being new to the western exhibitions partly accounts for Conklin Shows' success, but its innovations contributed. The guest relations booth and central merchandise compound had been introduced at the CNE in previous years, as had the colour-coordinated canvas and employee uniforms. Jim pushed the games and high stock giveaways, stampeding patrons with stuffed animals. The universal ticket system enabled him to fine-tune ride pricing. The show-owned design company dressed up the midway with a western theme, and patrons and fair boards commented that its visual attractiveness was worthy of a theme park.

The show had come a long way toward becoming a rationalized, professional, commercial enterprise, but had done so by suppressing many of the carnival's characteristics. In 1939, H.W. Waters, the CNE general manager when Patty first tried to win it, had predicted that midways would become bland as they "dressed up in a more sedate coat" and acquired "such an air of respectability" that they lost their "carnival or festival spirit."[14] An article lamenting the loss of the old-style midway and freak shows appeared in the August 24 Globe and Mail during the Ex of 1977 and quoted Dottie Marco, a concessionaire with the show, former sideshow producer, life-long carnie, and Pat Marco's wife. Dottie, "Godmother of the Midway," talked about the bureaucratization of the show, including time clocks and hourly wages. "This outfit is a big corporation," she said. "It's run like a downtown office building. All the shows are getting to be the same. The ones that don't change, die. Yeah, just like a downtown office building." The show's expansion and the increased regulation and oversight it required made modern business practices necessary, which met with Jim's penchant for "scientifically" managing midway operations. Business stability required running his company like a business.

Flush with cash, Jim continued in expansion mode. He planned to buy Lynch Shows, the major carnival company in the Maritimes, although the deal fell through and it remained in the hands of Clarence "Soggy" Reid. Jim began a ride rental operation for grocery stores and shopping malls in 1977. He produced a movie about the show to promote it to current and prospective fairs. Under political pressure, the CNE board put the midway contract up for tender in 1977. Only Conklin Shows bid. Labour and tax laws had become too harsh for the large American shows that would be closely scrutinized, and no other Canadian show was big enough.

Jim reported that the show had invested $2.5 million in rides and attractions for the 1977 season of the western unit. He added three new shows, a Cinema 180 film show, a magic show, and a mouse town that he had bought in Germany featuring 600 mice and a cat for mayor. Only the Cinema 180 lasted more than a season, but he had better luck with rides. He bought a 110-foot-high Giant Wheel in Holland, a Jet Star II roller coaster in Germany, and a Skydiver wheel from Chance Rides Manufacturing in Kansas. He bought two other rides — variations on older devices — one from Italy and one from England. As a preliminary foray for his own ride manufacturing company, he built a Tiki Tiki ride for the eastern road show. Neither it nor his ride-building business succeeded.

The second season in the West proved to be another success, with the show delivering the promised 25 percent increase in ride capacity. With the exception of Winnipeg, attendance was up, for a total of 2.3 million for the circuit. The show experimented with further promotions, including a pay-one-price Midnight Madness at Calgary. An idea Jim had been kicking around for years, this special allowed patrons to pay six dollars to ride as much as they wanted from 1 a.m. to 8 a.m. on the first Friday. A crowd of 70,000 showed up, but it was hard on staff and led to decreased crowds the following Saturday. In subsequent years, sales were capped at 20,000, but Midnight Madness specials spread throughout the industry. Pay-one-price — at a much higher price — would become a standard promotion.

The older Conklin & Garrett parks operations started to fade away from neglect because of the energy required to service the West but would get a boost from new parks in 1979. Sunnyside Wasaga opened outside of Collingwood, Ontario, in 1975, but it never did well and was closed after the 1979 season. Conklin Shows got out of Lake Ontario Park in Kingston and Crystal Beach, both after the end of the 1977 season, and out of Belmont Park after 1978. The show kept its operations at the lion safaris in Hemmingford and Rockton. A new arcade, the Undercurrent, with over 100 token-operated machines and an investment of $750,000, debuted in the basement of Toronto's CN Tower in 1977, a year after the tower opened. By its second year of operation, the arcade was "capturing about 80 per cent of the 1.5 million annual visitors" to the tower.[15]

Equipment that went West played for a few weeks on the CNE grounds in the spring of 1979, and a three-month summer midway was instituted the next year, another variation on the perennial attempt to make the grounds an attraction beyond the Ex. The Conklin company entered into joint ventures for a theme park at Maple Leaf Village Park in Niagara Falls and Playland at the Pacific National Exhibition grounds in Vancouver, both in 1979. Maple Leaf Village had the largest Ferris wheel in the world, a 175-foot-high ride bought in Holland for two million dollars, and the stint at Playland included the PNE itself, the fourth-largest fair in North America, one that Conklin Shows had played but once, in 1931 as Patty was bidding farewell to Vancouver. Taking advantage of changes in Ontario gambling laws, in 1978 Jim began a casino business for leasing to charitable organizations. While he was recovering territory his father had abandoned, he was also breaking into new frontiers.

BACK IN THE USA

They threw a big banquet for me. I was the showman of the year. Look at all the pictures up there. That was 1979 in February. The fair in Puerto Rico was in '78. I put the fair on. Here's a picture of me and Alfie. Here's one with me and Frank Conklin in Puerto Rico. That's when he was 18 years old. He didn't know nothing. He'll tell you about me when I used to make him piña coladas at my bar. I owned a nightclub in Puerto Rico, Danny's Living Room. It's still there....

I ended up working on the Royal American show in the States. I was there for 17 years. Then I had a bar in Puerto Rico and then I came up with a gimmick, a state fair for Puerto Rico. I went to see Conklin, I went to see Jimmy Murtry, I went to see Sedlmayr, nobody'd listen to me, except young Conklin. "Let me look at it," he said. He came down and then the old man come down, Jim come down. Jim took a shot.

Boy, was it a winner! I worked with Bob Rice with Conklin and Sheila McKinnon. Sheila was the boss in Puerto Rico. She put it together with me and my partner. It was a big success, a big fair. Everybody made lots of money, but I wasn't working a flat store.

I worked a flat store for years, in Puerto Rico, Dominican Republic. I was with Hollywood Park, a Spanish outfit, based in Puerto Rico. I showed the owner how to run things — he didn't know nothing — me and my partner who run the bar with me.

Then we bought a bar. Then I got connected in Las Vegas with Dean Martin. I was bringing shows down. Martin was a friend of mine. We were working together with shows, like Rich Little, Louis Prima, Sam Butera. I took them all to Puerto Rico and booked them in big hotels.

Jimmy came into my bar when the fair was on. Frank was there every night with all the carnies. They were having a few problems with the show at the time. Frank, he was worried, but they were okay after Puerto Rico.

I remember, the night before we opened, Jim saying to me, "Bissonnette, it better be good." I said, "Look at the people." This was the night before we opened, American Thanksgiving, 13 November.

Jim says to me, "It's drizzling." I said, "Don't worry about it. It'll be all right. Just watch."

The following night, the chief of police says to me, "What did you bring here? There's people lined up five miles from here." They had to open up new ticket boxes. They brought more rides from the States. Everybody made lots of money.

I wasn't involved with them when they came back another year. They went to Santo Domingo. Then I took the Royal American show to Panama a couple of years later in 1980. That was a good show. I know the family that run it.

Carl Sedlmayr used to send me cigars and money in prison before he died. I was in tight with him. I used to know the grandfather, before he died. He was old. It was a beautiful show, the only show everybody talked about. We used to play Winnipeg, Calgary, Edmonton, Regina, Saskatoon. I played the A circuit with them for many years. They let me run a flat store. With me it was always flats. I didn't know nothing else. "Hey buddy, you ever see this one?"

Interview with Timmins Bissonnette, April 26, 2006

Beginning in 1977, after the CNE some of the Conklin spectacular rides went to the United States. They needed to keep them working and there was demand for them at American fairs, where there were not enough spectaculars to go around. Bob Rice, an American whose father Patty had worked with in the Southwest early in the century, had been hired as the show's U.S. representative in 1975 and he booked the seven-ride unit.

Jim's son Frank, a mere 18 years old, was responsible for getting the rides, which included the Giant Wheel, the Monster, and the Musik Express, down the road. He had experienced and capable staff who were loyal to him and his ambitions. Moving the Enterprise and the Super Loops, which the show had bought in 1976, over such distances was a first and young Frank got a taste for setting firsts. They also acquired a Zyklon, a huge portable coaster that unwittingly shared a name with a poisonous gas used in Nazi death camps; they renamed it the Cyclone.

The rides worked major exhibitions in Albuquerque, New Mexico, and Phoenix, Arizona, as well as smaller fairs. In Albuquerque the first year, a riot at the Monster resulted in stab wounds to five staff, a clash with American culture that would be repeated in coming years. Some of the crew had problems getting through immigration and the show hired American help to fill the gaps and serve as cultural mediators, if needed.

Despite the difficulties it brought, Jim felt the U.S. operation held great potential and he bought a 20-acre lot in Texas to store equipment that could remain in the United States during the winter, "purely as an independent operation," he explained to *Amusement Business* in the December 24 issue. That winter he deleted "Canada" from the show's official name to "better reflect the international nature of our operations."[16] The nationalist angle had paid off when needed, but now it was expedient to represent themselves as a continental, that is, American, outfit. He had accomplished another of his father's ambitions. What was at first known as the Southern Comfort Unit would evolve in a few years into an independent show, Conklin Shows International.

By the spring of 1978, on the basis of figures from the previous season Jim could announce that his was now the largest show in North America. It had ridden 16 million people in 1977, up from two million in 1967 and compared to 10.9 million visitors to Disneyland. Show equipment was worth over $10 million, not counting $3.5 million invested at the CNE. Growth since the death of Patty had come from Jim's planning and restructuring, the good fortune of getting the big western exhibitions, and a buoyant economy.

A slowdown was in order. The economy had started to recede. Government licensing, inspection, and permitting expenses were increasing exponentially and energy prices had risen 28 percent in 1977 alone, just as the show had committed to moving rides larger than any show had ever moved before, which required scores of diesel-guzzling tractor-trailers. Jim planned to consolidate for the 1978 season, cut capital outlay, and concentrate on in-house projects. To enable work on these, the show bought a 65,000-square-foot building in Brantford. "One of the main projects ... was totally refurbishing" the Jet Star, bought only two years before, because it was not working properly.[17] The only major ride purchase was a $300,000 Wave Swinger. But as show secretary-treasurer Al Ross explained to an *Amusement Business* reporter in the May 20 issue, Jim was "always coming up with ideas." Ross continued: "He has this company rolling in the right direction and I don't think he could stop it if he wanted to."

Then another opportunity arose from which Jim could not turn away. The Deggeller brothers' Spectacular Magic Midway, almost 20 years old and one of the top five shows in the United States, had over-expanded and, with the U.S. economy slumping, was facing bankruptcy. Conklin & Garrett Shows came in with a friendly takeover bid, announced in March 1978. The Deggeller organization would remain intact, but Jim appointed additional staff of his own: John Drummey would be vice-president of U.S. operations, Bob Rice general manager, and Frank Conklin operations manager. The Magic Midway had an eight-month season stretching from Florida to Michigan. The Southern Comfort winter quarters moved from Texas to the Deggeller lot in Fort Lauderdale. Having captured all major exhibitions in Canada, Ross told *Amusement Business*, with only smaller fairs left to take over, the show was targeting the United States for "major expansion ... in the next 10 years." The rationale was that "there are just more populated areas there and much more potential."

After a record crowd of almost 500,000 at the Dade County Youth Fair in Miami in March 1978, with a record gross of over a million dollars, which "served as an excellent showpiece for Canadian Showman Conklin," the Magic Midway was hit by a fierce storm on the first of May in Florida; two men were struck by lightning but survived.[18] Then management discovered the show did not own enough trucks to move all its equipment and they had to buy 18 more tractor-trailers. They put 15 major Deggeller rides up for sale in August. The Conklin staff had other problems managing the Magic Midway, including dealing with fair officials who expected to be paid off, and Drummey was fired amid allegations he could not do his job. Alfie Phillips found the U.S. operation "mind boggling."[19]

The next year, Conklin management turned down the opportunity to bid on a return to the Kentucky State Fair, which the Deggellers had played for several years, because they did not approve of the bidding practices. They replaced it with the Eastern States Exposition, known as the Big E, in West Springfield, Massachusetts; the Illinois and Arkansas state fairs; and a fair in Pennsylvania. Conklin Shows bought a new Tidal Wave ride in 1979 and brought in its own management to replace stragglers from Deggeller times, returning the Magic Midway to profitable status. The Conklin executive remained optimistic about the show's prospects.

Carnivals continued to be scrutinized more closely in Canada. In the spring of 1978, the Department of National Revenue and the RCMP informed Conklin Shows that it would be audited at the western fairs and the CNE. Government officials would stand with counters at the rides and do their own count of patrons. The show agreed to co-operate but was concerned that fair boards would assume it was under special investigation. The officials reassured the fair boards and, other than annoyance to ride staff, the audit had no serious repercussions.

The law was not so lenient with the games. At the 1977 CNE, a charge of cheating was pressed against the show on an accusation that the balls for a basketball game were over-inflated. A guilty verdict was returned in the spring of 1978, but the Ontario Court of Appeal overturned it a year later. At the 1978 Calgary Stampede, several game operators were charged with fraud and obstructing justice, and similar charges were laid against operators at Belmont Park the same summer. In both cases, negotiations with police resulted in the charges being dropped. Jim insisted that these charges were owing to misunderstandings and varying interpretations of the Criminal Code. He repeatedly called for the statutes to be updated to reflect the reality on his midways.

Once more breaking his vow to consolidate, Jim ended the 1978 season with another purchase. Bernard & Barry Shows had collaborated with Patty at the Kitchener centennial in 1946, but then competed with him and Jimmy Sullivan for the next 15 years. Hank Blade, one-time Sullivan staff, joined the company in 1969, by which time it had been renamed Bernard Shows. Blade took over the show when the owners retired in the early 1970s, but his health began to fail and he sold Bernard Shows and its route to Conklin in the fall of 1978, beginning with the Welland fair in mid-September. While rumours persisted in the industry that Conklin was poised to eat up several other companies, Bernard Shows was the last that Conklin & Garrett would buy.

The Antique Carnival

The 1978 season had two highlights: an Antique Carnival and a trip to Puerto Rico. Sergei Sawchyn and Jim had begun mulling over the idea of the Antique Carnival in 1973. Then Sawchyn ended his short time as special assistant to the president to run his own performing arts touring agency, bringing the Moscow Circus to Montreal and Toronto in 1977. Jim went ahead with the idea, using his own staff, and Sawchyn came back to help with coordination in the last months. Most of the restoration work on the ancient rides was done the previous winter at the Brantford shops, under Red Rathee's supervision. The sideshows were put together by Sam Alexander.

The Antique Carnival tried to re-create the midway of 50 years before, but without the grift, gaff, and girls. As described in the September 16, 1978, *Amusement Business*, it had 14 rides, including a merry-go-round from the 1920s, a 1938 Lindy Loop, a chair swing, "its center pole originally a mast from a World War I German Dreadnought," and "the Coronation Arc one of a kind and built to honor Queen Elizabeth's father, King George VI." There were six old-style sideshows, admission of 25 cents, and nine food joints with prices 25 percent lower than on the regular midway. Midway talkers had to insist that "it is not a museum and everything works," including the 30 games no longer found on carnivals, like "the Shiv Rack, Huckley Buck, Coconut Pitch, Pony Wheel, Cigarette Shooting Gallery, Ham and Bacon Wheel, Candy Wheel, Blanket Wheel, Jingle Board, Stagger Board and Hoop-La." Nine actors from Calgary performed skits, both on the carnival site and in downtown Toronto. The 180 staff were dressed by a theatrical costume designer in period costumes. The midway was lit by vintage-style Edison light bulbs and covered in sawdust.

The Antique Carnival left Brantford in 28 trailers that spring to begin dress rehearsals in Calgary. It had a nine-weekend test run on the Stampede grounds before opening fully for the Stampede. It then went to Edmonton for Klondike Days, returning to Toronto in time to celebrate its reason for being, the 100th anniversary of the CNE. Pat Marco, who managed it, admitted they did "just a fair business" in Calgary, but they had more success at the CNE. Admission to the enclosed grounds was a dime, with rides a quarter apiece and kiddie rides 10 cents. It had cost over $2.5 million to put together.

According to Sawchyn, the Antique Carnival was Jim's "consummate pride and joy," and he underwrote it as "a philanthropist ... to preserve a part of the nation's social history." Jim wanted "to find a permanent home for his antique carnival at a place such as the Circus World Museum in Baraboo, Wis." The Canadian Carnival Historical Society, which Conklin had helped found in 1976, wanted to take it over, but had nowhere to store it. It was put up for sale to anyone with the proper offer, which required keeping it intact, but went back in storage in Brantford. The show could not afford to continue operating the Antique Carnival at a loss, so it dropped plans to tour it in the United States in 1979.

The Caribbean

Memories were made, not recalled, by the first Conklin foray into the Caribbean. The idea might have originated with one Timmins Bissonnette, who had operated a flat store — a game that could not be won unless the operator allowed — in the 1940s and '50s, sometimes with Sullivan's show and sometimes with Royal American. He had moved to Puerto Rico in 1966 to partner in a nightclub. Bissonnette, who grew up in Timmins, Ontario, a bilingual town, had been a French interpreter for Frank Conklin senior with the local police and health department in Quebec and used to borrow money from Frank in the winter. He pitched the concept of a Puerto Rican fair to two local promoters and arranged for them to meet Frank Conklin Jr. in Albuquerque in 1977. Jim, who was the same age as Bissonnette and had known him for years, made the final decision to go ahead. Bob Rice was brought in to manage the arrangement and by the next summer the dates were set.

La Feria Internacional del Caribe opened in San Juan on November 22, 1978, to mile-long lineups and ran for 25 days. The northern show shipped 18 trailers of equipment from New Jersey, while the Southern Comfort–Magic Midway conglomeration shipped 110 trailers on barges from Jacksonville, Florida. Transportation costs ran to a quarter of a million dollars. Staff leaped tremendous logistical hurdles and solved the hitches that arose, and business was spectacular. The 180 Conklin staff who travelled to Puerto Rico remember the weather, the hospitality, and the partying. It rained every after-noon at the same time, but this did not hurt the crowds used to the weather or the locals hired to work the joints. The carnies suffered from the heat and humidity but were able to relieve their pain with local rum at Bissonnette's bar.

Awarded showman of the year by the Canadian Showman's League for his efforts in Puerto Rico, Bissonnette's next newsworthy act, two years later, was to murder a friend and associate. Guy Lamarche was a crooked stock-broker from Bissonnette's hometown who had turned down his latest request for money. As Bissonette on the down escalator in Toronto's Royal York Hotel passed Lamarche on the up, he calmly shot him, then walked through the lobby to the street, where he was apprehended a few blocks away. At his trial, Bissonnette described how he was wearing a hat like Jimmy Cagney and a scarf like Humphrey Bogart, so, dressed like that it was natural for him to shoot his erstwhile friend and partner. He was sentenced to 25 years in jail.

The show tried to repeat the innovations of 1978 the following year. The United Nations had declared 1979 the International Year of the Child and, in the middle of the Antique Carnival, Sawchyn and Conklin began talking about using the concept as a theme at the CNE. One of Jim's goals was to retain control of the space the CNE association had allotted for the Antique Carnival. With association and corporate sponsorship, the World of the Child was a four-acre amusement park with a TV studio, a restaurant run by kids, a clown makeup alley, elephant rides, disco dancing, roller skating, a fantasy space flight, and a huge ice cream parlour. Sawchyn brought in a circus, which drew bad press for charging a separate admission. That was almost the only publicity the World of the Child got. Neither the Antique Carnival nor the World of the Child recovered costs.

As late as August 1979, Rice was working on a return to Puerto Rico, but a consortium that included Florian Vallée's Beauce Carnaval provided local officials a sweeter payoff and they scooped the spot. Rumours arose of an extended Conklin tour of the Caribbean, possibly even South and Central America. Rice turned his sights on the Dominican Republic and the show booked three weeks in Santo Domingo, the capital. It was a disaster. Hurricane David, a Category 5 storm and one of the deadliest hurricanes on record, had struck the island at the end of August, killing over 2,000 people and leaving

200,000 more homeless, destroying roads and crops, causing floods, and ravaging Santo Domingo. Heavy rains from Hurricane Frederic followed a week later. The country was still reeling when the show arrived in mid-November. Armed security guards were required to guard the office compound and the Dominicans did not trust the rides. The returns for the show were dismal.

Still, many remember the 1979 season as the pinnacle of Jim's show. Maple Leaf Village in Niagara Falls opened with North America's tallest Ferris wheel and the amusement park in Vancouver did well. The show had four new U.S. state fairs, and the PNE in Canada. By combining the routes of the two eastern road show units, each cut distances between spots and both had good seasons. The Magic Midway seemed on a solid footing and management staff responsible for the western exhibitions and the CNE had hit their stride. Camaraderie among full-time staff, bolstered by their sense that they were in on something big and thriving, reached an all-time high. The show could afford to throw lavish employee parties, employ a design firm, photographer, and an editor to publish *Jackpot*, a monthly newsletter, and run the western show as a travelling amusement park, "a Marriott-on-wheels."[20] Jim had developed a reputation for great ideas that he gave to staff to produce, along with the necessary resources. An admirable reputation if it could be maintained.

By the end of the decade, Jim had transformed his father's show into a multi-faceted corporation, the old-time carnie long left behind. Part of him must have felt it was a compliment when Dottie Marco described his company as "run like a downtown office building." The World of the Child and Santo Domingo looked like minor missteps in the show's steady march into the future. Some might have seen in them signs of what, in retrospect, is clear. Rising first on his father's reputation, but increasingly through his own ambition and acumen, within 10 years of Patty's death, Jim had lifted his show to a pinnacle from which it had nowhere to go but down.

Turbulence

....

(1979–1990)

....

During the last decades of the century, the immunity of the largest carnival company in the world to the economic and social instability that beset its peers turned out to be illusory. After almost 10 years of unfaltering success and unbroken good fortune, and while taking risks that still sometimes paid off, Conklin Shows' trajectory began to waver. Jim Conklin's seeming infallibility would be fractured, but he also discovered a resiliency that few suspected he had.

THE LETTER

In San Antonio we were set up in the streets. It was a real eye-opening experience. I remember setting up, and farther out in the street there was three Mexican boys walking one way and four Mexican boys walking the other way, and, for no known reason to me, a big knife fight started. One guy got slashed, the other guy got stabbed, and I'm going, "Oh, man, you're not in Kansas anymore."

We had some young girl who was right out of it. She came up and wanted to go on the Enterprise. I was standing at the top of the stairs and said, "No, no, no, you can't come up here, you're too messed up." She pulled out a knife and was going to walk through me. I think that's just something they do in San Antonio. Fortunately for me, there was a policeman not too far away who saw everything as it was transpiring, and he immediately pounced on her and took her away.

They have a parade every year the weekend after opening, I think it's the Battle of the Roses. Some old guy was camped out on the parade route in his RV. As the parade started up, he had a whole selection of weapons in his motor home, and he opened fire on the crowd. I think four people ended up getting killed and 11 or 12 people were wounded. There were some policemen in the mix. The whole time this is going on, me and Hippy are underneath the ride, laying as flat to the ground as we could get. The fair was open, the rides were open, we thought it was fireworks in the beginning, until everybody started running and screaming. I don't know if the gentleman ended up committing suicide or the police ended up helping, but that was pretty well the end of the parade.

We travelled up to Spokane after and that was fairly uneventful. Then Portland was the Rose Festival. We set up the Giant Wheel and the Tidal Wave, the Wave Swinger, the Enterprise, and I'm not sure if we had anything else, I know the four were there for sure. We had to set up in this park, right downtown…. The port's right there. We were set up, probably 20 feet away from the edge of the dock. You go over to the wall and look down, the water was 75 or 80 feet down, so they were parking some big boats.

During the fair they had a U.S. Navy tanker ship, 1,380 feet, parked right beside us. A Korean officers' training ship was there, a little small boat, about 400 feet. They had a couple of cruisers parked in there beside it. I think the only thing they couldn't get in there was an aircraft carrier. Of course, once the U.S. Navy shows up, the protesters show up. Who knows what they were protesting. The sailors were instructed by their commanding officer not to do anything to impede these protesters' right to protest, but that didn't apply to the rest of us.

The sailors off the boat had become very good customers. They told us that it really irked them, so we took it upon ourselves to maybe get rid of some of the protesters. We threw a bunch of their pamphlets and some of their signs over the edge of the dock, to a lot of cheers from a lot of sailors on the boat. Then we made ourselves scarce. The police looked very vigilantly for who did it, but I'm certain not too vigilantly, because they knew exactly who it was.

On the way to Winnipeg, whoever was driving the Musik Express got off on a soft shoulder and flipped the scenery load.... So, we got to Winnipeg and put as much together as we could and plywooded the rest, and managed to make opening. Played the Canadian route, Winnipeg, Calgary — Calgary we had a Midnight Madness and that was absolutely insane. People were just going home at eight o'clock in the morning. I'd never seen anything like it.

Edmonton, another great fair. I remember tearing down in Edmonton, pouring rain. I think it finally stopped raining about 15 minutes after we finished tearing down. The whole grounds had flooded out. We were literally jacking the Enterprise up in the air, standing in three feet of water. It was hydraulic, but it was man-operated hydraulics and you just kept jacking it up until you got in the air. We got everything out; extremely exhausting.

I get in the truck and start driving to Regina. One of our other drivers was in a truck right beside me and he swears to this day that my head was down and I was sound asleep for at least three or four minutes at 60 miles an hour going across highway number one on the way to Regina. He didn't want to honk the horn to wake me up because he didn't know what my reaction would be. I guess I eventually just woke up and continued on. We all got safely into Regina.

We opened the next day, so we started set-up immediately. We worked all day in Edmonton. Tore down all night. Drove, it was probably an eight- or 10-hour trip. Then immediately started setting up and then opened. Sometime in the middle of the night, when we were really on our last legs — we weren't going to make it — the ride superintendent came over and he had a little bag of something. He gave us each a pill, I don't know exactly what it was, but 20 minutes later we were all on fire, setting up the ride, wide awake, and we got it all done.

Regina was the last stop in the West, so we started coming to Toronto. At that point, we were driving in small convoys, groups of four or five trucks were assigned to one another. One guy had the money to fill up all the trucks. Well, I had the slowest truck. These boys got on ahead of me and they let me know where they were going to stop. It was my first time driving through northern Ontario and I overshot the truck stop where they were. So, I pulled over on the side of the highway and immediately the truck and trailer started to tilt like it was going to tip over and roll down this little ravine. The soft shoulders in northern Ontario were infamous, like quicksand. I guess I had forgotten what they told me.

I immediately jumped out of the truck. I wanted to be the lone witness, not the victim. Eventually the other trucks caught up to me. We tried to pull it back onto the road. We hooked up a bunch of chains and had people blocking off the highway so no cars were coming so we could try to get it out. That wasn't working. We got a couple of big wreckers and finally the OPP showed up. We got the truck out of the ditch.

You can imagine the attitude of the ride foreman and some of the other guys. I was getting non-stop shit from all of them and deserved it. After a little while, I was getting a little tired of it and I said to the foreman, "You know, I understand I messed up. Now stop." He just kept going. I finally threatened that I would break something on him if he didn't shut up and go away. We got the truck back onto the road and I continued back into Toronto. We got the ride set up. Then he unceremoniously fired my ass; not personally, he sent someone to do it, just in case I still carried a grudge. So, I got as far as the CNE that year and open, and when I got fired I said okay and went back home.

Interview with Howard "Lurch" Pringle, Aug. 30, 2005

★   ★   ★

Tremors from the earthquake that would shake the Conklin edifice to its foundation were felt first at the CNE, the bedrock upon which the structure had been built. The 1978 attendance record of 3,593,000 would prove to be the all-time high as attendance began to fall with the 1979 fair. When it was reported in the *Toronto Star* on July 21, 1979, that he had grossed five million dollars from the 1978 Ex, while the CNE association lost over a million, Jim deflected the interviewer to complain about the 35 percent and more he paid to the association: "The CNE cut is comparable to what other fairs receive, but they all take too much.... A lot of midway operators are going down the drain." Resolutions to consolidate, statements like this — he knew his company was on shaky ground. He had grown too fast, overextended the business with the banks, and the economy was faltering. His perception of a weak Canadian economy had been one rationale for moving into the United States. Ironically, it would be the U.S. economy that hurt the show worst.

The 1979 season should have been the Conklin Shows' best yet. After the record-setting Dade County fair, they had what looked like a strong run of U.S. fairs and planned to tour the Dominican Republic, Puerto Rico, and other Caribbean dates in the off-season. They had picked up the Playland Amusement Park at the Pacific National Exhibition at the beginning of its season. Maple Leaf Village made news with its Giant Wheel and the show used the Antique Carnival equipment to fill in its midway. Even the Bicycle Unit, the smaller of the two Ontario units, was doing better with 1,500 miles cut from its route, some weaker spots dropped and some new rides added. But the feeling that this would be their banner year was not reflected in dollars when the season was over. Several U.S. fairs did poorly, CNE grosses were down, the return to Puerto Rico fell through, the Dominican Republic date failed miserably, and the show suffered a major public relations embarrassment.

Oil Crisis

As with any enterprise of its size and with its liabilities, Conklin Shows' business model depended on perpetually rising nets, but world events, among other things, were cutting into the net. The problems with oil supplies and costs that began with the oil embargo of 1973 and proceeded through a series of global crises hit the West with another shock when Iran, after its 1978 fundamentalist revolution, cut all oil exports. Oil prices climbed precipitously in 1979 and the spectre of scarcity arose in the amusement business press with stories of carnivals that could not afford or even find fuel to travel. Conklin Shows was able to make its dates that year but had not factored high fuel prices into the books. Beyond the CNE, where American tourists failed to show up in the numbers the Ex had come to rely on, consumer anxiety and gas prices in both countries led to attendance drops at many of the Conklin fairs. A disturbing trend had started.

Fuel prices, high fair board percentages, economic uncertainty, and fear pushed the head of the world's largest carnival company into his first serious stumble. In late June 1979, Jim wrote a letter to the managers of his U.S. fairs, telling them that the show might not be able to meet the conditions of their contracts, the ink still wet on some of them, and asking them to swallow a 5 percent cut in their take. Some of these contracts were in the first of five years, but he wanted to renegotiate. He positioned the letter as a response to desperate times and a plea for the fairs to co-operate with his company to protect their mutual interests. The letter angered and confused the fair boards, some of whose fairs were months down the road. When news of the letter surfaced two months later, he was mocked in the industry press as "waiting by the chimney for Santa Claus."[1]

Consequences

Fuel shortages never became as acute as anticipated and Jim was seen as having sensationalized the problem to gain the upper hand with the boards. He later admitted, "Since the letter we have had no problems. It never got as serious as it was a couple months ago. We've had no fuel problems."[2] He was reported to have said "he was just worked up when he wrote the letter." Apparently, his advisers had been unable to cool him down. The carnival industry saw his hope that the fairs would reduce their percentage as foolish, and his rivals began stalking his U.S. dates. Two fairs accused him of breach of contract, and one of them cancelled for 1980, while he cancelled the other. Their acrimonious discussions were aired in the press.

At a management meeting in January 1980 to assess the 1979 season, Ross Caldwell, vice-president, finance, summarized the accounts and delivered foreboding news. Expenses had increased by $1.25 million and had to be controlled. The company's financial systems had not been upgraded to match its growth, and if finance and accounting were not involved more centrally the company would soon be losing money. Higher grosses in Canada had been siphoned off to cover losses in the United States. Dave Bastido, the show's accountant, spoke about rationalizing the financial operations. Alfie Phillips and Barry Jamieson both pointed out that staff cuts had been managed without undue stress and further cuts could be made. Jim emphasized finding ways to generate more revenue from current operations. He said that company financial information had been leaked to the press and he wanted tighter in-house secrecy. From now on, rather than report actual dollar figures, the company would release percentages relative to previous years' grosses.

With his letter to the U.S. fair boards, Jim had jeopardized his reputation as the worthy successor to his father, equally astute but more ambitious. Many who remembered Patty were satisfied to see this turn in his son's fortunes, so long in coming. Memories of Conklin Shows leaping into the gap created by Royal America's expulsion from Canada still fresh, and the show's incursions into U.S. territory not universally welcomed, the American-dominated industry took satisfaction from this misstep and probed for further signs of weakness. Complaints from fair boards about the show were given ample press, and even when an exhibition had not received the letter requesting to renegotiate, press coverage of the Conklin showing at the event never failed to mention it. Possibly based on the leaks about the show's finances that Jim claimed had happened, there were rumours that the show was more overextended than it would admit, possibly crippled beyond recovery. The rumours were accurate.

BUSTED

When Frank got the Dade contract in '79, we didn't think it was going to be that big, really. We opened up Friday and it was pretty dead. On Saturday we opened, and the next time I went home was Tuesday afternoon. We grossed more money in the very first weekend than the previous company reported for the whole event the year before. It was nuts. Trying to get the sellers out, to get tickets for the booths — counting the money was just completely out of the question. We just tried to get it out of the ticket boxes and throw it in bags for which day it came from. We were kind of making it up, balancing the sellers, so we had the appearance of some kind of control over the money. There was only two of us taking money out of the entire fairgrounds. There was another guy inside the office doling out tickets.

The day after the fair was over we got two and a half inches of rain in 45 minutes. We were just in the midst of tearing down. This underpass completely fills up with water and one of the guys is in there swimming the backstroke. We're going to return this Avco trailer. We head downtown and I take a look in the rear-view mirror and the trailer is turned sideways. The chassis has disconnected from the trailer and we're on I-95. We pull over at the very first exit into the world's worst neighbourhood. I run over to the gas station and call the lot and the welder is going to come out. The welder comes and we pull the trailer and the truck back into shape. Some guy comes over with a baseball bat and says, "You guys owe me some money for parking here in my parking spot." We say we don't have any money. We hook up the trailer as fast as we can and get out of there.

The next morning we decide to take the money to the bank because we don't have armoured cars. We had all the money from the last weekend and it was, like, one million three. I have this little Pinto and load up the money in the back, all the coin and everything. We're heading downtown. We hit some bumps and the Pinto's coming off the road a little bit, we've got so much coin in the back. We hand bomb bags of coin into the front seat.

We get down to the bank. My companion goes into the bank and says, "We've got a deposit to make. We got a lot of money." The girl asks, "How much?" She says, "About a million three." All of a sudden there's security guards running all over the place with guns drawn. So, we pull the Pinto into this drive. They've got to count the bags and the rest of it. We go into the front of the bank and they've got this big white chesterfield and we lie down and go to sleep. They come and wake us up with the receipt.

That was the first time I was exposed to how bad this business can be. On Tuesday morning, about 10:15, a call comes across the radio that we need first aid and some paramedics at the Tidal Wave. I grab my little first-aid kit. All of a sudden I was on top of the scene and there's this kid that's been stabbed twice. He's one of our guys. That was the first person I'd ever seen dead. He wasn't breathing and you could just tell that the life was out of him. He was a local kid that worked for us. Some guy got off the ride and tried to leave through the entrance. He told him he had to leave through the exit. They got into a shoving match. He comes back 20 minutes later with some friends and they hold him, while this one kid stabs him to death. They were back in the school that afternoon and they arrested all three of them. They were just juveniles, so nothing really happened to them.

After Miami we went out West again and that was great. We came here to the CNE in '79 and it was even bigger than the year before. Ever since then, this fair has constantly declined. If another carnival owner ever got this spot, he'd be elated with it. But all of us are so disappointed because we know what it was and what it could be. That's what hurts the most. It's just a giant flea market now.

I didn't go to Miami in 1980. We ran the summer midway all summer long, right into the opening of the CNE. I really got a feel for the rest of the show because I went out to the Lion Safari, Belmont, Crystal Beach, and Niagara Falls. We had all these operations going on everywhere. The CNE rolled around and I worked here at the ticket office again. We were down one million dollars with no warning whatsoever. It was awful.

After we got off the road, there was a lot of tension back in the shop and everywhere inside the company. At that point in Brantford, things were not good. Massey Ferguson was getting ready to shut its doors and a number of other companies were getting ready to close. Things were going to hell in a hand basket with Jim and the CIBC. Bastido even said to us, "If you guys come to work and the doors are locked, we'll call you and let you know what's going to happen." It was Halloween night when Jim had to restructure the joint. Lots of heads rolled that night. We went from 17 to 7 that night.

We actually had a party at Bastido's place that night. Everybody came and it was pretty ugly. People were getting drunk and they just lost their jobs. That night was pretty bad. Amongst the group, those who got to stay and those who got the axe, there wasn't any animosity; toward the company there was. Now I know why I was spared the axe: it's because they weren't paying me very much money and I could do a lot of things. I don't know how Jim made his decisions, but I know it was him. He had to do it. He had to reorganize.

He also got rid of a lot of equipment, which was good. A lot of that stuff wasn't making any money. He got out of the parks at that time. What he was good at was running three carnivals, and that's what he put all of his energy into. He made some very smart moves. He pulled it off, but it was pretty thin. There were a couple of times when he was considering pulling the plug.

The CIBC said no, they weren't going to play. Then Continental said no. Jim hit a brick wall and that's the first time he thought he was going to have to pack it in. He owed a lot of money. I thought these people were gazillionaires, but they were living off the bank's money because before then the banks wouldn't say no to them. They bought Deggeller Shows and Bernard Shows along the way; they expanded into the United States. Jim was buying a brand new ride every year from Germany. It all came home in 1980.

Interview with Greg "Scooter" Korek, Sept. 2, 2005

*   ★   *

Then we had that trouble in the early '80s. That was really tough around there. The big problem was the Bank of Commerce. They were really running scared. They were the chief bank involved with Massey Ferguson, and they were going under. I really believe they were scrambling. It was the worst time of all our lives. It was just terrible. It's your job, it's your livelihood, but when you see a company like that and you see Jim, just so … It was really bothering him. He didn't show a lot of emotion ever, but you knew that was drawing heavy on him. He kept us all around and I don't know that he should have. I think he was being very loyal to us. The bank, though, what are they going to do with the show? Are they going to run it? They would only have gotten pennies on the dollar.

He got help from a lot of friends, like Sam Ganz. He used a lot of his own money, too. I don't know what the bank was asking payment on. Going out West cost him a lot of money, brand new rides, trailers, trucks. That takes a long time to recoup, but it was only five years. The Deggeller Shows, there was a lot of dead wood around. The company got real big, real fast.

Interview with Dave McKelvey, Aug. 24, 2005

★　★　★

The show had lost money on the two theme carnivals, the latest U.S. tour, and the trip to the Dominican Republic. They were still buying spectacular European rides like the Giant Wheel and the Tidal Wave, the latter of which cost three-quarters of a million U.S. dollars. They were still paying for their acquisitions of other shows and their investments in the Vancouver and Niagara Falls parks. While grosses were up in Canada — thanks to hikes in the price of ride tickets — the net for 1979 was flat. Oil prices would soon begin increasing again. Everything Jim had done with his show during the previous decade was predicated on a buoyant economy and the Western world was entering a recession.

Consolidation

Prospects in the States no longer seemed so bright, even beyond the massacre they had witnessed at the San Antonio Battle of the Roses parade the previous spring. Having already dropped two fairs, Jim reviewed the 1979 season and in the January 12, 1980, issue of *Amusement Business* announced plans to "drastically reduce its U.S. operations," to cut most of the U.S. fairs, dissolve the Magic Midway, and weave the U.S. show into the western Canadian circuit. Alfie admitted that "it's certainly a big change for us," but pointed out the advantages of purchasing the show's "spectacular rides … through the U.S. arm of the company, and that will continue." They would also "continue to book our major rides onto American carnivals during the season." After the Dade County fair in March, the show would park the majority of its equipment at the CHUM Summer Midway on the CNE grounds for a few months, play the four western exhibitions and the CNE, then finish up with four U.S. state fairs in the fall.

Jim had already heard the bad news Caldwell was soon to deliver at the company's January 1980 meeting. For the second time in as many years, he vowed to stabilize operations: "If one word could summarize our 1980 plans, it is consolidation."[3] Winter quarters activities would be kept to a minimum to reduce overhead. The show sold many of its transport trucks and began hiring outside drivers to make its jumps, so avoiding the bother and expense of dealing with transportation regulations in Canada and the United States. The company kept its fairs on the two Ontario routes, but dropped more still dates to cut transportation costs. For the time being, it held on to its stake in the Vancouver and Niagara Falls amusement parks, the midways at the two lion safaris, and the arcade at the CN Tower.

Meanwhile, the Deggeller brothers reformed their show and took back many of the fairs abandoned by the Conklin Magic Midway, as well as the Maryland and South Carolina state fairs that Conklin Shows had planned to keep. Jim could clearly see that things had changed, and in the February 1980 issue of *Jackpot*, the company newsletter, he predicted that the coming decade would be "dominated by problem times rather than good times." That the Conklin empire was wobbling elicited both satisfaction and anxiety within the industry: If the mighty could fall, what about the rest of us?

An event organized by Jim in the last months of the decade exhibits another consolidating tactic. In November 1979, he held an auction in an 85,000-square-foot warehouse north of Toronto. He was trying to divest himself of 60 years of carnival memorabilia, as well as eight antique automobiles, the remains of 14 "Cars of the Great" from a museum near Niagara Falls that he and his partner at the CNE's Bavarian Gardens had tried to sell in January. He hoped to bring in 10,000 people and more than one million dollars. He had remarked to the *Toronto Star* on October 20 that "parting with some of the stuff will be like selling off ... family history." Practically, he would add to his capital and clear space in his winter quarters for working equipment. Symbolically, he would refurbish his reputation among the Toronto elite and cast off further remnants of his carnie heritage. He could no longer afford, at least for a time, his quixotic role as preserver of carnival history. Despite the planning and the sacrifice, his memorabilia had less value than he had imagined and the auction earned him far less than he had hoped.

The CNE continued to disappoint. Attendance dropped again in 1980 and this time ride grosses also fell, by 20 percent. A roller coaster accident injured 22 people. Attendance and grosses were off at two of the four western exhibitions. The eastern road show units were merely maintaining the status quo. Some of the other big exhibitions, notably the PNE and the Big E, did well, but cash flow was not growing to cover increased capital outlay and interest payments. The show once more raised ride prices to counter falling ridership. A company spokesman put the best light on its affairs, claiming in *Amusement Business* in September that diversification tempered the gusts buffeting the flagship CNE operation. Jim admitted to *Amusement Business* in January 1981 that the 1980 season "was particularly off because we had such a bad CNE and so much of the season is wrapped into that. Then everything else fell kinda flat."

By the 1980s, some observers and commentators were ready to write off not only the travelling carnival, but the old-style, family-run amusement park. The North American theme park industry was finally starting to emulate the Disneyland model and big investors were building big parks with big rides that did not have to travel, one popping up in the Conklin backyard. Plans for Canada's Wonderland were announced in the spring of 1979. The initial investment of $115 million would build a 320-acre park north of Toronto, set to open in 1981. Toronto would finally get the park that Jim had been unable to find a way to build. The summer midway on the CNE grounds was puny in comparison and the prospect of Wonderland sent the CNE board scrambling for ways to cope, including renegotiating the Conklin contract.

The Bank Calls In Its Loan

By the end of the 1980 season, the Canadian Imperial Bank of Commerce (CIBC), which held the Conklin debt, had had enough. It decided the show was not getting the returns required to keep that debt under control and it called in its note for seven million dollars. Some of the show executives were driving to the Norfolk County Fair in Simcoe on a cool, grey morning in early October when Jim read the letter to them. The bank demanded payment of four million dollars by November 9. Alfie broke the silence: "You think the fucks would have waited until Remembrance Day!"[4]

Having just lived through the best of times, show employees recall this period as their introduction to the worst of times. Uncertainty pervaded the organization, and word of its impending bankruptcy got out. As reported in the January 17, 1981, issue of *Amusement Business*, Jim knew of "the rumours of his going out of business or selling out" and the "anonymous phone calls ... made to his fairs in an effort to discredit him and his organization." He admitted that he had "reorganized his organization, financially, last fall," but claimed to have done so only in response to losses at the CNE. The season had been especially off because of the CNE, but other dates had also been down. He insisted that the show's "present plans are to continue with the entire operation, although there are no plans to do anything adventuresome." Despite his public denials, he had missed the chance to consolidate in an orderly way, and now Conklin Shows was being forced to shrink or sink.

Bastido, the accountant, argued with the CIBC that if it put the company into receivership, the bank would get nothing for the show's assets. The only way anybody would realize value on those assets was if the bank allowed the show to stay in business. But the bank would not give Jim any leeway and he thought he might have to shut down. Operating expenses that winter were covered by the take from the Undercurrent arcade, hidden away at the bottom of the CN Tower, its revenue siphoned through a secret account of which the CIBC was unaware.

Management streamlined operations, restructuring the business to focus on the travelling units, and dropping all side projects. Within three years Jim cut full-time staff from over 100 to 30. He set up Conklin Shows International, an independent subsidiary for the American show and appointed 20-year-old Frank its president. The show sold as much equipment as it could do without and still keep operating. It had already cut down its U.S. route and now reduced operations at the lion safaris in Quebec and Ontario. It kept its co-management gig with York–Hannover for the parks in Vancouver and Niagara Falls for 1981, then bowed out, letting the PNE go at the same time.

Jim pulled out all the stops to save his company. After the end of the 1980 regular route for Frank's rides, Jim made a deal with James Strates to keep them working late in the season at the Strates show's dates in the American South. He booked rides with Amusements of America at spring still dates and the Central Canada Exhibition in Ottawa. He called in personal favours to raise as much cash as he could, including a loan from Sam Ganz whose plush animal toy business had been built on sales to Conklin Shows. He held the bank at bay and the show narrowly avoided bankruptcy. It took until the end of the 1981 season for management to stabilize finances. The crisis brought tremendous stress to bear on Jim and, suitably chastened, he would never again expand as ambitiously as he had during the first decade after his father's death. He had shown his resourcefulness in the face of adversity, but it had taken a toll.

DOWN FROM THE PINNACLE

The first rule of the carnival business is, if anybody wants to give you money, take it…. The second rule is, try not to give it back….

There're other rules, too. One of them is, whenever it rains, you should take a nap. That's a pretty good rule. It's depressing in this business when it rains. It's really hard when you're working a game or a food stand or standing on a ride and it's raining. There's probably not much business and you're probably going to get wet. So it's very uncomfortable. Then it becomes demoralizing because time drags.

Another rule is, never assume anything in this business.

There's the rule that you'll never get it completely right. It's like a lot layout. You come and you lay out the lot, and you'll never get it right. The reason why is that there are too many variables. You can always walk around a lot and say, Jeez, I wish I had done that differently. It always looks different once you open. It's never as good as you want it to be. Sometimes you do a better job than others. Thank God for that, otherwise it would be very demoralizing. You got a job that you've been doing all your life and you never got it right yet.

I learned lot layout from Pat Marco. I first started with him in Ontario. Then it was Jim Conklin. I don't know how many years I was on the dummy end of that tape with Jim Conklin. It was a long time. We used to go out to western Canada and we always went in ahead, did it, and then came back. Jim was laying out the lots then. I think I was on the dummy end for at least 10 years. You learn a lot. He enjoyed doing it because he had a background in architecture and design. He'd see things that you wouldn't see.

Sight lines are more important today even than then. They can really make or break a layout. How the public sees it when they're walking in. You get some ugly spots and you've got to try to cover them up. Really what they are is bad sight lines. You know what it looks like on the front, but you've got to be thinking about if anybody can see the back and if they can, how much. That's probably the key thing with the layout, apart from the fact that you've got to get it all to fit. The sight lines are very important. The corners shouldn't be sharp, they should be rounded.

If you had an empty field and there was nothing in it, you'd put all the rides in the back and all the games in the front. But you don't have an empty field, you have a parking lot and it has buildings on it. It also has two, three, or four places where the people come in, so you have to take in those considerations.

In the '70s the CNE was 20 days, not 18, we opened on the Wednesday. It started to lose attendance in 1980, the recession year. It started right here, we felt it first because we're a cash business. The next two years there was quite a recession. Attendance suffered badly in '80, '81. Wonderland opened in '81, so that didn't help. The first part of the '80s was tough here. The back part of the '80s, it started to build up a bit.

Winnipeg moved out to the edge of town, out to the racetrack. They used to be at Polo Park, close to downtown. We were there 22 years. It was getting a little rough down there. They used to have a free gate starting at 11 and everybody came in, the good, the bad, and the ugly. Now, in this new facility, you don't see very much of the ugly anymore. It's a family kind of park. You have to drive there or take the bus. So you don't see the bad element.

You don't see the ugly here anymore either. They left with the other two million, they don't bother coming down. We had some tough years here. The Labour Day tradition was bad here all through the '80s. It started in '79. We saw swarming in '79 and we didn't know what it was. I didn't know what the hell was going on, although we found out after.

Interview with Alfie Phillips Jr., Sept. 1, 2005

★   ★   ★

The economic context in which the wounded Conklin Shows struggled to survive was the worst since the Depression. Government attempts to bring inflation under control by driving up interest rates failed, instead plunging North America into a deep recession in 1981. Canadian gross domestic product dropped by 6.7 percent over a period of 18 months and unemployment peaked at over 12.5 percent. Canadian output would not be restored until 1984 and unemployment only gradually fell back to the 9-to-10 percent range by 1986. In this context, carnival companies were failing, especially in the United States, and gloom pervaded the industry.

Struggling to Survive

In his president's report in the June 1981 issue of *Jackpot*, Jim cited "the perils (natural and economic) of another operating season," noting that his "instinct of self-preservation" gives him a thrill every May because he's gotten "through the winter." He gave credit to satirist Will Cuppy's *The Decline and Fall of Practically Everybody* for helping him make it. In summing up that season in the public press, he observed that "business has been flat," rides in particular.[5] He thought the rides were down because of "the demographic configuration, with less kids. There is no solution," he concluded. Looking ahead, he thought "the business will be relatively static … with ever increasing expenses."

He continued to juggle the routes of the two Ontario units, keeping most of the fairs, but cutting still dates and leaving some weeks open. The U.S. route was down to Dade County, the Big E, and the Arkansas State Fair. He had stripped the American unit so bare that of the 40 to 50 major rides at these fairs, only a dozen or so were Conklin-owned. The Strates show helped out at the Big E, Cumberland Valley Shows at Arkansas, and both shows, along with Amusements of America, at Dade County. Jim added the Gulf State Fair in Mobile, Alabama, in 1982, lost the Arkansas fair in 1985, and replaced it in 1986 by taking a fair in Yonkers, New York, from Deggeller Attractions. This latter acquisition was revenge for Jim and his ally, James Strates, who had helped start the Yonkers fair in 1981 and lost it to the Deggellers in 1985, the same year they took back a small county fair in their Florida hometown that Conklin Shows had acquired when it bought the Magic Midway.

Problems with the CNE would not go away. Despite a record $1.3 million profit in 1979, the Toronto Metro council got panicked by a few years of falling attendance. In early 1981, council replaced the association's general manager with its own appointee and gave two years' notice of termination of the contract with Conklin Shows. Vice-president Alfie Phillips told *Amusement Business* on January 31 that the notice was only "a mild surprise," but, estimating that "25 to 30 per cent of the Conklin empire's income derives from the Exhibition," admitted that if the show could not renew its contract it would have to be radically restructured.

Metro council wanted to relocate the midway, impose operating standards, obtain a better revenue-sharing deal, and, to address increasing public complaints, regulate prices and length of time for rides. But they might go even further. On March 28, *Amusement Business* reported a leak about ambitious plans to turn the CNE grounds into "a glittering year-round recreational complex and trade center over the next 10 years at a total cost of $700 million." There would be a huge, covered sports dome, "formal gardens and landscaping, with a skating rink, bars, and restaurants," and an underground link to the CN Tower. The sports dome would eventually be built east of the grounds, but a convention centre and trade fair building would come. Officials said that the midway contracts were cancelled because they could not "implement any large scale renovations with the midway ... remaining as it is today." The new manager, "a younger aggressive management consultant who is considering installing a casino to boost sagging attendance," let it be known that "whatever happens, the old-style midway seems to be doomed."

When Wonderland opened in 1981, people found its rides safer, cleaner, better run, and more thrilling than those at the Ex. Adding credibility to this perception, there were five accidents on CNE rides that season, including collisions on the Wild Cat and the Flyer, for a total of 19 injuries, all minor. Jim told *Amusement Business* that September, "I don't think Wonderland ... hurt us at all, to speak of. It's hard to tell." After the Ex that year, at which the CNE association lost $1.9 million, it negotiated a new short-term contract with Conklin that included improved safety standards. Attendance had fallen below three million for the first time in 20 years, while the Ohio State Fair exceeded that mark for the first time. Having fallen from its pinnacle, the CNE would never again be the world's largest fair and Conklin Shows shared heavily in its decline.

With 12 consecutive days of rain and a slumping economy, attendance at the 1982 CNE fell to 2.2 million, the lowest since 1937 and a figure that both the Ohio and the Texas state fairs beat. Metro council took management away from the CNE association and placed it in the hands of an appointed board of governors. As reported in the *Globe and Mail* on August 18, council approved a feasibility study for a new trade centre and sports complex in the spring of 1983. It developed a seven-year, $313 million plan. The new facilities would require demolishing "one of the Ex's most cherished attractions — the Midway."

The proposal became a political football. Metro politicians had targeted the structures built by Patty, features that made the midway of the CNE unique, including the Flyer, "the most-loved permanent installation on the Midway." Getting rid of them would enable council to transform Exhibition Park into a commercial space, free of its carnie trappings and its reliance on Conklin Shows. The economic and social circumstances had changed, as had the personalities, since the days of Patty's struggles with city hall, and Jim's campaign would turn out differently than his dad's. Council could pretend to cater to public concerns about safety and other issues to achieve its own economic ends. Although Jim showed no inclination to dominate the CNE midway as Patty had, even Patty might have failed to comprehend and control the forces challenging the family's hold on it. A shadow had fallen over the Flyer that would never lift.

Old Ways and New

As plans to gut the CNE developed, maybe the masses could be led to cherish the old-time sleaze of the midway, in contrast with sanitized theme parks like Wonderland or the CNE as envisaged by Metro council. Jim continued to insist that "even with giant, super-sophisticated amusement parks ... the travelling carnival" still had a place: "We really offer a different product.

Ours is brassier, noisier, less expensive and more surprising."[6] He thought sideshows might make a comeback supported by nostalgia and irony. He felt "there should be more emphasis on adults' and kids' attractions and less on thrill rides" and "it might be time to bring back the side show because of the changing demographics."[7]

In 1983, 10 years after freak shows had been banned at the Ex, Jim brought back a sideshow, calling on Ward Hall and Chris Christ, old-time impresarios who almost alone had kept the tradition alive. Their ten-in-one, with a fat man, a human pincushion, a sword swallower, a blockhead, a fire-eater, an ossified woman, a knife thrower, a tattooed lady, a dwarf, and an electric chair illusion, travelled the West with Conklin and then played Toronto. They also brought an oddities museum, a wax museum, and headless girl and snake girl illusions.

Jim's instincts were off, however, and the Hall and Christ show, a synthetic production that quoted a time long gone, was out of place on a midway dominated by expensive, technically advanced thrill machines. Neither could Jim use the old-time carnie aura to salvage the midway at the Exhibition from those who would pave it over. Corporate sponsors saved the 1983 CNE, contributing two million dollars, beside which any sideshow's contribution to the Ex's income was paltry. That year Conklin & Garrett donated the remaining Antique Carnival equipment to a heritage park in Calgary for a tax concession. The Hall and Christ sideshow survived a few more years in the United States, in its last season joining up with a circus to enable it to tour. The sideshow did not come back to the Ex again, nor did the masses.

By the early 1980s, many carnival owners felt that the industry's survival depended on creative measures and new ways of doing business. Some shows focused on contracts and a few actually negotiated reduced percentages with their fairs — what Jim had seemed foolhardy for attempting to achieve unilaterally a few years before. Others boosted corporate sponsorships and promotions, like the Midnight Madness special that had succeeded so well for Conklin Shows from its inception at the Calgary Stampede in 1978. Midways offered early-bird specials, two-for-one date nights, and reduced prices on slow days or through advance sales. Any pretence was used to declare special days with special deals to boost attendance.

Theme parks had educated the public on the advantages of pay-one-price (POP) tickets. One reason the Ohio State Fair was the world's largest in 1981 was the innovation of POP for the whole fair. Wear on equipment and staff was the main disadvantage, as the rides ran without stop. If the ride ticket was bundled with gate admission, farmers and older adults complained that it penalized them, but at many large fairs the agricultural component and attractions for the elderly were becoming negligible.

Jim went on the record as opposed to POP, especially for "the duration of a fair": "I don't think most carnival operators are in favor of it either. You have to look at it over a long-term agreement, and I don't think it will stand up. It's hard on the equipment and it's hard on the staff."[8] He thought POP was "a great promotion, but it won't work for the run of the fair; it would burn itself out."[9] Despite resistance throughout the industry, POP became a standard promotion.

Through all these means, especially POP and advance sales, and through continual restructuring, the Conklin executive managed to bring the company back to health. Income was static through the early 1980s, but they found ways to cut costs, like buying cheaper light bulbs, which added up, given the thousands they used. The purchase of two computers in late 1982 enabled them to eliminate three staff and within a few years computerize what were once time-consuming administrative tasks. Jim told *Amusement Business* on September 10, 1983, that the "costs of doing business" would "continue to be one of the most serious problems facing us today." His way of keeping costs down was to "control the number and the efficiency of our staff."

Operations remained stable through the middle of the decade. Barry Jamieson managed one Ontario unit and, after Pat Marco's death, experienced veterans, including Dottie Marco, Pat's widow, ran the other, while Frank ran the U.S. show. They all had a core of reliable, dedicated managers. Grosses continued to climb at Dade County and the Big E, fluctuate at the western Canadian fairs, and trend downward at the CNE. The smaller Ontario fairs held their own. The U.S. subcontractors who travelled with Frank were hurt by the low Canadian dollar when they played the West during the summer but finished with strong fall dates when they returned with the show to the States. The economy of the Canadian West declined with the oil industry, while the Ontario economy, led by the manufacturing sector, recovered. For the 1984

Alfie Phillips, 1987.

Stampede, the show "lowered prices of rides, at the request of the Stampede board, because of tough economic times in the once oil-rich area."[10] By 1983 the Undercurrent arcade at the CN Tower was the only stationary operation held by Conklin & Garrett.

In 1985 Alfie was made president of Conklin & Garrett, the parent company, while Jim remained chairman. That year Jim became involved with a company set up to refurbish and export rides for an amusement park in Guangzhou, China. Conklin & Garrett was focusing on its core business, travelling carnivals, while Jim would find other ways to explore the opportunities that money provided.

RECOVERY

That was the heyday of the show. The best this show ever did was '87, '88, and '89. The show had it all together. We had a really good ride lineup, we had all the Zacchini shit. The show looked good. Jim was still buying new stuff. We were having banner western Canadas, we were having banner Canadian National Exhibitions, we were having banner South. Things were pretty good. We were going to Puerto Rico. It was really together at that point. That was when I was proudest of the show.

It was September 3, 1989, we broke a million dollars gross for one day for the very first time with the show. It was elation. It was something else. It was right here on a Sunday. The Rolling Stones played the grandstand and when we read the financial reports the next day, numbers were jumping off the sheet, like, Birthday grosses of $18,000, $22,000 from a waffle stand. Numbers that we'd never seen before. I just remember the excitement of being part of that day, hitting a million bucks in one day. Seeing a million dollars in cash sitting all in one place, that was pretty wild too.

Interview with Greg "Scooter" Korek, Sept. 2, 2005

★   ★   ★

While the U.S. economy recovered, fuel prices, inflation and unemployment continued to hurt the show in Canada until mid-decade. Ride grosses began to grow again in the United States, but remained flat in Canada, where games revenue was proportionally higher and saw increases, largely to the benefit of independent concessionaires. Jim tried out new food stands, including health food and vegetarian offerings that, oddly enough, did not appeal to midway patrons. Resisting all trends, carnival food joints continue to observe the mantra, "We fry it, they buy it."

Finances had recovered enough by the 1982 season that Jim could buy a $700,000 Ranger, one of the first in North America, from the German ride manufacturer Huss. He traded it the next year for a similar ride, the Rainbow, from the same company, just so he could have something new, "Because that's the first thing everybody asks, What's new?"[11] Accompanied by the CNE general manager to the 1983 Oktoberfest, Jim bought a new German music ride and 3-D cinema, and then found a deal that appealed to the sense of daring he had been forced to suppress after his struggles with the bank.

Since introducing the Wild Mouse, the Schwarzkopfs had led the world in the production of portable coasters and the Conklins had owned many of them. In 1981 the Schwarzkopfs built the Doppel Looper, a coaster with two 360-degree loops, for a German showman. After its sale to a Belgium amusement park fell through, it became available for other takers. Despite the two-million-dollar price tag and ignoring what the bank might say, Jim Conklin wanted to own it and his son wanted to move it down the road.

The Doppel Looper is a massive ride, best suited to a stationary park, and was partly the Conklin response to Wonderland. It weighs 450 tons, travels on 25 trailers, and needs two generators to run. It requires eight experienced personnel, an 80-ton hydraulic crane, and six days to set up. No show before or since has tried to move such a piece of equipment over the road. Taking on the challenge, Frank Conklin at 24 put another notch in his belt. For the first appearance of the Doppel Looper at the 1984 Dade County Youth Fair, crowds stretched for two blocks and at the CNE, its only other date that year, it had a similar impact. In 1985 Frank added the Calgary Stampede to the Doppel Looper route for one year and then increased its dates to four per year, all in

Frank Conklin, 1980.

the United States, except for the CNE. He could not afford to carry it on the western Canadian route.

In 1984, to meet requirements for space to store Frank's new rides and equipment yet to be bought, Conklin Shows International moved into new winter quarters at West Palm Beach with 10 acres of land. The fuel crisis over, Jim complained about the cost of rides and their "storage and main-tenance in winter quarters, not to mention their continued refurbishment," as one of "the hidden costs of show business that has been skyrocketing in the past few years."[12] The cost of winter quarters, he claimed, had "doubled" in "five years." For his and Frank's conglomeration of shows and the equip-ment they owned, now over 100 rides, it probably had, although not entirely owing to inflation.

The Conklins' attraction to expensive Schwarzkopf machines continued. Possibly because of his own hubris, "the old Schwarzkopf Company, head-ed up for years by master builder Anton Schwarzkopf, declared bankruptcy" and went into receivership in November 1983, just before completing the sale of the Doppel Looper to the Conklins.[13] A triple loop coaster designed by Schwarzkopf before his company went bankrupt debuted at the Munich Oktoberfest in 1984 and was the first ride ever to be closed because of exces-sive crowds, but it was not for sale. The company restructured under a new owner and came out with the first portable Flume water ride in 1985. The Conklins bought a used Flume for Frank's show in 1988. It cost over a million dollars, required 14 trailers to move, and 10 experienced personnel needed eight days to set it up. The Flume was retired in 1990 because of the effort to move it. A Wild River Raft ride from an Italian firm, Soriani and Moser, also worth a million, replaced the Flume, but had so many mechanical problems it was returned to the factory.

The Conklins eventually put both the Flume and the Doppel Looper up for sale, price to be negotiated. They sold the Flume to Farrow Shows, which booked it back in at some of the major Conklin events. The Doppel Looper needed to gross $10,000 a day to make it worthwhile to set up and was eventu-ally mothballed in Florida.

Ride Safety and Insurance

Just as the industry was coming back from the recession, a new crisis arose over ride safety and insurance. After a number of sensational accidents in the United States in the first half of the 1980s, a few with fatalities, some states began imposing mandatory inspections with high fees attached. The Canadian Standards Association (CSA) had begun in 1982 to develop a midway safety code. John MacDonald, Jim's former ride superintendent, chaired the CSA committee. He held workshops at the Canadian Association of Fairs and Exhibitions convention for several years, beginning in 1983. The CSA code was gradually adopted by most of the provinces, to the general satisfaction of ride operators because it provided transparency and predictability. Safety codes tended not to be so clear in many of the states. The American Society for Testing and Materials struck a committee in the middle of the decade to address problems with ride safety programs and develop national ride standards. Ride safety became a more serious issue locally when there was an accident, like when the Dade County fair board had to deal with concerns following a fatal accident on a Strates Octopus in the next county.

Standards and codes could not, however, stave off the North American insurance crisis. "Excessive claims" for accidents and injuries had been successful and "large losses [were] paid out by the insurance industry."[14] Because U.S. courts were "awarding massive punitive damages," rates in the States were expected to "double, triple and quadruple" in 1985.[15] The "insurance outlook" was a "concern" throughout the amusement industry.[16] There were attempts to form an insurance company just for carnivals and amusement parks and to develop new formulas for liability rates. Some insurance companies stopped writing policies for carnivals altogether, while others doubled their rates for half the coverage. At the same time, fair officials began to raise their requirements for liability insurance.

Although the insurance crisis was worse in the United States than in Canada, the main financial hit against Conklin Shows for 1985 was "an unspecified increase in insurance premiums."[17] The show had to carry coverage of $10 million at the CNE that year and threatened to pull out the next year until it was reduced to three million dollars. The board of the Westchester

County Fair in Yonkers wanted $10 million in liability insurance, and they only got the fair "after protracted negotiations ... over how much insurance the show should have."[18] Cumberland Valley Shows had to hold the Dade County contract for Conklin Shows in 1986 because it was the only organization among the combined companies that had the necessary $10 million policy. Despite this, Darwin Fuchs, the fair's general manager, knew who to credit for "one of the strongest lineups of supers in North America ... Conklin always has the highest-capacity rides. They are superb."[19]

While the Conklin ride record remained clean, with no fatalities, Jim's ride had a close call in December 1982. One snowy, early winter night he was rear-ended in his BMW sedan at a red light in Brantford. He regained consciousness in a local hospital and took several months to recover. Luckily, it was the off-season, so he could look after company affairs from a stationary position, but the accident was a rough way to start his sixth decade.

Other long-time Conklin executives and associates were not so fortunate at cheating death. Neil Webb, who had joined Patty as treasurer to save the show from bankruptcy in 1933 and had retired in 1972, died in 1981 at the age of 79. Pat Marco, who came to Conklin Shows when it took over the Sullivan operation and had been lot manager in the east and then the west, never retired before his death in 1982 at 67. Art Lewis, to whom Patty and Frank had subcontracted their Quebec fairs from 1936 to 1938, died in 1984. Brothers George and Gus Pappas, who had food concessions with the show for many years, died within three months of each other in late 1985. George Hall, who had worked gambling operations with the show for 50 years, died in 1988. Andrew King, who had printed posters for Patty and Sullivan for 30 years, died in 1981 at the age of 96. King's son had gotten into the carnival business through Patty and, coming full circle, his grandsons bought rides from Jim and played the CNE and the western circuit with the show.

Other associates of Patty lived on. Sam and Jack Ganz had started out making stuffed animals by hand in their home and selling them to Patty at the Ex in the late 1940s. By 1980 they and their sons ran Canada's largest plush manufacturer, the exclusive supplier to the Conklins in Canada, as well as to the PNE and big fairs in the Maritimes. From a family of Italian trapeze artists who came to America in 1931, Teo Zacchini began building and operating dark rides in 1949, travelling with Royal American Shows for 10 years before joining Conklin Shows when Jim stripped the show down in 1980. In 1982 Zacchini bought and rebuilt a Cakewalk, an old ride from the 1940s that had once belonged to Patty, and took it out on Jim's midway. He stayed with the Conklins for another 10 years before he died in 1993, and his son kept dark rides and funhouses with the show after that. Don Campbell, who had built his company by providing rides for Patty's midway throughout the 1960s and left after the 1972 season because Jim wanted too much money, came back to Conklin Shows in 1984 with a new Gravitron. To make it pay for itself, Campbell needed to work the ride at bigger fairs than he could contract on his own.

Meanwhile, Metro council was having its way in remaking the CNE. When the CNE board of governors appointed councillor Winfield Stockwell general manager after the 1982 Ex, they gave him a mandate to boost corporate sponsorship and actually reduce attendance figures. This was to satisfy the theory that when the numbers were too high, dense crowds of unhappy patrons were getting stuck on the midway and missing the corporate exhibits in the buildings. Stockwell stopped releasing daily attendance figures in 1983 and total attendance in 1984. An intensified corporate sponsorship campaign in 1983 brought in two million dollars, $1.4 million over the previous year, and that rose to four million dollars by 1986. As intended, attendance dropped by more than 300,000 in 1984 and the Conklin midway lost $500,000 off its gross. Attendance hovered a little over two million for the rest of the decade and the gross remained flat. Stockwell catered to corporations at the expense of carnies.

The symbiosis between Conklin Shows and the CNE board of directors, their mutually beneficial interdependence, was over. When the show "celebrated its 50th anniversary at the fair" in 1987, they designed "a special crest" and produced a yearbook.[20] An *Amusement Business* headline on September 28 said, "Conklin Looks to Future After 50 Years At CNE," but its best years were behind it. The stature of the Ex was in decline and the Conklin reputation — and any chance to increase its revenues — now hung on the Canadian West and the big U.S. state fairs.

Then there was trouble with rides at the CNE. When the Ontario Amusement Devices Act was implemented in 1988, 31 of 72 rides, including eight majors, were unable to open at the Ex because the show failed to supply the necessary documentation. Show management had gambled that the inspectors would not shut them down and the inspectors had called their bluff. They scrambled to get their papers in order and all rides were running by the weekend, but the show estimated it lost $400,000. They turned their fortunes around the following year to play their best Ex of the 1980s, with a record one-day gross of one million dollars on the closing day, which in hindsight would turn out to be something of a last hurrah.

The Top 50 Fairs

In 1982 *Amusement Business* had published its first year-end compilation of the top 50 fairs in North America based on attendance, inherently a questionable number since fairs used a variety of means to report, misreport, or not report attendance figures. The CNE was third and four other Conklin fairs — the Big E, the Stampede, Dade County, and Klondike Days — were in the top 25. The following year, the trade paper published a list of top carnival companies, ranked by the number of top 50 fairs they played and attendance at those fairs. Still playing five of the 50, Conklin Shows led the industry with a total attendance of 5,892,000. The show held its rank in 1984, falling just shy of 5.6 million. In both years, attendance totals for other shows playing three or four of the top 50 were half or less than the Conklin total. In 1985 Conklin Shows fell to second place. Deggeller Attractions, having taken the Ohio State Fair from Pugh Shows, leapt to number one with total attendance of 5,846,000. Conklin returned to number one in 1986.

These rankings say little about the financial success of the shows but do contain multiple ironies. Deggeller Attractions had been formed several years before by sons of the owners of the Deggeller Spectacular Magic Midway who, after they overextended themselves, Jim Conklin had bought out in 1978. The liabilities that came with that purchase and Conklin Shows' inability to run the Magic Midway at a profit had contributed to the near collapse of the Conklin empire. The Deggeller sons, learning from the mistakes of their fathers and the Conklins, built a leaner show and took back most of the Magic

Midway fairs, as well as fairs like Ohio State and Yonkers that more estab-lished shows had considered their own.

Jim and Frank learned, too, and returned the U.S. show to Patty's prac-tice of booking the fairs and letting other companies fill their midways with equipment that did not burden the Conklin overhead. They, like Patty, in-vested in a small collection of extremely expensive spectacular rides as a draw and built their reputations with fair boards primarily as producers of well-run, impressive midways. Attendance at all the show's major ex-hibitions other than the Ex continued to grow, with a few setbacks due to weather. The Big E saw one dramatic setback in 1989 with 10 days of tor-rential rains resulting in a 20 percent drop in both attendance and Conklin ride grosses.

The two Ontario units were more self-sufficient, had fewer spectaculars, and played smaller spots. They warmed up at spring still dates and counted on a couple of strong weekends early in July, playing through both the Canada Day and Independence Day holidays at the 10-day International Freedom Festival in Windsor, but their main season began with the Kingston fair at the end of July. They maintained good relations with the communities in which they worked but counted their attendance numbers in the tens rath-er than hundreds of thousands that the big show pulled. Jim's staff managed the shows, while he dropped in for occasional visits with them and the fair committees. In 1986 he resurrected the World's Finest brand, applying it to the Bernard route, and formed a third Ontario unit, calling it Supershows. Supershows targeted company picnics and small festivals, but only played six or seven of these in its first few seasons.

The routes of the two main Ontario units remained stable throughout the 1980s and '90s, each playing some 25 fairs, celebrations, and still dates from late May to early October. Conklin & Garrett added Prince Albert, Saskatchewan — a fair Patty had played 50 years before — to the western Canada route in 1987, then dropped it in 1994. In 1988, Conklin International took the South Carolina State Fair back from the Deggellers, who had taken it from them in 1979. As the first step in an expansion plan, the Canadian com-pany bought Crown Amusements in 1989 to play smaller fairs in Alberta and Saskatchewan but got rid of it a few years later. As for the amusement park business, the company had gotten out at the right time, as Crystal Beach and Belmont Park were going under during these years.

By the end of the 1980s, the shows under Conklin & Garrett were running smoothly and did not require much of Jim's attention. He reported that 1988 had been their best season yet. He still handled negotiations with fair boards and was engaged in strategic planning, like the company's unrealized ambition to develop an Oktoberfest theme park in Florida in the late 1980s and its strategic game plan for the '90s, but he spent less time on his midways. He redirected his energy into restoring vintage merry-go-rounds and other antique pieces, buying new rides in Europe and old celebrity cars in the United States, and investing in a fishing lodge on the shores of the Gulf of Mexico and a conference centre on the shores of Georgian Bay. He set up a publishing company to publish *Household Info: A Personal Classified Directory* and *Patty Conklin's Great Carnival Dictionary* and began to write "a book about the life and times of his illustrious, colorful and often flamboyant father."[21] He had always been willing to delegate to trusted staff and would always haunt his midways, but as he entered his late 50s he let his grip loosen, slipping into the shadows so that the majority of Conklin employees, other than a handful of insiders spread throughout the various units, never really knew for whom, ultimately, they worked.

The Last Generation

(1990–2004)

The carnival industry responded to the approaching turn of the millennium by evolving further away from its arcane ancestry, adapting to a business model like the other industries of distraction. Other companies with regional monopolies like his own had emerged, while Jim Conklin, persistent in respecting the carnival's bloodlines because he could afford to be, tried running a niche outfit that recalled an earlier time. But the DNA of carnivals and of their owners was changing. The multi-headed hydra that the Conklin group of companies had become continued to mutate, until the generation to which it had been left, left it.

SUCCESSION

So, Jim took the ride rentals and turned it into Supershows. He revamped it all with some more equipment. He got the Superman emblem that we use. He acquired the rights, we have permission as long as we buy authentic Warner Brothers shirts and that…. There's no problem at all as long as we don't cause them any embarrassment or infringe on any of their stuff. We pay top dollar for our shirts. I think it's a neat idea.

I usually take out 14 or 15 rides, which is still not a bad size. We usually have roughly seven or eight concessions. And a candy floss and normal stuff like that. It's getting to the point where, especially malls and stuff like that, we can't fit in. We're booked throughout the summer. We lose a few here and there, and then we get better ones back. It's an experiment, you try a spot that you think is going to be good, and it's terrible.

We never expected Merrickville to be any good. It's a beautiful little town and it's the nicest fair board. They do everything out of their way for this fair. It's never going to be an A fair. It's always going to be a B or C fair for attendance. We get along very well with them and it's sad. This year the weather held up and they did their end of it, but it wasn't very good. It's been around for a hundred and fifty years, I'm not sure.

What happened was that, 25 years ago Conklins used to do that fair, but then because of geographics, it was way out of our range to go up there for a small fair. So, we let it go. They were getting a show from Quebec in there and for a couple of years they had nothing but trouble. They had the rides shut down, they had electrical problems, and they had the whole show shut down at one point. They'd half their rides running. It takes one year or two years to ruin a spot; it takes a lot of years to get it back. People don't forget that stuff. We've done such a good job, and the fair board has done such a good job to bring people back, but so far it just hasn't worked.

Then Newington, which is about an hour south of here, that's one of our good spots, Stormont County. It's a big fair. The town has one store and it's closed up. It doesn't even make sense, because there's no real big place around it, but they've just built such a good name. Almonte turned out real good; this was one of the best years they've had for a lot of years. Mr. Conklin really wanted to go for that one and I'd heard that it wasn't that good. We just brought all their numbers right back up to where they should have been. Jim will risk it. This is the first year that we played Arnprior, that had really gone by the way with other shows. Mr. Conklin tells us where to go after stuff.

Collingwood is another one of our big spots. Mr. Conklin brought that fair in. Actually, it was the World's Finest's fair, but scheduling put us back in there. We're glad to be there. The boss is only ten minutes away. He says he watches us from his house with the binoculars. He's up on the hill. We like Collingwood, it's a real farming community. A lot of tourists, too.

We brought back a lot of fairs that everybody kind of dumped. Some of them there's a reason for dumping, but a lot of it's just scheduling. Like Dorchester, just by London, we turned them right around. For years nobody wanted to touch them — there wasn't the grosses — but nobody was putting much into it. We put 12 rides in there one year and some joints, and I think that place has got some potential.

With a lot of these fair boards, the board members are getting older and there's nobody there to take it over. Dorchester is getting younger members, but a lot of these other ones are not. Their shows, the judging of cattle and that, is just falling away. Merrickville really has a good 4-H club and good judging, and they get a lot of sponsors.

The government still puts a little prize money in, but not as much as they used to. I don't understand it. There's not enough money for judging and stuff. The government tries to help with tax breaks and they do a lot for the fairs, if they can just keep them going. I think it's just the membership.

I remember that in Simcoe we always tore down in the snow. The weather's changed though. We set up in the snow, we started the first of April this year. We were in London, setting up in the snow. It was nasty weather, snow on the midway when we opened. People came out, but not a lot. Those early dates are tough. You're trying to get everything done in the winter. We do a lot in the winter; it's a lot of work. Plus, you're away from your family enough as it is, eh.

The business has been good to me — Mr. Conklin, you know. I've never worked for another show and I never would. I've never worked for anybody but him. When I first went down South, I was kind of like Frank's assistant; Frank had his show. He was very good to me, I couldn't have asked for a better person. He treated me very well.

The younger guys at that time, they all wanted to come down South and work for Frank. I saw my opportunity with some older guys that were the same age as Jim. I figured that these guys were going to be retiring and I wanted to be right there. Then I got back and I was here. I never thought, a couple of years ago, back in '98 or so, I never thought about it, but Jim talked about retirement. It didn't even dawn on me, "How could he retire?" I thought, jeez, maybe I made a mistake. But I've never regretted it since then. I would never work for anybody else in this company or in the business.

I've worked for him for 36 years, but up until the past few years I was never close. And still, you get intimidated by him. Not that he tries. He's a very quiet, soft-spoken man, but what he wants is what he wants. People mistake his being shy and quiet, as not real strong. But I'll tell you, you get him mad and you're in trouble. He knows what he wants and he knows the business like nobody else. When he has to express himself forcefully, he does, and I've been on the receiving end of it. Everyone says, "How can you take that?" And I say, "Well, you know what, I've still got a job." You get what you deserve.

Interview with Dave McKelvey, Aug. 24, 2005

★　★　★

Jim Conklin had taken his father's show, playing the CNE and a handful of Ontario fairs, and created a large, complex corporation operating across the continent, one that could only survive with a continually increasing influx of capital. He had overseen the transformation of the carnival into an amusement park on wheels with huge, expensive rides. He had cleaned up his midways, figuratively and physically, eliminating flat stores and roughies; adding uniforms, guest relations, themed rides and games, and rest spots with benches and planters; and implementing guaranteed prize giveaways at games and universal coupons at rides, a pay-one-price and advance sales promotions, a computerized office and corporate sponsorships — the Conko brand reigning over all.

Along with the growth of his corporation, Jim had seen the beginning of the decline of the traditional fair. Many factors were hurting country fairs: changing demographics and urbanization; changes in the agricultural industry and in government policies toward fairs; decreasing income from admission fees and lost grants; and increasing costs for salaries, insurance, infrastructure, and energy. Attendance at most Ontario fairs was falling. Meanwhile, Jim had gotten older and grown distant from the operational level of his company, especially at its big regional exhibitions, events that were still thriving and where the show entertained masses. He left running the show at the big events to others, while he accompanied the country fair into its autumn years.

When the third generation took over, the transformation of Conklin Shows seemed to be complete, while the decline of the country fair was still underway. When asked early in his career if he was king of the carnies, Frank rescinded the title: "In the first place, we don't call ourselves carnies.... We're businessmen. There's big money invested."[1] He was 22 at the time. "Patty was a showman, a promoter," Frank has said, while he is "just a businessman, running a business."[2] He has repeated this refrain throughout his career. He spoke of the time of his grandfather's carnival as "an era gone by": "I don't believe it exists any more. It's a business now, just like any other."[3] Frank's identity as a businessman would prevail over his attachment to an industry he believed had disappeared.

Jim and Norma's three children were close in age, born a few years apart in the late 1950s and early '60s. In 1959, Jim and Norma bought a large house in Brantford for the children to grow up in. Their daughters, Patricia and Melissa, were also involved with the show. Trish, Frank's senior by two years, implemented the first guest relations booth in the carnival industry in 1977 and managed it until the early 1980s, and had games on the midway for the rest of the decade. She was variously executive director of marketing, food concessions, and international relations. She took out food stands built to her specifications at the Brantford shop, then sold her games in 1992. She continued her education in the off-season, completing her masters in anthropology with a thesis on the carnival as an "insular ... community within a community," as her father told the *Toronto Star* on May 4, 1992. Melissa, the youngest, came out in 1983 to work in the road show office. She ensured improvements in merchandising, customer service, and operations kept up with the growth of the road show during these years. She worked with vendors and staff and coordinated many aspects of the road show events. Neither Melissa nor Trish had anything to do with running the powerful ride lineup.

Norma had thought Patricia the child most likely to follow in their father's footsteps on the midway, but the opportunities she wanted went to her brother. In 1994, with Jim's backing, she set up Trish's Mini Donuts on Pier 39 in San Francisco. In 1998, she established Trish's Dishes, as an umbrella

Trish, Frank, and Melissa Conklin on one of their midways, 1983.

food service company, under which she opened the San Francisco Chocolate Store; the Hook Restaurant at Pier 39; Sparky's Hollywood Chocolates and Sparky's Mini Donuts at City Walk, Universal Studios, Hollywood; and several hot dog and chowder kiosks in San Francisco. Conko the Clown makes a cameo appearance in the branding of all her businesses.

Melissa left the midway in less than 10 years, married, and settled in Vermont in 1989. In 1992 she became the general manager, co-founder, president, and partner with her father of Redfish Lodge on the Texas gulf coast, which he had purchased as an investment. She continued there until Hurricane Harvey wiped the lodge out in 2017. A few years later, Melissa became the general manager of the Stowehof, a luxury Alpine resort in Vermont.

It was up to their brother, like their grandfather most closely associated with the show's expensive, spectacular rides, to carry on the midway tradition into the third and last generation. To pay for it, Frank had to extend his season and keep his expensive equipment in operation year-round. In 1981 the dozen or so spectaculars that toured under him were worth more than four million dollars. By the end of the decade, with inflation and the addition of pieces like the Rainbow, the Doppel Looper, and the Flume, their value exceeded $15 million. The show booked 20 majors, 35 kiddie rides, and the Doppel Looper for two dates in Puerto Rico over three months in the winter of 1987–88 and sent a similar package in late 1990.

After Conklin Shows' pioneering success in Puerto Rico 10 years earlier, other shows and combinations had been taking their equipment south in the winter. The trend continued despite disasters, like the tour of the Caribbean by Century 21 Shows that Timmins Bissonnette helped set up that led to that company being dissolved, and the trip to South America by a company with which Irvin Deggeller was involved that ended with the Venezuelan government holding its equipment for over a year. The Conklins did not send as much equipment offshore again as they had in 1990, but most years throughout the next decade Frank sent a couple of rides to Puerto Rico under contracts held by other shows. He booked his Mark I roller coaster and Crazy Flip with Amusements of America on its first tour of Puerto Rico in 1995, for instance. His two rides were among the three most popular, but over the next few years he only sent one.

The show combined charity and off-season promotion in a benefit event it sponsored in 1992. On the initiative of show president Alfie Phillips, it stepped up as the "angel" for Inner City Angels, an organization that brought arts performances and workshops to Toronto-area schools, but that was about to fail if it could not find funding. Conklin Shows put on a three-day Toronto Youth Fair in May, offering a pay-one-price for admission and rides, all proceeds going to the arts group. Alfie told the *Globe and Mail* on February 19 that the sponsorship deal was "a natural tie-in" for the show but hoped that it would "provide the stage for rallying further support to such a deserving cause." It was also a sign of his and the show's growing awareness of the value of good corporate citizenship.

Dismantling Patty's Ex

The CNE board of governors continued to erase the carnie stain from the Ex, converting Patty's once-popular playground into a corporate one. Starting after the 1977 Ex with the Laff in the Dark, the board began to tear down the permanent attractions he had built just after the war. At the beginning able to treat the trend as a joke, the show had its photographer snap a commemorative photo of Jim and Alfie hamming it up while taking the last ride on the Laff. But then the Derby Racer, the Auto Skooter, the Magic Carpet, the Glass House, and the concession buildings all followed suit, their salvageable pieces and parts of their decorative fronts rescued to gather dust while waiting for some future museum of the midway.

Jim and Alfie taking the last ride on the Laff in the Dark, 1977.

The Flyer was a landmark of Exhibition Place and the city's waterfront. Despite the efforts of heritage buffs and coaster enthusiasts to stave off its destruction, the board had it demolished in June 1992. The argument that the 39-year-old coaster was structurally unsound was a cover for city politicians to whom it stood as an obstacle to their plans for year-round trade fairs and conventions. With the Flyer gone, CNE officials could reasonably entertain cutting ties with Conklin & Garrett when the current contract ran out after the 1994 fair. In 1993, they began talking about changing the face of the midway, speculating on the new form it might take. The theme for the Ex that season was "More Than Just the Midway."

There was one last monument to the glory days of the Ex that had to go. Jim described "the dismantling of the Alpine Way in 1995 — the last of Patty's permanent rides — as a heartbreak."[4] Having already given up bit by bit the rest of his father's legacy at Exhibition Place, Jim had seen the futility of any attempt to save the cable ride. In 1996 exhibition management began to reduce the number of games on the midway, starting with a 10 percent cut. The National Trade Centre, covering the area where the eastern terminus of the Alpine Way once stood, opened with 1.5 million square feet of exhibit space in 1997.

Patty had started his rehabilitation of the CNE grounds by paving the midway. The rides and buildings he had constructed on top of that pavement under an illusion of their permanence had been stripped away to reveal the massive parking lot with which he had begun. But now it was bordered by the huge trade centre on one side and a six-lane freeway on the other. The wrecking ball took Exhibition Stadium, built in 1948 and former home to major league sports and big concerts, in 1999, replacing it with more pavement.

While the repaving of Patty's paradise actually made it easier for the Conklin executives to integrate it into the Canada-U.S. route and cut down overhead, it also substantially reduced their pull with the CNE board and reduced the midway to a shadow of its former self. Alfie described the transformation:

> You lose all those attractions we had here, the baseball sta-
> dium and the football stadium, the Flyer gone, the Alpine,

gone. All that stuff's gone, which was part of the CNE. You lost the markets that were attracted to the stadium, the baseball team and the football team. You lost the concerts. And all that accounts for a lot of attendance: 60,000 for the Rolling Stones, 40,000 for a Blue Jays game, you'd get 100,000 people going to that stadium in one day. The recession started it, but all those things contributed to it going down over the period of a few years. We get a million whatever, now. I never know.[5]

The Road Shows

The Canadian arm of the company had begun to plan in the late 1980s for expansion, trying to find a route of smaller fairs in western Canada. In 1989 they bought Crown Amusements, a small show based in Edmonton with 15 rides, for $450,000, playing its route of 18 dates in mining towns and First Nations reservations through northern Alberta and Saskatchewan. The purchase was part of preparations for the possibility of the major western fairs lengthening their dates.

Crown was re-branded as Conklin's Northern Lights in 1990, but the economy had begun to falter and the western expansion was put off. So at the end of that season the executive unveiled Operation Swordfish, a master plan to rejuvenate the Ontario operation. They were going to invest four million dollars over two years on the Ontario units, which had been languishing with little money spent on them for years. While they bought a few rides and new bunkhouses for staff, the changes were mainly cosmetic. The show invited fair boards from across the province to the launch of Operation Swordfish at the Brantford winter quarters. Representatives from several fairs that did not have Conklin midways came, but the show signed no new dates. Beyond the fairs the show already had, there were few Ontario fairs large enough to support a full Conklin midway and there was ample competition for the smaller fairs.

In a full-page story in the Life section of the *Toronto Star* on May 4, 1992, Jim said he did not "travel with the shows" anymore: "But I do like to get out and visit them. I get itchy feet, I need to see what's going on." He referred to his engagement with the carnival as "a hobby of mine, vintage merry-go-rounds and rides in general." He contrasted the attention lavished on the circus with the lack of "any well-documented history of amusement parks or carnivals" and said he would "like to do something." He still hoped to use his free time to preserve carnival history.

Confirming his retirement from road-show travel, the Ontario operation was restructured in a management buyout in 1992.[6] Jim partnered with Sam Ganz and Barry Jamieson to form World's Finest Shows, still in the Conklin Group, which took over the assets and contracts of the Ontario road shows. Jim no longer needed the money or the aggravation. Jamieson would run the new company as president and chief operating officer. He had started with Conklin Shows in 1974, been ride superintendent for two years in the West, and then manager of the eastern road units throughout the '80s. When the new company was formed, one unit remained based in Simcoe, Sullivan's old winter quarters, with the barns at the fairground used for storage and a workshop in the winter. World's Finest needed a larger winter quarters and two years later Jamieson bought a vacant fabricating plant in an industrial park in Nanticoke, home to the show ever since. He built his own house nearby.

World's Finest Shows' multiple routes covered more than 60 Ontario fairs, festivals, and celebrations. The Bicycle Unit had been renamed the Trillium Unit in 1989 and the World's Finest unit became the Talbot Tour after the buyout. Throughout the 1990s, the annual ride gross for the Trillium Unit ranged between $2.3 and $2.8 million, while the Talbot Tour grossed between $1.25 and $1.75 million.[7] The Central Canada Exhibition in Ottawa, which World's Finest finally got in 1997 and which required both units to play, boosted the gross. To make room for the Ottawa date, the show persuaded the Peterborough and Barrie fair boards to change their dates. The annual ride gross for Jim's Supershows never reached half a million and he shut it down in 1997 after 11 years, turning it back into a ride rental operation. Overall attendance at Ontario fairs generally declined throughout the decade.

The Conklin Canadian rides had occasional off-season action beyond rentals. Super Fairs Inc., an Oklahoma promoter, had been organizing indoor carnivals since the early 1970s, but only gained attention 20 years later when some of the larger carnival companies started to book equipment at them. The five- or six-day fairs were held in sports domes in the cooler regions of North America in late winter or early spring. Jim put rides in for the Toronto Super Fair in the SkyDome from 1994 to 1996.[8] The six-day March event saw attendance of around 35,000. In February 2000, the partners booked World's Finest rides in at the SkyDome for a Chinese New Year Festival organized by a public relations firm, which drew 213,000.

The Conklin companies on both sides of the border had to deal with renewed turmoil when the U.S. economy entered a recession in 1990 and the Canadian economy followed, once more taking longer to recover. Unemployment in Canada reached 11 percent. The federal Goods and Services Tax, implemented in 1991, applied a tax on ride tickets for the first time since the amusement tax was withdrawn. The GST also brought administrative overhead that was as annoying as it was costly. Jim gave up the Northern Lights unit in 1992 as the prospect of longer western fairs receded with the economy.

Once again, financial factors made it difficult for Frank to bring his U.S. show into Canada and to keep his showcase rides on the road. He managed to keep the show's budget stable, but his profits were reduced. Some of the U.S. ride owners stopped coming with him into Canada for a time and were replaced by Canadians, including the Vallées' Beauce Carnaval from Saint-Georges, Quebec, and Sammy Arrigo's Big A Amusements from Brantford. Arrigo was approaching his 80s and had been on the road for over 60 years, although he stayed in central Ontario and kept his jumps to an average of 40 miles. He had a fire in winter quarters in 1994 after which his show was resurrected with help from ride manufacturers and several shows, including World's Finest. He, in turn, helped the Conklins out at the CNE.

ADJUSTING TO NEW REALITIES

Frank took it to another level. Frank got into the big, big rides. And took it to that level where it is now. Frank was young enough and had the balls to roll with it. He made the move into big equipment. The Enterprise was

Conklin's first real spectacular, other than the Himalaya. The next year the Giant Wheel came and I'm sure that Frank had some input, but I know that Jim knew that they needed to be bigger and better than everybody.

Then after that, we were on a roll; that's when we got the Zyklon and two or three Himalayas moving — the first of the real big rides besides Sky Wheels. The high-roll money, 350- to 500,000-dollar rides and progressively on and on. And still any new big ride, Frank's the first one to get it. There's nobody better.

I'll tell you something about Frank Conklin. You make a deal with him, he's like his grandfather, whether it's a good deal for him or a bad deal, he'll stick with it. He would never fall back. Frank says something, there's no changing; if it's bad for him, he doesn't care. Frank's honourable. He's a man of his word.

He's taken it to another level. There's nobody in the amusement business in North America who's as good.... I don't think anybody else holds a candle to him. Frank is the whole show; it's still all Conklin money. Frank's big show, there's nobody has the kind of capacity rides. He's got one roller coaster on 26 semi-trailers, double-loop roller coaster. There's nobody who can afford to buy one of those and transport it across the country. Frank's got one.

Drop of Fear travels on six trailers, but the fucking thing don't make no money. There's no capacity. But why's he got it? Because it's impressive and it signs fairs. You look at the thing, and it's massive. The fairs love it.

Frank's the innovator. Frank's theory when we were younger, "Bigger is better."

Interview with Tommy Coffing, Feb. 18, 2000

Patty's long shadow as the spectral patriarch of the show and the Conklin identification with big rides that was started by him were reinforced by an award from the International Association of Amusement Parks and Attractions (IAAPA) in 1993. A record of almost 25,000 attended the 75th anniversary convention of the association, where Patty was inducted into the IAAPA

Hall of Fame as a posthumous pioneer, recognized for his association with Kennywood Park, near Pittsburgh, and Palisades Park in New Jersey. He was in the company of roller coaster pioneers. Fellow inductees included John Miller, who originated the high-speed roller coaster, another coaster designer, and Anton Schwarzkopf, "Herr Achterbahn" himself.

Heavy Metal

Frank continued to focus on ride technology, in line with industry trends, and to streamline operations, reflecting best business practices. He had never been interested in shows, games, or food concessions — the carnie side of the business — leaving them to independent concessionaires or his sister or wife. He did not invest in the revival of illusion shows in the mid-90s, although he bought a funhouse and lost money trying to bring back other back-end shows. In 1993 he sold the remaining office games to his concessions manager for him to run as an independent. Trish had sold her games the year before, when she was sidelined in the restructured Ontario operation of which Barry Jamieson became president. She kept her food joints on Frank's show for a few more years, until his wife, Jodi, began to operate food stands for the show. Bobby Cassata, an independent game concessionaire, had toured with the Conklins in the United States, the West, and the CNE since 1975. His other business, developing trailer-mounted games at a plant in Daytona Beach, thrived largely because of that relationship. Cassata and a couple of other long-time independents produced the rest of the Conklin games lineup.

Frank booked rides with more shows and on independent midways in the United States, including at major state fairs in Florida and Minnesota. He did not want the bother of bringing standard rides and smaller pieces to the United States from Canada, so he let Cumberland Valley, Amusements of America, and a roster of independent ride owners fill in his midways for a full lineup of attractions. He had an ongoing reciprocal arrangement with Cumberland Valley Shows: they played his fairs and he played theirs. J.D. Floyd of Cumberland Valley saw it as an equal partnership, as he told *Amusement Business* on January 31, 1994: "The management of the two organizations really complement each other. We've had a relationship for 10 or 12 years now." Frank even subcontracted outright a few fairs to Cumberland Valley, as Patty had with Art Lewis and some of his Quebec fairs. Floyd and his partner, Billy Baxter, had, in fact, booked rides with Patty at the CNE long before they bought Cumberland Valley around the same time as the Conklins bought the Deggeller Magic Midway.

Frank maintained his reputation for taking big rides down the road. By 1994, when he acquired a Wild Cat coaster, another ride that was difficult to move and only played a handful of dates, he had increased his lineup of spectacular rides available for his own fairs to 18. These were big, technologically advanced, thrilling machines that had not been seen before, even at large state fairs. Like Patty in the 1930s and '40s, Frank provided attractions that people could experience almost nowhere other than on his midway. He was easily able to attract local branches of large corporations — McDonald's, Kentucky Fried Chicken, Safeway, Coca-Cola, Kodak, AMC Theaters — to sponsor promotions associating them with his marquee rides. He also boosted his lineup of kiddie rides, another industry trend, buying a dozen or so during the mid-1990s.

The company began to see a demand for rides like simulators, another new technology, that different generations could enjoy together. According to Alfie, the show had "done a study of rides in the past few years and we've seen an increase in popularity in rides for the whole family. Kiddie rides have maintained their popularity and it's the spectaculars which have only maintained or decreased in popularity…. Parents and grandparents are going on the rides with their kids…. That's the future of our market."[9] The recurrence of the family-friendly theme appears to be cyclical, possibly tied to demographic trends. Patty had catered to it in the 1950s with his original kiddielands, and Jim in the 1970s by cleaning up the midway and getting rid of sideshows. Now President Phillips was helping Frank play the family card.

The Travelling Town

Frank's show treated families on staff in a way that would have been foreign to his grandfather. In the early 1990s, parents on the show began fundraising for a school and Conklin International Academy opened in 1994 in a 46-foot, $110,000 custom trailer. "Registered as a private Christian school in Florida," it used "course materials from that state's Pensacola Christian College"; it had one full-time teacher for pre-school and one for the primary and secondary grades.[10] The Deggellers had pioneered a "Schoolhouse on the Midway" a few years earlier.[11] The teacher who helped start the Conklin school got her first experience with the Deggellers. Partly supported by a commissary and after-hours events for staff, with some fair boards making donations, tuition at the Conklin Academy was $55 a week per child. The private school's students, numbering as high as 30, included not only the children of employees, but employees who had not completed their education.

The school's teacher described its "main purpose" as "to keep families together," which an August 25, 1996, *Toronto Star* article about the school contrasted with "the shady times when male workers typically left their wives and children behind and travelled footloose and fancy-free across the continent for most of the year." By 2004 the school had expanded to two trailers, three teachers, and a budget of $200,000 a year. Patty's shady times had passed, as Frank accepted business realities by making over even the operating end of his show to present a family-friendly image. Gone were the days when wives and children were not welcome to travel with the carnival.

Some of the executives who had joined Frank when his father bought the Deggeller show retired or left for other companies. Bob Negus, a marketing executive who had come with the Deggeller purchase and was well known throughout the industry, died in March 1998 at the age of 68.[12] He had been the main spokesman for the American company for 18 years. In his last years, Negus had been semi-retired, so Alfie, as president of Conklin & Garrett, had taken on more active communications duties, especially in Canada. Alfie evolved into a sage commentator on the industry. The same year Negus died, Alfie packed the house for a panel he led at the Canadian Association of Fairs and Exhibitions convention on "The Midway of the Future." In his opinion, referring to electronic debit cards, "The future lies in the card system."[13]

As he became more involved with public relations, Alfie needed an assistant to manage employees. Howard "Lurch" Pringle, who had been with the show for 10 years and had been saved from an alcohol-use disorder several years before through an intervention by Frank, was given the new position of operations supervisor to help Alfie enforce dress code, client relations, and midway security. According to Alfie, their "biggest problem" had "been appearance and attitude," and Pringle "made a significant improvement."[14] Alfie continued: "It looks like we've got appearance under control now. Attitude will be more difficult to deal with, because we are working with a lot of temporary help."

An imposing six foot 10, Lurch imagined himself as the chief of police of a travelling mill town, Alfie his mayor. "Basically, our life revolves around the guy that owns the mill," he said. "We have a school, we have a commissary, we have laundry facilities; we have the boss's big house on the hill and the trailer park community down at the bottom of the hill. Every two weeks, we take our town and go someplace else."[15] Pringle helped promote the view that the show had "cast off the rowdy road show reputation of yesteryear in favor of a small-town feel."[16]

The major dates on the Canada-U.S. route remained the same through most of the '90s: five U.S. fairs, five western Canadian fairs, and the CNE. Show management continued to toy with the idea of running another unit to play smaller country fairs in Alberta and Saskatchewan. They considered bidding on the Medicine Hat and the Lethbridge exhibitions when they came open in 1994 but did not. The value of the Canadian dollar fell throughout the decade, but despite the U.S. exchange and the GST, the Calgary Stampede remained the best 10 days of the season, as it had since the decline of the CNE. Advance sales at Calgary in 1993 were $1.1 million, the largest the show had and great rain insurance. The overall concessions and rides gross was up 12 percent from the previous year.[17]

The Dade County fair in Miami was catching up, posting a record one-day ride take of half a million U.S. dollars in 1993. By 1995, it grossed just over five million dollars, beating the CNE's best and setting an all-time North American record.[18] The CNE ride gross had come close to five million Canadian dollars in 1978, but after 15 years of high inflation got less than four million in 1993. Dade County had lengthened its stand from 11 to 18 days in 1992 and the Big E in Massachusetts went from 12 to 17 days in 1994. That same year, the CNE board reduced its length from 20 to 18 days. By the end of the decade, Conklin executives were lobbying for a 14-day Ex.

By 1991 Conklin Shows was back at number one on the *Amusement Business* list of carnivals playing the top 50 fairs. The Westchester County Fair in Yonkers, New York, and the South Carolina State Fair in Columbia were securely in the top 50 by 1994, giving Conklin Shows seven of them with a total attendance of over 6.5 million. The show held its number one position for the rest of its independent existence.

Redefining the CNE

CNE attendance had fallen to 1.7 million by 1990 and fell or remained static every year of the decade, by the end of which it was the number five fair in North America based on published attendance. In 1992 the near riots that had marred the Labour Day finish to the exhibition for the previous five years were eliminated by shutting the gates at 5 p.m. and clearing the midway by 8 p.m. Labour Day, the perceived last day of summer, had been an excuse for a blowout. But it had never been a money-maker and the carnies were relieved to avoid having their turf "turned into a battleground, with young people destroying property and threatening exhibition workers," as the *Globe and Mail* expressed it in an article on September 4, 1993.

Exhibition management continued to present its control of attendance as an attraction to the corporate sponsors and exhibitors it needed to fill the new trade centre. In 1993 Conklin Shows changed how it paid the CNE, from a percentage of the ride gross to a per capita fee based on attendance, an arrangement that acknowledged the falling gate numbers and ensured they did not hurt the show as much as they might have. An expanded pay-one-price promotion that year helped the ride gross, and the show overall was up nine points over 1992.

CNE management entertained vague ideas about redefining the midway with technology and speculated about new rides and attractions. They did not have a clear picture of what they wanted because they believed it did not yet exist. They had visions of shaping the future of outdoor amusements and felt "the distance between computers and technology and rides and games and shows is blurring."[19] Having loosened the Conklins' chokehold on the midway by demolishing the attractions Patty had built, they sought other bidders in 1994, at the end of the latest five-year contract with Conklin Shows, and cast their net wide. Frank and Jim won the contract anyway.

There had been minor injuries on CNE rides over the years and the Flyer had a bad spate of mishaps in the early 1980s, but the worst damage to the show occurred from a fluke accident in 1995. A 16-year-old girl walking down the midway was knocked out by a square metre of fibreglass that "flew off after bolts became loose on the canopy" of the Enterprise. In 1997, "Conklin and Garrett Ltd. pleaded guilty ... to two violations of the Ontario Amusement Devices Act" for the accident and was fined $15,000.[20] The fine was a slap on the wrist, but the conviction enabled the family to file a civil suit against the show. The girl suffered "brain damage and loss of memory"; her personality changed "causing her to lose friends and smoke, drink and do drugs."[21] A week before the suit was to go to court in 2000, the family accepted an offer of $775,000 from the show. In the interim, an accident on the Wave Swinger, which dropped 48 riders three metres onto a steel platform, sending 14 to hospital, resulted in no charges or lawsuits.[22]

Frank bought his father "out entirely from the carnival end of the business" in early 1995, announced in *Amusement Business* on February 20. Already owner of the U.S. show, Frank had acquired the remains of Canada's Conklin Shows, which included the western route and the CNE, and the rides that were added to his lineup when he brought it into Canada. After the restructuring of the Ontario show in 1992, Jim admitted in 1995 that he had been pulling back from operations and for the past few years had been involved in decision-making only. Alfie remained the president of Conklin & Garrett, and Jim, Jamieson, and Ganz retained ownership of World's Finest Shows. Jim still looked after many of the contracts with the Ontario fair boards, while Jamieson remained in charge of operations. In 1999, Jim publicly announced his retirement from carnival operations, "handing the reins to his son, Frank."

Jim was now in "the business of restoring rides and manufacturing merchandise carts." He had set up Sunnyside Manufacturing in 1995 to produce carts, gates, fences, benches, ticket boxes, and other paraphernalia.

"Refurbishing and manufacturing, that's what I'll be involved in from now on," he told *Amusement Business* when Frank bought him out. He developed concepts for new games, although unlike Patty's bushel basket game they did not become popular, and built at least one glass house. Ray Coffing, who had left the show in 1985 to be operations manager for Kane Fernandez in Hawaii, rejoined Jim in late 1995 to be marketing director for Sunnyside.

The company made one of its first deals in 1996 when it traded "ride fencing, benches, electrical equipment, trucks and canopies" for old rides, including a merry-go-round, with Bill Lynch Shows.[23] John Drummey, another former Conklin employee, was running the Lynch show, since its owner, "Soggy" Reid, had been killed in a car accident the previous December. Jim also continued with his parks restoration project in China, which had become a hot market. In retirement, his hobbies and new ventures all connected with his past and that of the carnival.

BUSINESSMEN

Carnival Owner Snapshot
  Frank Conklin
  President, Conklin Shows, Brantford, Ont., and Royal Palm Beach, Fla.
  Education: High school graduate in Brantford.
  First industry job: Setting up equipment at the Canadian National Exhibition, Toronto, when I was 12.
  Changes: They've been mostly positive. Equipment is bigger, better and safer. We have more educated guys who are technology oriented.
  Philosophy: Hire good help, give them responsibilities and let them do their jobs.
  Hobbies: Hunting, fishing, skiing, boating and fast cars, plus enjoying doing things with my wife, Jodi, and two children.
  Career highlights: Taking over the show's southern route in 1980 and the whole thing in 1990.
  Influences: His family.

Dream Carnival: Aware that many other carnivals have listed his as their dream carnival, Conklin said he is very happy with what he has, but noted that there is always room for improvement.

Amusement Business, *Apr. 23, 2001, online edition, no page number*

⋆   ★   ⋆

Even 30 years after his death, Patty remained a touchstone for the amusement business press, an April 12, 1999, *Amusement Business* article on the success of the present-day show recalling him as "a flamboyant, charismatic, hustling showman" in contrast with his grandson: "Frank operates the carnival in more of a businesslike manner than Patty, who relied more on guile, savvy and a charming personality in his days." The present reality was not only practical, but sensible and necessary, although this statement implies it was clearly inferior to the more colourful past.

Cautious Growth

By the mid-1990s, with the economy stabilized, the Conklin road shows streamlined, and Jim no longer involved in making decisions, the shows entered a decade of cautious, incremental growth. Frank followed the sensible practices of a businessman, including bowing to economic realities by leaving some of his big rides parked when they could not pay their way. Barry Jamieson ensured that his Ontario routes sustained themselves and made a profit for him and his partners.

The shows picked up a few new dates. When World's Finest Shows took the Central Canada Exhibition in Ottawa from Amusements of America in 1997, at 39th place it was the first top 50 fair on the World's Finest route. But the Ottawa exhibition had been overstating its attendance for years and had actually entered a state of terminal decline. Conklin International added a fair in Red Deer, Alberta, in 1997, and the Canadian Lakehead Exhibition in Thunder Bay, Ontario, in 1998. Its biggest coup was winning, against five major American companies including the Deggeller and Strates shows, the bid for the South Florida Fair and Palm Beach County Exposition. The fair-grounds shared a property line with the Conklin winter quarters in West Palm Beach and South Florida kicked off the show's 2000 tour. Attendance at the fair increased by over 10 percent and on February 7 *Amusement Business* lauded the show for the "marvelous job" it did with "its super spectaculars." That year, the show saw its highest attendance ever, getting a shot at the wallets of nearly eight million fair goers at nine of the top 50 fairs.

Except for the CNE, the Conklin International fairs continued to set records, while the World's Finest fairs kept pace with inflation, largely through price increases. At the Ex, it took a pay-one-price promotion for the entire 1997 run for the show to get an increase in ride receipts, but that feat could not be repeated. Calgary and Dade County retained their reputations as fairs where the patrons loved the rides. The Dade County ride gross remained over five million dollars every year but one in the second half of the decade, despite the rain and cold that sometimes descended on the March date.[24] It reached $5.7 million by 2000, with per capita spending at $7.30. Both figures set industry records. The Calgary ride gross saw annual increases, reaching eight million Canadian dollars in 2000, or just over five million U.S.[25] Per capita spending was USD$4.31. This might have been a rebound from the previous year when a freak July snowstorm and near freezing temperatures had kept attendance down.

Frank and Alfie thought the 18-day Dade County fair one of the best in North America, but at 10 days Calgary was the best for its length. Rated the 10th largest fair, no other could equal the Stampede's gross. Unlike at Dade County, where games and food joints were booked independently by the fair board, at the Stampede the concessions' take for the show could match or beat the rides. Many of the same concessionaires played both events, working for the fair board at one and for Frank's show at the other. About half of the up to 100 rides that operated under the Conklin banner at Dade County were owned by the show. Frank had seven of the top 10 earning rides. The company put the same amount of its own equipment into the Stampede, the CNE, and the Big E for total ride lineups that ranged from 60 to 70 units, including kiddieland. When they landed the contract for the Westerner Days Fair & Exposition in Red Deer, it created holes in the Calgary midway, which they filled with more rides from American independents.

The Ontario fairs could only support smaller operations. Their experience was closer to the norm for the industry, with attendance flat and growth achieved by increasing prices. World's Finest Shows was the largest of the 25 or so carnivals in the province, its two units carrying around 50 devices between them, all company owned. The combined ride gross for the World's Finest units broke five million Canadian dollars in 2001. It took World's Finest over five months and a total of 60 dates to get it. Conklin Shows International had 16 dates, with five 18-day fairs, two of which made over five million U.S. dollars on their own.

Frank continued to build and maintain an arsenal of spectaculars. German rides had been falling out of favour because of their expense and weight. Italian companies built lighter copies of German rides and sold them for less. As Alfie told *Amusement Business* on March 2, 1998, "The Germans create the ride and the Italians duplicate it and it's cheaper." Frank bought a Crazy Flip from Soriani and Moser of Italy in 1995 and a USD$1.5 million G-Force from the same company in 1997. That year he also bought a Flume ride from the French company Reverchon, giving it a Niagara Falls theme. He kept his profitable spectaculars, like the Wild Cat and Mark 1 coasters, operating on independent midways when he did not have a fair for them to play. To save labour costs, he hired local roughies to set up and tear down the big rides. Transportation costs continued to mount, although the show was now contracting it out to avoid the expense of regulations, insurance, and paying qualified drivers when they weren't driving.

In 1999 Frank brought the first portable gravity tower to North America, picking it up for $1.4 million. Built by Moser, it stood 17.5 stories or 180 feet tall and had a drop of 165 feet. On its purchase, Frank made one of his rare statements to the press. "It's a spectacular ride," he told *Amusement Business* on February 22. "It is the first in the country and it will stand out dramatically on our midway. It is quite a significant ride and will have a very positive effect on our show's skyline." Called the Drop of Fear and visible for miles, it was enormously popular, although it had a low capacity.

As a spectacle, the Italian Drop of Fear vied with the expensive, heavy German Doppel Looper, but the tower only required six trucks to move and two and a half days to set up, so it appeared at all the major Conklin fairs. Beginning in 1997, the coaster played fewer dates. It was out of commission for two days with a burnt-out motor at the 1998 South Carolina State Fair. The next year it missed the Yonkers fair and the CNE for repairs, and the show had to quell speculation that Frank had finally sold it.

The midway cleanup continued, partly propelled by industry trends recognizing the importance of image. To deal with customer complaints, Alfie instituted an employee incentive program for the Canadian West and CNE in 1995 and brought it to the United States in 1997; it soon spread to World's Finest. The program provided awards for employee of the day and of the fair.

Appearance and public relations became increasingly key to the show's ongoing success. Instead of buying rides in 1998, the U.S. show spent $200,000 on phase 1 of its upgrade plan, a beautification program with more rest areas and new multicoloured tents, flags, and uniforms; employees shared the cost of the uniforms. Added to the incentive program, guest relations and patron surveys, the goal was to improve the midway experience. Phase 2, begun in 2000, aimed at transforming kiddieland into Family Land to encourage parents and grandparents to stay longer. The number of rides was reduced to make space for canopies, planters, benches, and other amenities. The rides had higher capacities and more could handle both adults and children.

The Patty Conklin Memorial Fund, started by Conklin & Garrett in 1981 with money raised from show employees through parties, raffles, and benefit bingos, provided another way to give back to the public. By 1998 the fund had spent $300,000 on local and national charities, children's activities, and scholarships for the children of employees. In 1990, the show organized the National Youth Talent Awards under the fund and in partnership with its Canadian fairs. The fairs hosted youth talent who were judged by fair board and Conklin officials. Each year, nine regional winners were sent to the national competition at the Canadian Association of Fairs and Exhibitions convention, held in different cities across the country. The fairs paid for travel and accommodations for the competitors. Cash prizes paid for from the Memorial Fund were awarded to the top three competitors, with $3,000 going to first place. The talent awards were a good public relations device, bringing the company and the fair boards together around something other than grosses, percentages, and attendance figures.

Other promotions and corporate sponsorships followed paths set in the late 1980s. Multinationals as well as local businesses and media outlets signed up to sponsor rides and offer specials. Advance sales remained the best promotion, with several fairs achieving advance sales of over a million dollars. Pay-one-price, despite its unpopularity for ride owners and operators, was now an expected offer, thanks to competition from amusement parks. The CNE converted to pay-one-price for the entire event, including gate admission, for 1997 and 1998, but went back to a separate gate after receiving volumes of complaints from people who had no interest in the midway rides. It kept the pay-one-price ride offer for the length of the fair, and several other exhibitions, including those in Winnipeg, Brandon, Edmonton, and Ottawa, followed suit. Other Conklin fairs used a pay-one-price pass to boost attendance on slow weekdays.

The U.S. arm of the company began developing the next generation of ride ticketing in 1996.[26] They worked with Danny Brown, a programmer based in Washington, D.C., who had helped them computerize their office 10 years before. The electronic system would enable patrons to buy magnetic stripe cards, pre-loaded with digital money, to swipe through a card reader at each ride. Apart from the considerable benefit of taking physical cash and tickets off the midway, the data collected and fed via a wireless network into a central server enabled show staff to precisely monitor all ride activity in real time. They also hoped the system would boost per capita spending by providing benefits for patrons, including reduced lineups and ease of transaction, so easy as to be almost invisible.

The initial ambitious goal of the Conklin managers was to have all rides on the cashless system by 2000. They would introduce it first to Canadians who were perceived to be more receptive to debit card transactions. The plan to introduce it in kiddieland in 1997 was scuttled when the developers failed to integrate the hardware and software into a stable system in time. They brought out a pilot version for a 20-ride kiddieland unit in 1998 but pulled it back and pushed projections for full implementation to five years out. In 2001 the system appeared at the western fairs as a kiddieland promotion sponsored by local businesses. The following year all rides in Canada were tied into the system and it was used at the Greater Gulf States Fair in Mobile, Alabama. The cards were introduced for some games in Canada and for rides at all Conklin U.S. fairs in 2003, by which time the system had cost more than double the estimated USD$400,000 to develop. On December 24, 2001, Alfie spoke to *Amusement Business* of the show "going down that road of innovation again with our electronic ticketing system."

The Conklin executives behind the e-ticket system believed it represented the future of midway transactions and results at some larger fairs were impressive. After the Canadian rollout in 2002, Howard Pringle said, "I see the cards becoming a necessity on the midway over the next five years."[27] One entertainment executive looking to buy a number of shows planned to supply his acquisitions with the system. The CNE, using the system at the gate and for all rides, committed to it largely because of the data it generates. Although there were problems with it at the gate in 2003, by the 2004 CNE it was working without a hitch. Other fairs expressed an interest, but many in the industry, especially concessionaires, had reservations about the system's reliability, convenience, and patron acceptance. Many glitches had yet to be worked out, and the ultimate fate of e-ticketing was still unclear by the middle of the decade.

Along with electronic ticketing and spectacular rides, the Conklin group of shows took advantage of other new technologies. They switched from walkie-talkies to cell phones for communication across the show grounds. World's Finest and the Canadian and U.S. branches set up their own websites to publicize their routes and enabled website visitors to post comments, an early use of social media. They also sold e-tickets on the websites, having local businesses sponsor them. This practice took advanced sales to another level, just as online ticket selling was becoming practical.

The New Millennium

After the September 11 terrorist attacks on the World Trade Center and the Pentagon, Conklin show officials anticipated that reduced travel, especially by air, would keep people closer to home, which could benefit local amusement parks. But, as one of their competitors put it, the parks were not their competition: "It's playing over the Internet. Kids can stay at home and never spend a dollar outside."[28] Technology and the play-at-home trend taken too far could work against them.

Conklin Shows and World's Finest Shows followed their established courses in the early years of the new millennium. Spectacular rides continued to be the dominant feature of the U.S. show. The Canadian show had fewer spectacular rides, fewer rides total, and fewer rides booked by other owners. Jamieson bought a Spin Out, similar to the G-Force, from the Netherlands in 2000 for close to one million U.S. dollars but toured it with Frank's show that year so it could earn enough to pay for itself. He bought an American-made Cliffhanger for USD$310,000 in 2002 and took it out on his own route. Frank bought a Zamperla Kite Flyer in 2001, a Fireball from KMG of Holland for over one million U.S. dollars in 2002, and an Italian giant slide in 2003. He installed permanent cable car rides over the midways of the South Carolina and South Florida state fairs. His spectaculars grossed high on every midway they played.

The aggregate attendance at the top 50 North American fairs peaked at over 45 million in 2000, then slipped in subsequent years. Although grosses fell in the United States and returns in Ontario remained uneven, the Canadian West got stronger as its oil economy began to pick up. A recession loomed in 2001, but according to the *Amusement Business* forecast published on January 8, "most fair executives appear to be more concerned about a cooling of the weather." That year, for the fifth in a row, Dade County had the highest ride gross in the history of travelling carnivals with a six-million-dollar take.

Dade County ran in the spring. In the fall of 2001, the Big E in Springfield, Massachusetts, opened four days after the September 11 attacks, but fair management attributed the 6 percent drop in attendance to rain. Most carnival businessmen continued to be more concerned about the weather than terrorism. The owners of 400 touring shows expected the 350 million people who visited their midways in 2001 would be back the following year if the weather was right, regardless of threats to national security or fluctuations in the economy.

By early into the new millennium, it was taken for granted that Conklin Shows had "the premier route among carnivals, playing the best fairs in the U.S. and Canada."[29] Frank became more available to the media and, like his father, complained about fair percentages, although the show had contributed to their inflation in the 1980s. When prodded, his litany of beefs included increased regulation, the low Canadian dollar, and rising labour, insurance, and transportation costs. He also promoted the e-ticket system and announced in *Amusement Business* in April 2003 his engagement with a company in South Carolina set up to market the system to other shows: "We're involved with the Barber family ... who are our partners in FairSwipe."

Pringle was being trained by Alfie to handle the media, but the latter remained the company spokesman. He criticized government regulations whenever he had the chance, especially at the CNE where new rules declaring the grounds a construction site were introduced in 2001 and caused the show trouble. Always comfortable with attention, Alfie began a sideline as master of ceremonies for hire, accepting his appointment to the role for the Showmen's League annual banquet in 2004, for instance.

Jamieson gained more media exposure, speaking on behalf of World's Finest. He put on a fundraiser for an agricultural program for Toronto schools in October 2001, pointing out in *Amusement Business* on November 26 that this was the first time a carnival had played in a Toronto park since Patty's Fair for Britain in 1943. He planned for the Pumpkin Fest to be an annual event, but there was no repeat. With taxes, the exchange rate, and other expenses, he thought "any business today is doing all it can to hang on," but he was "happy with the carnival business. I don't think there's any business any better and I wouldn't do anything else."

Fuel prices, labour costs, insurance premiums, and inspection fees continued to rise, and they converged to make moving and operating all that heavy equipment the biggest expense. The U.S. show had rid itself of its transport trucks by 2001 and contracted out most of its transportation, sometimes to former employees who formed their own trucking companies when the show let them go. Popular rides such as the Zipper and Octopus, as well as the Kamikaze and Rainbow, had to be phased out to cut costs. Independents who had long travelled as a part of Conklin Shows were also phased out to save money. Other rides such as the Drop of Fear and the Wild Cat coaster had become too expensive to move and were either sold to competitors or shelved in West Palm Beach.

Despite retaining its position as the show that played to the most patrons at the largest fairs in North America, Frank's show was no longer all-powerful and lost on a number of bids. He was unsuccessful in taking the North Carolina State Fair in both 2002 and 2003. In 2003 he also lost a Florida county fair. For his second bid on North Carolina, he had combined with Thebault-Blomsness Enterprises and Powers Great American Midways. That year, seven shows or combinations bid on the fair, competing on the basis of a straight payment on per capita attendance. The Strates show, which had played the fair for 53 years before losing it the previous year, won it back. Frank joined once more with the Powers show in 2004 to bid on the New York State Fair, where the Strates contract was up. The combination was disqualified for not meeting the requirements for a minimum number of rides.

The trend toward per capita bidding for fair contracts, guaranteeing fairs a set price tied to attendance, was a concern throughout the industry. It was seen as an arbitrary method of awarding contracts to the highest bidder regardless of any other considerations and it locked carnivals into a fixed fee no matter how much they actually earned. Strates had won the North Carolina fair in 2002 by bidding so high his competitors were convinced he would lose money. He offered $6.50 per attendee, which would translate into a payment of over four million dollars to the fair board, almost $70,000 more than the latest ride gross. Alfie told *Amusement Business* on August 11, 2003, that he thought Strates "gave a large percentage, if not all of the ride gross," and concluded, "It's hard to comprehend how you can stay in business that way." The fair in fact was up for grabs again the next year; Conklin Shows did not put in a bid, while Strates lowered its per capita offer and lost it. Meanwhile, other fair boards saw the advantage of per capita contracts and the practice spread because carnivals desperate for contracts were forced to play along.

Conklin Shows approached a dangerous new low in the 2003 season. "Conklin's Phillips Cites Carnival Woes" headlined an article in *Amusement Business* on August 18, in the middle of the season. Alfie "said the per capita bidding process" was "only one of several problems facing the carnival busi- ness.... The industry is in huge trouble." He continued: "A lot of shows this year are having a very bad season, and that includes us. It's scary out there." Beyond fair board greed, the show had to deal with "the U.S.-led war in Iraq, the continuing worldwide war on terrorism, a soft economy and rough weather early on." All this, along with rising costs across the board.

Other one-off factors compounded the Conklin dilemma in 2003. Concerns about mad cow disease peaked, hurting the beef industry in western Canada, where a case discovered in May led the United States and other countries to ban Canadian beef imports. Partly as a result, the Winnipeg, Calgary, and Edmonton exhibitions all had drops in attendance, but so too did the South Florida and Dade County fairs, the Dade County ride gross experiencing a significant decline for the first time. Although the World Health Organization declared the global epidemic of severe acute respiratory syndrome (SARS) over in July, it still hurt attendance at the CNE, which shrank to 1.25 million, as Toronto was an epicentre of the disease. As if that wasn't enough, the largest blackout in North American history struck Ontario and much of the northeastern United States on the day before the CNE was to open, keeping it closed for its first four days for a loss of as much as 200,000 in attendance. The Central Canada Exhibition with World's Finest on the midway was open for 12 minutes before the power went out, but it only lost two days. And then the Big E was down over 10 percent thanks to the remnants of Hurricane Isabel, the worst storm of the season.

Alfie took some of the blame for losing money, admitting that "we also shot ourselves in the foot with ride pricing."[30] They had replaced the pay-one-price promotion with an underpriced $20 electronic ticket worth 20 rides in Edmonton and a $16 ticket for 18 rides in South Carolina. Referring to ride pricing at Calgary, Edmonton, and Winnipeg, he continued: "We did it to ourselves. We are the enemy and it cost us at those three dates. With our pricing scheme, we, effectively, gave away the rides, and then we went to the washroom." The Edmonton ride gross dropped 9 percent and South Carolina 12 percent. The electronic ticket system also gave them grief wherever they tried to implement it that year, as the technology refused to function properly and proved difficult to use. While aggregate attendance at the top 50 North American fairs in 2003 was down by over 700,000, Conklin Shows played to over a million fewer customers. "It was a rough season, not a banner one," Frank and Alfie told *Amusement Business* on December 22, and Alfie concluded that "we barely survived a very tough year."

The show executives dropped a plan to buy a German coaster for the coming season, and they put all capital expenditures on hold. They would need a good 2004 to pay for their losses and to support a strategy for recovery. As Alfie put it, sounding like Jim 20 years before, "We don't plan to buy anything. We will try and repair damage we did in 2003."[31] But they had found another way to satisfy the demand for novelty. In 2003 they swapped three rides with West Coast Amusements from Langley, British Columbia. They renewed the agreement for 2004, trading a different set of rides. As West Coast co-owner Bobby Hauser said, "It gives us both new pieces without the investment. They're a great organization, great people to work with."[32]

Also beginning in 2003, the show had found a new way to freshen up its midway staff. Because of problems finding good local help, about which all owners complained, shows had started sponsoring foreign labour exchanges. Some brought in workers from Mexico. Conklin Shows used a Florida staffing agency to bring in South Africans. These were eager white college students who could not find jobs in post-apartheid South Africa. If they stayed with the show for the entire season, they could save what amounted back home to a year's salary. They thrived in their new environment and were perceived to be better workers than their North American colleagues. And they could charm patrons with their accent.

The 2004 season started off badly, with accidents. At the South Florida State Fair, "hydraulic fluid leaked in the Orbiter during a Midnight Magic promotion early Sunday morning and the ride was engulfed in flames."[33] Despite the conflagration, there were only a few minor injuries. At the Dade County Fair, the accident happened on a Gravitron, a ride evolved from the Rotor that spun riders at high speed against the inside walls of an enclosed capsule. On the next to last night, a wall panel gave way and three passengers were hurled from the ride. One was critically injured and in a coma for weeks, and the incident resulted in a fine and lawsuits. The Florida Department of Agriculture shut down all Gravitrons in the state until the cause could be determined.

Things got better from there. Numbers were up at Dade County where they raised the cost of the pay-one-price armband and broke a six-million-dollar ride gross. With pay-one-price back in place for the fairs of western Canada, they saw significant increases, with grosses up by 20 percent in Edmonton and 14 percent in Calgary. Attendance at the CNE, the Big E, and the South Carolina State Fair was also up. The e-ticket system was rolled out on a larger scale and functioned well at most events. With two hours of the Ex left to go, the G-Force malfunctioned by coming to an abrupt halt in mid-air. Riders had to be removed by ladders and 24 people were sent to hospital, some in neck braces and some on stretchers.

The economy was improving in 2004 and Conklin Shows benefitted along with the rest of the outdoor entertainment industry. They were back in the black and able to recoup some of the losses of 2003. But as Alfie told *Amusement Business* on November 22, "It wasn't hard for us to be up, but even being up significantly from last year was not enough.... We're still paying for last year." The business had recovered, the energy of Frank, the wisdom of Alfie and Jim (still providing advice), and the talents of their managers bringing the huge, ride-heavy Conklin Shows back from the brink. World's Finest remained a stable, increasingly independent operation under Jamieson. But they had entered a time of transition, and no one knew where they would end up.

THE END

On a personal level, there's the three eras of any business. The first generation builds. The second generation administers. And the third generation liquidates. That's not the carnival business, that's business in general. You can see all kinds of corporations out there where it has happened the same way.

Frank is a very smart individual. He's also got other concerns than the carnival business. He's got two young daughters. He's got great experience because he knows his grandfather's trials and tribulations, his father's, and from his own experience. Frank's personal choice is not to subject his daughters to this business. It's getting harder every year.

Outside agencies — anybody outside this business with their hand out, whether it be the trucking companies, the fair boards, the governments, the different fees required to get this business across the road, the fuel salesmen, stock salesmen — prices don't go down. Year after year the bottom line is shrinking. I'm extremely happy for Frank Conklin that he found a way to get out of this business, provide for his family for probably the rest of his life. I don't know how much he got for the company, but I don't think that he sold it cheaply.

Frank's a smart enough guy; if he gets bored, he'll find something to do. Maybe he'll call. He's got a vast repertoire of ex-employees, maybe they'd come to work for him, maybe they wouldn't. He knows he's got some pretty good friends out there; we'd offer him assistance in whatever way we can.

It does represent the end of an era. The Conklin family has been in business since the '20s. It's certainly the end of an era at the CNE, where they've played since 1937. But all things come to pass, and it was a good run. Not many companies can enjoy a 70-year-plus run being in business and finish on top of the game. Muhammad Ali had the opportunity to finish at the top of his game and didn't. Wayne Gretsky finished at the top of his game. Maybe you have to come from Brantford. You know a lot of people finish at the top of their game and know when it's time. Some don't and they're not remembered as fondly as I'm sure the Conklin family will be, for many, many years.

The one thing that doesn't need saying is that everybody out here, whether they've been here since Patty's days, whether they've been here since Jim Conklin's days like myself, whether they've been here for Frank's turn at the wheel, the one thing that I'm certain of is the amount of love for the Conklin family, the respect, that they rightfully deserve. It was a great run. I'll miss 'em.

Interview with Howard "Lurch" Pringle, Aug. 30, 2005

As economic realities were forcing Frank to restrain his brio in lugging his showy rides around for public spectacle, he was also playing his carnival king cards close to his chest. Neither he nor Alfie talked much to the media about Conklin Shows' return to profitability during the successful 2004 season, which helped him close negotiations that had been initiated during the less stable environment of the previous season.

On October 15, 2004, a news release announced that a new conglomerate, North American Midway Entertainment, a subsidiary of Stone Canyon Entertainment Corporation, had bought Canada's Conklin Shows and Conklin Shows International, along with two other companies. Former Ticketmaster president and chief operating officer Fred Rosen and a New York–based private equity firm, the Cypress Group, had formed Stone Canyon. Along with the Conklin companies, North American Midway Entertainment bought Farrow Amusement Company, based in Mississippi, and Thebault-Blomsness Inc., based in Illinois, the latter of which had two units, All Star Amusement Company and Astro Amusement Company. Conklin Shows was the largest of the three, which when combined had over 200 rides and played over 140 events. Rosen would be chairman of the board and Farrow's Mike Williams would be president and CEO. The management of the separate shows would remain in place for the time being.

The recent interest of investors from outside the carnival industry in buying carnivals might have begun with movie producer Michael Solomon in early 2003. He had talked to several of the larger shows, but nothing had come of it. Conklin had worked on joint bids with Thebault-Blomsness around the same time, and they and some other shows had been looking into the possibilities of merging but needed capital to support the transaction. The Cypress Group equity firm had come up with the money and then recruited Rosen, who was available because the company he formed after Ticketmaster, Key3Media, which had produced technology events, had gone bankrupt. Cypress's other investments included a large theatre chain, a drug company, an insurance company, and Meow Mix. Williams and Jeff Blomsness became the spokesmen for the conglomerate, while Frank and Rosen remained in the background. Blomsness said they had been working on the deal for three years.

Conklin Shows no longer existed as an independent business. The deal was finalized in December and Rosen approved a $3.5 million capital expenditure budget. Negotiations over the past year had been kept private, but insiders had known the deal was imminent, and it was seen as a model solution to the many problems of the carnival industry. The industry needed consolidation. Shows on their own could no longer afford to spend large amounts of money continually buying new rides. North American Midway Entertainment would have tremendous buying power and would also be in a significantly stronger position to negotiate with insurance companies. Expenses could be cut and rides swapped around among the various units. The shows in the merger would no longer be competing with each other, although they would continue to operate as separate units and keep their established routes. The deal was announced with a full page in the January edition of *Amusement Business*.[34] That same month, Rosen was a featured speaker at a conference in Beverley Hills on "The Future of Branded Entertainment."

One analyst hoped the merger would be "the vanguard of a trend" of shows merging "to gain greater leverage in the marketplace."[35] According to this view, "An influx of investment could help the industry raise standards, attract and retain quality workers, bulk up marketing muscle and contend with rising insurance and other costs." One theme rose to the top: "The marketing aspect of the deal, however, may well be the most compelling." The analyst predicted that "it won't be long before we see major national advertisers with a presence on the midway at county and state fairs across North America."[36] In fact, part of Rosen's plans for North American Midway Entertainment was "to create an attractive vehicle for marketers of entertainment and other products to reach the crowds who attend carnivals and fairs each year in the United States and Canada." Rosen estimated those crowds to be 150 million strong. Alfie relayed that he thought Rosen would "like to do some marketing and promotional work with fairs. Taking in consideration the volume of the market, how can you go wrong?" If successful and replicated, deals like this one would integrate the carnival industry into the global entertainment and marketing universe.

Beyond competitors who would have a hard time coming up against the conglomerate, others stood to lose from the deal. Shows like Cumberland Valley, Butler Amusements, and All-American that had booked rides with Conklin Shows for years would no longer be needed. Fair boards would find themselves with less choice in midway providers and often no choice at all. Others saw the deal as signalling the death of midways with character and individuality, a death that, as far as the larger shows were concerned, had happened largely unnoticed many years before. For Frank, who had lost interest in the future of the industry, it was just another good business decision, one that he stood to profit from handsomely.

According to Alfie, "Before this consolidation, our company was on a road to nowhere.... We had financial problems. We had difficulty in acquiring enough liability insurance. We could not afford to buy new rides and were having problems refurbishing the rides that we owned. The reasons were because during the last five years, expenses have risen dramatically and grosses remained stagnant."[37] He appreciated the investment capital and huge ride inventory now available to the group.

When the deal was announced in December as officially signed, Williams also announced that they had already begun to spend the $3.5 million capital budget on new rides. He kept busy over the next few months issuing news releases that cited the company's mission statement: "To provide an outstanding fun experience for families and develop the best standards for ride safety."[38] The first test of the new company was the 2005 South Florida Fair in the Conklin backyard, where North American Midway Entertainment would supply all the rides — no room for independents — and Rosen would be on the grounds. Frank was still able to joke that "the group would be in trouble if Rosen himself started picking out the rides."[39]

"The Jan. 14–30 South Florida Fair in West Palm Beach, the first venture for the newly formed North American Midway Entertainment, was a resounding success, according to all parties involved," the fair manager told *Amusement Business* on February 25. Frank said, "The midway looked better than ever. There's no doubt this is the way of the future." He and Alfie stayed in the background, letting their managers work with the fair and Williams. While attendance was down by 10 percent, gate, ride, and food revenue were all up in the double digits. They did not use the e-ticket system.

A review of the South Florida Fair in the February issue of *Amusement Business* called it "an out-of-home entertainment experience." The reviewer marked the fair as the debut of North American Midway Entertainment, "a venture that illuminates the growing sophistication of the industry." She saw the event, although "temporary," as successfully competing "for entertainment dollars head-to-head with destination amusement parks." She remarked with approval on the layout, service, variety of merchandise and entertainment, and cleanliness of the food outlets and restrooms. This perspective on the fair as an entertainment experience refused to acknowledge any trace of the carnie in favour of the corporate, and would have been encouraging to the shareholders of the Cypress Group. It augured well for finally lifting the lingering shadow of Patty Conklin and his like, dissolving his legacy into the dominant entertainment and marketing environment, and foreclosing on any chance for his kind to appear again.

Coda

What is Patty Conklin's legacy and that of the show to which he gave his borrowed name? His life and career belong to the history of the twentieth century, subject to its social and economic trends, which he exploited to his profit. He was there when the carnival emerged as a specific North American amusement industry, tinged with dishonesty, danger, and disrepute, and when it evolved in later years to embrace the middle-class masses with their growing prosperity and leisure time. He laid the foundation for his son and grandson to transform his jury-rigged enterprise and reputation into a continental conglomerate entertaining millions and dominating the industry, in the process becoming "a big corporation … run like a downtown office building." In hindsight, the years since Patty's death seem to have been in preparation for his show to be absorbed by something larger than itself and alien to its roots — for it to disappear.

LOOSE ENDS

I couldn't believe it. I didn't think there would be anybody in this flipping world that would ever buy this thing. At that moment when I found out that the cheque had hit the table, my very first thought was, "Is there really somebody crazy enough out there that would really want to do this?" My second thought was, 77 years of history just stopped in one flash of a moment. I was aware of the negotiations, but I didn't think it was ever

going to happen. I really expected that somebody was going to call at any moment and say the whole deal is off. That's the end of the story, I guess.
Interview with Greg "Scooter" Korek, Sept. 2, 2005

★ ★ ★

North American Midway Entertainment kept the top management staff of its various shows through the 2005 season, but then head office began pushing many of them out. Fred Rosen had hired Wayne Kunz, whose father had worked with Patty, as operations manager for the Conklin route soon after the merger, and he and Tony Diaz, from Farrow Shows, ran the route in Canada. Howard Pringle was let go before the 2006 season.

Alfie Phillips had characterized the show as on "the road to nowhere" before the merger. Turns out, that's the road his career with the show was on. He hung on for a few more years before deciding that what was once the Conklin midway wasn't big enough for two big personalities like his and Mike Williams's. He left the carnival for good by the end of the decade, and went on, among other activities, to review golf courses for a national golf magazine.

Frank Conklin, while owning part of North American Midway Entertainment, left the management of the combined company to others. He ran his former show for the new owners for four years after the merger, before finally selling his holdings and getting out in 2009.

Frank's investment in FairSwipe, the company formed to develop the e-ticket system, might have been part of his post-retirement plans. E-ticketing turned out to be too far ahead of its time. The data that was supposed to be the added benefit of the system turned out to be worthless without tactics to turn it to use. At the afternoon operations meetings, managers would be told the exact number of people on the midway and what they were spending money on, but could do nothing with the information other than what they were already doing. The hardware running the system lacked resilience to withstand the abuse — exposure to the elements, set-up and tear-down every 10 days, non-stop operation in rough conditions when open. North American Midway Entertainment dropped the system two years into the new regime, when Rosen and Williams found out they had to replace the equipment every two years at a cost of nearly a million dollars. FairSwipe was shut down in November 2005, although e-ticketing went on to become a standard practice in the coming decades.

Conklin senior staff had centuries of collective experience in dealing with the local fair boards, media, and public, and, while cleaning out the executive suite, Williams kept a core of Conklin managers to handle the locals. But he also brought people up from the California office to take over senior management, and tensions began to arise with the fair boards, especially those in Canada. The tensions subsided as the boards had little choice but to accept the new reality. Some of the U.S. boards were probably happy not to be dealing with Canadians anymore.

North American Midway Entertainment reduced the number of rides and concessions it provided for the Canadian National Exhibition in both 2005 and 2006. By 2007 relations with the CNE board were bad enough that, before the Ex opened that year, the CNE association issued a request for proposals to secure the services of a new midway provider.

A consortium called Conko Inc. submitted its proposal two days after the 2007 Ex ended. Jim had brought back Supershows in 2000 and built it up to 20 rides, playing 30 events, including 12 fall fairs and the Western Fair in London. To bid on the CNE, he combined the resources of Supershows and World's Finest Shows to form Conko Inc. He was the chief executive officer and Barry Jamieson the president and chief operating officer. Jamieson's son Stacy and Jim's daughter Trish were on the board of directors, with Alfie Phillips and other ex-Conklin International staff included among the management personnel. Frank was not involved. Later that fall, the CNE association announced that North American Midway Entertainment had been given the contract again. Conko Inc. was dissolved. The last chance for the resurrection of any semblance of the show that Patty Conklin had founded was past.

Jim Conklin continued to be involved in the industry he had helped shape. Norma died in 2009 and he slowed down. He ran Supershows for a few more years, then turned to renting rides and placing waffle stands at community events. Always a promoter of carnival history, he had donated many antique rides to Heritage Park in Calgary in 1983. He launched the North American Carnival Museum and Archives in 2008 with charitable status. He incorporated it and moved it to its own building in Brantford in 2009, on a street just around the corner from a small park on land donated by the family and named in their honour. The building was in an industrial park not zoned for museums, so he called it The Carnival Fun Factory. He opened it to the public in June 2015. It had a small outdoor amusement park, midway food, and a gift shop, with a substantial collection of midway memorabilia on display. He promoted it for events and birthday parties. The City of Brantford closed the Fun Factory the following spring for a zoning infraction, although the archives and artifacts continued for a time to be available for research purposes. The North American Carnival Museum and Archives is now dormant.

Jim suffered a massive stroke in early March of 2023 and died on March 22. His family held a private funeral service, and scores of friends and business associates attended a memorial at a gallery on the CNE grounds to give him his last call. He had been living independently and coming up with ideas to promote to the end. His family remembered him as an avid fisherman and tennis player who liked to cook and to read. He also loved his dogs, keeping multiple Westies —West Highland Terriers — with him throughout his life.

World's Finest continued to use the Conko logo after the sale of the show, but finally retired it in 2015, except for one left on the Century Wheel. It was also used on canvas tote bags produced by Brave Brown Bag as a fundraiser for the Conklin Foundation. You have to look hard to find Conko on the CNE midway today. The cross-eyed clown graces two ice cream waffle joints at the Ex, a confection that was but one of the firsts Patty brought to the public at his annual world's fair.

In Sum

But Conko is not the sum of Patty's bequest. While the show that marked so many milestones in the history of the North American carnival is no more, its legacy, good and bad, persists. Big midways for small fairs; banal, family-friendly funways under themed colours; a business model that makes grift and girls unprofitable; massive machinery moved heedless of effort; the ability to play in every corner of Canada and the United States to many millions of patrons annually — these milestones are part of the legacy of three generations of Conklins.

Patty built his show by pilfering a patrimony from an ailing widow and cheating Speed Garrett on his deathbed, and the show was known in the West in its early days as Patty Conklin and his 40 Thieves. By the time he died he was a respectable businessman. Beginning with little more than a beat-up merry-go-round and a big, rotten fish, he was central to the introduction of European spectaculars to North American fair goers. He transformed the midway experience into an occasion to ride the most thrilling machines available in the world, and the CNE from a regional fair into the world's largest annual outdoor exhibition. After his death, the CNE became the location for massive trade fairs year-round, where rides appeared for 18 days each summer. It remains Canada's largest fair, but the midway is almost an afterthought.

Patty began by entertaining immigrant farmers in the West with girl shows and freak shows. Along with other carnival owners, he paved the way for strippers to be accepted by the public. While girl shows died out with the loosening of public morality, freak shows disappeared when public opinion evolved to find the display of humans distasteful. There are few shows of any kind on midways today.

Exciting rides offering a visceral experience not available anywhere else became the best weapons the midway had to defend itself against other entertainment media empires, but amusement parks excelled better than midways at thrill machines. Canada's Wonderland, owned by an American company, now has a ride lineup that the CNE will never match and entertains more than twice the annual visitors as the Ex.

When brother Frank found horses, his attention to the carnival became half-hearted. He could afford to adopt the life of gentleman farmer and his health required it. In doing so, he contributed significantly to thoroughbred breeding in Canada and is remembered as a leader in that world more than in the outdoor amusement industry.

Patty all but let his regional fairs go, happy to enjoy the spotlight through the CNE. He died as he lived, a character who became the role he played, never sure that someone wouldn't call him on it and his fame and fortune would turn out to be as ephemeral as he suspected them to be.

Jim took over road show operations and had more appreciation for their heritage than did his father. His talents were better suited to his time. He built his company up, so it was ready to take over the western fair circuit after the fall of Royal American Shows. Conklin Shows became the biggest midway provider in the world to the biggest fairs in the world. Jim and son Frank's show dominated the carnival industry and defined what a North American midway should be. It became a different kind of operation, made possible by the success of big exhibitions at the expense of traditional fairs.

Jim's retirement hobby was supporting the smaller fairs that had provided the ground in which his father's show had grown and which his own show had outgrown. The agricultural industry has been changing, and fairs have suffered from the loss of their rationale. Agricultural associations have begun using events other than fairs to promote their interests. The Covid-19 pandemic hurt all events that relied on the gathering of large crowds of people. All fairs and exhibitions in Canada were cancelled for 2020 and 2021. They began to recover in 2022. The future of local fairs versus regional exhibitions remains in question.

Frank was the right person to take the newest and biggest rides on the road. He was able to manage the logistics of moving massive pieces of equipment, but he pushed the limits beyond what was sustainable. After he had gone as far as he could with rides and was forced to pull back, there was nothing more to interest him on the road. Luckily for him, he was able to get out cleanly, selling the family company and leaving the business his forebears had followed for close to a century. In the process, he contributed to North American Midway Entertainment, an aggregation that describes itself today as "the world's largest travelling outdoor amusement park" and that annually entertains over 15 million patrons with over 200 rides.

This story of Patty Conklin and his show is a record of a remarkable personality, so perfectly suited to his time that his like will not appear again. His show became a significant institution and left an indelible mark on North American midways. Patty, Jim, and Frank evolved the family show into a multinational corporation reflecting the society around them. There is no final version of this story. It reaches one kind of conclusion with the end of Conklin Shows, but there are many more stories to tell and many more ways to tell them.

Acknowledgements

I've been fortunate to have had the support and assistance of scores of people during my work on *Carnie King*. In the beginning, Jim Conklin granted me access to the Conklin archives and connected me to people who could answer my questions about the show. When he died his daughters Melissa and Trish picked up where he left off. They have encouraged me and readily responded to all my requests, especially during the last stages of development.

The people associated with Conklin Shows whom I've been lucky to know over the years are too many to name, including all those whom I interviewed. I first worked for the show under the management of John Miller, who helped me earn my tuition and who had the chance to endorse my project for this book before he died. Dave Bastido, Dave McKelvey, Bill Napper, May Robertson, and Dave Vance became friends who greeted me warmly when I showed up on the midway in later years and were always ready to answer my questions and help me however they could. Barry Jamieson and Alfie Phillips smiled on my efforts to write about the show with which they have been involved all their lives. Greg "Scooter" Korek is a wealth of information about Conklin Shows and midways and fairs generally. I'm happy to count him as a friend who has always been eager to share what he knows with me.

Everyone I've dealt with at Dundurn Press has been helpful and a joy to work with. Kathryn Lane, Dundurn's associate publisher, has stood by me since she first offered to publish *Carnie King*. She was a great comfort when we encountered obstacles along the way. Elena Radic, managing editor, has been a friendly guiding hand throughout the process of getting the book into print. Carrie Gleason was my copy editor and saved me from many mistakes. Susan Fitzgerald, my substantive editor, in innumerable instances showed me how to best serve my readers by producing clear and readable text. She was everything an author could hope for in an editor.

I'm grateful to my sons Liam and Quinn for their love and for their support throughout the book's entire production. Finally, and most importantly, my partner, Lorie Boucher, has remained by my side through everything, including the many ups and downs I've experienced with this book. Without her, I would never have had the fortitude to see it through to publication. I owe her my gratitude in this and every aspect of my life.

Glossary

The glossary defines terms used in the text more than once. Terms used only once are defined in context.

advance man: Carnival office employee who worked ahead of the show to book engagements.

agents: Games operators.

back end: Rides and shows that usually occupied the middle and end of the midway.

bally: A raised platform in front of the show upon which the talker presented their spiel.

bally show: A preview of a show presented on the bally by the talker to gather a crowd interested in paying to see the show.

blowdown: A storm strong enough to cause havoc with a carnival's tents and equipment.

brass: Show money paid to staff when the show was short of regular currency; only valid at the cookhouse or pie car.

fixer: Carnival office employee who made the necessary arrangements, including bribery, with the local police and other authorities to ensure that a show did not come into conflict with them.

flat store; flat joint: A game no one could win unless the operator wanted them to.

front end: Games and concessions that usually occupied the part of the midway closest to the main entrance.

gaff joint: A crooked or controlled game that allowed the operator to determine who won; the "gaff" in a "G wheel" was the control on the wheel that enabled the operator to stop it wherever he wanted.

gilly show: Shows that had no transportation equipment, so they were loaded on rented railway boxcars then carted to and from the lot by local draymen.

grind store; grind show: Games and shows that relied on a steady flow of customers, none of whom would spend a great deal of money.

hey rube: A fight between carnies and marks.

joint: Another name for a game.

legal adjuster: *See* fixer.

lot boss: The general superintendent who looked after day-to-day operations.

lucky boy: Dishonest games agent.

mark: A customer on the midway who thinks they can win at the games and is willing to spend money to prove it.

mitt joint: A palm reader's concession.

nut: The overhead or operating expense for each game or attraction, including the cost of a ride; once it is covered, the operation was said to be "off the nut."

patch: *See* fixer.

pie car: The railway car used as the staff lounge; a tradition from the circus trains of the late nineteenth century.

privilege: The flat rate per foot of midway real estate paid by owners of concessions — including games, novelty joints, and food stands — to work on the midway.

still date: A spot booked to fill in periods when a show did not have fairs to play; usually did not have an event associated with it.

store: Another name for a game.

strong show: A carnival that allowed gambling, grift, and explicit girl shows was said to "play strong."

suitcase show: The owner of a suitcase show owned no more than their suitcase full of bookings and contracts.

Sunday school show: Type of show that did not play strong; a term borrowed from vaudeville.

talker: Also known as a spieler, but never a barker, the talker worked on the bally to attract a crowd interested in seeing a show.

tear down: The process of taking apart and loading all the games, rides and equipment belonging to a show at the end of a date for travel to the next date.

ten-in-one: Ten acts for one admission; a type of freak show.

tip: The crowd gathered in front of the bally to hear a talker who sought to "turn the tip" or get everyone streaming to the ticket box.

townie: Another name for a mark; someone who was not with the carnival.

Notes

PREFACE: A CARNIVAL KINGDOM

1 See Joe McKennon, *A Pictorial History of the American Carnival* (Sarasota, Fla.: Carnival Publishers, volumes I and II, 1972, volume III, 1981). McKennon's work is the only published attempt to cover the history of the American carnival. It is a source for much of the background information on the carnival industry. See also Paul Horsman, *The Fabulous World of the Carnival* (Nashua, N.H.: Midway Publications, 2000). A number of histories of individual American carnival companies have been published, although none on any Canadian show.

2 Many Canadian fairs have had celebratory volumes written about them, but for broader studies of fairs in Canada, see Grant MacEwan, *Agriculture on Parade: The Story of the Fairs and Exhibitions of Western Canada* (Toronto: Thomas Nelson, 1950), David Jones, *Midways, Judges and Smooth-Tongued Fakirs: The Illustrated Story of Country Fairs in the Prairie West* (Saskatoon: Western Producer Prairie Books, 1983), Guy Scott, *A Fair Share: A History of Agricultural Societies and Fairs in Ontario, 1792–1992* (Peterborough, Ont.: Ontario Association of Agricultural Societies, 1992), and Guy Scott, *Country Fairs in Canada* (Markham, Ont.: Fitzhenry and Whiteside, 2005).

3 On the CNE, see James Lorimer, *The Ex: A Picture History of the Canadian National Exhibition* (Toronto: James Lorimer Publishers, 1973), John Withrow, ed., *Once Upon a Century: 100 Year History of the Ex* (Toronto: J.H. Robinson Publishing, 1978), and Keith Walden, *Becoming Modern in Toronto: The Industrial Exhibition and the Shaping of Late Victorian Culture* (Toronto: University of Toronto Press, 1997).

1: THE APPRENTICESHIP OF JOE RENKER

1   Details about the lives of Karl and Maria Renker and their children come from vital records in the New Jersey State Archives in Trenton, New Jersey. These include death certificates for them and birth certificates for their children Adelia, Joseph, Rudolph, Catherine, and Frank. I have also found information in the federal censuses of 1900, 1910, 1920, and 1930, the state censuses of 1905 and 1915, Paterson city directories from various years, and the Social Security Death Index.

2   Information about the Renkers' passage and arrival comes from the passenger list of the SS *Gallia* and the Renkers' entrance papers. The passenger list is held in the archive of the Port of New York and the entrance papers in the New Jersey State Archives.

3   Much of what is known about Patty's childhood comes from James Conklin's recollections of stories his father told him. Patty also provided various accounts to reporters later in his life.

4   Jane Addams, *The Spirit of Youth and the City Streets* (New York: Macmillan, 1909), pp. 5–6.

5   Toronto *Star Weekly*, Aug. 31, 1957, p. 19.

6   Background information in the following paragraphs comes from David Nasaw, *Going Out: The Rise and Fall of Public Amusements* (Cambridge, Mass.: Harvard University Press, 1993). See also Robert W. Snyder, *The Voice of the City: Vaudeville and Popular Culture in New York* (New York: Oxford University Press, 1989).

7   See Nasaw and John F. Kasson, *Amusing the Million: Coney Island at the Turn of the Century* (New York: Hill & Wang, 1978).

8   See Woody Register, *The Kid of Coney Island: Fred Thompson and the Rise of American Amusements* (New York: Oxford University Press, 2001).

9   See Garret Keizer, "Labor's Schoolhouse: Lessons from the Paterson Silk Strike of 1913," *Harper's*, 335 (July 2017), pp. 53–58.

10   "J.W. Conklin, 1892–1970," *Amusement Business*, Nov. 21, 1970, p. 76.

11   Information on James Wesley Conklin Sr. comes from articles in *Billboard* throughout this period.

12   Robert Bogdan, *Freak Show: Presenting Human Oddities for Amusement and Profit* (Chicago: University of Chicago Press, 1988), p. 58.

13   Much of the background on the carnival in the following pages and throughout is from McKennon, *A Pictorial History of the American Carnival*. The information in McKennon is confirmed in other sources.

14 See A.W. Stencell, *Girl Show: Into the Canvas World of Bump and Grind* (Toronto: ECW Press, 1999).

15 "Clark & Conklin Shows," *Billboard*, March 6, 1915, p. 31.

16 "Where and When They Open," *Billboard*, March 18, 1916, p. 73.

17 "Winter Quarters List," *Billboard*, March 24, 1917, p. 122.

18 "Clark & Conklin Shows," *Billboard*, Apr. 21, 1917, p. 29.

19 "Clark & Conklin Shows," *Billboard*, Apr. 21, 1917, p. 29.

20 "Conklin in Cincy," *Billboard*, March 2, 1918, p. 34.

21 "Clark & Conklin Shows Will Retain Title as Heretofore — Partnership with Flynn Cancelled," *Billboard*, March 23, 1918, p. 68.

22 "Many Carnivals Start 1918 Tour During the Past Week," *Billboard*, May 11, 1918, p. 28.

23 "Clark & Conklin Shows," *Billboard*, May 25, 1918, p. 41.

24 "Clark & Conklin Shows," *Billboard*, Oct. 26, 1918, p. 32.

25 McKennon, vol. I, p. 71.

26 "Mr. and Mrs. J.W. Conklin in Auto Accident Near Shelby, Miss.," *Billboard*, Dec. 21, 1918, p. 44.

27 Federal census 1920, New Jersey State Archives.

28 Membership card of Joseph Renker, in author's possession.

29 "Billboard Callers," *Billboard*, Oct. 16, 1920, p. 73.

30 "Billie Clark Buys Tom Hasson's Interest in Famous Broadway Shows — Hasson Will Take Out Circus," *Billboard*, Nov. 20, 1920, p. 90.

31 "Clark's Broadway Shows," *Billboard*, Dec. 18, 1920, p. 122.

32 "The Clean-Up Wins at Toronto Meeting," *Billboard*, Dec. 9, 1922, p. 6.

33 "'Patty' Conklin Opens Plant," *Billboard*, Oct. 30, 1920, p. 74.

34 "Original Conklin One Ball Bucket Game," *Billboard*, Jan. 1, 1921, p. 65.

35 "Original Conklin One Ball Bucket Game," *Billboard*, Feb. 19, 1921, p. 88.

36 "Clark's Broadway Shows," *Billboard*, March 5, 1921, p. 72.

37 On Lou Dufour here and throughout, see Lou Dufour with Irwin Kirby, *Fabulous Years: Carnival Life, World's Fairs, and Broadway* (New York: Vantage, 1977).

38 Dufour, p. 25.

39 "'King Patty'—an industry gives thanks," *Amusement Business*, Nov. 16, 1968, p. 41.

40 "Conklins for Canada Fairs," *Billboard*, June 25, 1921, p. 102.

41 "Grave of J.W. Conklin Decorated by Family and Friends on Decoration Day," *Billboard*, June 11, 1921, p. 93.

42 Stencell, p. 13.

43 Toronto *Star Weekly*, Aug. 31, 1957, p. 19.

44 "Lavoie in Chicago," *Billboard*, Dec. 23, 1922, p. 82.
45 "Covered Many Miles LaVoie's International Attractions in Quarters at Detroit," *Billboard*, Nov. 10, 1923, p. 104.
46 "International Amusement Co. to Open at Detroit, Mich., April 12," *Billboard*, March 22, 1924, p. 242h.
47 "Carnival Caravans," *Billboard*, Feb. 3, 1923, p. 89.
48 "Levitt-Brown-Huggins Shows Inaugurate Season at Kelso, Wash.," *Billboard*, May 19, 1923, p. 93.
49 "Conklin Concession Co.," *Billboard*, Sept. 15, 1923, p. 102.
50 "International Am. Co. Has Good Opening at Vancouver, Wash.," *Billboard*, Apr. 22, 1922, p. 90.

2: CONKLIN & GARRETT'S ALL-CANADIAN SHOWS

1 J.W. Conklin, "Carnival Problems in Western Canada," *Billboard*, Dec. 5, 1931, p. 54.
2 "In the Name of Agriculture," *Farm and Ranch Review*, Sept. 6, 1915, p. 499.
3 Letter, Molly Lavoie to Patty Conklin, Nov. 30, 1923. Original in Conklin archives, copy in author's possession.
4 "Levitt-Brown-Huggins Open in the Northwest Inaugurate Tour for 1924 at Tacoma, Wash.," *Billboard*, May 3, 1924, p. 120.
5 Biographical details about Speed Edward Garrett come from various articles in *Billboard* and his letters to Patty. Information also comes from interviews by Greg Korek and Bill Napper with Speed's grandsons, Wayne and Don Garrett.
6 Telegram, Molly Lavoie to Patty Conklin, March 1, 1924. Original in Conklin archives, copy in author's possession.
7 "Elks' Circus Opens Monday," *Vancouver Sun*, Apr. 23, 1927, p. 10. Details about what shows opened come from Conklin accounts book for 1924, which also contains information about their route. Original in Conklin archives.
8 "A Symposium on Outdoor Amusements," *Billboard*, March 23, 1929, p. 67.
9 This story and its assessment of Patty is from the Montreal *Standard*, Sept. 21, 1946, p. 20.
10 Conklin accounts book for 1924. Original in Conklin archives.
11 The activities of the Conklins and Garrett between seasons can be followed through scattered mentions in *Billboard*.
12 "Conklin & Garrett Shows Slated to Open May 2 at Vancouver," *Billboard*, Feb. 21, 1925, p. 104.

13 "Levitt-Brown-Huggins Shows Close Season and Enter Winter Quarters at Portland, Ore.," *Billboard*, Nov. 4, 1922, p. 82.

14 On Louis D. "L.D." Taylor, see Daniel Francis, *L.D.: Mayor Louis Taylor and the Rise of Vancouver* (Vancouver: Arsenal Pulp Press, 2004).

15 "Conklin & Garrett Shows Brief Resume of Stands Played," *Billboard*, June 6, 1925, p. 100.

16 "Conklin & Garrett All-Canadian Shows Clean Organization," Victoria *Colonist*, May 14, 1925, p. 12.

17 "Circus Comes Once More to Victoria 'All Canadian Shows' Here For One Week," Victoria *Colonist*, May 12, 1925, p. 12.

18 Letter, John Shirras to Conklin & Garrett, May 25, 1925. Original in Conklin archives.

19 Toronto *Star Weekly*, Aug. 13, 1957, p. 19.

20 James Coleman, "Success Didn't Spoil Patty Conklin," *Amusement Business*, special issue, Nov. 16, 1968, p. 59.

21 "Conklin & Garrett Shows Close Winter Quarters Established at Vancouver, British Columbia," *Billboard*, Oct. 17, 1925, p. 88.

22 Conklin accounts book for 1925. Original in Conklin archives.

23 Testimonial letters for 1925. Originals in Conklin archives.

24 Information about Al Salvail and Pete Kortes comes from mentions in *Billboard* throughout this period.

25 "Conklin & Garrett Shows," *Billboard*, Apr. 17, 1926, p. 81.

26 "A Symposium on Outdoor Amusements," *Billboard*, March 23, 1929, p. 67.

27 James Coleman, "Success Didn't Spoil Patty Conklin," *Amusement Business*, special issue, Nov. 16, 1968, p. 59.

28 Letter, William Douglas to Patty Conklin, May 17, 1926. Original in Conklin archives.

29 "Midway Confab," *Billboard*, June 26, 1926, p. 84.

30 J.W. Conklin, "Carnival Problems in Western Canada," *Billboard*, Dec. 5, 1931, p. 54.

31 Letter, Gyro Club to Conklin, Sept. 25, 1926. Original in Conklin archives.

32 "Conklin & Garrett Shows Winter in Vancouver, B.C.," *Billboard*, Oct. 16, 1926, p. 86.

33 Conklin accounts book for 1926. Original in Conklin archives.

34 Information on these properties comes from Patty's correspondence. Originals in Conklin archives.

35 Telegram, Garrett to Conklin, Dec. 31, 1926. Original in Conklin archives, copy in author's possession.

36 Press material and accounts book for 1927. Originals in Conklin archives.

37 Advertisement, *Billboard*, Oct. 23, 1926, p. 84.

38 Conklin accounts book for 1927. Original in Conklin archives.

39 "Midway Confab," *Billboard*, Aug. 28, 1926, p. 88.

40 "Big Show Is Coming Here on Saturday," Nanaimo *Free Press*, May 2, 1927, p. 2.

41 For details of L.D. Taylor's career, see Francis.

42 "Conklin & Garrett Shows," *Billboard*, June 22, 1929, p. 75.

43 Conklin accounts book for 1927. Original in Conklin archives.

44 Want ads, *Billboard*, Nov. 12, 1927, p. 86; Dec. 10, 1927, p. 146a.

45 "Los Angeles," *Billboard*, Dec. 3, 1927, p. 70.

46 "Conklin & Garrett Shows Using Barnes-Carruthers Acts," *Billboard*, March 24, 1928, p. 118.

47 Letter, Conklin to Garrett, July 4, 1928. Original in Conklin archives.

48 Death certificate for Karl Renker, July 7, 1927, New Jersey State Archives.

49 Speed's location and condition can be followed in telegrams and letters he sent to Patty and Frank. Originals in Conklin archives, copies in author's possession.

50 "Glamour of Circus Attracts Old and Young — Vancouver to Be Mecca During the Next Seven Days for Adherents of King Carnival," *Vancouver Sun*, May 5, 1928, p. 28.

51 "Argument on Circus Games Is Adjourned," *Vancouver Sun*, May 7, 1928, p. 18. See "Elks vs. City Issue Friday" and "Airs Protest Over Carnival," *Vancouver Sun*, May 9, 1928, pp. 19 and 22, and "No Wheels of Chance at Fair," *Vancouver Sun*, May 12, 1928, p. 1.

52 Letter, Conklin to Garrett, June 12, 1928. Original in Conklin archives, copy in author's possession.

53 Telegram, Conklin to Garrett, June 12, 1928. Original in Conklin archives, copy in author's possession.

54 Letter, Conklin to Garrett, Sept. 29, 1928. Original in Conklin archives, copy in author's possession.

55 Telegram, Conklin to Garrett, Sept. 20, 1928. Original in Conklin archives, copy in author's possession.

56 Letter, Conklin to Garrett, Jan. 3, 1929. Original in Conklin archives, copy in author's possession.

57 Telegram, Conklin to Garrett, July 3, 1928. Original in Conklin archives, copy in author's possession.

58 Payments to each of the principals are recorded in the accounts book for 1928.

59 Advertisement, *Billboard*, Jan. 21, 1928, p. 86.

60 Letter, Conklin to Garrett, Jan. 3, 1929. Original in Conklin archives, copy in author's possession.

61 "Paddy Conklin Visiting N.Y.," *Billboard*, Nov. 3, 1928, p. 85.

62 Legal details recounted in correspondence between Conklin and Hand. Originals in Conklin archives.

63 "Paddy Conklin Night At L.A. Showmen Club," *Billboard*, Jan. 19, 1929, p. 74.

64 "Pacific Coast Showmen's Notes," *Billboard*, March 9, 1929, p. 79.

65 Letter, Conklin to Garrett, Jan. 3, 1929. Original in Conklin archives, copy in author's possession.

66 On Carl Sedlmayer and Royal American Shows, here and throughout, see Bob Goldsack and Fred Heatley, *Royal American Shows: World's Largest Midway: A Pictorial History* (Nashua, N.H.: Midway Museum Publications, 1996).

67 "Tent City Springs Up on Cambie — Finishing Touches Are Being Put to Elks' Circus; Open On Saturday," *Vancouver Sun*, May 3, 1929, p. 3.

68 "Elks Publish Magazine of Great Merit — Frank Hardie, Talented Journalist, Proves Stimulating Editor-in-Chief," *Vancouver Sun*, May 4, 1929, section 3, p. 3.

69 "Conklin & Garrett Shows," *Billboard*, May 18, 1929, p. 76.

70 Letter, Conklin to Garrett, July 13, 1929. Original in Conklin archives, copy in author's possession.

71 J.W. Conklin, "Carnival Problems in Western Canada," *Billboard*, Dec. 5, 1931, p. 54.

72 Andrew King, *Pen, Paper & Printing Ink* (Saskatoon: Western Producer Prairie Books, 1970), p. 91.

73 Letter, Conklin to Garrett, July 13, 1929. Original in Conklin archives, copy in author's possession.

74 "Pacific Coast Showmen's Notes," *Billboard*, Nov. 23, 1929, p. 75.

75 Letter, Conklin to Garrett, Dec. 5, 1929. Original in Conklin archives, copy in author's possession.

76 Letter, Conklin to Garrett, Dec. 5, 1929. Original in Conklin archives, copy in author's possession.

77 "Partnership Is Dissolved — Speed Garrett's interest in Conklin & Garrett shows passes to J.W. Conklin," *Billboard*, Feb. 8, 1930, p. 72.

78 Letter, Garrett to Conklin, Apr. 30, 1930. Original in Conklin archives, copy in author's possession.

79 Letter, Conklin to Garrett, May 6, 1930. Original in Conklin archives, copy in author's possession.

80 Letter, Garrett to Conklin, June 11, 1930. Original in Conklin archives, copy in author's possession.

81 Letter, Conklin to Garrett, June 21, 1930. Original in Conklin archives, copy in author's possession.

82 "J.W. Conklin Contracts Big Freak Animal Show," *Billboard*, Jan. 4, 1930, p. 73.

83 "Pacific Coast Showmen's Association," *Billboard*, Aug. 30, 1930, p. 75.

84 Letter, Patty Conklin to Frank Conklin, July 18, 1930. Original in Conklin archives, copy in author's possession.

85 Letter, Conklin to Garrett, June 21, 1930. Original in Conklin archives, copy in author's possession.

86 J.W. Conklin, "Carnival Problems in Western Canada," *Billboard*, Dec. 5, 1931, p. 54.

87 Letter, Conklin to Garrett, June 21, 1930. Original in Conklin archives, copy in author's possession.

88 Letter, Conklin to Garrett, July 18, 1930. Original in Conklin archives, copy in author's possession.

89 Letter, Conklin to Garrett, July 18, 1930. Original in Conklin archives, copy in author's possession.

90 Letter, Patty Conklin to Frank Conklin, July 18, 1930. Original in Conklin archives, copy in author's possession.

91 Photo caption, *Amusement Business*, Oct. 19, 1968, p. 47.

92 "J.W. Conklin to Be Very Busy for a Few Weeks," *Billboard*, Oct. 18, 1930, p. 69.

93 "Pacific Coast Showmen's Association," *Billboard*, Oct. 25, 1930, p. 69.

94 On Edgar "Painless" Parker, see Arden G. Christen and Peter M. Pronych, *Painless Parker: A Dental Renegade's Fight to Make Advertising "Ethical"* (Halifax: McCurdy Printing and Typesetting, 1995).

95 Mike Hanley, "Charm and Flim-flam: The Carnie's Life," *Toronto Star*, May 23, 1999, p. D18.

96 Montreal *Standard*, Sept. 21, 1946, p. 20.

97 "SLA Banquet and Ball Proves Roaring Success," *Billboard*, Dec. 13, 1930, p. 3.

98 "Conklin's Canadian at Vancouver, B.C.," *Billboard*, May 16, 1931, p. 46.

99 Dufour with Kirby, p. 46.

100 "Circus Removes to Central Park," *Vancouver Sun*, May 11, 1931, p. 4.

101 "Conklin Ends Fair Circuit," *Billboard*, Aug. 22, 1931, p. 44.

102 "They're Vancouver Girls in Conklin Show at Fair," *Vancouver Sun*, Aug. 25, 1931, p. 9.

103 "New General Agent for Conklin Shows," *Vancouver Sun*, Aug. 29, 1931, p. 15.

104 "'I'm Not Downcast, We'll Come Through Safely and Well' — Premier S.F. Tolmie Says Exhibition Is Destined to Grow Steadily," *Vancouver Sun*, Aug. 22, 1931, p. 1.

105 "244,385 Attended Exhibition — Two Autos, Trip, Await Winners," *Vancouver Sun*, Aug. 31, 1931, p. 18.

106 "Record Crowd Out for Opening of Canada Pacific Exhibition," *Billboard*, Sept. 5, 1931, p. 86.

3: TURNING TO THE EAST

1   On the Johnny J. Jones Exposition, see Bob Goldsack, *A History of the Johnny J. Jones Exposition* (Nashua, N.H.: Midway Museum Publications, 1990). On Rubin & Cherry Shows, see Chris Audibert, *Rubin & Cherry* (Nashua, N.H.: Midway Museum Publications, 1989). On Royal American Shows, see Goldsack and Heatley, *Royal American Shows.*

2   See "Parasitic Twin Severed from Body of Boy, 12," *Pittsburgh Post-Gazette,* Feb. 11, 1944; "Knife Gives Normal Life to Partial Twin," *Palm Beach Post,* Feb. 11, 1944; "Boy Normal after Partial Twin Removed from Body," *Free Lance-Star* Feb. 11, 1944; "Surgery Makes Him One: Through with Sideshows Now, Young Defort Is Happy at School," *Winnipeg Tribune,* Feb. 10, 1944.

3   "At Last the Carnival Cleanup," *Billboard,* June 3, 1922, p. 74.

4   R.D. Luce, "Those Troublesome Concessions," *Billboard,* March 23, 1929, p. 63.

5   "Organization Is Indorsed," *Billboard,* Oct. 14, 1933, p. 38.

6   "Fleming to Western Canada," *Billboard,* March 5, 1932, p. 44.

7   "All Class A Canadian Shows, Losers in 1931, To Carry On," *Billboard,* Jan. 30, 1932, p. 62.

8   "Conklin's Canadian Shows," *Billboard,* July 2, 1932, p. 49.

9   "Conklin's Canadian Shows," *Billboard,* Apr. 30, 1932, p. 59.

10 Letter, Conklin to Garrett, March 22, 1932. Original in Conklin archives, copy in author's possession.

11 "Hartmann's Weekly Broadcast," *Billboard,* July 30, 1932, p. 71.

12 "Hartmann's Weekly Broadcast," *Billboard,* July 30, 1932, p. 71.

13 Letter, Conklin to Garrett, Sept. 3, 1932. Original in Conklin archives, copy in author's possession.

14 "Conklins Return from Trip Abroad," *Billboard,* Jan. 21, 1933, p. 38.

15 Series of letters between Conklin and Garrett from March 26 to June 14, 1932. Originals in Conklin archives, copies in author's possession.

16 Letter, Garrett to Conklin, July 14, 1932. Original in Conklin archives, copy in author's possession.

17 Letter, Garrett to Conklin, Sept. 20, 1932. Original in Conklin archives, copy in author's possession.

18 The story of the miner and his loss is told by James Conklin as recounted to him by his father.

19 Letter, Agnes Tulloch to Conklin, June 8, 1933. Original in Conklin archives, copy in author's possession.

20 Letter, Conklin to Garrett, June 27, 1933. Original in Conklin archives, copy in author's possession.

21 "Conklin's Shows in Quarters," *Billboard*, Oct. 28, 1933, p. 42.

22 "Showmen's League of America," *Billboard*, Nov. 4, 1933, p. 41.

23 "SLA Nominates Its Officers — Carruthers Selected for 1934 President at Rousing Meeting," *Billboard*, Nov. 4, 1933, p. 40.

24 "Ernie Young Wins Battle For Presidency of the SLA — Popular revue producer elected by overwhelming majority—Patty Conklin becomes vice-president—Streibich re-elected secretary," *Billboard*, Dec. 16, 1933, p. 38.

25 "Convention Muttering," *Billboard*, Dec. 16, 1933, p. 40.

26 "Carnival Mutterings," *Billboard*, Apr. 21, 1934, p. 46.

27 "Paddy Conklin Springs Surprise," *Billboard*, March 17, 1934, p. 47.

28 "Conklin Makes Dandy Showing in Toronto," *Billboard*, July 14, 1934, p. 43.

29 "Conklin's All-Canadian Shows," *Billboard*, July 14, 1934, pp. 48, 52.

30 "Conklin's All-Canadian Shows," *Billboard*, Aug. 18, 1934, p. 47.

31 "Conklin's All-Canadian Shows," *Billboard*, Sept. 1, 1934, p. 54.

32 *Sherbrooke Daily Record*, Aug. 29, 1934, p. 6.

33 H.W. Waters, *History of Fairs and Exhibitions: Their Classifications, Functions and Values* (London, Ont.: Reid Brothers, 1939).

34 "Showmen's League of America," *Billboard*, Oct. 6, 1934, p. 49.

35 "On to Toronto! Moguls of Outdoor Showdom Drawn to Mass Conventions," *Billboard*, Nov. 24, 1934, p. 45.

36 "Kin to Buffalo Bill Canon Cody States — Tells Gathering of Showmen to Keep Production Clean," *Toronto Star*, Nov. 28, 1934, p. 23.

37 "SLA Function Big Success," *Billboard*, Dec. 8, 1934, p. 46.

38 "Showmen's League of America," *Billboard*, Dec. 8, 1934, p. 47.

39 "Hartmann's Weekly Broadcast," *Billboard*, May 25, 1935, p. 62.

40 "Name Hamilton Man as Head of Showmen — J.W. Conklin to Be Youngest and First Canadian President — Pay Honor to Dead," *Toronto Star*, Nov. 26, 1934, p. 25.

41 "Outdoor Observations," *Billboard*, Sept. 8, 1928, p. 169.

42 "Conklin Springs Pay Gate in the Eastern Provinces," *Billboard*, July 27, 1935, p. 56.

43 "Conklin's Shows Conclude Season," *Billboard*, Oct. 12, 1935, p. 44.

44 "Conklin's Shows Conclude Season," *Billboard*, Oct. 12, 1935, p. 44.

45 "Organization Behind Scenes Puts Over Expositions, Says Conklin," *Billboard*, Dec. 14, 1935, p. 59.

46 Leonard Traube, "Out in the Open — Chapter from Conklinville," *Billboard*, Dec. 7, 1935, p. 57.

47 "Pacific Coast Showmen's Assn," *Billboard*, June 13, 1936, p. 47.
48 "Out in the Open," *Billboard*, Apr. 4, 1936, p. 56.
49 "Weather Man Gives Conklin Bad Break," *Billboard*, June 13, 1936, p. 45.
50 Conklin accounts book for 1936. Original in Conklin archives.
51 "Conklin Shows Finish Season," *Billboard*, Oct. 24, 1936, p. 46.
52 "Hartmann's Broadcast," *Billboard*, Dec. 5, 1936, p. 68.
53 "CNE Beats 1934 by 148,000 — Toronto Midway to Be Changed," *Billboard*, Sept. 14, 1935, p. 61.
54 "CNE May Add a Day to Run," *Billboard*, Dec. 21, 1935, p. 40.
55 "Toronto as Music Center, CNE Aim," *Billboard*, Jan. 18, 1936, p. 45.
56 Jack Mosher, "Carnival King," *Maclean's*, July 15, 1941, p. 30.
57 *White Tops*, April–May 1936, p. 5.
58 Roger Littleford Jr., "Out in the Open," *Billboard*, Dec. 19, 1936, p. 65.
59 "Conklin Plans for Toronto — Avers that Playland Midway Is to Be of Gigantic Proportions," *Billboard*, Jan. 30, 1937, p. 42.
60 "Yorkton Show Is Voted Tops — Weadick's Stampede Feature of Exhibition — Innovations Pleasing," *Billboard*, Aug. 8, 1936, p. 44.
61 Jim Conklin, "The School History in Brief," *Conklin Shows Yearbook 1987* (Brantford, Ont: Jackpot Books, 1987), p. 20.
62 "Canadian Barnum," London *Daily Express*, March 25, 1937, p. 3.
63 Jerry Holtman [pseudo.], *Freak Show Man: Uncensored Memoirs of Harry Lewiston — The Incredible Scoundrel* (Los Angeles: Holloway House, 1968), p. 217.
64 Photo of Patty Conklin and Sally Rand, *Billboard*, June 12, 1937, p. 49.
65 "Conklin on Flying Trip in Quest of Attractions," *Billboard*, June 5, 1937, p. 50.
66 "Hartmann's Broadcast," *Billboard*, Aug. 14, 1937, p. 73.
67 "Conklin Starts CNE Work at Toronto," *Billboard*, Aug. 14, 1937, p 48
68 "Two Spielers Fired for Racy Sex Talk," *Toronto Star*, Sept. 8, 1937, p. 7.
69 "'Gator Runs Away and Scares Crowd," *Toronto Star*, Sept. 7, 1937, p. 15.
70 Roger Littleford Jr., "Out in the Open," *Billboard*, Sept. 18, 1937, p. 72.
71 Conklin accounts book for 1937. Original in Conklin archives.
72 "Midway Confab," *Billboard*, Oct. 16, 1937, p. 52.

4: THE WAR YEARS

1 "Conklin Gets CNE 6th Time — Frolexland Head Has Consecutive Role at Toronto," *Billboard*, Nov. 15, 1941, p. 32.

2 On Johnny J. Jones, see Goldsack, *A History of the Johnny J. Jones Exposition*. On Rubin & Cherry Shows, see Audibert, *Rubin & Cherry*. On Morris & Castle Shows, Castle-Erlich-Hirsch Shows, and Beckmann & Gerety Shows, see McKennon, *A Pictorial History of the American Carnival*. *Billboard* also provides much information on the major shows throughout these years.

3 On Royal American Shows, see Goldsack and Heatley, *Royal American Shows*.

4 Jim Conklin, "The School History in Brief," p. 32.

5 Frank D. Shean, "Along the Midway at the CNE," *Billboard*, Sept. 17, 1938, p. 44.

6 Herb Dotten, "Close Ups: Hard-Way School Gave Scenic Artist Ray Practical Approach," *Billboard*, Dec. 17, 1949, p. 51. This article is the source of much information on Jack Ray.

7 Fred H. Phillips, "Jimmy Sullivan Defies Accepted Formula to Gain Success in Canada," *Billboard*, Feb. 27, 1954, p. 64.

8 Montreal *Standard*, Sept. 21, 1964, p. 16.

9 J.W. Conklin, "Carnival Showmen Voice Opinions of Biz Outlook," *Billboard*, Apr. 9, 1938, p. 142.

10 "Outdoor Prospects," *Billboard*, Apr. 8, 1939, p. 131.

11 *Toronto Star*, Aug. 16, 1969, p. 8.

12 Jim Conklin, "The School History in Brief," p. 27.

13 "Frolexland Is Prepped by Conklin," *Billboard*, Aug. 19, 1939, p. 33.

14 Conklin accounts book for 1940. Original in Conklin archives.

15 "Conklin Gate Is Hyped 20% — Froliland Big Draw at Brandon, Calgary, Edmonton—Still Dates Satisfactory," *Billboard*, Aug. 2, 1941, p. 29.

16 "CNE Heads Aim at 2,000,000," *Billboard*, Aug. 23, 1941, p. 46.

17 "CNE Runs Ahead of 1940 Figures," *Billboard*, Sept. 6, 1941, p. 3.

18 "CNE Gate Seen over 2,000,000," *Billboard*, Sept. 20, 1941, p. 42.

19 "The Crossroads," *Billboard*, Oct. 18, 1941, p. 49.

20 "Conklin Preps for 1942," *Billboard*, Nov. 8, 1941, p. 30.

21 "Aerial Rides," Edmonton *Bulletin*, July 13, 1942, pp. 1–2.

22 "Britain Fair to Repeat — Conklin Again Sets CNE Sub — Dominion Grants Okay Under Charities Act — 42G Realized in First Promotion," *Billboard*, March 20, 1943, p. 30.

23 "Conklins Place Rides at Four Canada Funspots," *Billboard*, June 26, 1943, p. 40.

24 "Quebec and Conklins Further Post-War Planning by 10-Year Contract for Midway Offerings," *Billboard*, Feb. 5, 1944, p. 42.

25 "Conklins Pres Post-War — Projects Are Started Early — Midway Paving Seen as Top Bet for Boards," *Billboard*, Sept. 30, 1944, p. 32.

26 "5-Year Winnipeg Pact for Conklin," *Billboard*, May 12, 1945, p. 36.

27 On Frank Conklin as a horse breeder, see the Canadian Horse Racing Hall of Fame website. He is also widely covered in the press during these years.
28 "Quebec Expo Maps Ambitious Plans — Many Postwar Improvements — Will Operate Amusement Park Starting in '46 — New Buildings to Be Erected," *Billboard*, June 30, 1945, p. 54.
29 Advertisement, *Billboard*, Feb. 16, 1946, p. 57.
30 "Conklins Rack It Up at Hamilton's Fete," *Billboard*, July 13, 1946, p. 53.
31 "Midway Confab," *Billboard*, Oct. 5, 1946, p. 54.

5: THE EX MARKS THE SPOT

1   The following discussion of amusement parks is informed by Nasaw, *Going Out*.
2   "Kids Biz's Top Asset—Huedepohl; Urges Ideas to Attract Them," *Billboard*, April 15, 1950, p. 69.
3   "Arthur and Anne Fritz Request Exclusive on Kiddieland Name," *Billboard*, March 18, 1950, p. 78.
4   "Hefty Picnic Biz Built by Belmont," *Billboard*, June 23, 1945, p. 47.
5   "Conklins Operating Rides in Three Parks," *Billboard*, June 9, 1945, p. 47.
6   "Billings Gives Montreal Folks a Chance to Put 'Bite' on Him," *Billboard*, Aug. 6, 1949, p. 54.
7   "Conklins Operating 23 Rides in Canada," *Billboard*, June 22, 1946, p. 82.
8   Jack Dadswell, *Hey There, Sucker!* (Boston: Bruce Humphries, 1946), p. 26.
9   "New Rides a Reality," *Billboard*, special section, March 29, 1947, p. 52. Much of the information about rides in the following paragraphs, including information about the Conklin equipment, comes from this and subsequent articles on ride technology in *Billboard* during this period.
10 J.W. Conklin, "Letter to the Editor," *Greater Show World*, Oct. 1947, p. 2.
11 Conklin accounts book for 1945. Original in Conklin archives.
12 "Conklin Tips Plans with 10-Yr. Pacts — Frolicland Theme for All," *Billboard*, Feb. 16, 1946, p. 51.
13 The movements of Conklin–Sullivan personnel can be followed in *Billboard*.
14 "Midway Confab," *Billboard*, Aug. 2, 1947, p. 50.
15 Grosses here and in the following paragraphs are from the Conklin accounts book for 1950. Original in Conklin archives.
16 "Eastern Canada Biz Soars — Quebec Gives Top Increase — Sherbrooke, Three Rivers top '46—Censors Make It a Little Rough for Back-End," *Billboard*, Sept. 13, 1947, p. 74b.

17 Information on the coasters at Belmont Park and Crystal Beach can be found in the Roller Coaster Database (rcdb.com), a comprehensive source of information about roller coasters around the world.

18 Letter, Conklin to Hughes, May 9, 1946. Original in Conklin archives.

19 "Conklin Seeking Bids and Ideas for CNE Midway," *Billboard*, Dec. 28, 1946, p. 50.

20 "Brydon Faces Busiest Year; In at Little Rock, Memphis," *Billboard*, Apr. 24, 1948, p. 53.

21 "Permanent Midway Buildings at CNE Go Up Under Conklins," *Billboard*, May 24, 1947, p. 57.

22 Retlaw Elah, "Skipping 'Round the CNE," *Billboard*, Aug. 16, 1947, p. 50.

23 "Conklins' Modernistic Theme Points Up CNE's New Midway," *Billboard*, March 29, 1947, p. 55.

24 "Unusual Fronts at Toronto Draw Raves From de L'horbe," *Billboard*, Oct. 4, 1947, p. 57.

25 Details about the 1947 CNE come largely from *Billboard* articles published before, during, and after the exhibition.

26 "Olsen, Johnson Promise to Fumigate New Show for 1948 Visit to 'Ex'," *Toronto Star*, Aug. 29, 1947, p. 3.

27 "CNE Pin-Up Girls Get Police OK — Olsen & Johnson Show Fails to Shock Inspector, 'Just Funny Roughhouse'," Toronto *Telegram*, Aug. 30, 1947, p. 11.

28 CNE grosses here and in the following paragraphs are from the Conklin accounts books. Originals in Conklin archives.

29 Advertisement, *Billboard*, May 8, 1948, p. 73.

30 "CNE Post-Season Confab? — Parkmen Seek Okay in Dec. — Huedepohl and Others Believe Few Days in Toronto Would Prove Beneficial," *Billboard*, Sept. 25, 1948, p. 56.

31 "Summer NAAPPB Confab Set — Board Okays Toronto Site — Hughes, Conklin to Arrange Meeting Place on Grounds," *Billboard*, Dec. 18, 1948, p. 68.

32 *Canadian Weekly*, Aug. 14, 1965, p. 15.

33 James Coleman, "Success Didn't Spoil Patty Conklin," *Amusement Business*, special issue, Nov. 16, 1968, p. 57.

34 Letter, Conklin to Hughes, Nov. 4, 1950. Original in Conklin archives.

35 Herb Dotten, "Contrasting Conklins Are Alike in Amazing Ability to Make $$," *Billboard*, July 9, 1949, p. 102.

36 "Frank Conklin's Horses Cop Money," *Billboard*, Sept. 13, 1947, p. 74b.

37 Joe Perlove, "They Waited for Darkness to Unwind Big Bankrolls," *Toronto Star*, Sept. 11, 1948, p. 11.

38 "Big New Fair Set at Ottawa; Plenty of Acts — Makes Bow May 30," *Billboard*, Jan. 22, 1949, pp. 3, 33.

39 "Act To Break Sesqui Log Jam — Exec Maps Four-Step Method to Speed Action on Mounting Bids for Midway Attractions — Batt, Conklin Group Withdraws Amusement Zone Offer," *Billboard*, Dec. 17, 1949, p. 55.

40 On the Johnny J. Jones Exposition, see Goldsack, *A History of the Johnny J. Jones Exposition*.

41 Letter, Conklin to Morse, Apr. 18, 1951. Original in Conklin archives.

42 "'Midway Millionaires' Attacked by Lamport — Mayor Asks 'Gravy' From CNE Midway Go to City Deficit," Toronto *Telegram*, Jan. 24, 1952, p. 1.

43 "CNE Directors Yield Power to Hughes—Mayor," Toronto *Star*, Jan. 25, 1952, p. 2.

6: ROUTINE

1 "City Tax on Midway in New CNE Contract — Mayor, CNE 'Fireworks' Behind Closed Doors — Curb Hughes' Powers, Call Bingo Tenders," Toronto *Telegram*, Jan. 25, 1952, p. 1.

2 "'Bingo' Beasley Offers $8,000 More To CNE," Toronto *Telegram*, Jan. 29, 1952, p. 1.

3 "Hydro For Conklin 'Could Cost $50,000' — Mayor Fights Terms," Toronto *Telegram*, Feb. 13, 1952, p. 19.

4 "'Nasty Situation' in CNE Contracts," Toronto *Telegram*, Feb. 25, 1952, p. 1.

5 "Change Conklin Terms — Hope to Gain $125,000 For CNE Over 5 Years," *Toronto Star*, Feb 29, 1952, p. 4.

6 "Hire Business Examiners for CNE, Mayor Promises," *Toronto Star*, Mar. 5, 1952, p. 2.

7 "CNE Contract Tony Martin as Name Draw," *Billboard*, July 19, 1952, p. 50.

8 "Conklin Kidland Is CNE Highlight," *Billboard*, Aug. 30, 1952, p. 54.

9 "CNE First Two Days on Par with 1951," *Billboard*, Aug. 30, 1952, p. 45.

10 "CNE Directors Meeting: Say Need Hughes as McCallum Inexperienced," *Toronto Star*, Sept. 18, 1952, p. 2.

11 "McCallum Gets Hughes Job at Same $15,000 Pay," *Toronto Star*, Oct. 1, 1952, p. 2.

12 "Started CNE Marathons — Elwood Hughes, 71, Dead," *Toronto Star*, May 1, 1956, p. 2.

13 "Harbor Board Permits 16 Rides for Children to Stay at Sunnyside," *Globe and Mail*, Mar. 16, 1956, p. 1.

14 "License Expires in August — Children's Sunnyside Will Operate," *Globe and Mail*, Apr. 12, 1956, p. 1.

15 "To Kiddieland," *Globe and Mail*, Mar. 16, 1956, p. 6. Annotated version in Conklin archives.

16 "Conklin Coaster Clicks — New $185,000 CNE Ride Off to an Impressive Start in Toronto," *Billboard*, Sept. 5, 1953, p. 62.

17 "Conklin–CNE Gross Rises 20% Over '53 — Roller Coaster Sets Record One-Day Gross; New Rides Placed in Operation," *Billboard*, Sept. 18, 1954, p. 54.

18 "Wall St. Journal Says: Want a Good Business? Buy Amusement Park," *Billboard*, Sept. 5, 1953, p. 56.

19 J.W. Conklin, "International Association of Fairs and Exhibitions," *Greater Show World*, Dec. 1952, p. 10.

20 Conklin, "International Association of Fairs and Exhibitions," p. 10.

21 Conklin, "International Association of Fairs and Exhibitions," p. 10.

22 "Kiddie Carnival Promotion Brought Resounding Success," *Merchandising*, Apr. 18, 1955, p. 43.

23 Robert Douglas, "There Are Some Exciting New Rides and a Lot of Old Favorites Are Back," Toronto *Daily Star*, Aug. 21, 1971, p. 47.

24 "Showmen Help Amusement Enterprises in U.S. and Abroad — Al Sweeney Remembers When: Number 15," *Amusement Business*, Jan. 3, 1981, pp. 24, 22.

25 "Rosenthal Raps Operator Apathy for Dearth of New Major Rides," *Billboard*, Nov. 21, 1953, p. 60.

26 Jim McHugh, "Makers Lack New Rides," *Billboard*, Apr. 11, 1953, p. 54.

27 "West Coast Firm to Build, Operate Portable Rotors — Velare Brothers, Kight, Murphy Join Myers in New Ride Venture," *Billboard*, Dec. 6, 1952, p. 52.

28 "Portable Rotor Set for '54 Operation," *Billboard*, Nov. 21, 1953, p. 60.

29 "Imports German Units — Conklin Gets New Type Funhouse, Flying Cars," *Billboard*, Jan. 15, 1955, p. 63.

30 "Conklin Signs for Canada's 1st Roto-Jet," *Billboard*, July 17, 1954, p. 72.

31 "Conklin Reports — Lengthy Tour Fun; Show Ideas Lacking," *Billboard*, Apr. 24, 1954, pp. 61, 66.

32 "Patty Conklin Negotiates Buy of Wild Mouse — Purchases Ride on Flying Eight-Day Trip to Germany," *Billboard*, Oct. 20, 1956, p. 62.

33 "Conklin Tells AREA About Foreign Rides," *Billboard*, Dec. 8, 1956, p. 68.

34 "Patty Conklin Buys Two Wild Mouses," *Billboard*, Mar. 17, 1958, p. 37.

35 "Conklin Sells Wild Mouse to Rye, N.Y., Op," *Billboard*, Apr. 21, 1958, p. 71; "Advertisement," *Billboard*, Nov. 3, 1958, p. 72.

36 Advertisements, *Billboard*, Mar. 16, 1959, p. 64, and Dec. 7, 1959, p. 62.

37 "Conklin Plans Belgian Trips," *Billboard*, Feb. 17, 1958, p. 75.

38 "Patty Conklin Buys Two Wild Mouses," *Billboard*, Mar. 17, 1958, p. 57.

39 "McCallum Praises Brussels' Buildings — CNE General Mgr. Lauds French Exhibit; Midway Operators Bemoan Light Takes," *Billboard*, May 12, 1958, p. 58.

40 David Proulx, "Tely Reporter's Conscientious Guide to the CNE Midway," Toronto *Telegram*, Aug. 23, 1958, p. 2.

41 J.W. Conklin, "1961 Forecast — Canadian Outlook Brightens," *Amusement Business*, Jan. 9, 1961, pp. 29, 30. *Billboard* became *Amusement Business* in 1961.

42 "CNE Surplus Tops 553G Despite Rainy Weather — Conklin Midway Take Is $476,039; Grandstand Patrons Pay $454,863," *Billboard*, Feb. 9, 1959, p. 54.

43 Conklin accounts book for 1960. Original in Conklin archives.

44 "Rain Mars CNE Line-Up; Eyes 900G Mark," *Amusement Business*, Aug. 28, 1961, p. 25.

45 "Conklin Gross 794G at Toronto Despite Rain," *Amusement Business*, Sept. 11, 1961, p. 29.

46 "Canada's Big Show," *Amusement Business*, Aug. 28, 1961, p. 18.

47 Advertisement, *Billboard*, July 9, 1955, p. 65.

48 "Winnipeg Ex Shifts Site to Race Track; Signs Conklin Shows — Will Continue to Feature Name Acts; Maps Full-Scale Midway Operation," *Billboard*, Feb. 13, 1954, p. 69.

49 "Racine Wins 5-Year Quebec Contract — 25-Year Conklin Reign Ended When City Council Votes for Local Show," *Billboard*, Sept. 15, 1958, p. 87.

50 Herb Dotten, "Freaks Are Thinning Out," *Billboard*, Sept. 15, 1956, p. 68.

51 Herb Dotten, "His Goal: A Great Horse," *Billboard*, May 5, 1956, p. 54.

52 Joe Perlove, "Tip: Keep a Close Eye Out for Blue Man Offspring," *Toronto Star*, Mar. 23, 1962, p. 13.

7: RETURN

1 "Seattle 1961 Fair Seeks Funzone Ideas," *Billboard*, Apr. 14, 1958, p. 49.

2 "Seattle Expo Midway Themes To Old Days," *Billboard*, Oct. 31, 1960, p. 65.

3 "Midway Moguls," *Amusement Business*, May 12, 1962, p. 22.

4 Jim Conklin, "The School History in Brief," pp. 27–28.

5 "Midway Moguls," *Amusement Business*, May 12, 1962, p. 22.

6 "Midway Moguls," *Amusement Business*, May 12, 1962, p. 22.

7 "'Tired' after 70 Years — Conklin 'Retires' to Social Scene After Seattle Coup," *Amusement Business*, Dec. 1, 1962, p. 22.

8 J.W. Conklin, "1963 Industry Forecast — Canada," *Amusement Business*, Jan. 5, 1963, p. 19.

9   "Space Problem — Piers for CNE Midway?" *Amusement Business*, Sept. 21, 1963, p. 28.

10   "A Star-Less CNE? — Powell Looks to New Image," *Amusement Business*, Dec. 5, 1964, p. 6.

11   "CNE 'Too Big' for Toronto," *Amusement Business*, July 3, 1965, p. 6.

12   J.W. Conklin, "1961 Forecast — Canadian Outlook Brightens," *Amusement Business*, Jan. 9, 1961, p. 30.

13   "Conklin Gross Up 15% — Record Looms at Toronto," *Amusement Business*, Sept. 11, 1965, p. 42.

14   Conklin financial statement for income tax purposes. Original in Conklin archives.

15   "Frank Conklin Breeder of Canada 'Horse of the Year'," *Amusement Business*, Dec. 22, 1962, p. 66.

16   "In the Chips," *Amusement Business*, Sept. 5, 1964, p. 29.

17   Lou Dufour, "What Oldtimers Jackpotted About," *Amusement Business*, Aug. 10, 1974, p. 32.

18   On the last years of World of Mirth Shows, see Bob Goldsack, *World of Mirth Shows ... a Remembrance* (Randolph Center, Vt: Greenhills Books, 1984).

19   "Sullivan Equipment Selling," *Amusement Business*, Apr. 18, 1964, p. 127.

20   Information on the Campbell gross and net is from the Conklin accounts book for 1968. Original in Conklin archives.

21   Conklin accounts book for 1964. Original in Conklin archives.

22   Conklin accounts book for 1967. Original in Conklin archives.

8: NEVER HIS LIKE AGAIN

1   *Amusement Business*, July 10, 1965, p. 9.

2   *Toronto Star*, Aug. 20, 1960, p. 19.

3   "Around the Fairs," *Amusement Business*, Feb. 13, 1965, p. 13.

4   "Conklin in CNE Pact," *Amusement Business*, July 10, 1965, p. 9.

5   "Carnival King Patty Conklin Ran CNE Midway 33 years," *Toronto Star*, Nov. 9, 1970, p. 22. In the obituary, Powell is quoted from 1965.

6   "CNE Ready to Run; Expect Changes in '67," *Amusement Business*, Aug. 13, 1966, p. 12.

7   "CNE Must Modernize, Expand — Consultants," *Amusement Business*, June 25, 1966, p. 8.

8   "CNE Ready to Run; Expect Changes in '67," *Amusement Business*, Aug. 13, 1966, p. 12.

9   *Toronto Star*, Dec. 22, 1966, p. 2.

10   Toronto *Telegram*, Aug. 19, 1966, p. 19.

11   "Personals," *Amusement Business*, May 28, 1966, p. 25.

12   "Greene, Linkletter, Faith Exclusives — CNE Talent Line-Up Set; Midway Bolstered," *Amusement Business*, July 8, 1967, p. 7.

13   "Conklin: CNE Hopes High," *Amusement Business*, Sept. 2, 1967, p. 25.

14   *Toronto Star*, Aug. 12, 1967, p. 2.

15   "CNE: No Coin Table Games," *Amusement Business*, Aug. 12, 1967, p. 28.

16   Toronto *Telegram*, Aug. 26, 1968, p. 25.

17   "'2-for-1' Tried on Rides," *Amusement Business*, Aug. 12, 1967, p. 10.

18   "Belmont Park: Living with Expo," *Amusement Business*, Sept. 9, 1967, p. 21.

19   "Emcee in Demand," *Amusement Business*, Feb. 5, 1966, p. 30.

20   "Honor Patty, Burn Mortgage in Toronto," *Amusement Business*, Nov. 5, 1966, p. 23.

21   "Conklin Lists Committee for AB's Diamond/75th," *Amusement Business*, Dec. 6, 1969, p. 22.

22   "Vast Toronto Spread Chases $2 Mil Gross," *Amusement Business*, Aug. 29, 1970, p. 44.

23   "Bingo Bomb Threat Doesn't Faze Patty," *Amusement Business*, Aug. 29, 1970, p. 44.

24   "Conklin Ahead on $2 million CNE quest," *Amusement Business*, Sept. 5, 1970, p. 29.

25   "CNE's Conklin in Hospital," *Toronto Star*, Aug. 26, 1970, p. 26.

9: A CARNIVAL EMPIRE

1   "The Conklin View: It's a Business," *Amusement Business*, Sept. 23, 1972, p. 18.

2   Robert Douglas, "There Are Some Exciting New Rides and a Lot of Old Favorites Are Back," *Toronto Star*, Aug. 1, 1971, p. 47.

3   Douglas, p. 47.

4   Linda McQuaig, "Retarded Girl, 5, Taken from CNE Freak Display," *Globe and Mail*, Aug. 17, 1973, p. 1. Other articles by McQuaig and letters to the editor about Pookie appear in the *Globe and Mail* throughout August.

5   "Good Homeniuk Season in Canada, but Dollar Difference Hurts Show," *Amusement Business*, Dec. 14, 1998. Online edition, no page numbers.

6   "Canada's Campbell Builds Show Slowly," *Amusement Business*, May 27, 1978, p. 31.

7   On Royal American Shows and the Laycraft Commission, see Goldsack and Heatley, *Royal American Shows*. For the report, see James H. Laycraft, *Royal*

American Shows Inc. and Its Activities in Alberta: Report of a Public Inquiry of the Commission of Inquiry into the Affairs and Activities in the Province of Alberta of Royal American Shows Inc. (Edmonton: Government of Alberta, 1978). See also Fiona Angus, "Midway to Respectability: Carnivals at the Calgary Stampede," in Max Foran, ed., Icon, Brand, Myth: The Calgary Exhibition and Stampede, (Edmonton: Athabasca University Press, 1978), pp. 111–46.

8   "Canada Route Decision Seen by End of Year," Amusement Business, Dec. 20, 1975, p. 20.
9   Tom Powell, "Conklin Captures Canadian Contract — To Provide Midway at Four Major Fairs," Amusement Business, Jan. 3, 1976, p. 17.
10   Powell, p. 15.
11   Irwin Kirby, "Opinion," Amusement Business, Apr. 3, 1976, p. 27.
12   "Carnivals, Fairs Sick, Reithoffer Tells OABA," Amusement Business, June 12, 1976, p. 28.
13   See Goldsack and Heatley, Royal American Shows.
14   Waters, History of Fairs and Exhibitions, p. 129.
15   "Undercurrent Business up 30 per cent," Amusement Business, Nov. 11, 1978, p. 16.
16   "Conklin Deletes Canada Ident from Company," Amusement Business, Jan. 21, 1978, p. 30.
17   "Winter Quarters Expanded, Conklin Unit in Fast Start — 65,000 Square Foot Building Added in Brantford," Amusement Business, May 20, 1978, p. 36.
18   "$1,028,950 Gross for the Midway at Dade County," Amusement Business, Apr. 15, 1978, p. 26.
19   "What's It All About, Alfie?" Amusement Business, Aug. 26, 1978, p. 34.
20   Linda Deckard, "Employee Relations a Conklin Concern," Amusement Business, Aug. 19, 1978, p. 33.

10: TURBULENCE

1   Tom Powell, "T.P. on AB," Amusement Business, Aug. 25, 1979, p. 2.
2   Tom Powell, "Fair Managers Upset Over Letter from Conklin — Cites Problems, Seeks Renegotiation of Contracts," Amusement Business, Aug. 25, 1979, p. 12.
3   Tom Powell, "Conklin Reduces U.S. Operations, Will Dissolve the Magic Midway," Amusement Business, Jan. 12, 1980, p. 17.
4   Interview with Barry Jamieson by the author, Aug. 18, 2006.
5   Tom Powell, "Conklin: CNE Ride Biz Static, While Games 'Have Done Well'," Amusement Business, Sept. 26, 1981, p. 46.

6   "Conko-Dollars to Replace Tickets on CNE Rides," *Toronto Star,* May 4, 1992, p. C3.

7   Ancil Davis, "Conklin Says Business Costs to Be Continuing Headache," *Amusement Business,* Sept. 10, 1983, p. 29.

8   "'Fair Season,' Says Conklin Shows Owner," *Amusement Business,* Nov. 20, 1982, p. 35.

9   Tom Powell, "Conklin Swaps Specs: Income on Par with '82," *Amusement Business,* July 30, 1983, p. 45.

10 Tom Powell, "Conklin's Gross up at Calgary Despite Reduction in Ride Prices," *Amusement Business,* July 28, 1984, p. 60.

11 Tom Powell, "Conklin Swaps Specs: Income on Par with '82," *Amusement Business,* July 30, 1983, p. 45.

12 Ancil Davis, "Conklin Says Business Costs to Be Continuing Headache," *Amusement Business,* Sept. 10, 1983, p. 32.

13 "Germany's Schwarzkopf Ride Firm Is Reorganized," *Amusement Business,* May 12, 1984, p. 1.

14 Richard J. Keyworth, "Guest Corner," *Amusement Business,* Mar. 1, 1986, p. 3.

15 "Adoption of Ride Regs Proceeding in Canada," *Amusement Business,* Mar. 23, 1985, p. 47.

16 "Insurance Outlook Causes Concern at N.Y. Fair Meeting," *Amusement Business,* Feb. 1, 1986, p. 1.

17 Ancil Davis, "Conklin's Grosses Soar at Eastern States Expo," *Amusement Business,* Oct. 5, 1985, p. 32.

18 Ancil Davis, "Record 638,167 Attend Yonkers, N.Y., fair," *Amusement Business,* June 21, 1986, p. 18.

19 Ancil Davis, "Weather Curbs Business at Dade County Youth Fair," *Amusement Business,* Apr. 12, 1986, p. 13.

20 Tom Powell, "Excellent Run for Toronto's CNE Despite Fire on Grounds, Strikes," *Amusement Business,* Sept. 19, 1987, p. 22.

21 Tom Powell, "T.P. on AB," *Amusement Business,* Sept. 10, 1988, p. 2.

11: THE LAST GENERATION

1   *Miami Herald,* Mar. 26, 1981, p. 28.

2   Interview with Frank Conklin by the author, Feb. 20, 2000.

3   Kathleen Goldhar, "No Escape from Class for CNE families," *Toronto Star,* Aug. 25, 1996, p. A5.

4   Donna Jean MacKinnon, "Legendary Midway a Family Affair," *Toronto Star*, Aug. 16, 2007, p. A10.

5   Interview with Alfie Phillips by the author, Sept. 1, 2005.

6   Details of the restructuring come from accounts told to the author by Barry Jamieson and Jim Conklin.

7   Accounts books of Conklin Group. Originals in Conklin archives.

8   "Super Fairs' Finerty: There's No Place Like Dome," *Amusement Business*, Apr. 15, 1996, online edition, no page number.

9   "Advance Sales, Strong Spring Bolster Conklin Shows' Season," *Amusement Business*, Aug. 2, 1993, online edition, no page number.

10 Moira Macdonald, "Carny School Days — Kids of Travelling Carnival Workers Get Educated on the Road," Toronto *Sun*, Aug. 29, 1999, p. 47.

11 "Deggeller Attractions Offers 'Schoolhouse on The Midway'," *Amusement Business*, Feb. 25, 1989, p. 48.

12 On Bob Negus, see "Lifelines, John Robert Negus," *Amusement Business*, Mar. 2, 1998, online edition, no page number.

13 "Midway of the Future Hot Topic at CAFE '98," *Amusement Business*, Mar. 2, 1998, online edition, no page number.

14 "Conklin's Ride Grosses Up Despite Stampede's Attendance Decrease," *Amusement Business*, July 25, 1994, online edition, no page number.

15 Interview with Howard Pringle by the author, Aug. 30, 2005.

16 Goldhar, "No Escape from Class for CNE Families," p. A5.

17 Figures for the Calgary Stampede from "Stampede Turnout, Spending Up Despite Rain," *Amusement Business*, July 26, 1993, online edition, no page number.

18 Figures for Dade County Are from "Conklin's Grosses at Winchester Fair Up Despite Rain; Strong '93 Expected," *Amusement Business*, June 28, 1993, and "Dade County Fair Revenues Soar to Record $13 Million," *Amusement Business*, Apr. 10, 1995, online edition, no page number.

19 "CNE Wants to Redefine Midway, Plans Changes," *Amusement Business*, July 26, 1993, online edition, no page number.

20 "CNE Firm Fined in Teen's Accident," *Toronto Star*, Jan. 28, 1997, p. A11.

21 Alan Barnes, "Conklin Settles CNE Injury Case — Family accepts $775,000 Before Suit Goes to Court," *Toronto Star*, July 5, 2000, p. B7.

22 Brian Gray, "Kids Injured in Ride Crash — No Sign of Trouble During Inspection, Official Says," Toronto *Sun*, Aug. 2, 1999, p. 5.

23 "Bill Lynch Shows Regroups, Hopes Changes Bring Strong '96," *Amusement Business*, Apr. 29, 1996, online edition, no page number.

24 "Dade Co. Fair Ride Gross Hits $5.7 Mil," *Amusement Business*, Apr. 10, 2000, online edition, no page number.

25 "Calgary Stampede, Conklin Set Records," *Amusement Business*, July 24, 2000, online edition, no page number.

26 Some of the information on electronic ticketing comes from an interview by the author with Greg Korek, who was involved with the initiative.

27 "Smart Cards to Be Necessity," *Amusement Business*, Oct. 7, 2002, online edition, no page number. This article contains much background information. Systems for providing online ticket sales proliferated during the 2010s and the Covid-19 pandemic provided further motivation for using them. Since 2022, they have become standard features on midways throughout North America.

28 "Innovations, Improvements Key to Keeping Carnivals Competitive," *Amusement Business*, Jan. 7, 2002, online edition, no page number.

29 "Travel Trepidation Could Be Boon for Midways This Year," *Amusement Business*, Jan. 7, 2002, online edition, no page number.

30 Tom Powell, "Conklin's Phillips Cites Carnival Woes," *Amusement Business*, Aug. 18, 2003, p. 20.

31 "Carnival Purchasing Plans — A Sampling of New Rides, Equipment & Attractions Within U.S. and Canadian Shows," *Amusement Business*, Jan. 5, 2004, p. 12.

32 Tom Powell, "Forest Fires Impact Some Dates, But Hauser Still Has Solid Year," *Amusement Business*, Jan. 5, 2004, p. 11.

33 "Gate Drops at South Florida Fair Due to Weekend Weather Woes," *Amusement Business*, Feb. 9, 2004, online edition, no page number.

34 The issues of *Amusement Business* in late 2004 and early 2005 have many articles on and references to the formation of North American Midway Entertainment and its significance. In June 2005, the print version of *Amusement Business* became a monthly.

35 James Zoltak, "Turnstiles: Consolidation Doesn't Necessarily Mean Shrinkage," *Amusement Business*, Nov. 22, 2004, online edition, no page number.

36 Marla Matzer Rose, "Rosen Shows Knack for This Ticket to Rides," *Amusement Business*, Nov. 22, 2004, online edition, no page number.

37 Tom Powell, "A Year of Blessed Events? — Carnival Owners Say Economy, Optimism at Fair Conventions Points to a Robust 2005," *Amusement Business*, Feb. 2005, p. 36.

38 "North American Midway Taps Safety Director," *Amusement Business*, Jan. 7, 2005, online edition, no page number.

39 Tom Powell, "Morton Comes Out Firing in the Tradition of Buffalo Bill," *Amusement Business*, Jan. 2005, p. 22.

Index

Page numbers in italics refer to photographs and their captions.